William Thomas St. Clair

Caesar For Beginners

A First Latin Book

William Thomas St. Clair

Caesar For Beginners
A First Latin Book

ISBN/EAN: 9783337302870

Printed in Europe, USA, Canada, Australia, Japan

Cover: Foto ©Paul-Georg Meister /pixelio.de

More available books at **www.hansebooks.com**

CAESAR FOR BEGINNERS

A FIRST LATIN BOOK

BY

WILLIAM T. St. CLAIR, A.M.

Professor of the Latin Language and Literature in the Louisville (Kentucky) Male High School; Author of "Medical Latin," 'Summary of Latin Syntax,' and 'Notes to the Third Book of Caesar's Gallic War'

NEW YORK
LONGMANS, GREEN AND CO.
LONDON AND BOMBAY
1899

Affectionately Inscribed
to
My Son

PREFACE.

LATIN is an excellent mental training for teaching accuracy, conciseness and exactness. How can this discipline be best secured in schools where the Latin course is confined within three or four years? Those preparatory schools in which Latin is taken up early—say at the age of ten or twelve—may with great profit use 'New Gradatim,' 'Viri Romae,' or 'Nepos' before 'Caesar's Gallic War.' The material for schools of limited time, however, clearly must be taken from the Latin author to be studied first. This book is designed to fit the beginner to take up Caesar as his first Latin. Caesar is not claimed as indispensable to the preparatory course, to the exclusion of other pertinent authors; but the choice of Caesar is the best solution of the problem under the limitations and restrictions given. Besides the fact that Caesar's Latin is hard to master, we have two difficulties to contend with. *First*, in many schools preparatory work is in the hands of young teachers of very narrow or very short experience; the chief result of their pains is wearisome and, to a great degree, unrewarded labor certainly to themselves and perhaps to their pupils. Indeed even the best teachers would welcome a good *teaching book* introductory to Caesar. *Second*, the change from the ordinary beginner's book is so great and so radical that the pupil is lost when he faces Caesar's

Latin. The aim of this book is to meet and, if it may be, lessen these hindrances, not to explain all the difficulties of the Latin language.

The points of practical value are:

1. A working vocabulary of five hundred words taken from the second book of Caesar.

2. Lessons of uniform length throughout, adapted to the average ability of pupils.

3. Lessons graded with a view towards reaching and mastering the complex constructions of Caesar. The subordinate clauses, such as ut, qui, cum, etc., are brought in early in carefully graded lessons, showing the combination of these clauses and illustrating their order and dependence.

4. Steady and uniform progression in the building of the complex sentence and stress laid upon the proper adjustment of words and clauses. Illustrative clauses and phrases from the second book of Caesar, often copied verbatim, oftener with the order and style of the text closely imitated.

5. Alphabetically and by conjugations all of the verbs in the second book of Caesar; principal parts and meanings to be learned as part of the vocabulary, beginning with paragraph (91).

6. The first fourteen chapters of the second book of Caesar simplified and adapted in twenty lessons. Prose composition in each of these lessons based upon the text. Principles and constructions met with in these particular chapters are explained in the *same terms and examples* used in the foregoing lessons which are prepared with a view to application in these chapters.

7. The second book of Caesar complete, with notes. The notes invariably use the terms and examples which

the pupil has been applying from the first lesson. There are no grammatical references and new or offhand expressions, but explanations in terms with which the pupil is already familiar.

There is no wide chasm between the lessons in the main part of the work and the text of Caesar. Between these come the simplified chapters of Caesar and the notes in which, when like points occur in Caesar's text, are repeated the illustrative sentences and explanations used in the former part of the work. Much Latin construction has been purposely omitted and left for the remaining books of Caesar. The lessons have been abridged and constructions made plain, so as to place them within the grasp of the average pupil; since it is not the *quantity* of material crowded into a lesson or a child's head, but the *quality* of the work done, which brings the best results and is therefore most needed. The author gratefully acknowledges his indebtedness to Professor Abraham Flexner, head master of "The Flexner School," Louisville, for valuable assistance in arranging the plan and order of the lessons and especially in the treatment of the relative pronoun; and to Professor Garland Bruce Overton of the Male High School, Louisville, for patient and exhaustive reviews of the proof-pages throughout that have added much to the value of the work. The author feels grateful to the publishers, also, for uniform courtesy and consideration, and for suggestions and help that have added strength to the book.

W. T. S.

LOUISVILLE, June, 1899.

CONTENTS.

PREFACE... Pages vii-ix
INTRODUCTION....................................... " xiii-xv
LESSONS I—X. First-declension and second-declension nouns and adjectives declined; first-conjugation verb, *portō*, in the present, imperfect, and future indicative; sentence-building and order of words; ablative of place, means, attendance....... Pages 1-16
LESSONS XI—XVIII. Present system of *portō* completed; purpose clauses; apposition; relation of words and clauses; relative pronoun; principal parts of verbs................ Pages 16-35
LESSONS XIX—XXVII. First conjugation completed in the active voice; *sum* completed; third-declension nouns; *quod* and *cum* clauses; dative with adjectives; dative with *imperō* and *mandō;* rule of sequence................................... Pages 35-54
LESSONS XXVIII—XXXVII. Second and third conjugations in the active; *iubeō* with accusative + infinitive; sentence-analysis; order and dependence of words and clauses; varying order of words; fourth declension; adjectives of the third declension; use of *suus*....................................... Pages 54-76
LESSONS XXXVIII—XLVIII. Complex sentence analyzed; *cum* and *ubi* clauses; personal and demonstrative pronouns declined; fifth declension; more vivid future condition; *nē* in negative purpose and commands; fourth conjugation; first conjugation passive; personal agent; gerundive construction.. Pages 76-103
LESSONS XLIX—LVI. Passive voice of the second, third, and fourth conjugations; *cum* clauses continued; intermediate clauses; subjunctive mood in indirect discourse and by attraction; ablative absolute; adjectives with genitive in *ius;* comparison of adjectives.. Pages 103-123
LESSONS LVII—LXVI. Ōrātiō Oblīqua; infinitive tenses in O. O.; subordinate clauses in O. O.; relative clause of purpose; indirect

CONTENTS.

question; perfect passive participle; purpose and result clauses; deponent verbs; less vivid future condition; dative with compound and with special verbs; causal and concessive *cum;* accusative of extent in space; verbs of commanding; verbs of fearing.................................... Pages 124–151

LESSONS LXVII—LXX. Double dative; deponents governing the ablative; four ways of expressing (1) purpose, (2) the ablative absolute, and (3) the *cum* clause; dative of possession; temporal clauses; dative of agency with the periphrastic; impersonal verbs; uses of the relative; verbs of hindering; ablative with the comparative............................. Pages 152–161

LESSONS LXXI—LXXV. Substitutes for the perfect active participle; adverbial accusative; ablative of quality; partitive genitive; *persuādeō* in the passive; periphrasis for supineless verbs, etc.; how 'ought' and 'must' are expressed; relative clause of result; commands and exhortations, same in O. O.; hortatory subjunctive, same in O. O.; conditionals in O. O.; table and rule for *mood* and *tense* in O. O..................... Pages 161–172

SPECIMENS OF 'INDIRECT DISCOURSE'............... " 175–177
ADAPTED AND SIMPLIFIED CAESAR................ " 178–198
TEXT OF CAESAR, Book Two complete.............. " 201–210
NOTES TO THE SECOND BOOK...................... " 222–255
VERBS IN BOOK TWO, WITH MEANINGS............ " 256–260
PARADIGMS OF NOUNS, PRONOUNS, AND ADJECTIVES. " 261–270
COMPARISON OF ADJECTIVES AND ADVERBS......... " 271–273
PARADIGMS OF REGULAR VERBS.................... " 274–291
PARADIGMS OF VERBS, IRREGULAR AND DEPONENT... " 292–309
PARADIGMS OF THE PERIPHRASTIC CONJUGATION... " 310–311
RULES OF QUANTITY............................. " 312–314
LATIN-ENGLISH VOCABULARY...................... " 315–341
ENGLISH-LATIN VOCABULARY...................... " 342–350
INDEX... " 351–357

INTRODUCTION.

Alphabet.—The Latin alphabet has twenty-four letters: a, b, c, d, e, f, g, h, i, k, l, m, n, o, p, q, r, s, t, u, v, x, y, z. i serves for both *i* and *j;* as the former it is called *vowel* i, as the latter *consonant* i. There is no w: properly v represented also the vowel u, but in this book v is used for the consonant and u for the vowel sound of v (*u*).

Vowels.—The vowels are a, e, i, o, u, and y, sounded thus:

ā as in *father.*   ă as in the first syllable in *aha.*
ē " " *prey.*   ĕ " " *net.*
ī " " *unique.* ĭ " " *him.*
ō " " *hope.*   ŏ " " *harmony.*
ū " " *rude.*   ŭ " " *put.*

y is sounded like the French *u,* German *ü.*

Diphthongs.—Some diphthongs are here omitted as being unimportant.

ae is sounded *eye.*
au as *ow* in *how.*
eu as *ew* in *new.*
oe as *oi* in *soil.*

Consonants.—The consonants b, d, f, h, k, l, m, n, p, qu are pronounced as in English. c, g, t have the hard sound, as *cold, get, take;* ti never like the English *sh* in *tion.* s has a sharp hissing sound, as *send, this;* never sound **s** like *z*. **i** *consonant* (for **j**) has the sound of *y*, as *million, yet*. **r** was probably slightly trilled. **v** has the sound of *w*, as **vinum,** *wine*.

Syllables.—In a Latin word there is a syllable for each vowel or diphthong. The last syllable of a word is called the *ultima;* the syllable before the last, the *penult;* the one before the penult, the *antepenult*. Monosyllables are words containing *one* syllable; dissyllables, words of *two* syllables; polysyllables, words of more than two syllables. Utter separately all vowels except those combined as diphthongs. In dividing a word into syllables, a single consonant is joined with the following vowel; as, lē-gā-tus. In the case of two or more consonants, join with the following vowel those consonants that can be pronounced with the vowel; as, ca-stel-lum.

Parts of speech.—Functions as in English : verb, noun, pronoun, adjective, adverb, preposition, conjunction, interjection.

Inflection.—The regular change in the form of a Latin word, by which its different relations to other words are shown, is called inflection. The inflection of nouns, pronouns, participles, and adjectives is called Declension; that of verbs, Conjugation. There are five declensions of nouns and four conjugations of verbs.

Comparison.—Adjectives and adverbs have three degrees of comparison: positive, comparative, superlative.

Number, voice, etc.—There are two numbers, singular and plural; three persons, first, second, and third; three genders, masculine, feminine, and neuter; two voices in the verb, active and passive.

Cases.[1]—In the inflection of nouns, etc., Latin has the following six cases:

---

[1] The cases, except the nominative and vocative, are called *oblique cases*.

Nominative = simple meaning of the word, as subject.

Genitive = *of* + meaning of the word with the values of the English prepositional phrase.

Dative = *to* or *for* + meaning of the word—as *indirect object*.

Accusative = simple meaning of the word—as *direct object*.

Vocative = *O* + the English meaning.

Ablative = *from, with, by, in* or *on* + meaning of the word.

Accent.—The accent of a syllable is the stress of voice laid upon it.

1. Words of *two* syllables are accented upon the *penult*; as, **tu′-ba**.

2. Words of *more* than *two* syllables are accented upon the *penult*, if that is long; otherwise upon the *antepenult*; as, **a-mā′-vī, a-mā′-ve-ram**.

3. The accent should not fall upon the last syllable.

Quantity.—Latin vowels marked with a horizontal line above them are long in quantity, i.e., long in duration of the time required to sound them. Vowels not so marked may be regarded as short and require half as much time in sound as long vowels. The length or shortness of a vowel or a syllable is called *quantity*. A syllable is long in quantity (1) if it contains a long vowel or diphthong; (2) if the vowel of the syllable precedes **x**, or two consonants, except a mute and a liquid. A syllable is short if its vowel precedes another vowel or **h**. A syllable is common when it contains a short vowel followed by a mute with **l** or **r**; as, **lă-cri-ma**. In this book all long vowels are marked, special attention having been given to determining hidden quantities. For rules of quantity see **(500–504)**.

LESSON I.

FIRST DECLENSION.

(See Introduction for the names and meanings of the cases.)

1. Fossa, *a* or *the ditch*, declined in the singular number.

Nom. fossă,   *a ditch* ("as subject")
Gen. fossae, *of a ditch* (pronounced foss-*eye*)
Dat. fossae, *to* or *for a ditch*
Acc. fossam, *a ditch* ("as object")
Voc. fossă,   *O ditch*
Abl. fossā,   *from, with, by, in,* or *on a ditch*

2. The *stem* of a noun is the common part to which terminations are annexed to distinguish the different cases. The stem of fossa ends in ă, and is the same as the word itself in the nominative case. The stem originally ended in ā.

The stem form appears in each case; the nominative and vocative have nothing additional; the ablative is distinguished from the nominative and vocative by the lengthening of the stem vowel ā; the genitive and dative annex e to the stem, and the accusative annexes m. These terminations may be called case-endings, though strictly speaking they are combinations of the stem and the true ending.

3.   **VOCABULARY.**

Nouns of the first declension end in **a** in the nominative singular and are *feminine* except when males are meant, as in **poeta,** a poet. In the vocabularies of this declension, when no gender is specified the feminine is meant.

Nom.	Gen.	Meaning.
causa	causae	*cause*
porta	portae	*gate*
Italia	Italiae	*Italy*
fuga	fugae	*flight*

CAESAR FOR BEGINNERS.

Nom.	Gen.	Meaning.
silva	silvae	*forest*
tuba	tubae	*trumpet*
prōvincia	prōvinciae	*province*
lāta	lātae (*adj.*)	*wide* or *broad*
māgna	māgnae (*adj.*)	*great* or *large*
amīcitia	amīcitiae	*friendship*

4. Agreement of the adjective.—An adjective agrees with the noun which it limits in *gender*, *number*, and *case*. Thus: silvae lātae, *of a broad forest;* tubā māgnā, *with a large trumpet.*

The adjective is usually placed *after* the noun it modifies. For emphasis it may precede the noun.

5.   **EXERCISES.**

I.—1. Causam.[1] 2. Ītaliae. 3. Portae. 4. Tubā. 5. Fuga. 6. Silvam lātam. 7. Prōvinciae māgnae. 8. Fugā.

II.—1. Of the province. 2. Flight (*obj.*). 3. For the province. 4. Of a wide ditch. 5. By flight. 6. A large trumpet (*obj.*). 7. To the cause.

LESSON II.

FIRST DECLENSION, CONTINUED.

6. Fossa declined in the plural.

Nom.	fossae,	*the ditches*
Gen.	fossārum,	*of the ditches*
Dat.	fossīs,	*to* or *for the ditches*
Acc.	fossās,	*the ditches*
Voc.	fossae,	*O ditches*
Abl.	fossīs,	*from, with, by, in,* or *on the ditches*

The *stem* **fossa** is unchanged throughout the plural except in the dative and ablative, where final **a** is omitted before the case-ending **īs**.

---

[1] There is no Latin word for *the* or *a*, which words must be supplied according to the sense, as also often *his, hers, theirs.*

7. Use of the genitive.—A noun in the genitive case limits another noun. One genitive may modify another genitive. Sometimes a noun in the genitive is translated by the English *possessive case* instead of *of*.

Thus: **Galbae tuba** may mean *the trumpet of Galba* or *Galba's trumpet*. Here **Galbae** is a noun in the genitive limiting the noun **tuba**.

The ablative *causā*.—**Causā** means *for the sake of*, and must stand *after a genitive;* as, **fugae causā,** *for the sake of flight*.

8.   **VOCABULARY.**

Nom.	Gen.	Meaning.
pūgna	pūgnae	*fight*
Gallia	Galliae	*Gaul*
Galba	Galbae, *mas.*	*Galba (man's name)*
galea	galeae	*helmet*
rīpa	rīpae	*bank*
cōpiae	cōpiārum, usually plur.	*forces*
Belgae	Belgārum, *mas.*	*Belgians*
amāta	amātae, *adj.*	*beloved*
nova	novae, *adj.*	*new*
alta	altae, *adj.*	*tall* or *deep*
multa	multae, *adj.*	*much* or *many*
et, *conjunction*		*and*
in, *preposition with the abl.*		*in*

9. Use of *in*.—The preposition **in** is used with the *ablative* to denote place where. Thus: **in prōvinciā novā,** *in the new province*.

10.   **EXERCISES.**

I.—1. Cōpiārum. 2. Prōvinciīs. 3. Galeae. 4. Amīcitiae causā. 5. Rīpās altās. 6. In silvā lātā. 7. Galbae tubā novā. 8. Galeīs multīs. 9. Belgārum cōpiās multās. 10. Galbae cōpiārum causā in Galliā.

II.—1. With a trumpet. 2. By Galba's flight. 3. For the beloved forces. 4. The flight (*obj.*) of the Belgians. 5. For the sake of a new province.

LESSON III.

FIRST-CONJUGATION VERB. FIRST DECLENSION, CONTINUED.

11. Present indicative active of *portō, I carry*.

SINGULAR.
1. portō, *I carry, am carrying,*
2. portās, *you carry* [*do carry*
3. portat, *he carries*

PLURAL.
1. portāmus, *we carry*
2. portātis, *you carry*
3. portant, *they carry*

The *present stem* of this verb is **portā**, which appears in each form except the *first person singular*, where final **ā** is lost before **ō**. The endings **s, t, mus, tis, nt**, annexed to the stem, denote the different persons of the verb and its subject, and are called *personal endings*. To conjugate this tense of a verb, change *final* **ō** of the *first person singular* to **ās, at, āmus, ātis, ant**.

Conjugate and give meanings of **pūgnō, parō**, and **superō** in the *present indicative active*. Decline and give meanings in both singular and plural of **tuba, galea**, and **silva alta** (*together*).

12. **VOCABULARY.**

pūgnō,	*I fight*
parō,	*I prepare*
superō,	*I overcome*
occupō,	*I seize*
cēlō (*pronounced ka-lo*),	*I conceal*
vītō (*pronounced we-to*),	*I avoid*

13. Commit to memory the following examples:

1. portat, — *he carries*
2. galeam parat, — *he prepares a helmet*
3. Galba Belgās superat, — *Galba overcomes the Belgians*
4. occupant, — *they seize*
5. fugam cēlant, — *they conceal their flight*
6. Belgae cōpiās Galbae vītant, — *the Belgians avoid Galba's forces*

In sentences (1) and (2), as no subject is separately expressed, *he* is to be supplied. In (3) the subject **Galba** is separately given and therefore *he* should be omitted. Again in (3) **Belgās** is the *direct object* of the verb **superat**, which it precedes: so in (2), (5), and (6), the *direct object* is in the *accusative* and stands before the verb, which comes last.

LESSON IV.

FIRST DECLENSION AND FIRST CONJUGATION, CONTINUED.

14. Conjugate and give meanings of **occupō**, **cēlō**, and **vītō** in the *present indicative active*.

Decline and give meanings of **rīpa**, **cōpiae**, and **porta māgna**.

Review vocabularies in Lessons I and II.

15. **Example of the direct and indirect objects.**

Galba cōpiīs galeās multās   *Galba prepares many helmets*
parat,   *for his forces*

In this sentence **cōpiīs** is in the *dative* and is called the *indirect object* of the verb **parat**; the *indirect object* usually precedes the *direct*, as **cōpiīs** here precedes **galeās**.

16. Fix in mind this common *order of words*:

a. Place the adjective *after* the noun it modifies.

b. **causā**, *for the sake of*, always comes *after a genitive*.

c. The verb stands at the end of a sentence with the direct object before it.

d. The indirect (*dative*) object comes before the direct.

e. The subject comes first; if not separately expressed, it is indicated by the *ending* of the verb.

17.   **EXERCISES.**

I.—1. Occupat. 2. Cēlāmus. 3. Superās. 4. Vītātis. 5. Belgās superāmus. 6. Belgae fugam cēlant. 7. Cōpiīs tubās novās occupat. 8. Galbae cōpiae galeās multās portant (are carrying). 9. Belgae in Galliā cōpiās māgnās parant. 10. Galba in Ītaliā Belgārum cōpiās superat.

II.—1. We seize. 2. You (*sing.*) are fighting (or fight). 3. You (*plur.*) are preparing helmets for the beloved forces. 4. They avoid a fight for the sake of friendship. 5. They seize helmets and trumpets for the Belgians. 6. Galba avoids a fight and conceals his flight.

LESSON V.

SECOND DECLENSION.

18. Servus, *slave,* declined in the singular.

Nom. servus, *a slave*
Gen. servī,[1] *of a slave*
Dat. servō, *to* or *for a slave*
Acc. servum, *a slave*
Voc. serve,[2] *O slave*
Abl. servō, *from, with, by,* etc., *a slave*

The stem of nouns in the second declension ends in o. In combination with the case-endings o undergoes changes, appearing as ō, u, e, or disappearing altogether. The stem of **servus** is **servo**.

19. Table of case-endings.—Commit to memory:

Nom. -us = *subject*
Gen. -ī = *of*
Dat. -ō = *to* or *for*
Acc. -um = *object*
Voc. -e = *O*
Abl. -ō = *from, with, by, in,* or *on*

---

[1] Pronounced ser-*we*, with the r slightly trilled.
[2] Pronounced ser-*wāy*, with the r slightly trilled.

SECOND DECLENSION.

20.   **VOCABULARY.**

Nouns of this declension ending in **us** are mostly masculine; when no gender for such nouns is specified, the *masculine* is meant.

Nom.	Gen.	Meaning.
mūrus	mūrī	*wall*
vīcus	vīcī	*village*
amīcus	amīcī	*friend*
gladius	gladiī	*sword*
dō (*conjugated like* pūgnō)		*I give*
novus	novī, *adj.*	*new*
măgnus	măgnī, *adj.*	*great* or *large*
multus	multī, *adj.*	*much* or *many*
amātus	amātī, *adj.*	*beloved*

21. Agreement of adjective. (4.[1])—Notice carefully the agreement of the adjective in the following examples; thus far the noun and its limiting adjective have the same ending:

1. **fossae lātae,** *of a wide ditch*
2. **mūrī lātī,** *of a wide wall*
3. **galeā novā,** *with a new helmet*
4. **gladiō novō,** *with a new sword*

22.   **EXERCISES.**

I.—1. Mūrō. 2. Gladium novum. 3. Amīcī causā. 4. Caesar amīcō galeam novam et gladium măgnum dat. 5. Galba in vīcō tubās multās occupat.

II.—1. Of a large village. 2. To a beloved friend. 3. Galba is preparing a high wall for the village. 4. Caesar conceals in the village the helmets of his forces.

---
[1] All references are made to paragraphs.

LESSON VI.

FIRST CONJUGATION AND SECOND DECLENSION, CONTINUED.

23. Imperfect Indicative of *portō*.

SINGULAR.
1. portābam, *I was carrying—*
   I carried
2. portābās, *you were carrying*
3. portābat, *he was carrying*

PLURAL.
1. portābāmus, *we were carrying* [*ing*
2. portābātis, *you were carrying*
3. portābant, *they were carrying*

The stem is **portā**, which appears in each form. To make this tense of a verb, change final ō to ā, which forms the *present stem;* thus the stem of **occupō** is **occupā**: to the stem annex **ba**, which is called the *tense-sign*, and to this add the personal endings m, s, t, mus, tis, nt.

24. Table of endings.

SINGULAR.
-bam
-bās
-bat

PLURAL.
-bāmus
-bātis
-bant

25. Servus declined in the plural.

Nom. servī, *slaves*
Gen. servōrum, *of slaves*
Dat. servīs, *to* or *for slaves*
Acc. servōs, *slaves*
Voc. servī, *O slaves*
Abl. servīs, *from, with,* etc., *slaves*

26. Table of case-endings.

Nom. -ī
Gen. -ōrum
Dat. -īs

Acc. -ōs
Voc. -ī
Abl. -īs

FIRST CONJUGATION.

27.   **VOCABULARY.**

Nom.	Gen.	Meaning.
lēgātus	lēgātī	*ambassador*
Rōmānus	Rōmānī	*Roman (noun or adj.)*
populus	populī	*people*
Gallus	Gallī	*Gaul (noun or adj.)*
numerus	numerī	*number*
nūntius	nūntiī	*message*
hiemō		*I winter*
aedificō		*I build*
conlocō		*I place*
in, *prep. with the accusative*		*into*
in Galliam, in Ītaliam		*into Gaul, into Italy*

28.   **EXERCISES.**

I.—1. Hiemāmus. 2. Hiemābāmus. 3. Aedificat. 4. Aedificābat. 5. Caesar Gallōrum cōpiās superābat. 6. Cōpiae populī¹ Rōmānī² in vīcō Belgārum hiemant. 7. Gallī amīcīs Galbae gladiōs novōs dabant.

II.—1. They were building. 2. Caesar is wintering in a new village. 3. Galba was building a high wall for his forces. 4. The ambassadors of the Belgians give swords and helmets to Galba's slaves.

LESSON VII.

FIRST CONJUGATION, CONTINUED.

29. Future Indicative of *portō*.

SINGULAR.
1. portābō, *I shall carry*
2. portābis, *you will carry*
3. portābit, *he will carry*

PLURAL.
1. portābimus, *we shall carry*
2. portābitis, *you will carry*
3. portābunt, *they will carry*

The stem is **portā**; the tense-signs are bō, bi, and bu, to which are annexed the personal endings s, t, mus, tis, nt.

---

¹ Genitive singular.   ² Adjective.

30. Table of endings.

SINGULAR.	PLURAL.
-bō	-bimus
-bis	-bitis
-bit	-bunt

31. Order of words.—For answers to questions in the following sentence see (16).

Caesar in Galliā cōpiīs Galbae *Caesar will seize in Gaul new*
vīcōs novōs occupābit, *villages for Galba's forces*

Point out the subject. What does the adverbial phrase in Galliā limit? "Use of adjunct" (84). Name and give position of the *indirect object*. The genitive **Galbae** limits what? (7). *Direct object* and position? *Agreement of adjective* and its position? (4).

32. VOCABULARY.

Nom.	Gen.	Meaning.
locus	locī	*place*
līberī	līberōrum (*plur. only*)	*children*
Germānī	Germānōrum	*Germans*
fīnitimī	fīnitimōrum	*neighbours*
nostrī	nostrōrum	*our (men)* [1]

idōneus or idōnea, *adj. mas.* or *fem.*   *suitable*
reliquus [2] or reliqua, *adj. mas.* or *fem.*   *remaining*
mātūrō   *I hasten*
contrā, *prep. with the acc.*   *against*

33. Conjugate in the present, imperfect, and future indicative **mātūrō, conlocō,** and **hiemō,** and give meanings.

---

[1] For this use of nostrī see (258).
[2] reliquus often means 'the rest of,' but the '*of*' does not necessitate the use of a *genitive:* cōpiae reliquae—cōpiās reliquās, may mean 'the rest of the forces.'

Decline and give meanings of **causa, prōvincia, mūrus, gladius,** and **fīnitimī.**

84. Use of the adjunct or adverbial phrase.—The preposition with its noun forms an adverbial phrase and modifies the verb. Only the accusative and ablative cases demand the use of prepositions. The accusative contains the idea of *place whither*, the ablative *place whence* and *where*. Prepositions are used to define more exactly the local ideas involved in these cases.

85. Uses of *in*.—In + ablative = *in* or *on*, and modifies a verb of *rest* within the limits of one place. In + accusative = *into* (*to, against*), and modifies a verb of *motion* from one place to another.

Caesar in Galliā (*abl.*) **hiemā-**   *Caesar was wintering (resting)*
bat,   *in Gaul*
Caesar in Galliam (*acc.*) **mā-**   *Caesar will hasten into Gaul*
tūrābit,

86.   **EXERCISE.**

1. Nostrī Germānōs et Belgās superābunt. 2. Germānī in locīs idōneīs līberōs cēlābant. 3. Reliquae Belgārum cōpiae contrā populum Rōmānum pūgnant. 4. Cōpiae Rōmānae (*adj.*) in Galliam pūgnae causā mātūrābunt. 5. Galbae amīcī nostrīs numerum gladiōrum māgnum parant.

LESSON VIII.

SECOND DECLENSION, CONTINUED.

87. Nouns in *um*.

Nouns ending in **um** are neuter. The *nominative, accusative,* and *vocative* are alike, ending in **um** in the *singular* and **a** in the *plural*.

Oppidum, *town.*

	SINGULAR.	PLURAL.
Nom.	oppidum	oppida
Gen.	oppidī	oppidōrum
Dat.	oppidō	oppidīs
Acc.	oppidum	oppida
Voc.	oppidum	oppida
Abl.	oppidō	oppidīs

Singular nouns ending in **a**, genitive **ae**, are *feminine* and are declined like **fossa**.

Plural nouns ending in **a**, genitive **ōrum**, are *neuter* and are declined like the *plural* of **oppidum**.

38. Table of case-endings.

	SINGULAR.	PLURAL.		SINGULAR.	PLURAL.
Nom.	-um	-a	*Acc.*	-um	-a
Gen.	-ī	-ōrum	*Voc.*	-um	-a
Dat.	-ō	-īs	*Abl.*	-ō	-īs

39.   **VOCABULARY.**

(The gender is *neuter*.)

Nom.	Gen.		Meaning.
scūtum	-ī		*shield*
vāllum	-ī		*rampart*
perīculum	-ī		*danger*
arma	armōrum (*plur. only*)		*arms*
loca	locōrum		*places*[1]
nōn (*adv.*)			*not*
expūgnō			*I storm*
per, *prep. with the acc.*			*through*
multus	multa	multum, *adj.*	*much*[2]
altus	-a	-um, *adj.*	*high*
māgnus	-a	-um, *adj.*	*great*

---

[1] **Locus,** *place*, may in the plural take the endings of the *masculine* gender, like the plural of **servus**; or the endings of the *neuter*, like the plural of **oppidum**. In Caesar's Latin the *neuter* plural is regularly used.

[2] The three genders of the adjective occur side by side.

SECOND DECLENSION.

40. **EXERCISES.**

I.—1. Nostrī in Galliam arma multa portābunt. 2. Cōpiae Rōmānae (*adj.*) Belgārum vīcōs et oppida expūgnābant. 3. Germānī per oppida Belgārum arma et līberōs portant. 4. Belgae pūgnae causā in silvīs altīs galeās et gladiōs et scūta cēlābunt. 5. Lēgātus populī Rōmānī nostrīs loca idōnea parat.

II.—1. Slaves were carrying Galba's arms through places of danger. 2. Neighbours of the Roman people (*sing.*) build large ramparts for Galba's forces. 3. Caesar will give helmets and shields to his beloved forces and storm the walls of the town.

LESSON IX.

SECOND DECLENSION, CONTINUED.

41. Puer,[1] *boy*, mas. **Ager**, *field*, mas. **Vir**, *man*, mas.

	SINGULAR.	PLURAL.	SINGULAR.	PLURAL.	SINGULAR.	PLURAL.
Nom.	puer	puerī	ager	agrī	vir	virī
Gen.	puerī	puerōrum	agrī	agrōrum	virī	virōrum
Dat.	puerō	puerīs	agrō	agrīs	virō	virīs
Acc.	puerum	puerōs	agrum	agrōs	virum	virōs
Voc.	puer	puerī	ager	agrī	vir	virī
Abl.	puerō	puerīs	agrō	agrīs	virō	virīs

42. Rule of gender.—Second-declension nouns ending in **us** are mostly *masculine*, sometimes *feminine*. Nouns in **er** and **ir** are *masculine*, those in **um** are *neuter*.

Decline the *nouns* of the first and second declensions (**453, 454**), and conjugate (with meanings) the present, imperfect, and future indicative of **amō (474)**.

43. Ablative with *cum.*—When *with* means *together*

---

[1] Observe that the noun and agreeing adjective need not *end alike*; as, puer amātus, *the beloved boy*.

with, it is expressed not by the *ablative alone*, but by **cum** + *ablative*. This is called the "ablative of attendance."

Galba in Galliam cum cōpiīs mātūrat,   *Galba hastens into Gaul with his forces*

In this example the two adverbial phrases **in Galliam** and **cum cōpiīs** *precede* and limit the verb **mātūrat**, which they *follow* in the translation.

Ablative without *cum.*—The "ablative of means or instrument."

Nostrī pīlīs multīs castra expūgnant,   *Our men are storming the camp with many javelins*

When means or instrument is to be expressed, the *ablative without* **cum** is used.

44.   VOCABULARY.

(The gender is *neuter*.)

Nom.	Gen.	Meaning.
proelium	proeliī	battle
pīlum	-ī	javelin
castra	castrōrum (*plur. only*)	camp [1]
hīberna	-ōrum	winter-quarters
praesidium	praesidiī	defence
cum, *prep. with the abl.*		with
redintegrō		I renew

45.   EXERCISES.

I.—1. Germānī cum nostrīs proelium nōn redintegrābunt. 2. Nostrī gladiīs et pīlīs praesidia Gallōrum expūgnābant. 3. Galba in Galliam cum cōpiīs mātūrābit et armīs castra Gallōrum expūgnābit. 4. Cōpiae reliquae in castra arma portant et praesidia nova parant.

II.—1. Caesar places his new forces in winter-quarters for the sake of a defence. 2. Our men were storming the walls of the town and renewing battle with the Germans. 3. The friends of the Romans (*noun*) will build many ramparts for our men.

---

[1] Decline **castra** (37).

LESSON X.

ADJECTIVE OF THE FIRST AND SECOND DECLENSIONS.

46. Altus, alta, altum, *high.*

	SINGULAR.			PLURAL.		
	Mas.	Fem.	Neuter.	Mas.	Fem.	Neuter.
Nom.	altus	alta	altum	altī	altae	alta
Gen.	altī	altae	altī	altōrum	altārum	altōrum
Dat.	altō	altae	altō	altīs	altīs	altīs
Acc.	altum	altam	altum	altōs	altās	alta
Voc.	alte	alta	altum	altī	altae	alta
Abl.	altō	altā	altō	altīs	altīs	altīs

47. Uses of the ablative.

1. Ablative of *place where* takes the preposition **in**, thus: **Caesar in Galliā hiemābit.**

2. Ablative of *attendance* takes the preposition **cum**, thus: **Galba cum cōpiīs mātūrat.**

3. Ablative of *means* or *instrument* has *no preposition*, thus: **Rōmānī gladiīs pūgnābant.**

In (1) and (2) the adverbial phrases **in Galliā** and **cum cōpiīs** modify the verb; in (3) **gladiīs**, though a noun in the ablative case, modifies **pūgnābant** in an adverbial sense.

48.   **VOCABULARY.**

Nom.	Gen.	Meaning.
nūntius	nūntiī, *mas.*	*messenger*
mora	-ae, *fem.*	*delay*
auxilium	auxiliī, *neut.*	*aid* or *help*
imperium	-ī, *neut.*	*power* or *command*
sine, *prep. with the abl.*		*without*
ē or ex, *prep. with the abl.*		*out of*
convocō		*I summon*
ut, *conjunction*		*so that*
Rēmī	-ōrum, *mas.*	*the Remi*
dubitō		*I hesitate*

49. **EXERCISES.**

I.—1. Nostrī cum Germānōrum fīnitimīs proelium nōn redintegrābunt. 2. Lēgātus Rōmānus sine morā ex hībernīs nūntiōs multōs convocābat. 3. Galba oppidī mūrōs expūgnābit et imperiī causā cōpiās Belgārum superābit. 4. Rēmī in proeliīs multīs populō Rōmānō auxilium dant. 5. Caesar per prōvinciam cum cōpiīs mātūrābit et in Ītaliā sine perīculō hiemābit.

II.—1. Slaves were carrying arms out of the town into winter-quarters. 2. Caesar will not give help to the remaining Remi. 3. Germans seize the fields of the Gauls and renew the battle against our men.

LESSON XI.

FIRST CONJUGATION, CONTINUED.

50. Present subjunctive of *portō*.

SINGULAR.	PLURAL.
1. portem, *I may[1] carry*	1. portēmus, *we may carry*
2. portēs, *you may carry*	2. portētis, *you may carry*
4. portet, *he may carry*	3. portent, *they may carry*

The present subjunctive is formed by changing final **ā**, of the stem **portā**, to **e** and annexing the *personal endings* **m, s, t, mus, tis, nt**.

This is the only tense in which the stem **portā** undergoes a change of the final vowel.

51. Table of endings.

SINGULAR.	PLURAL.
-em	-ēmus
-ēs	-ētis
-et	-ent

---

[1] This meaning of the *present subjunctive* is given with a view to its use in *final clauses of purpose*. Other English renderings will be given later.

FIRST CONJUGATION.

52.   VOCABULARY.

Nom.	Gen.	Meaning.
frūmentum	-ī, *neut.*	*corn*
equus	-ī, *mas.*	*horse*
oppidānī	-ōrum, *mas.*	*townsmen*
sīgnum	-ī, *neut.*	*signal*
ut (*with the subjunctive*)		*so that*
coniūrō		*I conspire*
vāstō		*I lay waste*
appellō		*I call*
praefectus	-ī, *mas.*	*general*

53. Use of *ut*.—When *ut* means *so that*, it introduces a subordinate clause of *purpose*, and the verb of this clause is in the subjunctive. This *ut* + subjunctive may be translated by the *English infinitive*.

54. Apposition.

Rōmānī Rēmīs amīcīs auxilium dant,   *The Romans give help to the Remi, their friends*

In the English sentence *friends* is in apposition with and limits *Remi*; the Latin equivalent for *friends* is put in the *dative* to agree with **Rēmīs**, as the *appositive* takes the *case of the noun which it limits*.

Example of the *ut* clause.

Pūgnant ut superent,   *They fight so that they may overcome* (or *to overcome*)

The *English infinitive* "to overcome" is not rendered by the *Latin infinitive*; it must be changed to the *subjunctive*.

55.   EXERCISES.

I.—1. Rōmānī gladiīs pūgnant, ut Gallōs superent. 2. Galba nostrīs equōs dabit, ut ex Ītaliā mātūrent. 3. Caesar cum cōpiīs per prōvinciam mātūrat ut Gallōrum vīcōs occupet. 4. Germānī cum Belgīs, fīnitimīs populī

Rōmānī, coniūrābunt. 5. Caesar signum proeliī dat et cōpiae Rōmānae oppidum māgnum expūgnant.

II.—1. The Gauls build high walls so that they may avoid a battle with our men. 2. The Romans will not lay waste the fields of the Remi, their friends. 3. Caesar hastens into Gaul to prepare¹ a suitable camp for our men.

LESSON XII.

ADJECTIVE AND VERB, CONTINUED.

56. Integer, integra, integrum, *fresh.*

The masculine gender is inflected like **ager**, the feminine like **fossa**, and the neuter like **oppidum**.

	SINGULAR			PLURAL		
	Mas.	Fem.	Neuter	Mas.	Fem.	Neuter
Nom.	integer	-gra	-grum	integrī	-grae	-gra
Gen.	integrī	-grae	-grī	integrōrum	-grārum	-grōrum
Dat.	integrō	-grae	-grō	integrīs	-grīs	-grīs
Acc.	integrum	-gram	-grum	integrōs	-grās	-gra
Voc.	integer	-gra	-grum	integrī	-grae	-gra
Abl.	integrō	-grā	-grō	integrīs	-grīs	-grīs

57. Principal parts of the verb.—Latin verbs have four principal parts, so called because when these parts are known, the other forms of the verb may be found.

They are *present indicative, present infinitive, perfect indicative,* and the *first supine.* The *present infinitive* of the first conjugation is formed by changing *final* **ō** of the verb to **ā-re** (pronounced *ah-re*); thus, **portō, portāre** (to carry).

---

¹ Not infinitive in Latin.

58. VOCABULARY.

Nom.	Gen.	Meaning.
subsidium	-ī, neut.	relief
cōnsilium	-ī, neut.	plan
initium	-ī, neut.	beginning
aedificium	-ī, neut.	building
impedīmenta	-ōrum, neut. plur.	baggage
ferus -a, -um, adj.		fierce
sed, conj.		but
trāns, prep. with the acc.		across
propter, prep. with the acc.		on account of
ad, prep. with the acc.		to or towards
quod, conj.		because
cōnfīrmō		I establish

Conjugate the following verbs in the present subjunctive, and review them in the present, imperfect, and future indicative with meanings: **dubitō, appellō, convocō,** and **parō.** Decline **altus** and **crēber** (466).

59. Use of *ad*.—When "to" means *towards* (of place), it is expressed *not* by the *dative,* but by **ad +** *accusative.* This phrase—**ad +** *accusative*—modifies a verb which denotes *motion* from one place to another. Thus:

Nostrī ad Galbae castra mā-   *Our men hasten to Galba's*
  tūrant,   *camp*

But:

Caesar Galbae (*dat.*) equum   *Caesar gives a horse to Galba*
  dat,

60. EXERCISES.

I.—1. Galba proeliī causā ē castrīs nostrōs convocāre nōn dubitābit. 2. Praefectī nostrī (*adj.*) ad Galbae castra gladiōs et scūta portāre parant. 3. Praefectus Rōmānus in Galliā aedificia nōn vāstābat sed cum Gallīs amīcitiam cōnfīrmābat. 4. Caesar cōpiīs amātīs arma nova dabit ut castra Germānōrum expūgnent.

II.—1. The Belgians do not hesitate to build high walls so that they may avoid a battle. 2. The remaining Gauls were preparing to renew the battle with the Germans, their neighbours. 3. The fierce Germans are carrying corn to the camp of the Belgians; they will not give aid to Galba.

LESSON XIII.

VERB, CONTINUED.

61. Imperfect subjunctive of *portō*.

SINGULAR.
1. portārem, *I might carry*
2. portārēs, *you might carry*
3. portāret, *he might carry*

PLURAL.
1. portārēmus, *we might carry*
2. portārētis, *you might carry*
3. portārent, *they might carry*

61. Table of endings.

SINGULAR.	PLURAL.
-rem	-rēmus
-rēs	-rētis
-ret	-rent

These endings are annexed to the stem **portā**.

Conjugate in both *present* and *imperfect subjunctive*, and give meanings of **fugō, mandō,** and **imperō**.

63. Principal parts of verbs.

Pres. Ind.	Pres. Infin.	Perf. Indic.	First Supine.	
fugō	fugāre	fugāvī	fugātum	*to rout*
pūgnō	pūgnāre	pūgnāvī	pūgnātum	*to fight*
occupō	occupāre	occupāvī	occupātum	*to seize*

64. Moods and tenses.—The indicative mood has six tenses, viz.: present, imperfect, future, perfect, pluperfect, and future-perfect.

The subjunctive has four tenses: present, imperfect, perfect, and pluperfect.

The first *three* of the indicative and the first *two* of the subjunctive are formed upon the *present stem*.

65. Ablative of time.—*Time when* or *within which* is expressed by the ablative without a preposition.

Vigiliā secundā trāns Rhēnum mātūrat,	*He hastens across the Rhine in (during) the second watch*
Nostrī initiō proeliī Germānōs fugant,	*Our men rout the Germans in the beginning of the battle*

Vigiliā and initiō, though nouns in the ablative case, in an adverbial sense modify the verb.

66.   VOCABULARY.

Nom.	Gen.	Meaning.
animus	-ī, *mas.*	*mind*
Rhēnus	-ī, *mas.*	*the Rhine*
tēlum	-ī, *neut.*	*weapon*
prō, *prep. with the abl.*		*in front of*
prīmus	-a, -um, *num. adj.*	*first*
secundus	-a, -um, " "	*second*
extrēmus	-a, -um, *adj.*	*farthest*
oppūgnō	-āre	*to attack*
mandō	-āre	*to direct* or *instruct*
imperō	-āre	*to command*
fugō	-āre	*to rout*
vigilia	-ae, *fem.*	*watch* (division of the night)

67.   EXERCISES.

I.—1. Nostrī prō castrīs vālla alta aedificant. 2. Caesar cum cōpiīs trāns Rhēnum ad oppida Germānōrum mātūrābat. 3. Germānī in castra lēgātōs Rōmānōs convocant et nostrīs auxilium dare parant. 4. Nostrī in Galbae castra tēla multa portābunt et prīmā vigiliā Belgās fugābunt. 5. Gallī prō mūrō oppidī cōpiās integrās conlocābant ut proelium cum nostrīs redintegrārent.

II.—1. Our (*adj.*) general will not hesitate to attack a

town of the Belgians in farthest Gaul. 2. Our men were carrying new weapons into the general's camp so that they might rout the Gauls. 3. The Belgians in many places build high walls for the sake of defence.

LESSON XIV.

VERB AND ADJECTIVE, CONTINUED. REVIEW OF THE FIRST CONJUGATION.

68. Conjugation of *imperō*.

Present Indicative.	Imperfect Indicative.	Future Indicative.
I command.	*was commanding.*	*shall command.*
SINGULAR.	SINGULAR.	SINGULAR.
1. imperō	imperābam	imperābō
2. imperās	imperābās	imperābis
3. imperat	imperābat	imperābit
PLURAL.	PLURAL.	PLURAL.
1. imperāmus	imperābāmus	imperābimus
2. imperātis	imperābātis	imperābitis
3. imperant	imperābant	imperābunt

Present Subjunctive.	Imperfect Subjunctive.
may command.	*might command.*
SINGULAR.	SINGULAR.
1. imperem	imperārem
2. imperēs	imperārēs
3. imperet	imperāret
PLURAL.	PLURAL.
1. imperēmus	imperārēmus
2. imperētis	imperārētis
3. imperent	imperārent

69. Agreement of the adjective.—Compare the *ending* of the *adjective* and the *ending* of the *noun* which it limits, in the following:

Nostrī Belgās ferōs fugābunt, *Our men will rout the fierce Belgians*

Do the noun **Belgās** and the adjective **ferōs** end alike? Look up the *gender* of **Belgās** and apply the rule for agreement of the adjective (4).

70. Imperative mood of *portō.*

SINGULAR.   PLURAL.

1. [wanting]   [wanting]
2. { portā,   *carry (thou)*   { portāte,   *carry (ye)*
   { portātō, *thou shalt carry*   { portātōte, *ye shall carry*
3. portātō, *he shall carry*   portantō, *they shall carry*

Examples of the use of the imperative.

Gladiōs portā, serve!   *Slave, carry the swords!*
Oppidum, praefectī, expūgnāte!   *Generals, storm the town!*

Do not place the person addressed (*voc.*) *first* in a Latin sentence.

71.   **EXERCISES.**

I.—1. Germānōs fugāte, Rōmānī! 2. Gallī, ut perīculum vītent, ex oppidīs mātūrant. 3. Galba tubā sīgnum proeliī dabit et nostrī in Germānōrum castrīs equōs et arma occupābunt. 4. Germānī cum Belgīs coniūrābant ut populī (*gen.*) Rōmānī praesidia expūgnārent. 5. Praefectī Rōmānī in hībernīs idōneō in vīcō cōpiās conlocābunt.

II.—1. General, give the signal! 2. The Germans will attack the remaining towns and winter in the villages of the Gauls. 3. The townsmen hasten to Galba's camp to establish [1] friendship with [2] the Roman people.

---
[1] Not infinitive in Latin.   [2] Use cum.

LESSON XV.

PORTŌ, CONTINUED. PRESENT SYSTEM OF TENSES, COMPLETED.

72. Present system of *portō* completed.

Present participle   portāns,   *carrying*
Present infinitive   portāre,   *to carry*
Gerund   portandī, *of carrying*

73. Gerund defined and declined.—The gerund is, in form, a neuter verbal noun of the second declension, corresponding in meaning to the English verbal noun ending in *ing*.

The gerund is thus declined. The *nominative* is supplied by the present infinitive active.

Gen. portandī,   *of carrying*
Dat. portandō,   *to or for carrying*
Acc. (ad) portandum,   *for carrying*
Abl. portandō,   *from, with, by,* etc., *carrying*

74. Use of the gerund.—The gerund in any form governs the same case as the verb of which it is a part. As:

Agrōs vāstandō, *By laying waste the fields*

75. Synopsis of *portō* in the present system.—The following *nine* forms are built upon the *present stem* portā:

1. *Present indicative*   portō,   *I carry*
2. *Imperfect indicative*   portābam, *I was carrying*
3. *Future indicative*   portābō, *I shall carry*
4. *Present subjunctive*   portem,   *I may carry*
5. *Imperfect subjunctive*   portārem, *I might carry*
6. *Imperative*   portā,   *carry (thou)*
7. *Present participle*   portāns, *carrying*
8. *Present infinitive*   portāre, *to carry*
9. *Gerund*   portandī, *of carrying*

Give complete synopsis, *present system*, in order of "tense-name," "tense-form," and "meaning," of **incūsō** and **sustentō**.

Decline the *nouns* of the *first* and *second declensions* (453, 454), also **altus** and **crēber** (466). Name *four* kinds of *ablatives*.

76.   **VOCABULARY.**

Nom.	Gen.	Meaning.
rēgnum	-ī, *neut.*	*kingdom* or *royal power*
facile, *adv.*		*easily*
castellum	-ī, *neut.*	*redoubt*
armātus	-a, -um, *adj.*	*armed*
proximus	-a, -um, "	*next*
parātus	-a, -um, "	*ready*
incūsō	-āre, -āvī, -ātum	*to blame*
sustentō	-āre, -āvī, -ātum	*to hold out*
impetrō	-āre, -āvī, -ātum	*to obtain*

77. Relation of words and clauses.

Lēgātī Belgārum ad Galbae castra veniunt, ut cum populō Rōmānō amīcitiam cōnfīrment,   *Ambassadors of the Belgians come to Galba's camp to establish* friendship with the Roman people*

Lēgātī = subject of the principal verb **veniunt** (indicative mood).

Belgārum = genitive plural modifying **lēgātī**.

⎧ **ad** = preposition governing the noun **castra** in the accusative.
⎨ **Galbae** = genitive singular limiting **castra**.
⎩ **castra** = object of **ad**: this phrase limits the principal verb **veniunt**—*a verb of motion*.

veniunt = present indicative active, 3d plural, *not of the first conjugation*.

---

* To establish, etc., subordinate clause denoting *purpose* (53).

ut = conjunction going with cōnfīrment: this entire clause denotes *purpose* and is subordinate to veniunt.

{ cum = preposition governing the noun populō in the *ablative*.

populō = object of cum: this phrase limits the verb cōnfīrment.

Rōmānō = adjective modifying populō in the *ablative singular masculine*.

amīcitiam = direct object of cōnfīrment.

cōnfīrment = present subjunctive active, 3d plural; subjunctive of *purpose after* ut.

78. REVIEW VOCABULARY.

LESSONS I—XV.

1. trāns (prep. with the acc.), *across*
2. contrā (prep. with the acc.), *against*
3. auxilium, auxiliī (neut.), *aid*
4. iuvō, iuvāre, iūvī, iūtum, *to aid*
5. adiuvō, adiuvāre, adiūvī, adiūtum, *to aid*
6. sum, esse, fuī [no supine], *be* or *am*
7. lēgātus, lēgātī (mas.), *ambassador*
8. et (conj.), *and*
9. armātus, armāta, armātum (adj.), *armed*
10. arma, armōrum (neut.), *arms*
11. oppūgnō, oppūgnāre, oppūgnāvī, oppūgnātum, *attack*
12. vītō, vītāre, vītāvī, vītātum, *avoid*
13. impedīmenta, impedīmentōrum (neut.), *baggage*
14. rīpa, rīpae (fem.), *bank*
15. proelium, proeliī (neut.), *battle*
16. quod (conj.), *because*
17. initium, initiī (neut.), *beginning*
18. Belgae, Belgārum (mas.), *Belgians*
19. amātus, amāta, amātum (adj.), *beloved*
20. incūsō, incūsāre, incūsāvī, incūsātum, *blame*
21. puer, puerī (mas.), *boy*
22. lātus, lāta, lātum (adj.), *broad* or *wide*
23. aedificō, aedificāre, aedificāvī, aedificātum, *build*
24. aedificium, aedificiī (neut.), *building*
25. sed (conj.), *but*
26. appellō, appellāre, appellāvī, appellātum, *call*
27. castra, castrōrum (neut.), *camp*
28. portō, portāre, portāvī, portātum, *carry*
29. causa, causae (fem.), *cause*
30. līberī, līberōrum (mas.), *children*
31. imperium, imperiī (neut.), *command*

32. imperō, imperāre, imperāvī, imperātum, *to command*
33. cēlō, cēlāre, cēlāvī, cēlātum, *conceal*
34. coniūrō, coniūrāre, coniūrāvī, coniūrātum, *conspire*
35. frūmentum, frūmentī (neut.), *corn*
36. perīculum, perīculī (neut.), *danger*
37. praesidium, praesidiī (neut.), *defence*
38. mora, morae (fem.), *delay*
39. mandō, mandāre, mandāvī, mandātum, *direct* or *instruct*
40. fossa, fossae (fem.), *ditch*
41. facile (adv.), *easily*
42. cōnfīrmō, cōnfīrmāre, cōnfīrmāvī, cōnfīrmātum, *establish*
43. extrēmus, extrēma, extrēmum (adj.), *farthest*
44. ager, agrī (mas.), *field*
45. ferus, fera, ferum (adj.), *fierce*
46. pūgna, pūgnae (fem.), *fight*
47. pūgnō, pūgnāre, pūgnāvī, pūgnātum, *to fight*
48. prīmus, prīma, prīmum, *first*
49. fuga, fugae (fem.), *flight*
50. causā (stands *after* the gen.), *for the sake of*
51. cōpiae, cōpiārum (fem.), *forces*
52. silva, silvae (fem.), *forest*
53. integer, integra, integrum (adj.), *fresh*
54. amīcus, amīcī (mas.), *friend*
55. amīcitia, amīcitiae (fem.), *friendship*
56. Galba, Galbae (mas.), *Galba*
57. porta, portae (fem.), *gate*
58. Gallia, Galliae (fem.), *Gaul* (country)
59. Gallus, Gallī (mas.), *Gaul* (citizen)
60. praefectus, praefectī (mas.), *general*
61. Germānī, Germānōrum (mas.), *Germans*
62. dō, dare, dedī, datum, *give*
63. māgnus, māgna, māgnum, *great* or *large*
64. mātūrō, mātūrāre, mātūrāvī, mātūrātum, *hasten*
65. galea, galeae (fem.), *helmet*
66. auxilium, auxiliī (neut.), *help*
67. dubitō, dubitāre, dubitāvī, dubitātum, *hesitate*

68. altus, alta, altum (adj.), *high*, *tall*, or *deep*
69. sustentō, sustentāre, sustentāvī, sustentātum, *hold out*
70. equus, equī (mas.), *horse*
71. in (prep. with the *abl.*), *in;* (with the *acc.*) *into*
72. prō (prep. with the *abl.*), *in front of*
73. Ītalia, Ītaliae (fem.), *Italy*
74. pīlum, pīlī (neut.), *javelin*
75. rēgnum, rēgnī (neut.), *kingdom* or *power*
76. vāstō, vāstāre, vāstāvī, vāstātum, *lay waste*
77. amō, amāre, amāvī, amātum, *love*
78. vir, virī (mas.), *man*
79. multus, multa, multum (adj.), *much* or *many*
80. nūntius, nūntiī (mas.), *message* or *messenger*
81. animus, animī (mas.), *mind*
82. fīnitimī, fīnitimōrum (mas.), *neighbours*
83. novus, nova, novum (adj.), *new*
84. proximus, proxima, proximum (adj.), *next*
85. nōn (adv.), *not*
86. numerus, numerī (mas.), *number*
87. impetrō, impetrāre, impetrāvī, impetrātum, *obtain*
88. propter (prep. with the *acc.*), *on account of*
89. noster, nostra, nostrum (adj.), *our*
90. nostrī, nostrōrum (mas.), *our men*
91. ē or ex (prep. with the *abl.*), *out of*
92. superō, superāre, superāvī, superātum, *overcome*
93. populus, populī (mas.), *people*
94. locus, locī (mas.), *place;* (plur. neut.) loca
95. conlocō conlocāre, conlocāvī, conlocātum, *to place*
96. loca, locōrum (neut.), *places*
97. cōnsilium, cōnsiliī (neut.), *plan*
98. parō, parāre, parāvī, parātum, *prepare*
99. prōvincia, prōvinciae (fem.), *province*
100. vāllum, vāllī (neut.), *rampart*
101. parātus, parāta, parātum (adj.), *ready*
102. castellum, castellī (neut.), *redoubt*
103. subsidium, subsidiī (neut.), *relief*

104. Rēmī, Rēmōrum (mas.), *Remi*
105. reliquus, reliqua, reliquum (adj.), *remaining*
106. redintegrō, redintegrāre, redintegrāvī, redintegrātum, *renew*
107. Rhēnus, Rhēnī (mas.), *Rhine*
108. Rōmānus, Rōmānī (mas.), *Roman*
109. Rōmānus, Rōmāna, Rōmānum (adj.), *Roman*
110. fugō, fugāre, fugāvī, fugātum, *rout*
111. prōflīgō, prōflīgāre, prōflīgāvī, prōflīgātum, *rout*
112. secundus, secunda, secundum (adj.), *second*
113. occupō, occupāre, occupāvī, occupātum, *seize*
114. servus, servī (mas.), *servant* or *slave*
115. scūtum, scūtī (neut.), *shield*
116. sīgnum, sīgnī (neut.), *signal*
117. ut (conj.), *so that*
118. expūgnō, expūgnāre, expūgnāvī, expūgnātum, *storm*
119. idōneus, idōnea, idōneum (adj.), *suitable*
120. convocō, convocāre, convocāvī, convocātum, *summon*
121. gladius, gladiī (mas.), *sword*
122. per (prep. with the *acc.*), *through*
123. ad (prep. with the *acc.*), *to, towards*
124. oppidum, oppidī (neut.), *town*
125. oppidānī, oppidānōrum (mas.), *townsmen*
126. tuba, tubae (fem.), *trumpet*
127. vīcus, vīcī (mas.), *village*
128. mūrus, mūrī (mas.), *wall*
129. tēlum, tēlī (neut.), *weapon*
130. hiemō, hiemāre, hiemāvī, hiemātum, *winter*
131. hīberna, hībernōrum (neut.), *winter-quarters*
132. cum (prep. with the *abl.*), *with*
133. sine (prep. with the *abl.*), *without*

LESSON XVI.

RELATIVE PRONOUN.

79. Quī, quae, quod, *who, which, what,* or *that.*

	SINGULAR.			PLURAL.		
	Mas.	Fem.	Neuter.	Mas.	Fem.	Neuter.
Nom.	quī	quae	quod	quī	quae	quae
Gen.	cūius	cūius	cūius	quōrum	quārum	quōrum
Dat.	cui	cui	cui	quibus	quibus	quibus
Acc.	quem	quam	quod	quōs	quās	quae
Abl.	quō	quā	quō	quibus	quibus	quibus

80. Review of the declension of the relative in English grammar.

who.

	SINGULAR.	PLURAL.
Nom.	*who*	*who*
Poss.	*whose*	*whose*
Obj.	*whom*	*whom*

which.

	SINGULAR.	PLURAL.
Nom.	*which*	*which*
Poss.	*whose, of which*	*whose, of which*
Obj.	*which*	*which*

Observe that the English pronoun *who* may be *masculine* or *feminine, singular* or *plural*, as is seen in the following examples: 1. This is the *boy who* is diligent. 2. These are the *boys who* are truthful. 3. Tell me the name of the *girl who* is reciting. 4. There are many *girls who* read good books.

In example (1) '*who*' is *singular* and *masculine*, agreeing with its antecedent, 'boy.' In example (2) '*who*' is *plural* and *masculine* to agree with its antecedent, 'boys.' In (3) '*who*' is *singular feminine* to agree with its antecedent, while in (4) '*who*' is *plural feminine*.

81.   **VOCABULARY.**

Review words 1–66 in 'review vocabulary' (78).

82. Commit to memory:

1. **Lēgātus quī mātūrat,**   *The ambassador who hastens*
2. **Gallī quī hiemant,**   *The Gauls who winter*

3. Cōpiae quae parant,   The forces which prepare
4. Tuba quae sīgnum dat,   The trumpet which gives a signal
5. Praesidia quae cēlant,   The defences which conceal
6. Pīlum qucd superat,   The jarelin which overcomes

83. Agreement of the relative.—The relative *must* agree with its antecedent in *number*, *gender*, and *person;* the case of the relative is determined *by its function in its own clause,* which function is always different from that of its antecedent. There can be no relative pronoun without at least two verbs in the sentence.

LESSON XVII.

RELATIVE PRONOUN, CONTINUED.

84. *Castra* and the relative pronoun.—As **castra** is *plural* in form and *singular* in meaning and also *neuter*, a relative pronoun referring to **castra** as its antecedent must be *neuter* and *plural*, as in example (1).

When **castra** becomes the *subject* of a verb, the latter takes a *plural form* in Latin, although it is *singular* in English, as in example (2).

85. Examples of *castra*, etc.

1. **Caesar castra quae impedīmenta cēlant expūgnat,**   *Caesar storms the camp which conceals the baggage*
2. **Castra Galbae equōs cēlābant,**   *The camp concealed Galba's horses*

86.   VOCABULARY.

Review words 67–133 in 'review vocabulary' (78).

87. Conjugate and give meanings of **fugō** and **mandō** in the *imperative* (70); also decline their *gerunds* and give their *present participles* and *present infinitives* (72, 73).

RELATIVE PRONOUN.

88. What is the *present stem* of cŏnfīrmō ?
How many forms are derived from this stem?
Give full synopsis of these *with meanings.*
How express in Latin a subordinate clause of *purpose*?
Explain fully the agreement of the *relative* quae in Latin sentence (3) below.

89.   EXERCISES.

I.—1. Praefectus quī in Galliā hiemat cum Belgīs proelium redintegrābit. 2. Galba pīlīs multīs aedificia Germānōrum quī contrā populum Rōmānum coniūrant expūgnat. 3. Praefectī nostrī (*adj.*) in hībernīs in prōvinciā cōpiās quae castella nova aedificant conlocābunt. 4. Germānī quī in castra cōpiās convocant, ut pūgnam vītent, proelium nōn redintegrābunt sed ē castrīs fugā mātūrābunt.

II.—1. With the aid of the Remi Galba overcomes the remaining Belgians who are laying waste the fields of the Romans. 2. Slaves were carrying many weapons into the camp which concealed the baggage of the Roman general. 3. Our men overcome in many battles the forces which are building defences in Gaul. 4. The fierce Belgians will establish friendship with their neighbours and storm the town which gives aid to the Roman forces.

LESSON XVIII.

RELATIVE PRONOUN, CONTINUED.

90. **Examples of the relative as the object:**

1. **Oppidum quod Galba occupat,** *The town which Galba seizes*
2. **Agrī quōs Germānī vāstant,** *The fields which the Germans lay waste*

3. **Castra quae Rēmī in Galliā conlocant,** — *The camp which the Remi place in Gaul*
4. **Cōpiae quās Caesar in prōvinciam convocat,** — *Forces which Caesar summons into the province*
5. **Tuba quam Galba servō dat,** — *The trumpet which Galba gives to (his) slave*
6. **Lēgātus quem praefectī incūsant,** — *The ambassador whom the generals blame*

91. VOCABULARY.

Learn the *principal parts* and *meanings* of verbs 1–10 (448).

92. How words are joined together in a sentence.

Belgae contrā integrās cōpiās quās Caesar in castra convocat nōn sustentābunt, — *The Belgians will not hold out against the fresh forces which Caesar is summoning into camp*

Belgae: subject of **sustentābunt**, which is the *principal verb* in the sentence and is placed *at the end*. **contrā integrās cōpiās**: adverbial phrase, modifies **sustentābunt**. **integrās**: *precedes* **cōpiās**, because **cōpiās** is the antecedent of the relative **quās** and should immediately precede the relative. **quās**: begins the relative clause and is the *direct object* of **convocat**. **Caesar**: subject of **convocat**. **in castra**: adverbial phrase limiting the *next verb*, **convocat**. **nōn**: adverb limiting **sustentābunt**.

93. EXERCISES.

I.—1. Cōpiae quās Galba in hībernīs conlocat Belgārum praesidia nōn oppūgnābunt. 2. Nostrī cum Rēmīs coniūrandō castra quae Germānī in Galliā conlocābant oppūgnāre parābant. 3. Praefectī Galbae in Galliam mātūrāre nōn dubitant, ut oppida quae amīcī Germānōrum imperiī causā aedificant oppūgnent. 4. Caesar cōpiīs amātīs vīcōs quōs nostrī in Galliā facile expūgnābant (*stormed*) dabit. II.—1. The slaves whom Galba conceals in a suitable place will carry relief to the Remi. 2. Caesar was giving swords and javelins to the Remi, whom he calls friends, so that they might attack the large camp which the Germans were preparing to place in Gaul. 3. O Romans! storm the redoubt which the Belgians are preparing. 4. Galba's forces will attack the wall which the Germans are building.

LESSON XIX.

RELATIVE PRONOUN, CONTINUED. IRREGULAR VERB SUM, *I AM*.

94. Present indicative, *sum*, *I am*. **Imperfect indicative,** *eram*, *I was*. **Future indicative,** *erō*, *I shall be*.

I am.		*I was.*		*I shall be.*	
SINGULAR.	PLURAL.	SINGULAR.	PLURAL.	SINGULAR.	PLURAL.
1. sum, *I am*	sumus, *we are*	eram	erāmus	erō	erimus
2. es, *you are*	estis, *you are*	erās	erātis	eris	eritis
3. est, *he is*	sunt, *they are*	erat	erant,	erit	erunt

95. Use of *sum*—**Predicate nominative.**—Forms of *sum* are followed by a *noun* or an *adjective* in the nominative case; such a nominative is called a *predicate nominative*. If the predicate nominative is an *adjective*, it takes the *gender* and *number* of the *subject* to which it belongs. The case with *esse* will be explained later.

96.   VOCABULARY.

Verbs 11-20 (**448**).

97. Examples of the predicate nominative:

1. Mūrus altus est,   The wall is tall
2. Porta lāta est,   The gate is wide
3. Oppidum māgnum erat,   The town was large
4. Cōpiae ferae erant,   The forces were fierce
5. Belgae ferī erant,   The Belgians were fierce
6. Castra māgna erunt,   The camp will be large

In the above sentences the *predicate adjective* is in the *nominative*, having the *number* and *gender* of the subject to which it belongs. In (2) **lāta** is *nominative singular feminine*, to agree with **porta**. In (6) **castra** is *plural*, hence **erunt** is *plural* and **māgna** is *nominative plural neuter*, agreeing with **castra**.

98. The pronoun in the genitive (possessive) case.

EXAMPLES.

1. Germānī quōrum castra Galba occupābit,   The Germans whose camp Galba will seize
2. Cōpiae quārum tēla nova sunt,   The forces whose weapons are new
3. Oppidum cūius mūrī altī sunt,   The town whose walls are tall
4. Praefectus Rōmānus cūius cōpiae Gallōs superābant,   The Roman general whose forces overcame the Gauls

99.   EXERCISES.

I.—1. Silvae in Galliā multae sunt (*there are many,* etc.). 2. Mūrus oppidī altus est. 3. Sumus amīcī populī Rōmānī. 4. Nostrī tēlīs et armīs vīcum cūius mūrī nōn māgnī sunt expūgnābunt. 5. Caesar praefectō cūius cōpiae ad Belgās auxilium nōn portābant pīla multa dabat. 6. Nostrī frūmentō Belgās quōrum oppida in prōvinciā sunt iuvābant (*were aiding*).

II.—1. The walls are tall. 2. Galba's camp is new. 3. The Roman forces are fresh. 4. Caesar will give help to the Remi whose fields are in farthest Gaul. 5. Our generals will carry corn into the town whose walls the fierce Belgians are preparing to storm. 6. The forces whose generals Galba summons out of winter-quarters will renew the battle, so that they may rout the Germans.

LESSON XX.

PORTŌ, CONTINUED. PERFECT STEM.

100. Perfect Indicative of *portō*, *I carried, have carried, did carry.*

SINGULAR.	PLURAL.
1. portāvī	1. portāvimus
2. portāvistī	2. portāvistis
3. portāvit	3. portāvērunt (ēre)

Personal endings.

SINGULAR.	PLURAL.
-ī	-imus
-istī	-istis
-it	-ērunt (ēre)

101. Portāv, the stem of this tense, called the *perfect stem*, is found by dropping *final* ī from the first person singular of the *perfect indicative*.

Conjugate, with meanings, vītō, parō, and occupō in the *perfect indicative*.

102. Meanings of the perfect and imperfect Indicative.— The *perfect* tense has *two* uses, denoting (1) an action completed *just now* (*Definite perfect*), or (2) one *completed* at some point of *past time* (*Indefinite* or *Historical perfect*): as, (*definite perfect*) **pater pervēnit**, *father has (already) arrived;* (*indefinite perfect*) **Caesar omnem Galliam vīcit**, *Caesar conquered all Gaul.*

The *imperfect* tense represents an action as *continued* in the *past*. The action may be (1) *continuous* in the past; as, **oppidānī oppidum aedificābant**, *the townsmen were building a town;*—(2) *customary* or *usual* action; as, **Germānī Rhēnum trānsībant**, *the Germans used to cross (kept crossing) the Rhine ;*—(3) *attempted* action (*Conative imperfect*); as, **hostēs pontem incendēbant**, *the enemy tried to burn the bridge.*

103.   **VOCABULARY.**

Verbs 21-30 (448).

104. Use of *quod*,[1] *because.*—**Quod** introduces a subordinate clause to show 'reason why,' and such a clause is called a *causal clause.*

Causal clauses do not usually stand last.

1. **Quod nostrī ad pūgnandum**   *Galba gives the signal, because*
    (*gerund*) **parātī sunt, Galba**   *our men are ready for fight-*
    sīgnum dat,   *ing*
2. **Quod Belgae coniūrāvērunt,**   *Because the Belgians conspired,*
    Galba oppida oppūgnāre   *Galba prepared to attack their*
    parāvit,   *towns*

In (1) above **quod** introduces **sunt parātī**, giving the *cause of* and modifying the *principal verb*, **dat**. So in (2) **quod . . . coniūrāvērunt** limits **parāvit**, stating the *reason* for the action.

105.   **EXERCISES.**

I.—1. Servī fugae causā praefectīs equōs parāvērunt. 2. Quod Germānī quōs fugāvit ex Galliā mātūrābant, Caesar in hībernīs cōpiās conlocāvit. 3. Caesar praefectōs incūsābat, quod contrā Belgās proeliō nōn sustentāvērunt (*did not hold out*) sed fugā in castra mātūrāvērunt. 4. Belgārum cōpiae quās nostrī initiō proeliī superāvērunt

---

[1] Quod, quia, quoniam, discussed in (276).

equōs parābant (*were making ready*), ut trāns Rhēnum
mātūrārent. 5. Galba, praefectus Rōmānōrum, quod
Germānī multōs populī Rōmānī agrōs vāstābant, proelium
redintegrāre parāvit.

II.—1. The generals in Galba's camp routed the remaining Belgians with the forces[1] which the Remi gave (dedērunt) to the Roman people. 2. The general to whom
Caesar gave fresh forces will easily storm the redoubt of
the Belgians. 3. The townsmen to whom Caesar gives
corn and weapons are friends of the Roman people.
4. The Germans will hasten out of the village, in which
they are wintering, to lay waste the fields of the Belgians.

LESSON XXI.

PORTŌ AND SUM, CONTINUED.

106. Pluperfect Indicative of *portō*. Future perfect indicative.

had carried.	*shall have carried.*
SINGULAR.	SINGULAR.
1. portāveram	portāverō
2. portāverās	portāveris
3. portāverat	portāverit
PLURAL.	PLURAL.
1. portāverāmus	portāverimus
2. portāverātis	portāveritis
3. portāverant	portāverint

107. These two tenses *complete* the indicative mood of
portō in the active voice. See indicative mood, active, (*six
tenses*,) of amō (474). Conjugate the entire indicative mood
of sustentō, convocō, and dō. Distinguish the indicative
tenses with respect to *stems*.

---
[1] Ablative of means (43), 'ablative without cum.'

108. Present subjunctive of *sum*. Imperfect subjunctive.

may be. *might be.*

SINGULAR.	PLURAL.	SINGULAR.	PLURAL.
1. sim	sīmus	essem	essēmus
2. sīs	sītis	essēs	essētis
3. sit	sint	esset	essent

109. **VOCABULARY.**

Verbs 31–40 (**448**).

110. Subordinate clauses.—*Three* kinds of *subordinate clauses* have thus far been used, viz.: the **ut** *clause, the relative*, and the **quod** *clause*. What can be said of the **ut** *clause*? of the agreement and position of the *relative*? of the meaning of the **quod** *clause*?

111. **EXERCISES.**

I.—1. Germānī prō oppidī mūrīs vālla alta conlocandō praesidia parāverant. 2. Quod perīcula proeliī māgna sunt, Caesar in silvīs altīs pūgnam nōn redintegrābit. 3. Praefectus cōpiīs integrīs equōs et arma dedit, ut ad Rēmōs, amīcōs, subsidium portārent. 4. Germānī propter māgnum nostrōrum numerum vīcum novum in quem līberōs et impedīmenta portāre parābant aedificāvērunt. 5. Lēgātus Rōmānōrum oppidānōs, quod amīcīs populī Rōmānī subsidium nōn dederant, incūsābat.

II.—1. Because the Germans gave aid to the Belgians who were not friends of the Roman people, Caesar[1] hastened[1] to attack with many forces the redoubt which they had placed in front of their camp. 2. With the help[3] of the slaves whom Galba had summoned into Gaul, our generals[1] built[2] a large camp in which they placed weapons for storming (**ad** + *gerund*) the towns of the Belgians.

---

[1] Place *first* in sentence. [2] Place *last*.
[3] Ablative of means (**43**), 'ablative without cum.'

LESSON XXII.

THIRD DECLENSION. SUM, CONTINUED.

112. Mīles, *soldier*, mas. Case-endings.

	SINGULAR.	PLURAL.	SINGULAR.	PLURAL.
Nom.	mīles	mīlitēs	—	-ēs
Gen.	mīlitis	mīlitum	-is	-um
Dat.	mīlitī	mīlitibus	-ī	-ibus
Acc.	mīlitem	mīlitēs	-em	-ēs
Voc.	mīles	mīlitēs	—	-ēs
Abl.	mīlite	mīlitibus	-e	-ibus

113. The stem[1] of **mīles** may be found by dropping **is** from the *genitive singular:* **mīlitis**, stem **mīlit**.

The *nominative* and *vocative* singular are alike, differing somewhat from the *stem;* the remaining cases of the *singular* and *all* the cases of the *plural* are formed by annexing the *case-endings* to the *stem*. The *nominative, accusative,* and *vocative plural* end in **ēs**, the *dative* and *ablative plural* in **ibus**.

114.   VOCABULARY.

Verbs 41–46 (448).

Nom.	Gen.	Meaning.
pedes	peditis, *mas.*	*footman,* plural *infantry*
eques	equitis, *mas.*	*horseman,* plural *cavalry*
obses	obsidis, *mas.*	*hostage*
bellum	-ī, *neut.*	*war*
Sēquanī	-ōrum, *mas.*	*the Sequani*
inimīcus	-a -um, *adj.*	*unfriendly*
bonus	-a -um, *adj.*	*good*
armō	(give principal parts)	*to arm*
dēcertō	" " "	*to contend*
exercitō	" " "	*to train*

Decline **pedes, eques,** and **obses.**

---
[1] For the classification of stems see Third Declension (455).

115. Notice carefully the *agreement* of *adjective* and *noun* in the following:

1. **servī bonī,** *of a good slave*
2. **mīlitis bonī,** *of a good soldier*

Nouns and their modifying adjectives end alike only when declined alike, as in (1) above. In (2) the requirement is that each should have the ending proper to *identity* of *gender, number,* and *case.*

116. Imperative of *sum*.

SINGULAR.
1. [wanting]
2. { es, *be thou*
   { estō, *thou shalt be*
3. estō, *he shall be*

PLURAL.
1. [wanting]
2. { este, *be ye*
   { estōte, *ye shall be*
3. suntō, *they shall be*

Present Infinitive.

esse, *to be.*

This completes the *present system* of tenses of the verb **sum.**

117. Synopsis of *sum* (*present stem* es):

1. *Present indicative*   sum
2. *Imperfect indicative*   eram
3. *Future indicative*   erō
4. *Present subjunctive*   sim
5. *Imperfect subjunctive*   essem
6. *Imperative*   es
7. *Present participle*   [lacking]
8. *Present infinitive*   esse
9. *Gerund*   [lacking]

118.   EXERCISES.

I.—1. Galbae mīlitēs ad pūgnandum parātī sunt. 2. Praefectus noster mīlitibus Rōmānīs galeās quās in castrīs Germānōrum occupāverat (*had taken possession of*) dedit. 3. Mūrī quōs Gallī praesidiī causā prō oppidīs aedificāvērunt altī et lātī erant. 4. Praefectī nostrī Gallōs incūsāvērunt et oppida quae sine praesidiō erant oppūgnāvērunt, quod populō Rōmānō līberōs obsidēs[1] nōn dederant.

II.—1. Caesar will have given a new shield to the good soldier. 2. Galba was summoning the fresh infantry out of camp. 3. Caesar was blaming the general to whom he had given the signal, because he hesitated to renew the battle with[2] the cavalry of the Sequani. 4. The Germans gave their children to Galba as hostages, so that they might establish friendship with[2] the Roman people.

LESSON XXIII.

FIRST CONJUGATION AND THIRD DECLENSION, CONTINUED.

119. Perfect subjunctive of *portō*. Pluperfect subjunctive.

may have carried.	*might have carried.*
SINGULAR.	SINGULAR.
1. portāverim	portāvissem
2. portāveris	portāvissēs
3. portāverit	portāvisset
PLURAL.	PLURAL.
1. portāverimus	portāvissēmus
2. portāveritis	portāvissētis
3. portāverint	portāvissent

Perfect Infinitive.

portāvisse, *to have carried*

This completes the *perfect system of tenses* formed upon the perfect stem **portāv**.

---

[1] Appositive, as *hostages* (54).
[2] Use prep. cum. Why? (48.)

120. Synopsis of the perfect system of *portō* (*six tenses*):

1. Perfect indicative   portāvī
2. Pluperfect indicative   portāveram
3. Future perfect indicative   portāverō
4. Perfect subjunctive   portāverim
5. Pluperfect subjunctive   portāvissem
6. Perfect infinitive   portāvisse

121.   VOCABULARY.

Verbs 47-52 (448).

Nom.	Gen.	Meaning.
imperātum	-ī, *neut.*	*order* or *command*
levitās	levitātis, *fem.*	*fickleness*
facultās	-tātis, "	*opportunity*
aestās	-tātis, "	*summer*
potestās	-tātis, "	*power*
auctōritās	-tātis, "	*influence*
flūmen	flūminis, *neut.*	*river*
homō	hominis, *mas.*	*man*
rūmor	rūmōris, *mas.*	*report*
cum, *conj.*		*while*

122. Declension of nouns.

Cīvitās, *state*, fem.   Agmen, *line (of march)*, neut.

	SINGULAR.	PLURAL.	SINGULAR.	PLURAL.
Nom.	cīvitās	cīvitātēs	agmen	agmina
Gen.	cīvitātis	cīvitātum	agminis	agminum
Dat.	cīvitātī	cīvitātibus	agminī	agminibus
Acc.	cīvitātem	cīvitātēs	agmen	agmina
Voc.	cīvitās	cīvitātēs	agmen	agmina
Abl.	cīvitāte	cīvitātibus	agmine	agminibus

Nouns in **ās**, *gen.* **ātis**, are *feminine*. Nouns in **men**, *gen.* **minis**, are *neuter*.

Lapis, *stone*, mas.

	SINGULAR.	PLURAL.		SINGULAR.	PLURAL.
Nom.	lapis	lapidēs	*Acc.*	lapidem	lapidēs
Gen.	lapidis	lapidum	*Voc.*	lapis	lapidēs
Dat.	lapidī	lapidibus	*Abl.*	lapide	lapidibus

Nouns in **is**, *gen.* **idis**, and **es**, *gen.* **itis** or **idis**, are *masculine*.

Combined declension of **miles ferus** (mīles, third-declension noun; **ferus**, an adjective with the second-declension endings):

	SINGULAR	PLURAL
Nom.	mīles ferus	mīlitēs ferī
Gen.	mīlitis ferī	mīlitum ferōrum
Dat.	mīlitī ferō	mīlitibus ferīs
Acc.	mīlitem ferum	mīlitēs ferōs
Voc.	mīles fere	mīlitēs ferī
Abl.	mīlite ferō	mīlitibus ferīs

123.   **EXERCISE.**

1. Praefectus cui Caesar proelium redintegrandī sīgnum dat Germānōrum peditēs facile fugābit. 2. Noster praefectus in Galliam cum peditibus integrīs quōs in hībernīs in prōvinciā Rōmānā conlocāverat mātūrāvit et obsidēs multōs postulāvit. 3. Belgae lēgātō nostrō līberōs obsidēs dabant, ut in potestāte populī Rōmānī essent. 4. Caesar multīs cum cīvitātibus quae in armīs nōn erant et contrā populum Rōmānum nōn coniūrāverant amīcitiam cōnfīrmāvit. 5. Quod Germānī obsidēs quōs postulāverat nōn dedērunt,[1] Caesar oppida trāns flūmen Rhēnum oppūgnāvit.

LESSON XXIV.

THIRD DECLENSION. SUM, CONTINUED.

124. Pater, *father*, mas.   **Rūmor,** *report*, mas.

	SINGULAR	PLURAL	SINGULAR	PLURAL
Nom.	pater	patrēs	rūmor	rūmōrēs
Gen.	patris	patrum	rūmōris	rūmōrum
Dat.	patrī	patribus	rūmōrī	rūmōribus
Acc.	patrem	patrēs	rūmōrem	rūmōrēs
Voc.	pater	patrēs	rūmor	rūmōrēs
Abl.	patre	patribus	rūmōre	rūmōribus

Nouns in **er** and **or** are *masculine*.

---

[1] *Would not give.*

Latus, *side* or *flank,* neut.

	SINGULAR.	PLURAL.
Nom.	latus	latera
Gen.	lateris	laterum
Dat.	laterī	lateribus
Acc.	latus	latera
Voc.	latus	latera
Abl.	latere	lateribus

Corpus, *body,* neut.

	SINGULAR.	PLURAL.
Nom.	corpus	corpora
Gen.	corporis	corporum
Dat.	corporī	corporibus
Acc.	corpus	corpora
Voc.	corpus	corpora
Abl.	corpore	corporibus

Nouns in **us,** gen. **eris** or **oris,** are *neuter.*

Legiŏ, *legion,* fem.

	SINGULAR.	PLURAL.
Nom.	legiŏ	legiōnēs
Gen.	legiōnis	legiōnum
Dat.	legiōnī	legiōnibus
Acc.	legiōnem	legiōnēs
Voc.	legiŏ	legiōnēs
Abl.	legiōne	legiōnibus

Nouns in **ŏ** are *masculine,* save those in **dŏ, gŏ,** and **iŏ,** which are *feminine.*

125.   **VOCABULARY.**

Verbs 53–66 (448).

126. Dative with adjectives. — Adjectives of *likeness, fitness, nearness,* and the like with their opposites take the *dative;* as,

Belgae sunt proximī Germānīs,   *The Belgians are next to the Germans*

127. Sum in the perfect tenses.—Principal parts: **sum, esse, fuī,** *no supine.* Upon the *perfect stem* **fu** are formed *six tenses.* For synopsis of the *present system,* see (117).

Synopsis of the *perfect system* of **sum** (*stem* **fu**):

Perfect indicative	fuī, *I have been—was*
Pluperfect indicative	fueram
Future perfect indicative	fuerō
Perfect subjunctive	fuerim
Pluperfect subjunctive	fuissem
Perfect infinitive	fuisse

THIRD DECLENSION.

128. Use of cum + subjunctive.—Cum,[1] *when*, is followed by a verb in the *imperfect* or *pluperfect subjunctive*. Cum + *imperfect subjunctive* means '*when*' in the sense of *while*, denoting action *unfinished;* cum + *pluperfect subjunctive* means '*when*' in the sense of *after*, denoting action *finished*. If the first verb after cum is in the *imperfect subjunctive*, then cum = *while* (*when*), not *with*, and the verb is translated *as if it were imperfect indicative;* as, **cum Caesar in Galliā esset**, *while Caesar was in Gaul.*

129. EXERCISES.

I.—1. Cum Caesar equitēs integrōs exspectāret, peditēs oppidum cūius mūrī nōn altī fuērunt expūgnāvērunt. 2. Praefectī tubīs mīlitibus integrīs sīgnum dedērunt et ē castrīs celeritāte māgnā mātūrāvērunt, ut Germānōrum hīberna quae in Galliā erant occupārent. 3. Cum reliquae cīvitātēs quae Galbae amīcae[2] erant ad castra Rōmāna auxilium portārent, Caesar trāns Rhēnum cum peditibus et equitibus mātūrāvit et Germānōrum castella, quod populō Rōmānō obsidēs novōs nōn dederant, oppūgnāvit. 4. Caesar auctōritātem amplificandī causā cum cīvitātibus multīs in Galliā amīcitiam cōnfīrmāvit.

II.—1. The state in which Caesar placed his camp will give much corn to the Roman infantry. 2. While our soldiers were preparing to attack the walls of the town, the townsmen hastened out of the town, so that they might avoid (to avoid) the dangers of battle. 3. While the Sequani were awaiting the forces of the neighbouring Belgians, the Roman legions hastened with great swiftness through the province and seized the camp which the Sequani had prepared for the sake of defence.

---

[1] For treatment of *historical* cum see (208).
[2] Adjective, *friendly*.

LESSON XXV.

FIRST CONJUGATION AND THIRD DECLENSION CONTINUED.

130. Collis, *hill,* mas.   **Rēx,** *king,* mas.

	SINGULAR.	PLURAL.	SINGULAR.	PLURAL.
Nom.	collis	collēs	rēx	rēgēs
Gen.	collis	collium	rēgis	rēgum
Dat.	collī	collibus	rēgī	rēgibus
Acc.	collem	collēs -īs	rēgem	rēgēs
Voc.	collis	collēs	rēx	rēgēs
Abl.	colle	collibus	rēge	rēgibus

Flūmen lātum, *a wide river,* neut.

	SINGULAR.	PLURAL.
Nom.	flūmen lātum	flūmina lāta
Gen.	flūminis lātī	flūminum lātōrum
Dat.	flūminī lātō	flūminibus lātīs
Acc.	flūmen lātum	flūmina lāta
Voc.	flūmen lātum	flūmina lāta
Abl.	flūmine lātō	flūminibus lātīs

181. Nouns ending in **is** *not increasing* the number of syllables in the *genitive* are called "*vowel-stems in* **i**," and have **ium**[1] in the *genitive plural* and **īs** or **ēs** in the *accusative plural*. Many have the *ablative* in **ī** (457). The stem of nouns in **is** or **es** *increasing* the number of syllables in the *genitive* is found by dropping **is** from the *genitive;* thus, **lapis, lapidis,** stem **lapid; mīles, mīlitis,** stem **mīlit.** The stem of nouns in **is** or **es** *not increasing* in the *genitive* ends in **i**; as, **collis, collis,** stem **colli.**

Nouns in **is** or **es** (*vowel-stems in* i) are *masculine*, sometimes *feminine*.

---
[1] For summary of the genitive plural in um and ium see (460).

182. VOCABULARY.

Verbs 67–80 (448).

183. Supine system of portō.—The *supine stem*, upon which *four* forms are based, is found by dropping **um** from the first supine: **portātum**, supine stem **portāt**.

The following, formed upon the stem **portāt**, *complete the active voice of* **portō**:

1. *First supine*   portātum,   *to carry*
2. *Second supine* portātū,   *to carry*
3. *Future participle* portātūrus, -a, -um, *being about to carry*
4. *Future infinitive* portātūrum, -am, -um esse, *to be about to carry*

Write a *complete synopsis* of **superō** in the active voice in order of *stems*, giving *name of tense and meaning*, with *nine* forms upon **superā** (75), *six* upon **superāv** (120), and *four* upon **superāt**.

184. Dative with *imperō* and *mandō*.—**Imperō**, *I command*, and **mandō**, *I direct*, take their *object*, the person commanded, in the *dative;* thus:

Caesar legiōnibus imperat, *Caesar commands the legions*
Galba praefectīs mandāvit, *Galba directed his generals*

185. Rule of sequence of tenses.—When the verb in the *principal clause* denotes *present* or *future time*, the verb in the *dependent clause* is *present* or *perfect subjunctive*.

When the verb in the *principal clause* denotes *past time*, the verb in the *dependent clause* is *imperfect* or *pluperfect subjunctive*.

186. Table of sequence.

Present Future Future-perfect	are followed by	present subjunctive to show *contemporaneous* or *subsequent action* (*unfinished*); perfect subjunctive to show *antecedent action* (*finished*).

Imperfect
Perfect   } are follow-
Pluperfect   ed by

{ imperfect subjunctive to show contemporaneous or *subsequent* action (*unfinished*); pluperfect subjunctive to show antecedent action (*finished*).

187. Application of the rule of sequence in the *ut* clause.

Caesar obsidēs postulat ut auctōritātem amplificet,	Caesar demands hostages so that he may increase his power
Caesar obsidēs postulābit ut auctōritātem amplificet,	Caesar will demand hostages so that he may increase his power
Caesar obsidēs postulāverit ut auctōritātem amplificet,	Caesar will have demanded hostages so that he may increase his power
Caesar obsidēs postulābat ut auctōritātem amplificāret,	Caesar kept demanding hostages so that he might increase his power
Caesar obsidēs postulāvit ut auctōritātem amplificāret,	Caesar demanded hostages so that he might increase his power
Caesar obsidēs postulāverat ut auctōritātem amplificāret,	Caesar had demanded hostages so that he might increase his power

LESSON XXVI.
THIRD DECLENSION, CONTINUED.

188. Multitūdō, *multitude*, fem.

	SINGULAR.	PLURAL.
Nom.	multitūdō	multitūdinēs
Gen.	multitūdinis	multitūdinum
Dat.	multitūdinī	multitūdinibus
Acc.	multitūdinem	multitūdinēs
Voc.	multitūdō	multitūdinēs
Abl.	multitūdine	multitūdinibus

THIRD DECLENSION.

Vīs, *force, vigor,* fem. **Iter,** *march,* neut.

	SINGULAR.	PLURAL.	SINGULAR.	PLURAL.
Nom.	vīs	vīrēs	iter	itinera
Gen.	vīs	vīrium	itineris	itinerum
Dat.	—	vīribus	itinerī	itineribus
Acc.	vim	vīrēs	iter	itinera
Voc.	—	vīrēs	iter	itinera
Abl.	vī	vīribus	itinere	itineribus

For 'general rules of gender' in the *third declension* see (458).

139. Review declension of all the *nouns* in the third declension (458, 459). Give synopsis in the entire active voice of **imperō** in order of 'tense-name,' 'stem,' and 'meaning.' Give synopsis, active voice, of **amō**, by *moods, etc.* (474). What can be said of the *relative clause* and subordinate clauses introduced by **ut, quod,** and **cum**? Give the *rule of sequence*.

140. VOCABULARY.

Nom.	Gen.	Meaning.
hostis	hostis, *mas.*	*enemy*
īgnis	īgnis, *mas.*	*fire*
fīnis	fīnis, *mas.*	*end* (in the plural, *territory*)
turris	turris, *fem.*	*tower*
calamitās	-tātis, *fem.*	*calamity*
pāx	pācis, *fem.*	*peace*
pars	partis, *fem.*	*part*
subitō, *adv.*		*suddenly*
fortiter, *adv.*		*bravely*
ōrātiō	-ōnis, *fem.*	*speech*
profectiō	-ōnis, *fem.*	*departure*
dēditiō	-ōnis, *fem.*	*surrender*
mūnītiō	-ōnis, *fem.*	*fortification*

Īgnis has the ablative **īgne** or **īgnī**.

141. EXERCISES.

I.—1. Cum Caesar in Galliā esset, lēgātī multārum cīvitātum ad castra quae in hostium fīnibus parābat mātūrāvērunt. 2. Equitēs Rōmānī auxiliō Rēmōrum castellum in quō arma multa erant expūgnāvērunt et agmina hostium facile prōflīgāvērunt. 3. Quod hostēs proeliō cum Caesaris legiōnibus nōn dēcertābant sed in oppidō cōpiās cēlābant, mīlitēs nostrī altās turrēs quibus oppidī mūrōs facile expūgnāvērunt aedificāvērunt. 4. Germānī in quōrum fīnibus nostrī praesidia parant ad Caesaris castra līberōs obsidēs, ut pācem impetrent, portābunt. 5. Galba in fīnēs hostium cum peditibus et māgnā equitum parte mātūrāvit, ut māgnum obsidum numerum postulāret.

II.—1. Caesar blamed the soldiers of the first and second legion, because they did not renew the battle with the enemies' infantry. 2. While Caesar was preparing on the hill a place for his camp, the enemies' forces suddenly hastened out of the woods towards our men. 3. Our general whose soldiers routed the Sequani will hasten into the territory of the Belgians to prepare¹ new fortifications. 4. While Galba was contending in the boundaries² of the Belgians, Caesar's legions easily routed the infantry of the Sequani and gave to the rest of³ the enemy an opportunity of establishing peace with the Roman people.

LESSON XXVII.

USE OF IMPERŌ AND MANDŌ.

142. Review **sum**—*present system* (**117**), *perfect system* (**127**). Also conjugate with meanings all of **sum** in the order given in (**484**); observe carefully the *future participle* and *future infinitive*. What forms of **sum** are lacking?

143. Decline the nouns of the *first* and *second declensions*

---

¹ How is *purpose* expressed in Latin ? (**58**.)
² 'boundaries' = territory.
³ 'rest of': *dative* of **reliquus**.

(453, 454), and also altus and crēber (466). What is the *case* of the *predicate noun* or *adjective* after forms of **sum**? What adjectives govern the *dative*? Give example, both English and Latin, illustrating the *agreement* of the *relative with its antecedent*, and explain.

144.   **VOCABULARY.**

Verbs 81-92 (448).

145. Use of *imperō* and *mandō*.—Imperō and mandō take the person commanded in the *dative* and an **ut** clause to denote what is commanded to be done. This **ut** clause is translated by the *present infinitive*.

1. Caesar servō ut mātūret imperat, — *Caesar commands the slave to hasten*
2. Galba praefectīs ut frūmentum impetrent mandābit, — *Galba will direct his generals to obtain corn*
3. Praefectus nostrīs ut mūnītiōnēs expūgnārent imperāvit, — *The general commanded our men to storm the fortifications*

Notice very carefully the *sequence of tenses in the* **ut** *clauses* when the *English infinitive verb* is turned into *the subjunctive in Latin*. In (1) and (2) the *present subjunctive* is used because the *time* of the *leading* verb is in (1) *present* and in (2) *future* ; see '*table of sequence*' (first part) (**186**). In (3) the *imperfect subjunctive* is used because the *principal verb* denotes *past time* ('table of sequence,' second part).

146.   **EXERCISES.**

I.—1. Caesar Germānīs quī in fīnibus nostrīs hiemant imperābit ut in prōvinciam Rōmānam līberōs obsidēs portent. 2. Caesar praefectō equitum mandat ut in hostium fīnēs mātūret et cōpiās prōflīget. 3. Galba praefectō cūius mīlitēs mūnītiōnēs novās aedificābant mandāvit ut in hībernīs peditēs et equitēs conlocāret (*sequence*). 4. Cum Rēmī, amīcī nostrī (*adj.*), contrā Germānōrum et Belgārum cōpiās fortiter sustentārent, Caesar Galbae imperāvit ut in Galliam cum mīlitibus prīmae et secundae legiōnis mātūrāret et ad Rēmōs subsidium portāret.

II.—1. Because the fortifications in the enemies' territory were large, Galba directed (*past time*) his soldiers to build a tall tower. 2. The Remi direct their ambassadors to obtain peace for their state which had given aid to the Roman legions in many battles. 3. While Caesar was preparing to attack a large town, messengers hastened into our camp to announce[1] the departure of the enemy out of the town. 4. The general whom Caesar commanded to attack the new fortifications will seize the enemies' baggage.

LESSON XXVIII.

SECOND-CONJUGATION VERB.

147. Present indicative of *dēleō*, *I destroy*. Meanings of persons as in **portō**.

I destroy.

	SINGULAR.	PLURAL.
1.	dēleō	dēlēmus
2.	dēlēs	dēlētis
3.	dēlet	dēlent

The *stem* in this verb is **dēlē**, found by dropping *final ō*.

148.   VOCABULARY.

videō,	*I see*
habeō,	*I have*
teneō,	*I hold*
moveō,	*I move*
contineō,	*I keep*
prohibeō,	*I prevent* or *cut off*

---

[1] Infinitive to express *purpose*. Do *not* render by the *Latin infinitive*.

SECOND CONJUGATION.

149. Notice carefully the endings of the *present subjunctive* in the *first* conjugation and those of the *present indicative* in the *second* conjugation. Note the loss of a syllable in the second person singular of dēleō: not dē-le-ēs, but dē-lēs.

First conjugation—present subjunctive.		Second conjugation—present indicative.	
Table of endings.		*Table of endings.*	
SINGULAR.	PLURAL.	SINGULAR.	PLURAL.
-em	-ēmus	-eō	-ēmus
-ēs	-ētis	-ēs	-ētis
-et	-ent	-et	-ent

150. Thus if a verb ends in **et** or **ent**, for instance, it is *present subjunctive* when the verb is of the *first* conjugation; *present indicative* when the verb is of the *second* conjugation.

Conjugate the *present subjunctive* of **postulō** and **imperō**; *present indicative* of **habeō**, **moveō**, and **teneō**.

151.   EXERCISES.

I.—1. Praefectus Rōmānus, quod hostium profectiōnem videt, cum legiōne prīmā ad collem in quō[1] Galbae castra sunt mātūrat. 2. Nostrī Germānōrum profectiōnem prohibent, ut Caesarī obsidēs novōs impetrent. 3. Peditēs Caesaris gladiīs et pīlīs mūnītiōnēs quās Sēquanī praesidiī causā aedificāvērunt facile dēlent. 4. Quod Belgae ferī[2] in Galliā fīnēs lātōs[2] habent, Caesar castra movet et in Galliam mātūrat, ut agrōs vāstet. 5. Cum hostēs trāns flūmen impedīmenta portārent, Galba in colle proximō flūminī cōpiās conlocāvit et Caesaris imperāta exspectāvit.

II.—1. The soldiers of the second legion easily routed

---
[1] *on which.*
[2] Explain *agreement* of **ferī** and **lātōs**.

the enemies' infantry and seized the baggage which the enemy had concealed in their fortifications. 2. Because Caesar sees the enemies' forces on the hill in front of the town whose walls he is preparing to attack, he keeps his infantry and cavalry in camp. 3. Galba commands the generals of the infantry to hasten across the river and await the departure of the enemy.

LESSON XXIX.

SECOND CONJUGATION, CONTINUED.

152. Imperfect Indicative of *dēleō.* **Future Indicative. Present subjunctive.**

was destroying.		*shall destroy.*		*may destroy.*	
SINGULAR.	PLURAL.	SINGULAR.	PLURAL.	SINGULAR.	PLURAL.
1. dēlēbam	dēlēbāmus	dēlēbō	dēlēbimus	dēleam	dēleāmus
2. dēlēbās	dēlēbātis	dēlēbis	dēlēbitis	dēleās	dēleātis
3. dēlēbat	dēlēbant	dēlēbit	dēlēbunt	dēleat	dēleant

153. The stem in the above tenses is **dēlē.** The endings of the *imperfect* and *future* indicative are the same as in **portō.** The endings of the *present subjunctive* of **dēleō** are very much like the *present indicative* endings of **portō.** Compare these endings: **portō**, *present indicative* **ō, ās, at, āmus, ātis, ant; dēleō**, *present subjunctive* **am, ās, at, āmus, ātis, ant.** Therefore when the verb ends, for instance, in **at** or **ant**, it is *present indicative* if it belongs to the *first conjugation;* *present subjunctive* if it belongs to the *second conjugation.*

154. VOCABULARY.

habeō	habēre	to have
prohibeō	prohibēre	to prevent
valeō	valēre	to be strong
distineō	distinēre	to divide
sustineō	sustinēre	to withstand
iubeō	iubēre	to order

155. Use of *iubeō*, *I order*.—Iubeō is followed by the *accusative (subject)* + *infinitive;* as,

Caesar mīlitēs hostium profec-   *Caesar will order his soldiers to*
tiōnem prohibēre iubēbit,   *prevent the enemies' departure*

In this sentence mīlitēs is in the *accusative case, subject* of the infinitive prohibēre, which, being a transitive active verb, takes its *direct object*, profectiōnem, in the *accusative* also.

156.   EXERCISES.

In the following sentences distinguish carefully the verb-forms in et, at; ent, ant.

I.—1. Quod cīvitās auctōritāte et numerō mīlitum valēbat, Caesar lēgātīs ut obsidēs multōs postulārent imperāvit. 2. Praefectī nostrī peditēs distinēbunt, ut in Galliā populī Rōmānī imperium amplificent et hostium cōpiās sustineant. 3. Galba mīlitēs integrōs trāns flūmen ad collem in quō hostēs mūnītiōnēs novās aedificant mātūrāre iubēbit. 4. Praefectus peditum numerum amplificat et fīnitimōs in castra frūmentum portāre iubet, ut in Galliā hiemet et hostium profectiōnem prohibeat. 5. Gallī turrēs novās quās nostrī ad oppidum oppūgnandum aedificāvērunt īgnī dēlēbunt.

II.—1. Our infantry will obtain corn and arms from many states which are preparing to give hostages to Caesar, so that they may have peace. 2. While the states next to the Roman province were preparing a plan of surrender, Caesar was keeping his new legions in camp. 3. Galba commands[1] his generals to place the baggage in camp and with javelins and swords to withstand the infantry of the enemy. 4. Write sentence (3) again, substituting 'orders' for 'commands': Galba *orders*[2] his generals, etc.

LESSON XXX.
SECOND CONJUGATION, CONTINUED.

157. Imperfect subjunctive of *dēleō, might destroy.*

SINGULAR.	PLURAL.
1. dēlĕrem	dēlĕrēmus
2. dēlĕrēs	dēlĕrētis
3. dēlĕret	dēlĕrent

Imperative.

SINGULAR.	PLURAL.
1. [wanting]	[wanting]
2. dēlē, *destroy thou* / dēlētō, *thou shalt destroy*	dēlēte, *destroy ye* / dēlētōte, *ye shall destroy*
3. dēlētō, *he shall destroy*	dēlentō, *they shall destroy*

Present participle.
dēlēns, *destroying*

Present infinitive.
dēlēre, *to destroy*

Gerund.
Gen. dēlendī
Dat. dēlendō
Acc. dēlendum
Abl. dēlendō

158. This completes the *present system* of forms belonging to the *present stem*, dēlē, as is seen in the following synopsis:

1. *Present indicative*   dēleō
2. *Imperfect indicative*   dēlēbam

---
[1] Use imperō.   [2] Use iubeō.

SECOND CONJUGATION.

3. *Future indicative*   dēlēbō
4. *Present subjunctive*   dēleam
5. *Imperfect subjunctive*   dēlērem
6. *Imperative*   dēlē
7. *Present participle*   dēlēns
8. *Present infinitive*   dēlēre
9. *Gerund*   dēlendī

159.   **VOCABULARY.**

Nom.	Gen.	Meaning.
frāter	-tris, *mas.*	brother
imperātor	-tōris, *mas.*	commander
lēx	lēgis, *fem.*	law
nox	noctis, *fem.*	night
virtūs	-tūtis, *fem.*	courage
compleō	-plēre, *second conj.*	to fill
obtineō	-nēre, " "	to hold

160. Principal parts of second-conjugation verbs.—Only a few verbs of the second conjugation have the *perfect indicative* in **vī**; **dēleō** is given for better comparison with **portō**. Most verbs of this conjugation have **uī** in the *perfect*.

The ending of the *present infinitive* is **ēre**.

dēleō	dēlēre	dēlēvī	dēlētum
compleō	complēre	complēvī	complētum
habeō	habēre	habuī	habitum
valeō	valēre	valuī	valitum
sustineō	sustinēre	sustinuī	sustentum

161. Review of subordinate clause—order of words.

Cum nostrī prō oppidō fossās complērent, hostium cōpiae in mūrō pīla et lapidēs conlocābant,

While our men were filling the ditches in front of the town, the enemies' forces were placing javelins and stones upon the wall

The cum clause, ending with complērent, modifies and marks the *time* of the action in the principal verb, conlocābant; prō oppidō, adverbial phrase (*within the cum clause*), modifies complērent; in the principal clause hostium (*genitive*) limits the subject, cōpiae; in mūrō modifies conlocābant and denotes *place where;* the direct objects precede their verbs.

162.   EXERCISES.

I.—1. Caesar imperātōrī legiōnis prīmae ut vigiliā secundā castra moveat imperat. 2. Galba partem legiōnis oppidum subitō oppūgnāre et partem profectiōnem hostium prohibēre iubet. 3. Caesar mīlitibus quōs in hībernīs in prōvinciā conlocāvit imperābit ut castra moveant et in Galliā praesidia et mūnītiōnēs aedificent. 4. Cum Galba cōpiās distinēret et ad [1] mūrōs oppidī expūgnandum parāret, oppidānī ex oppidō mātūrāvērunt et māgnā virtūte nostrōs fugāvērunt.

II.—1. Galba directed 'the commanders of the new legions to renew[2] the battle with great courage. 2. The enemy build many fortifications, so that they may withstand the great multitude of our men. 3. Our commanders divided their forces in the first watch, that they might storm the enemies' redoubts in many places. 4. Galba demands the surrender of many hostages, because the Gauls have great influence and hold command in many states.

---

[1] ad ... expūgnandum, *to attack.*
[2] For *mood* see (145); for *tense* see (185).

LESSON XXXI.

SECOND CONJUGATION, CONTINUED.

163. Dēleō in the *perfect system;* stem dēlēv.

Perfect indicative.	Pluperfect indicative.	Future-perfect indicative.	Perfect subjunctive.
destroyed.	*had destroyed.*	*shall have destroyed.*	*may have destroyed.*
SINGULAR.	SINGULAR.	SINGULAR.	SINGULAR.
1. dēlēvī	dēlēveram	dēlēverō	dēlēverim
2. dēlēvistī	dēlēverās	dēlēveris	dēlēveris
3. dēlēvit	dēlēverat	dēlēverit	dēlēverit
PLURAL.	PLURAL.	PLURAL.	PLURAL.
1. dēlēvimus	dēlēverāmus	dēlēverimus	dēlēverimus
2. dēlēvistis	dēlēverātis	dēlēveritis	dēlēveritis
3. dēlēvērunt (ēre)	dēlēverant	dēlēverint	dēlēverint

Pluperfect subjunctive.
might have destroyed.
SINGULAR.
1. dēlēvissem
2. dēlēvissēs
3. dēlēvisset
PLURAL.
1. dēlēvissēmus
2. dēlēvissētis
3. dēlēvissent

Perfect infinitive.
dēlēvisse, *to have destroyed*

Synopsis of the *perfect system:*

1. dēlēvī 4. dēlēverim
2. dēlēveram 5. dēlēvissem
3. dēlēverō 6. dēlēvisse

164. Compare the personal endings of the following:

FIRST CONJUGATION.
Present indicative.
1. portō   portāmus
2. portās   portātis
3. portat   portant

Present subjunctive.
1. portem   portēmus
2. portēs   portētis
3. portet   portent

SECOND CONJUGATION.
Present indicative.
dēleō   dēlēmus
dēlēs   dēlētis
dēlet   dēlent

Present subjunctive.
dēleam dēleāmus
dēleās dēleātis
dēleat dēleant

165. VOCABULARY.

Verbs 1-10 (**449**).

Nom.	Gen.	Meaning.
nōmen	-minis, *neut.*	*name*
prīnceps	-cipis, *mas.*	*chief*
cohors	-hortis, *fem.*	*cohort*
altitūdō	-dinis, *fem.*	*height*
ibi, *adv.*		*there*
salūs	-ūtis, *fem.*	*safety*

166. Points to remember.

1. **Ut**, *so that*, introduces a *purpose clause* with the *verb* in the *subjunctive*. This **ut** + *subjunctive* is often translated by the *infinitive*.

2. **Cum**, *while*, takes the *imperfect subjunctive*, translated like the *imperfect indicative*.

3. **Quod**, *because*, introduces a *causal clause* whose *verb* is often in the *indicative*.

4. The *relative* **quī**, etc., usually follows its *antecedent* and stands *first* in its clause, the *verb* of which is often in the *indicative*.

5. **Imperō** and **mandō** take the *dative* and an **ut** clause; the verb in the **ut** clause is in the *subjunctive*.

6. **Iubeō** is used with the *accusative* + *infinitive*.

167. EXERCISES.

I.—1. Quod cīvitās auctōritāte[1] māgnā est, Caesar Belgīs ut imperātōribus Rōmānīs līberōs prīncipum obsidēs dent mandat. 2. Hostēs quī nostrōrum virtūtem et multitūdinem māgnam vidēbant (*saw*) cum līberīs et fīnitimīs trāns flūmen in Galliam mātūrāvērunt et ibi castra conlocāvērunt. 3. Cum cohortēs legiōnis prīmae

---

[1] auctōritāte māgnā = *of great influence;* 'ablative of quality' (**376**). Translate, 'because their state is one of great influence,' etc.

in castrīs essent, cohortēs reliquae ad oppūgnandum mūrōs māgnae altitūdinis turrīs (*acc.*) altās aedificābant. 4. Quod hostēs in castrīs mīlitēs continēbant et nostrīs facultātem pūgnandī nōn dabant, Caesar praefectīs ut agrōs hostium vāstārent imperāvit.

II.—1. On account of the great courage of our men the enemy did not attack the town in which the Roman legions were wintering. 2. Caesar will hasten out of camp with the remaining cohorts to destroy¹ the redoubt which the enemy are building for the sake of safety. 3. Our commanders gave aid to many states of Gaul and called the Gauls friends of the Roman people, because they had many fields and villages and much influence. 4. Caesar commanded Galba to keep¹ his cavalry ready upon the hill and to prevent the flight of the enemy.

LESSON XXXII.
SECOND CONJUGATION, CONTINUED.

168. Perfect system of *sustineō*; perfect stem *sustinu*.

Principal parts: **sustineō   sustinēre   sustinuī   sustentum**

From **sustinuī** *is derived the stem* **sustinu.**

1. sustinuī
2. sustinueram
3. sustinuerō
4. sustinuerim
5. sustinuissem
6. sustinuisse

169. Supine system of *dēleō* (*four forms*).

Supine, **dēlētum**; *supine stem,* **dēlēt.**

First supine	dēlētum, *to destroy*
Second supine	dēlētū, *to destroy*
Future participle	dēlētūrus, -a, -um, *being about to destroy*
Future infinitive	dēlētūrum, -am, -um esse, *to be about to destroy*

---
¹ Be careful about *choice of tense*—' rule of sequence ' (185).

170. The ending of the *future participle* is ūrus, -a, -um; that of the *future infinitive* ūrum, -am, -um esse. To form these, strike off um from the *supine* and *annex* the above *endings;* as, parō, parāre, parāvī, parātum; *supine stem,* parāt; *future participle,* parātūrus; *future infinitive,* parātūrum esse. videō, vidēre, vīdī, vīsum; *supine stem,* vīs; *future participle,* vīsūrus; *future infinitive,* vīsūrum esse.

171.   VOCABULARY.

Verbs 11–22 (449).

Nom.	Gen.	Meaning.
tempus	-poris, *neut.*	*time*
eōdem tempore, *adverbial phrase*		*at the same time*
explōrātor	-tōris, *mas.*	*scout*
pēs	pedis, *mas.*	*foot*
pōns	pontis, *mas.*	*bridge*
undique, *adv.*		*from (on) all sides*
tum, *adv.*		*then*

172. Repeat the rule of sequence. What adjectives govern the dative? What is the *case* of the *predicate* word with **sum**, etc.? Give rules for the agreement of *adjective* and *relative*. Name four kinds of *ablatives*. Decline the nouns of the first, second, and third declensions (**453, 454, 458, 459**), and **altus** and **crēber** (**466**).

173.   EXERCISES.

I.—1. Caesar Gallīs ut in castra Rōmāna līberōs prīncipum obsidēs portārent imperāvit. 2. Quod Caesar explōrātōrēs pontem dēlēre iusserat, hostēs prīmā vigiliā cum līberīs et impedīmentīs trāns flūmen mātūrāvērunt. 3. Nostrī quibus Caesar tēla nova dedit peditēs hostium, quod virtūte et numerō hominum nōn valēbant, facile prōflīgāvērunt. 4. Mīlitēs legiōnis prīmae hominēs virtūtis māguae erant et nōn fugā sed fortiter dīmicandō salūtem impetrāvērunt. 5. Quod Gallī mūnītiōnēs novās nostrās oppūgnābant, Caesar imperātōrem cūius cōpiae tēla multa et bona habēbant in Galliam mātūrāre, ut Gallōrum castella et vālla dēlērent, iussit.

II.—1. Caesar ordered the infantry of the second legion to attack the town whose walls were not high. 2. With great swiftness and courage our cavalry hastened out of the redoubts and easily routed the enemies' lines. 3. Galba commanded scouts to destroy the new bridge and prevent the departure of the Belgians who had not given hostages to Caesar. 4. While the Belgians were awaiting the aid of their neighbours, Caesar suddenly attacked their town on all sides with his infantry[1] and destroyed the new fortifications.

LESSON XXXIII.

THIRD CONJUGATION.

174. Present Indicative of *pōnō*, *I place*.

SINGULAR.	PLURAL.
1. pōnō	pōnimus
2. pōnis	pōnitis
3. pōnit	pōnunt

Personal endings.

-ō	-imus
-is	-itis
-it	-unt

---

[1] '*Ablative of means*' (48); 'ablative *without* cum.'

Like **pōnō**, conjugate **mittō**, *to send*, **dūcō**, *to lead*, and **cōgō**, *to collect*.

175.   **VOCABULARY.**

Verbs 23–32 **(449)**.

Nom.	Gen.	Meaning.
fertilitās	-tātis, *fem.*	*fertility*
ab latere, *adverbial phrase*		*on the flank*
ac, *conj.*		*and*
parātus -a, -um, *adj.*		*prepared*
inīquus -a, -um, *adj.*		*unfavourable*
inter, *prep. with the acc.*		*among* or *between*
cis, " " " "		*on this side of*
tam, *adv.*		*so*

176. Order of words.—Though the *subject* usually tends to stand first and the *verb* last in the Latin sentence, this arrangement of words is frequently greatly varied. Often the *most prominent* word in the speaker's mind comes *first* and other words follow in order of prominence. For position of forms of **sum**, for example, see the first line in "*Caesar's Gallic War,*" Book II, Chapter I: "**cum esset Caesar in Galliā**"; again in Chapter IX: "**palūs erat nōn māgna.**" Then we find the *verb first* in the sentence, as in Chapter II, third paragraph: "**dat negōtium Senonibus,**" *he employs the Senones;* and in Chapter XVII. line 12: "**adiuvābat etiam . . . cōnsilium,**" *it was of advantage, too, to the plan.*

177. Review the entire verb **sum** (484), and *all* of the active voice of **amō** and **moneō** (474, 476).

178.   **EXERCISES.**

I.—1. Caesar incūsāvit imperātōrem cui sīgnum dedit, quod ad mūrum oppidī turrēs nōn prōmōvit. 2. Eōdem tempore hostēs in multīs Galliae cīvitātibus cōpiās māgnās cōgunt ut legiōnēs Rōmānās sustineant. 3. Imperātor Rōmānus, quod profectiōnem hostium videt, trāns flūmen ad collem in quō sunt Galbae castra peditēs prīmae legiōnis mittit ut fugam prohibeant. 4. Praefectī hostium, quod virtūtem ac numerum nostrōrum peditum vidēbant, in castrīs cōpiās continēbant neque' nostrīs facultātem pūgnandī dabant. 5. Galba nōmine populī Rōmānī obsidēs multōs cōgit (*collects*) et in hībernīs inter cīvitātēs quārum auctōritās est nōn māgna legiōnēs novās pōnit.

II.—1. Caesar places (**pōnō**) in winter-quarters among the Remi the new cavalry which Galba is collecting from all sides. 2. Because the courage of the Roman legions is so great, the enemy send to Galba the children of their chiefs as hostages. 3. Caesar leads his new legions into the boundaries of farthest Gaul and commands the Gauls,[2] who are unfriendly to the Roman people, to prepare[3] winter-quarters for our men and to carry corn into our camp.

LESSON XXXIV.

THIRD CONJUGATION, CONTINUED. FOURTH DECLENSION.

179. Imperfect Indicative of *pōnō*.   **Future Indicative.**
   was placing.   *shall place.*

SINGULAR.	PLURAL.	SINGULAR.	PLURAL.
1. pōnēbam	pōnēbāmus	pōnam	pōnēmus
2. pōnēbās	pōnēbātis	pōnēs	pōnētis
3. pōnēbat	pōnēbant	pōnet	pōnent

180. The *present stem* (*verb-stem*), pōnĕ, ending in *short* e, is found by dropping re from the *present infinitive active*. The stem vowel ĕ is lost before ō, is changed to u before nt,

---

[1] neque = et ... nōn; see vocab. (202).
[2] Case after imperō?   [3] Mood with imperō?

to ĭ before the other endings of the *indicative* and *imperative;* in the *imperfect* and *future indicative* it becomes ē, and in the *present subjunctive* ā.

181.   VOCABULARY.

Verbs 33–42 (**449**).

exercitus -ūs, *mas.*		*army*
incendō,	third conjugation	*to burn*
relinquō,	" "	*to leave*
cōnscrībō,	" "	*to enroll*
expellō,	" "	*to drive out*
incolō,	" "	*to inhabit*
permittō,	" "	*to entrust*

Verbs of the third conjugation have *short* e in the *penult* of the *present infinitive*, the accent falling upon the *antepenult*: pōnō, pónĕre; mittō, míttĕre.

182. Fourth declension.

Cāsus, *fate,* mas.   Cornū, *horn* or *wing,* neut.

	SINGULAR.	PLURAL.	SINGULAR.	PLURAL.
Nom.	cāsus	cāsūs	cornū	cornua
Gen.	cāsūs	cāsuum	cornūs	cornuum
Dat.	cāsuī(ū)	cāsibus	cornū	cornibus
Acc.	cāsum	cāsūs	cornū	cornua
Voc.	cāsus	cāsūs	cornū	cornua
Abl.	cāsū	cāsibus	cornū	cornibus

The stem ends in u. Nouns in us are *masculine* with a few *feminine* exceptions; those in ū are *neuter*.

183. Comparison of tenses having similar endings.

Present subjunctive.		Present indicative.		Future indicative.	
(*First conjugation.*)		(*Second conjugation.*)		(*Third conjugation.*)	
1. portem	portēmus	dēleō	dēlēmus	pōnam	pōnēmus
2. portēs	portētis	dēlēs	dēlētis	pōnēs	pōnētis
3. portet	portent	dēlet	dēlent	pōnet	pōnent

THIRD CONJUGATION.

Thus it is seen that a verb ending in **et** or **ent** is *present subjunctive* if *first* conjugation; *present indicative* if *second* conjugation; *future indicative* if *third* conjugation.

184.   **EXERCISES.**

I.—1. Imperātōrēs Rōmānī extrēmā in Galliā ut potestātem amplificent legiōnēs novās cōnscrībent. 2. Praefectus quī māgnam hostium multitūdinem videt trāns flūmen Rhēnum mīlitēs nōn dūcet. 3. Caesar in fīnibus Germānōrum exercitum māgnum relinquet ut nōmen et auctōritātem populī Rōmānī amplificet. 4. Cīvitātēs Galliae quae virtūte et auctōritāte et numerō hominum valent nōn facile ē fīnibus Galliae legiōnēs nostrās expellent. 5. Nostrī in cīvitātibus proximīs Galliae (*dative*) māgnās cōpiās cōgent ac peditēs eōdem tempore cōnscrībent ut hostēs superent.

II.—1. The townsmen will burn their towns and carry their children and baggage into the boundaries of their neighbours. 2. The Gauls place their states under the power[1] of the Roman army and drive out the Germans who are in arms and are not friendly to Caesar. 3. The Roman commander leaves the cavalry among the Sequani, because they inhabit places next to our province, and hastens across the river with his infantry. 4. In the second watch our men will burn the bridge which the enemy built and will prevent their departure.

---

[1] Place under the power, **permittō in** + *accusative*.

LESSON XXXV.

THIRD CONJUGATION. ADJECTIVES OF THE THIRD DECLENSION.

185. Present subjunctive of *pōnō*. **Imperfect subjunctive.**
may place.   *might place.*

SINGULAR.
1. pōnam
2. pōnās
3. pōnat

PLURAL.
1. pōnāmus
2. pōnātis
3. pōnant

SINGULAR.
pōnerem
pōnerēs
pōneret

PLURAL.
pōnerēmus
pōnerētis
pōnerent

186. As in the *second conjugation*, the *present subjunctive* ends in **am, ās, at,** etc. If a verb ends in **at**, for example, it is *present indicative* in the *first conjugation*, *present subjunctive* in *any other conjugation*. Conjugate **incendō** and **expellō** in the present, imperfect, and future indicative, and present and imperfect subjunctive.

187. VOCABULARY.

Verbs 1–6 (450).

Nom.	Gen.	Meaning.
dux	ducis, *mas.*	*leader*
adventus	-tūs, *mas.*	*arrival*
equitātus	-tūs, *mas.*	*cavalry*
cōpia	-ae, *fem.*	*abundance*
omnis -nis, -ne, *adj.*		*all*
facilis -lis, -le, *adj.*		*easy*

188. Adjective of the third declension.

Fortis, *brave*.

	SINGULAR.			PLURAL.		
	Mas.	Fem.	Neuter.	Mas.	Fem.	Neuter.
Nom.	fortis	-is	-e	fortēs	-ēs	-ia
Gen.	fortis	-is	-is	fortium	-ium	-ium
Dat.	fortī	-ī	-ī	fortibus	-ibus	-ibus
Acc.	fortem	-em	-e	fortēs (-īs)	-ēs (-īs)	-ia
Voc.	fortis	-is	-e	fortēs	-ēs	-ia
Abl.	fortī	-ī	-ī	fortibus	-ibus	-ibus

Fortis, *stem* **forti** (vowel-stem in i), has *one* form for both *masculine* and *feminine*, and one for the *neuter* (e). Adjectives of *two* terminations, *being* i-*stems*, have ī in the *ablative singular*, ia in the *neuter plural*, ium in the *genitive plural*, and īs often in the *accusative plural masculine and feminine*.

189. Use of *suus*, 'his' or 'theirs.'—Suus, sua, suum is a possessive *reflexive* pronoun of the third person, denoting *possession* and referring to the *subject* of a sentence or clause. It is declined like **altus, -a, -um**, and *agrees* in *gender, number*, and *case* with the *noun limited*, that is, the *thing possessed, not the possessor*. It means *his* or *theirs* according to the *number* of the *possessor*.

Caesar ē castrīs suōs mīlitēs   *Caesar leads his soldiers out*
dūcit,   *of camp*
Hostēs suum oppidum incendunt,   *The enemy burn their town*

190. EXERCISES.

I.—1. Caesar, cum in prōvinciā legiōnēs reliquās cōnscrīberet, ducibus equitātūs imperāvit ut hostium oppidum in quō erant multa impedīmenta incenderent. 2. Caesar undique exercitum cōget ut Germānōs quī inter multās cīvitātēs valent ac multa oppida incolunt ē fīnibus Gallōrum expellat. 3. Caesar, ut Sēquanōs quī nostrīs sunt inimīcī expellat et ad fortēs Rēmōs auxilium portet, in Galliam sine morā suās cōpiās dūcet. 4. Quod imperātor hostium ē castrīs ad proelium exercitum nōn dūcēbat, Galba ut castra hostium expūgnāret mīlitēs aedificāre turrīs (*accus.*) altitūdinis māgnae iussit. 5. Quod explōrātōrēs adventum Caesaris exercitūs nūntiāvērunt, Belgae trāns Rhēnum sua castra movēbunt et cum Germānīs coniūrābunt ut mīlitum nostrōrum (*adj.*) impetum sustineant.

II.—1. On account of the enemies' arrival Caesar will leave his infantry in winter-quarters among the Remi and will enroll new legions. 2. With the aid of the soldiers whom he will enroll in farthest Gaul Caesar will overcome and drive out the remaining enemy. 3. Galba directs his brave generals to lead the cavalry of the second legion into the territories next to the Roman province and to attack the new fortifications of the enemy.

LESSON XXXVI.

THIRD CONJUGATION, CONTINUED.

191. Imperative of *pōnō*, *place* (*thou*).

	SINGULAR.	PLURAL.
2.	pōne	pōnite
	pōnitō	pōnitōte
3.	pōnitō	pōnuntō

Present participle.   **Present infinitive.**
pōnēns, *placing*   pónĕre, *to place*

Gerund.
of placing, etc.

Gen. pōnendī   *Acc.* pōnendum
Dat. pōnendō   *Abl.* pōnendō

This completes the *nine* forms composing the *present system* of pōnō, based upon the *present stem* pōne.

192. Synopsis—present system—of *pōnō*.

1. *Present indicative* — pōnō
2. *Imperfect indicative* — pōnēbam
3. *Future indicative* — pōnam (-ēs)
4. *Present subjunctive* — pōnam (-ās)
5. *Imperfect subjunctive* — pōnerem
6. *Imperative* — pōne
7. *Present participle* — pōnēns
8. *Present infinitive* — pōnere
9. *Gerund* — pōnendī

Give synopsis in the *present system* of **mittō** and **relinquō**. Conjugate the *present subjunctive* of **dubitō**, *present indicative* of **habeō**, *future indicative* of **dūcō**.

193.   **VOCABULARY.**
Verbs 7-14 (450).

Nom.	Gen.	Meaning.
aditus	-ūs, *mas.*	*access* or *approach*
commeātus	-ūs, *mas.*	*supplies*
mōns	montis, *mas.*	*mountain*
statim, *adv.*		*at once*
manus	-ūs, *fem.*	*band (hand)*

194. Decline **duplex** and **equester** (467). Observe that **equester** has *three* terminations in the *nominative*: ter, tris, tre; being a vowel-stem in i (ri), it takes ī *in the ablative*, etc., as in **fortis**. **Duplex**, increasing the number of syllables in the genitive, is a consonant-stem (**duplic**), and takes the form of *i-stems* in the cases pointed out above, except that the *ablative (singular)* often ends in **e**.

195.   **EXERCISES.**

I.—1. Caesar prō oppidō cūius mūrī sunt nōn altī castra pōnet, quod aditum facilem habet. 2. Adventū equitātūs Caesar ē castrīs omnēs cōpiās dūcit et ab latere inīquō in locō hostium agmina exagitāre parat. 3. Germānī quī trāns Rhēnum agrōs multōs habent et māgna oppida incolunt ex hībernīs omnēs nostrōs mīlitēs expellent. 4. Eōdem tempore Galba in extrēmōs Galliae fīnīs (*acc. plur.*) praefectōs mittit ut legiōnēs novās cōnscrībant et frūmentum et commeātūs impetrent. 5. Caesar in hostium fīnēs, ut agrōs vāstent et mūnītiōnēs dēleant et exercituī Rōmānō commeātūs cōgant, fortēs praefectōs mittet.

II.—1. Because the brave messengers had announced the approach of the enemies' cavalry, Galba ordered his commanders to prepare all the forces for renewing the battle. 2. Caesar commands the brave general to collect an abundance of corn for the army whose camp he will place (**pōnō**) in Gaul. 3. While Galba was enrolling infantry and cavalry for the sake of overcoming the Gauls, ambassadors from a large part of Gaul hastened to Caesar's winter-quarters to give hostages and obtain peace. 4. Because the town has an easy access, Caesar directs his generals to lead all the forces out of camp and storm the walls from all sides.

LESSON XXXVII.

THIRD CONJUGATION, CONTINUED.

196. Perfect system of *pōnō*. —*Perfect stem* **posu.**

Perfect indicative. *placed.*	Pluperfect indicative. *had placed.*	Perfect subjunctive. *may have placed.*
SINGULAR.	posueram	posuerim
1. posuī	posuerās, etc.	posuerīs, etc.
2. posuistī		
3. posuit	**Future-perfect indicative.**	**Pluperfect subjunctive.**
PLURAL.	*shall have placed.*	*might have placed.*
1. posuimus		
2. posuistis	posuerō	posuissem
3. posuērunt (-ēre)	posueris, etc.	posuissēs, etc.

Perfect infinitive.

posuisse, *to have placed*

197. *Supine system* of **pōnō** (*four* forms); *supine stem* **posit.**

1. *First supine*   positum,   *to place*
2. *Second supine*   positū,   *to place*
3. *Future participle*   positūrus, -a, -um, *being about to place*
4. *Future infinitive*   positūrum, -am, -um *esse, to be about to place*

198.   **VOCABULARY.**
Verbs 15–18 (450).

Nom.	Gen.	Meaning.
mōs	mōris, *mas.*	*custom* or *habit*
servitūs	-tūtis, *fem.*	*slavery*
dēdō ⎫		⎧ *to surrender*
ēdūcō ⎬ (see principal parts in	*to lead out*
petō ⎨ the general vocabulary)	*to seek* or *ask for*
timeō ⎭		⎩ *to fear*
novissimum agmen, *neut.*		*the rear*

Petō, with the meaning '*ask for*,' takes the direct object in the accusative, not the *dative*; as, **pācem petunt**, *they ask for peace.*

199. Decline **pūgnāns (467).** Give full synopsis, *entire active voice*, by stems, of **imperō, iubeō**, and **cōgō.** First repeat the *principal parts* of the verb and point out the *three stems*, stating the *number* of forms derived from *each stem.* Give the *name* of the form, next the *form itself*, and then the *meaning.*

200.   **EXERCISES.**

I.—1. Caesar in (*upon*) altum collem suās cōpiās dūxit et ibi castella ac mūnītiōnēs posuit ut prīmum hostium impetum sustinēret. 2. Dux Rōmānus in castrīs mīlitēs continuit, quod hostēs līberōs prīncipum obsidēs dēdiderant ac potestātī Caesaris oppida omnia permīserant. 3. Cum ducēs quōs Caesar in Galliam lēgātōs mīserat ut exercituī

Rōmānō commeātum cōgerent frūmentum postulārent, Sēquanī castra nostra oppūgnāvērunt et incendērunt. 4. Quod explōrātōrēs quōs trāns Rhēnum commeātūs causā mīserat hostium adventum nūntiāvērunt, Caesar fortibus praefectīs ut statim in proximum montem omnem equitātum dūcerent mandāvit.

II.—1. While the cohorts of the first legion with great courage were withstanding the enemies' brave attack, Galba directed the cavalry to await his commands upon the nearest hill. 2. Upon the arrival of the Roman infantry which Caesar had trained in many battles, the townsmen will send into our camp suitable men so that they may surrender hostages and ask for peace 3. Caesar hastened at once with his armed infantry into the farthest boundaries of Gaul, and many states that feared the power of our army sought peace.

LESSON XXXVIII.

THE IRREGULAR VERB POSSUM, *I AM ABLE.*

201. Learn the Indicative mood of *possum* **(485).**—Principal parts, **possum, posse, potuī**—*no supine.*

Decline **altior** (467) *and the fourth-declension nouns* (461).

202.   VOCABULARY.

Verbs 19–23 (450).

tantus, -a, -um, *adj.*	*so great*
ubi, *conj.*	*when*
dē, *prep. with the abl.*	*with respect to, about*
discēdō	*to depart*
redigō	*to reduce*
nec (neque) { conjunction, used in the *second* of two connected ideas }	*and . . . not*

203. Use of *cum* **and** *ubi.*—**Cum,** *when,* is used with the *imperfect subjunctive* to denote *contemporaneous* action (*when* in the sense of '*while*'); with the *pluperfect subjunctive* to denote *antecedent* action (*when* in the sense of '*after*'). This is called *Historical* **cum** and *describes* the *circumstances* under which an action took place.

Ubi, *when,* commonly takes the *perfect indicative,* or the *Historical present indicative* (*the present as a vivid representation of the past*). The **ubi** clause *defines the time* during which an action took place. When to use **cum** or **ubi**, in writing English in Latin, is often difficult to determine.

204. Analysis of a complex sentence.

Cum mīlitēs quōs Caesar in Galliam ut exercituī Rōmānō commeātūs cōgerent mīserat frūmentum postulārent, Sēquanī castra nostra incendērunt,	*While the soldiers whom Caesar had sent into Gaul to collect supplies for the Roman army were demanding corn, the Sequani set fire to our camp*

A complex declarative sentence, of which **Sēquanī . . . incendērunt** is the *main clause.* Since the *subject,* **Sēquanī**, is unmodified, the remainder of the sentence limits the *predicate* **incendērunt**. At a glance you see that the *subordinate* part of the sentence, **cum . . . postulārent**, has *three* component parts, viz., a **cum**, a *relative*, and an **ut** clause.

Begin with **cum**: looking for the verb introduced by **cum**, there appears a *relative clause* which is in turn divided in two by an intermediate **ut** clause, and the *latter* standing undivided ends with **cōgerent**. Since the **ut . . . cōgerent** clause *stands within* the *relative clause,* the *next verb* in order should complete the *relative clause,* beginning with **quōs** and ending with **mīserat**; here bear in mind that **ut . . . cōgerent** shows *affirmative purpose* of, and gets its *sequence* from, **mīserat**, and that **quōs . . . mīserat** describes **mīlitēs**. Thus you find that **cum** introduces postulārent, and that this entire clause modifies the *principal verb* incendērunt, *describing* the *circumstances* of the action of the latter and denoting *time contemporaneous*.

205.   **EXERCISE.**

1. Caesar ubi tantam hostium multitūdinem vīdit, ē castrīs omnēs legiōnēs ēdūxit et mandāvit praefectīs ut impetum hostium exspectārent.   2. Quod mīlitum nostrōrum impetum sustinēre nōn poterant, oppidānī proximīs cum fīnitimīs in extrēmōs Galliae fīnēs discessērunt. 3. Quod Gallī nōn possunt contrā legiōnēs fortēs nostrās sustentāre, Caesar in servitūtem omnēs cīvitātēs quae arma et obsidēs nōn dēdidērunt rediget.   4. Hostēs reliquī quī armīs ac hominum numerō nōn valēbant ad Caesarem prīncipēs cīvitātum lēgātōs ut pācem peterent mīsērunt. 5. Adventū hostium Galba suō mōre in castrīs partem equitum reliquit, partem in montem dūxit.   6. Castra Caesaris quae hostēs expūgnāre non potuerant proxima erant collī altō nec aditum facilem habēbant.

LESSON XXXIX.
POSSUM, CONTINUED. PERSONAL PRONOUN.

206. Learn the subjunctive and infinitive moods of *possum* **(485).**

Decline all the nouns of the third declension (458, 459).

207. Personal pronoun, first person.

Ego, *I*.

	SINGULAR.	PLURAL.
Nom.	ego, *I*	nōs, *we*
Gen.	meī, *of me*	nostrum, nostrī, *of us*
Dat.	mihi, *to or for me*	nōbīs, *to or for us*
Acc.	mē, *me*	nōs, *us*
Abl.	mē, { *with, from, by me*, etc. }	nōbīs, *from us*, etc.

208. Demonstrative pronoun (sometimes used for the personal pronoun, *third person*).

is, ea, id, *this* or *that, he,* etc.

	SINGULAR.			PLURAL.	
Nom.	is	ea	id	eī or iī eae	ea
Gen.	ēius	ēius	ēius	eōrum eārum	eōrum
Dat.	eī	eī	eī	eīs or iīs	
Acc.	eum	eam	id	eōs eās	ea
Abl.	eō	eā	eō	eīs or iīs	

209.   VOCABULARY.

Verbs 24-33 (450).

nōndum, *adv.*   *not yet*
nē, *conj.*   *in order that . . . not*
trādō   *to hand over*
circumdō   *to surround*

Nē in negative commands, prohibitions, etc., will be given later.

210. How cause and manner are expressed.—*Cause* is expressed by the simple ablative.

Virtūte nostrōrum hostēs sus-   *On account of (because of) the*
tentāre nōn poterant,   *courage of our men the ene-*
                                 my could not hold out

The *manner* of an action is expressed by the ablative usually with **cum**, unless a limiting adjective accompanies the noun. But even with the adjective **cum** may be used. Sometimes it is almost impossible to distinguish *means* and *manner*.

Hostēs cum celeritāte disces-   *The enemy departed with speed*
sērunt,

211. Use of nē.—**Nē**, *in order that . . . not*, introduces a subordinate clause of *negative purpose* with the verb in the *subjunctive*, the choice of *tense* being determined by the *rule of sequence*.

Dant obsidēs nē Caesar oppi- *They give hostages in order that*
dum dēleat, *Caesar may not destroy their town*

212. EXERCISES.

I.—1. Caesar māgnō equitātūs numerō oppidum circumdedit nē hostēs noctū[1] discēderent. 2. Hostēs quī mīlitum nostrōrum impetum sustinēre possunt ad Caesarem dē pāce lēgātōs nōn mittent. 3. Rēmī quī proximī Belgīs et hominēs virtūtis māgnae erant ex suīs fīnibus Germānōs facile expulērunt. 4. Ubi trāns flūmen hostium agmina vīdit, Caesar in collem proximum cōpiās omnēs suās ēdūxit ac praefectīs equitum ut proeliī sīgnum exspectārent imperāvit. 5. Rēmī quī Caesaris exercitūs adventum timent Belgās reliquōs, quod populō Rōmānō obsidēs trādidērunt et pācem petīvērunt, incūsant.

II.—1. Because they were not able to withstand the Roman infantry, the Sequani burned all their towns and departed out of Gaul. 2. Upon the arrival of the cavalry (*singular of* **equitātus**) which our leaders had collected from (**ex**) many states the Gauls sent ambassadors to Caesar with respect to a surrender. 3. While our men were preparing to storm the walls of the town with weapons and stones, the townsmen suddenly departed and placed (**pōnō**) safety in flight. 4. When the enemy saw upon the hill our cavalry whose approach (**adventus**) scouts had announced, they did not await an attack but[2] fled at once into the nearest (**proximus**) villages.

---

[1] An old ablative used adverbially, *by night*.
[2] Use ac.

LESSON XL.

THE IŌ VERB OF THE THIRD CONJUGATION.

213. Learn *capiō*,[1] *I take*, in the entire active voice (480).
—Principal parts, capiō, capere, cēpī, captum.

214. Reflexive (personal) pronoun of the third person.—
Suī, *of himself, herself*, etc.

	SINGULAR.	PLURAL.
Nom.	——	——
Gen.	suī, *of himself*	suī, *of themselves*
Dat.	sibi, *to or for himself*	sibi, *to or for themselves*
Acc.	sē, *himself*	sē, *themselves*
Abl.	sē, *from*, etc., *himself*	sē, *from*, etc., *themselves*

The reflexive (personal) pronoun sē, etc., like its corresponding possessive **suus**, etc., (189), refers to the *subject of the sentence or clause:* hence it is distinguished by the term 'reflexive' (from reflectō, *bend* or *turn back*).

Cum Caesar in Galliā esset, *While Caesar was in Gaul, am-*
lēgātī ad eum (not reflexive) *bassadors came to him*
vēnērunt,
Caesar lēgātōs ad sē (reflexive) *Caesar ordered ambassadors to*
venīre iussit, *come to him*

215. VOCABULARY.

Verbs 34-41 (450).

ā or ab, *prep. with the abl.*	*from*
ācriter, *adv.*	*fiercely*
faciō,	*to do* or *make*
impetum facere,	*to make an attack*
accipiō,	*to receive*
que, *conj.*	*and*

---

[1] Verbs in iō retain i before a, o, u, and ē : see capiō in the present indicative capiunt, imperfect capiēbam, future capiēs, present subjunctive capiat. So with compounds of capiō.

Que is always *enclitic*, being attached to the *second* of two words connected: **ferrō ignīque**, *with fire and sword.* When **que** joins clauses, it is attached to the *first* word of the *second* clause.

Caesar vīcōs incendit agrōsque   *Caesar burnt the villages and*
vāstāvit,   *laid waste the fields*

216. Use of *impetum facere.*—**Impetum facere,** *to make an attack,* usually takes **in** + *accusative.*

Hostēs in nostrōs impetum   *The enemy made a fierce attack*
**ācriter fēcērunt,*   *upon our men*

An *adverb* is often used in *Latin* where the English makes use of an *adjective*, as with **ācriter** in the above sentence.

217. Review of important points.—Define *meaning* and *use* of **suus** (189); distinguish **cum** and **ubi** clauses (203); explain use of **ut** and **quod,** and of **imperō** and **iubeō** (166); **nē** + *subjunctive* (211); predicate nominative with **sum,** etc. ; position and agreement of the *relative ;* rule of sequence ; name *six* kinds of ablatives.

218.   EXERCISES.

I.—1. Dux noster in dēditiōnem Rēmōs accipiet et cōpiīs omnibus in Sēquanōrum fīnēs, ut in hostēs impetum ācriter faciat, mātūrābit.   2. Caesar imperat Galbae ut cōpiīs quās ab Rēmīs, fīnitimīs, accēperat in oppidānōs impetum faciat.   3. Adventū equitātūs nostrī Caesar commeātibus hostēs prohibuit et māgnā hominum multitūdine oppidum circumdedit, nē oppidānī fugā salūtem peterent.   4. Caesar mūnītiōnibus mūrīsque altīs ea castra in quibus omnēs suās legiōnēs posuerat circumdedit ut exercitus noster ad hiemandum salūtis locum habēret.   5. Tum Rēmī ac Belgae quī cīvitātēs Galliae proximae prōvinciae sunt ad Caesaris castra dē dēditiōne hominēs idōneōs mīsērunt.

II.—1. While our infantry in an unfavourable place were

withstanding the javelins of the enemy with courage, Caesar directed his generals to lead out the cavalry and make an attack upon the enemies' rear. 2. Because Caesar ordered the Remi to inhabit a part of the territories which he had received from (*ab*) the Gauls, many states next to Gaul blamed Caesar and prepared to attack our camp. 3. While the cavalry were making an attack upon the Gauls, Caesar ordered his scouts to destroy the bridge, which the enemy had built, in order that they might not be able to depart out of Gaul without a surrender.

219.   REVIEW VOCABULARY.

Lessons XXII—XL.

1. possum, posse, potuī, [no supine], *to be able*
2. cōpia, cōpiae (fem.), *abundance*
3. aditus, aditūs (mas.), *access*
4. omnis, omnis, omne (adj.), *all*
5. inter (prep. with the acc.), *among*
6. ac (conj.), *and*
7. nūntiō, nūntiāre, nūntiāvī, nūntiātum, *announce*
8. adventus, adventūs (mas.), *approach*
9. armō, armāre, armāvī, armātum, *arm*
10. arma, armōrum (neut.), *arms*
11. exercitus, exercitūs (mas.), *army*
12. petō, petere, petīvī, potītum, *ask for* or *seek*
13. impetus, impetūs (mas.), *attack*
14. eōdem tempore, *at the same time*
15. statim (adv.), *at once*
16. exspectō, exspectāre, exspectāvī, exspectātum, *await*
17. manus, manūs (fem.), *band*
18. corpus, corporis (neut.), *body*
19. fīnis, fīnis (mas.), *end*, (plural) *boundary* or *territories*
20. fortis, fortis, forte (adj.), *brave*
21. fortiter (adv.), *bravely*
22. pōns, pontis (mas.), *bridge*

23. frāter, frātris (mas.), *brother*
24. incendō, incendere, incendī, incēnsum, *burn*
25. Caesar, Caesaris (mas.), *Caesar*
26. calamitās, calamitātis (fem.), *calamity*
27. eques, equitis (mas.), *horseman*, (plur.) Roman *cavalry*
28. equitātus, equitātūs (mas.), *cavalry*
29. prīnceps, prīncipis (mas.), *chief*
30. cohors, cohortis (fem.), *cohort*
31. cōgō, cōgere, coēgī, coāctum, *collect*
32. imperātor, imperātōris (mas.), *commander*
33. contendō, contendere, contendī, contentum, *contend*
34. virtūs, virtūtis (fem.), *courage*
35. mōs, mōris (mas.), *custom* or *habit*
36. pellō, pellere, pepulī, pulsum, *defeat*
37. postulō, postulāre, postulāvī, postulātum, *demand*
38. discēdō, discēdere, discessī, discessum, *depart*
39. profectiō, profectiōnis (fem.), *departure*
40. dēleō, dēlēre, dēlēvī, dēlētum, *destroy*
41. distineō, distinēre, distinuī, distentum, *divide*
42. faciō, facere, fēcī, factum, *do* or *make*
43. expello, expellere, expulī, expulsum, *drive out*
44. facilis, facilis, facile (adj.), *easy*
45. hostis, hostis (mas.), *enemy*
46. cōnscrībō, cōnscrībere, cōnscrīpsī, cōnscrīptum, *enroll*
47. permittō, permittere, permīsī, permissum, *entrust*
48. pater, patris (mas.), *father*
49. fertilitās, fertilitātis (fem.), *fertility*
50. timeō, timēre, timuī, [no supine], *fear*
51. levitās, levitātis (fem.), *fickleness*
52. ācriter (adv.), *fiercely*
53. compleō, complēre, complēvī, complētum, *fill*
54. īgnis, īgnis (mas.), *fire*
55. pēs, pedis (mas.), *foot*
56. mūnītiō, mūnītiōnis (fem.), *fortification*
57. undique (adv.), *from* or *on all sides*
58. bonus, bona, bonum (adj.), *good*
59. trādō, trādere, trādidī, trāditum, *hand over*
60. habeō, habēre, habuī, habitum, *have*

61. altitūdō, altitūdinis (fem.), *height*
62. collis, collis (mas.), *hill*
63. suus, sua, suum (possessive adj. pron.), *his* or *their*
64. teneō, tenēre, tenuī, [no supine], *hold*
65. cornū, cornūs (neut.), *horn*
66. obses, obsidis (mas.), *hostage*
67. amplificō, amplificāre, amplificāvī, amplificātum, *increase*
68. pedes, peditis (mas.), *footman*, (plur.) *infantry*
69. auctōritās, auctōritātis (fem.), *influence*
70. incolō, incolere, incoluī, [no supine], *inhabit*
71. nē (conj.), *in order that . . . not*
72. contineō, continēre, continuī, contentum, *keep*
73. rēx, rēgis (mas.), *king*
74. lēx, lēgis (fem.), *law*
75. dūcō, dūcere, dūxī, ductum, *lead*
76. dux, ducis (mas.), *leader*
77. ēdūcō, ēdūcere, ēdūxī, ēductum, *lead out*
78. relinquō, relinquere, relīquī, relictum, *leave*
79. legiō, legiōnis (fem.), *legion*
80. agmen, agminis (neut.), *line of march* (marching column)
81. homō, hominis (mas.), *man*
82. impetum facere, *make an attack*
83. mōns, montis (mas.), *mountain*
84. moveō, movēre, mōvī, mōtum, *move*
85. multitūdō, multitūdinis (fem.), *multitude*
86. nōmen, nōminis (neut.), *name*
87. nox, noctis (fem.), *night*
88. nōndum (adv.), *not yet*
89. ab latere, *on the flank*
90. facultās, facultātis (fem.), *opportunity*
91. iubeō, iubēre, iussī, iussum, *order*
92. pars, partis (fem.), *part*
93. pāx, pācis (fem.), *peace*
94. pōnō, pōnere, posuī, positum, *place*
95. potestās, potestātis (fem.), *power*
96. parātus, parāta, parātum (adj.), *prepared* or *ready*
97. prohibeō, prohibēre, prohibuī, prohibitum, *prevent*

98. novissimum agmen, novissimī agminis (neut.), *rear*
99. accipiō, accipere, accēpī, acceptum, *receive*
100. redigō, redigere, redēgī, redāctum, *reduce*
101. rūmor, rūmōris (mas.), *report*
102. flūmen, flūminis (neut.), *river*
103. salūs, salūtis (fem.), *safety*
104. explōrātor, explōrātōris (mas.), *scout*
105. videō, vidēre, vīdī, vīsum, *see*
106. mitto, mittere, mīsī, mīssum, *send*
107. Sēquanī, Sēquanōrum (mas.), *Sequani*
108. gravis, gravis, grave (adj.), *severe*
109. latus, lateris (neut.), *side* or *flank*
110. servitūs, servitūtis (fem.), *slavery*
111. tam (adv.), *so*
112. tantus, tanta, tantum (adj.), *so great*
113. mīles, mīlitis (mas.), *soldier*
114. ōrātiō, ōrātiōnis (fem.), *speech*
115. cīvitās, cīvitātis (fem.), *state*
116. lapis, lapidis (mas.), *stone*
117. valeō, valēre, valuī, valitum, *to be strong*
118. subitō (adv.), *suddenly*
119. aestās, aestātis (fem.), *summer*
120. commeātus, commeātūs (mas.), *supplies*
121. dēditiō, dēditiōnis (fem.), *surrender*
122. dēdō, dēdere, dēdidī, dēditum, *surrender*
123. circumdō, circumdare, circumdedī, circumdatum, *surround*
124. capiō, capere, cēpī, captum, *take*
125. tum, inde (adverbs), *then*
126. ibi (adv.), *there*
127. cis (prep. with the acc.), *on this side of*
128. tempus, temporis (neut.), *time*
129. turris, turris (fem.), *tower*
130. inīquus, inīqua, inīquum (adj.), *unfavourable*
131. inimīcus, inimīca, inimīcum (adj.), *unfriendly*
132. bellum, bellī (neut.), *war*
133. vigilia, vigiliae (fem.), *watch* (division of the night)
134. ubi (adv.), *when*

135. **cum** (conj.), *while*
136. **quī, quae, quod** (rel. pron.), *who, which, what, that*
137. **sustineō, sustinēre, sustinuī, sustentum,** *withstand*
138. **dē** (prep. with the *abl.*), *with respect to*

LESSON XLI.

FIFTH DECLENSION.

220. Rēs, *thing*, fem.   **Diēs,** *day*, mas.

	SINGULAR.	PLURAL.	SINGULAR.	PLURAL.
Nom.	rēs	rēs	diēs	diēs
Gen.	reī	rērum	diēī	diērum
Dat.	reī	rēbus	diēī	diēbus
Acc.	rem	rēs	diem	diēs
Voc.	rēs	rēs	diēs	diēs
Abl.	rē	rēbus	diē	diēbus

The stem of nouns in the fifth declension ends in ē. Nouns of the fifth declension are *feminine*, except **diēs**, which is *masculine*. **Rēs** and **diēs** alone have the entire plural; others occur usually in the nominative and accusative plural—many have no plural.

221. Ablative of separation.—Separation is expressed by the ablative with or without a preposition; as,

Caesar armīs hostēs dēspoliat, *Caesar deprives the enemy of their arms*

222.   VOCABULARY.

spēs	speī, *fem.*	hope
fidēs	fideī, *fem.*	confidence
propīnquitās	-tātis, *fem.*	nearness
exiguitās	-tātis, *fem.*	shortness
vulnus	-neris, *neut.*	wound
summus -a -um, *adj.*		top of
in summō colle		on the top of the hill
sī, *conj.*		if
nisi, *conj.*		unless
proelium committō		to begin battle
pellō		to defeat

223. Use of *si* and *nisi* in conditionals (335).—Sī, nisi, etc., introduce conditional sentences. In a conditional sentence the *dependent* clause, *containing the condition*, is called the *protasis;* the clause containing the *conclusion* is called the *apodosis*.

The more vivid future condition.—(*a*) In the *more vivid* future condition the *future indicative* is used in both *protasis* and *apodosis;* as,

Caesar pācem faciet, sī hostēs obsidēs dēdent,   *Caesar will make peace, if the enemy surrender hostages*

(*b*) If the conditional act is considered as *completed* before that of the *apodosis*, the *future perfect* is used in the *protasis;* as,

Nisi hostēs omnia arma trādiderint, Galba proelium committet,   *Unless the enemy hand over all their arms, Galba will begin battle*

('Hand over' = *will have handed over*, representing action *completed* in the *future*, before *another future action* begins.)

224.   EXERCISE.

1. Caesar in servitūtem eās cīvitātēs quae cum nostrīs peditibus in Rēmōrum fīnibus proelium commīsērunt facile redēgit. 2. Mīlitēs quī commeātūs petendī causā ē castrīs discesserant adventum hostium nōn cōnspēxērunt. 3. Nostrī propter propīnquitātem celeritātemque hostium capere oppidum in quō erant commeātūs et multa arma nōn potuērunt. 4. Cum Caesar in colle adventum hostium exspectāret, praefectīs equitum mandāvit ut statim ē castrīs omnēs cōpiās ēdūcerent et ad committendum proelium parārent. 5. Noster imperātor in suam fidem[1] Rēmōs fīnitimōsque accipiet, sī eae cīvitātēs quae sine causā in

---

[1] In suam fidem = *under his protection*.

nostrōs impetum fēcērunt ad Caesarem dē dēditiōne lēgātōs mīserint. 6. Caesar in Belgās omnibus cōpiīs impetum faciet, nisi Belgae lēgātōs mīserint ut obsidēs dēdant pācemque petant. 7. Peditēs Rōmānī propter temporis exiguitātem celeritātemque hostium imperātum Caesaris nōn exspectāvērunt sed in hostēs impetum ācriter fēcērunt, nē pūgnandī facultātem āmitterent.

LESSON XLII.

FOURTH CONJUGATION.

225. Mūniō, *I fortify.* Principal parts **mūniō, mūnīre, mūnīvī, mūnītum.** The present system is as follows. The *present stem,* **mūnī,** is found by striking off **re** from the *present infinitive active,* **mūnīre.**

Present Indicative.	Imperfect Indicative.	Present Subjunctive.
I fortify.	*was fortifying.*	*may fortify.*
SINGULAR.	mūniēbam	mūniam
1. mūniō	mūniēbās, etc.	mūniās, etc.
2. mūnīs		
3. mūnit	Future Indicative.	Imperfect Subjunctive.
PLURAL.	*shall fortify.*	*might fortify.*
1. mūnīmus	mūniam	mūnīrem
2. mūnītis	mūniēs, etc.	mūnīrēs, etc.
3. mūniunt		

Imperative.	Present participle.
mūnī, *fortify thou*	mūniēns, *fortifying*
mūnīte, *fortify ye,* etc.	

Present Infinitive.	Gerund.
mūnīre, *to fortify*	mūniendī, *of fortifying*

226. VOCABULARY.

Verbs 1-9 (451).

audiō — *to hear*
impediō — *to hinder*
veniō — *to come*
cōnsentiō — *to conspire*
quis, *interrogative pronoun* — *who?*

aliquis { *indefinite pronoun,* after sī, nisi, nē, num, *quis.* } *any one, some one*

227. Demonstrative pronoun hīc, *this.*

	SINGULAR.			PLURAL.		
	Mas.	Fem.	Neuter.	Mas.	Fem.	Neuter.
Nom.	hīc	haec	hōc	hī	hae	haec
Gen.	hūius	hūius	hūius	hōrum	hārum	hōrum
Dat.	huic	huic	huic	hīs	hīs	hīs
Acc.	hunc	hanc	hōc	hōs	hās	haec
Abl.	hōc	hāc	hōc	hīs	hīs	hīs

228. Use of *nē* (*not*) in negative commands.—Imperō, mandō, and many verbs of *commanding* take ut + *subjunctive* in *affirmative* commands, and nē + *subjunctive* in *negative* commands.

Caesar imperat mīlitibus nē   *Caesar commands his soldiers*
oppidum incendant,   *not to burn the town*

229. EXERCISES.

I.—1. Hīs in locīs sunt nōn multa oppida idōnea tantae hominum multitūdinī. 2. Germānī spē expūgnandī oppida multa trāns Rhēnum in Galliam suās cōpiās dūxerant. 3. Belgae omnibus cōpiīs in prōvinciam nostram ut in fidem populī Rōmānī līberōs obsidēs trādant veniunt. 4. Nisi Caesar in hās cīvitātēs quās Galba proeliīs multīs in servitūtem redēgit contenderit, hostēs manūs novās cōgent ut mūnītiōnēs Rōmānās incendant. 5. Sēquanī cum Belgīs, fīnitimīs, cōnsentiunt et oppida sua fossīs mūrīsque mūniunt nē Caesar in potestātem populī Rōmānī cīvitātēs redigat.

II.—1. Because the enemy fear the approach of the Roman legions, they will depart out of these fortifications and leave in camp a large part of their baggage. 2. While Caesar's soldiers were fortifying that town which the Sequani had left, the Belgians made an attack upon Galba's infantry who were coming towards the town with all the baggage. 3. When Caesar saw the large number of ambassadors whom the enemy had sent into our camp, he commanded his generals not to make (nē + *imperf. subj.*) an attack upon the enemies' forces. 4. Unless the chiefs of these states which are strong in courage and in number of men come [1] into our camp and ask for [1] peace, Caesar will lead out his infantry and lay waste their towns and fields.

LESSON XLIII.

FOURTH CONJUGATION, CONTINUED.

230. Perfect system of *mūniō.*—**Stem mūnīv.**

Perfect indicative. *I fortified.*	Pluperfect indicative. *had fortified.*	Perfect subjunctive. *may have fortified.*
SINGULAR.	mūnīveram,	mūnīverim, etc.
1. mūnīvī	mūnīverās, etc.	**Pluperfect subjunctive.**
2. mūnīvistī		*might have fortified.*
3. mūnīvit	**Future-perfect indicative.**	mūnīvissem, etc.
PLURAL.	*shall have fortified.*	**Perfect infinitive.**
1. mūnīvimus	mūnīverō	*to have fortified.*
2. mūnīvistis	mūnīveris, etc.	mūnīvisse
3. mūnīvērunt (-ēre)		

---
[1] Future or future-perfect indicative.

Give synopsis, *by stems*, in entire active voice of **audiō** and **cōnsentiō**.

Give synopsis in active voice of **mūniō**, *by moods*, etc., in the order given in (482).

231. Supine system of *mūniō*.—*Stem* mūnīt.

1. *First supine*   mūnītum,   *to fortify*
2. *Second supine*   mūnītū,   *to fortify*
3. *Future participle* mūnītūrus -a, -um, *being about to fortify*
4. *Future infinitive* { mūnītūrum, -am, -um esse, } *to be about to fortify*

232.   **VOCABULARY.**

Verbs 10–19 **(451)**.

233. Demonstrative pronoun *ille*, *that*, *he*.

	SINGULAR.			PLURAL.		
	Mas.	Fem.	Neuter.	Mas.	Fem.	Neuter.
Nom.	ille	illa	illud	illī	illae	illa
Gen.	illīus	illīus	illīus	illōrum	illārum	illōrum
Dat.	illī	illī	illī	illīs	illīs	illīs
Acc.	illum	illam	illud	illōs	illās	illa
Abl.	illō	illā	illō	illīs	illīs	illīs

234.   **EXERCISES.**

I.—1. Nisi illae cīvitātēs reliquīs cum Belgīs cōnsentient ac suīs amīcīs auxilium dabunt, Gallī Caesaris exercitūs adventum impedīre nōn poterunt. 2. Exercitus noster vīcōs omnēs incendit (*perf.*) et agrōs per quōs vēnerant vāstāvit, nē hostēs illa loca incolere possent. 3. Cum Rēmī in castra sua cum impedīmentīs exercitūs venīrent, nostrī in novissimum agmen impetum fēcērunt et agmina perturbāvērunt. 4. Caesar hōc proeliō in servitūtem omnēs eās cīvitātēs quārum prīncipēs cum Germānīs cōnsēnserant et obsidēs nōn dederant redēgit. 5. Quod hostēs, in castrīs suās manūs retinendō, nostrīs facultātem pūgnandī nōn dedērunt, Caesar ducibus prīmae legiōnis ut omnibus cum cohortibus ēius legiōnis ē castrīs contenderent et in mūrum oppidī impetum facerent imperāvit.

II.—1. When the enemy had lost hope with respect to withstanding the attack of our infantry, Caesar directed their chiefs to bring (**addūcō**) hostages into his camp and to surrender the town without delay. 2. At the same time ambassadors come to Caesar from all sides and bring corn and (**que**) supplies for our men, because Caesar had announced the approach of his army. 3. While the enemy were fortifying their camp on the top of the hill, our commanders surrounded the hill with (*omit*) infantry and (**que**) cavalry and began battle on all sides. 4. The Sequani into whose territories Caesar is preparing to lead a large army will ask for (**petō**) peace, in order that the Roman legions may not lay waste their fields, destroy their fortifications, and burn their towns.

LESSON XLIV.

FIRST CONJUGATION PASSIVE.

285. Present indicative passive of *portō*.

SINGULAR.	PLURAL.
1. portor, *I am (being) carried*	1. portāmur, *we are carried*
2. portāris (-re), *you are carried*	2. portāminī, *you are carried*
3. portātur, *he is carried*	3. portantur, *they are carried*

The *present stem* is **portā** as in the *active*, t*·* which are annexed the following endings.

Table of endings.

SINGULAR.	PLURAL.
-or	-mur
-ris (-re)	-minī
-tur	-ntur

Conjugate **postulō** and **cōnservō** in the *present indicative passive*.

286. **VOCABULARY.**

Review verbs 1–19 (451).

Decline **īdem**, *the same* (464).

287. Personal agent—how expressed.—The agent or doer with a passive verb is put in the *ablative with* **ā** *or* **ab**. Distinguish carefully *means* or *instrument* from *agent;* thus,

(*a*) **Gallī ā Rōmānīs superantur**, *the Gauls are overcome by the Romans:* by the Romans = *persons* by whom, hence **ā** or **ab** + *ablative*, to denote *personal agent*.

(*b*) **agrī ignī vāstantur**, *the fields are laid waste by fire:* by fire = *thing* by which, hence ablative of *means* or *instrument* without a preposition.

288. **EXERCISES.**

I.—1. Eae cīvitātēs quae arma commeātūsque trādidērunt ā nostrīs cōnservantur. 2. Proelium in summō colle ab imperātōre fortī redintegrātur. 3. Fīnēs per quōs Caesar suum exercitum dūxit ā peditibus nostrīs vāstantur. 4. Dēditiō omnium armōrum ā Caesare postulātur, quod Sēquanī in Rēmōs, fīnitimōs amīcōsque populī Rōmānī, impetum ācriter fēcērunt. 5. Hostēs ad Caesarem līberōs prīncipum obsidēs mīsērunt nē facultātem faciendī pācem āmitterent.

II.—1. New fortifications are being built by those soldiers whom Caesar had left in camp. 2. Those states into which the Roman commanders came to enroll new legions are spared by Caesar. 3. The number of soldiers is being increased by the Roman commanders in order that the enemy may not be able to defeat our army. 4. Unless

Caesar surrounds¹ the town on all sides, the enemy will depart by night² and seek safety in flight. 5. The enemies' forces which made an attack upon Caesar's infantry while they were fortifying their camp, are easily routed by Galba's soldiers.

LESSON XLV.

FIRST CONJUGATION PASSIVE, CONTINUED.

239. *Portŏ* continued in the indicative passive.

Imperfect indicative.	Future indicative.
was (being) carried.	*shall be carried.*
SINGULAR.	SINGULAR.
1. portābar	portābor
2. portābāris (-re)	portāberis (-re)
3. portābātur	portābitur
PLURAL.	PLURAL.
1. portābāmur	portābimur
2. portābāminī	portābiminī
3. portābantur	portābuntur

Table of endings.

SINGULAR.	PLURAL.	SINGULAR.	PLURAL.
-bar	-bāmur	-bor	-bimur
-bāris (-re)	-bāminī	-beris (-re)	-biminī
-bātur	-bantur	-bitur	-buntur

240. Use of *ā* or *ab*.—Ā or ab means *from* (denoting origin or source) when the adverbial phrase (*preposition + noun*) limits a verb in the *active voice;* but it means *by* (denoting personal agent) if it limits a *passive verb:*

1. Hostēs ab Gallīs auxilium accipiunt, *The enemy receive aid from the Gauls*
2. Auxilium hostibus (*dat.*) ab Gallīs datur, *Aid is given to the enemy by the Gauls*

---
¹ Fut. perf. indic.; see 228 (b).   ² noctū.

241. VOCABULARY.

Review words 1–46 in the 'review vocabulary' (219).

auxilia -ōrum, *neut.*   *auxiliaries*
medius -a, -um, *adj.*   *middle of*
dē mediā nocte   *about the middle of the night*
eō, *adv.*   *thither*
ad eum, ad eōs   *to him, to them*

242. Decline quis, *who?* (465).

Sometimes is, ea, id, *he, she, it*, is used as the personal pronoun of the third person; thus,

1. Cum Caesar esset in Galliā, lēgātī ad eum vēnērunt,   *While Caesar was in Gaul, ambassadors came to him*
2. Nisi Belgae pācem petent (petīverint), Caesar statim in eōs impetum faciet,   *Unless the Belgians ask for peace, Caesar will make an attack upon them at once*

243. EXERCISES.

I.—1. Causa coniūrandī erat haec, quod multīs in locīs oppida Gallōrum ā mīlitibus nostrīs vāstābantur. 2. Sīgnum ad proelium committendum ab imperātōre cūius cōpiae in silvīs cēlantur¹ subitō dabitur hostēsque ā legiōnibus fortibus prōflīgābuntur. 3. Cum exercitus noster in extrēmā Galliā esset, obsidēs nōmine populī Rōmānī ā ducibus nostrīs postulābantur et in castra Rōmāna sine morā ab hostibus portābantur. 4. Potestās populī Rōmānī inter eās cīvitātēs quārum virtūs māgna est ā Caesare amplificābitur, nē hostēs commeātibus nostrōs prohibeant. 5. Eōdem tempore oppida Sēquanōrum ab hīs cōpiīs quibus Galba tēla nova dedit occupantur, quod ad Caesarem de pāce lēgātōs nōn mīsērunt.

II.—1. The enemy fled with all their baggage out of the territories through which our men were coming, because

---

¹ The present indicative passive denotes the *continuance* of an action in the present; cēlantur = '*are being concealed.*'

they feared the power of our army. 2. The brave soldiers of the second legion were overcome by many wounds, which they received when they made an attack upon the Germans. 3. While Caesar was wintering among the Remi whose fields are next to the Roman province, corn and supplies were carried to him by many states. 4. When the enemy saw the high towers which were being built by our men so that they might storm the walls of the town, they at once surrendered to Caesar the children of their chiefs as hostages and asked for peace.

LESSON XLVI.

FIRST CONJUGATION PASSIVE, CONTINUED.

244. *Portō* continued in the present system passive.

Present subjunctive. Imperfect subjunctive.
may be carried. *might be carried.*

SINGULAR.	PLURAL.	SINGULAR.	PLURAL.
1. porter	portēmur	portārer	portārēmur
2. portēris (-re)	portēminī	portārēris (-re)	portārēminī
3. portētur	portentur	portāretur	portārentur

Imperative.

SINGULAR.

2. { portāre, *be thou carried*
   { portātor, *thou shalt be carried*
3. portātor, *he shall be carried*

PLURAL.

2. portāminī, *be ye carried*
3. portantor, *they shall be carried*

Present infinitive. Gerundive.
portārī, *to be carried* portandus, -a, -um, (*worthy*) *to be carried*

245. This completes the *eight* forms in the *passive*, based upon the *present stem* **portā**. The *present stem* **portā** undergoes a change in the *present subjunctive* where final ā becomes e. Compare the *ending* of the *present infinitive active* (āre) with that of the *present infinitive passive* (ārī).

246. Synopsis of *portō* in the present system passive.— *Stem* **portā.**

1. *Present indicative*   portor,   *I am being carried*
2. *Imperfect indicative*   portābar,   *I was being carried*
3. *Future indicative*   portābor,   *I shall be carried*
4. *Present subjunctive*   porter,   *I may be carried*
5. *Imperfect subjunctive* portārer,   *I might be carried*
6. *Imperative*   portāre,   *be thou carried*
7. *Present infinitive*   portārī,   *to be carried*
8. *Gerundive*   portandus -a -um, (*worthy*) *to be carried*

247.   **VOCABULARY.**

Review words 47–92, in 'review vocabulary' (**219**).

vadum, -ī, *neut.*   *ford*
concilium, -ī, *neut.*   *council of war*
post, *prep. with the acc.*   *behind* or *after*
prōtinus, *adv.*   *immediately*
atque, *conj.*   *and also*

248.   **EXERCISES.**

I.—1. Proximō diē Caesar fortibus equitātūs praefectīs ut in Sēquanōrum fīnēs cōpiās omnēs dūcerent imperāvit, nē auxilia ā Sēquanīs ad Aeduōs portārentur. 2. Aeduī, quod nostrī exercitūs quem timēbant adventum audīverant (*had heard of*), ad Germānōs, fīnitimōs, lēgātōs mīsērunt ut ab eīs cīvitātibus quae populō Rōmānō sē nōndum dēdiderant auxilia impetrārent. 3. Nisi Galba suōs mīlitēs in novissimum agmen Aeduōrum impetum facere iusserit commeātibusque eōs prohibuerit, Aeduī ex Italiā contendent et cum Germānīs coniūrābunt. 4. Cum Caesar castra mūnīret, lēgātī ex māgnā parte Galliae ad eum vēnērunt atque ut in dēditiōnem eōs acciperet petīvērunt.

FIRST CONJUGATION PASSIVE.

II.—1. Because the Belgians burned our fortifications in the territories of Gaul, a large number of hostages was demanded by Caesar according to his custom. 2. Galba will enroll new legions and hasten (mātūrō) into the boundaries of the Gauls whose fields are being laid waste by the Germans, so that aid may be given to his friends[1] and the enemy may be overcome. 3. A camp will be placed (conlocō) on the top of the hill and the battle will be renewed by those generals whose brave forces have defeated (pellō) the enemy in many battles.

LESSON XLVII.
FIRST CONJUGATION PASSIVE, PERFECT SYSTEM.

249. Principal parts of *portō* in the passive:

Present indicative.	Present infinitive.	Perfect indicative.
portor	portārī	portātus sum

The perfect stem portāv does not occur in the passive voice.

The remaining *eight forms* of the passive are based upon the *supine stem* portāt which is seen in the *perfect passive participle*, portātus; these compose the *perfect system* of the passive.

250. Perfect system of *portō* in the passive.—*Stem* portāt.

Perfect indicative.	Perfect subjunctive.
have been—was carried.	*may have been carried.*
SINGULAR.	SINGULAR.
1. portātus, -a, -um sum	portātus, -a, -um sim
2. " " " es	" " " sīs
3. " " " est	" " " sit
PLURAL.	PLURAL.
1. portātī, -ae, -a sumus	portātī, -ae, -a sīmus
2. " " " estis	" " " sītis
3. " " " sunt	" " " sint

---
[1] Suīs amīcīs.

Pluperfect indicative.
had been carried.

SINGULAR.
1. portātus, -a, -um eram
2. "   "   "   erās
3. "   "   "   erat

PLURAL.
1. portātī, -ae, -a erāmus
2. "   "   "   erātis
3. "   "   "   erant

Future-perfect indicative.
shall have been carried.

SINGULAR.
1. portātus, -a, -um erō
2. "   "   "   eris
3. "   "   "   erit

PLURAL.
1. portātī, -ae, -a erimus
2. "   "   "   eritis
3. "   "   "   erunt

Pluperfect subjunctive.
might have been carried.

SINGULAR.
portātus, -a, -um essem
"   "   "   essēs
"   "   "   esset

PLURAL.
portātī, -ae, -a essēmus
"   "   "   essētis
"   "   "   essent

Perfect infinitive.
portātum, -am, -um esse
to have been carried.

Future infinitive.
portātum īrī
to be about to be carried

Perfect participle.
portātus, -a, -um
having been carried.

251. The above compound tenses are formed by annexing parts of the verb **sum** to the perfect passive participle, portātus, -a, -um.

The participial parts of these tenses, such as portātus, -a, -um, portātī, -ae, -a, portātum, -am, -um, etc., are made to agree in *gender, number,* and *case* with the *subject* of the verb.

252.   VOCABULARY.

Review words 93–138 in 'review vocabulary' (**219**).

253. The gerundive construction.—Instead of the accusative-object with the gerund, put the *object* in the *case* in which the gerund would stand (*were it used*), and place the *gerundive* in agreement with this noun in the *same gender, number, and case.*

FIRST CONJUGATION PASSIVE.

1. By drawing up a line of battle: the gerund construction is **instruendō aciem**; change **aciem** to the *ablative* **aciē** (the case indicated by **instruendō**); place the gerundive **instruendus** in the *ablative, singular, feminine* to agree with **aciē** and the phrase is correctly written **aciē instruendā**.

2. By destroying the fortifications: the gerund construction is **dēlendō mūnītiōnēs**; gerundive, **mūnītiōnibus dēlendīs**.

254. Commit to memory the following:

1. **Imperātor amātus est,** *The commander has been* or *was loved*
2. **Virtus amāta est,** *Courage has been* or *was loved*
3. **Nōmen amātum est,** *The name was loved*
4. **Mīlitēs amātī sunt,** *The soldiers were loved*
5. **Cīvitātēs amātae sunt,** *The states were loved*
6. **Castra amāta sunt,** *The camp has been loved*

LESSON XLVIII.

FIRST CONJUGATION PASSIVE. ADJECTIVES USED AS SUBSTANTIVES.

255. Synopsis of the passive—first conjugation—by stems.

Present system, stem **portā**.

1. *Present indicative*   portor
2. *Imperfect indicative*   portābar
3. *Future indicative*   portābor
4. *Present subjunctive*   porter
5. *Imperfect subjunctive*   portārer
6. *Imperative*   portāre
7. *Present infinitive*   portārī
8. *Gerundive*   portandus

Perfect system, stem **portāt**.

1. *Perfect indicative*   portātus sum [1]
2. *Pluperfect indicative*   portātus eram

---

[1] The perfect indicative passive (*indefinite perfect*) represents the action as *past*, without reference to its *duration*, *merely as something ended*.

3. *Future-perfect indicative*   portātus erō
4. *Perfect subjunctive*   portātus sim
5. *Pluperfect subjunctive*   portātus essem
6. *Perfect infinitive*   portātum esse
7. *Future infinitive*   portātum īrī
8. *Perfect participle*   portātus, -a, -um

Conjugate the entire verb **amō**, *active* and *passive*, as given in (474, 475).

256.   **VOCABULARY.**

Review verbs 1–41 (450).

257. Perfect passive participle. — The perfect passive participle (p. p. p.) is found by changing final **m** of the *first supine* to **s**: **moveō, movēre, mōvī, mōtum;** supine **mōtum,** p. p. p. **mōtus, -a, -um,** *having been moved.* **cōgnōscō, cōgnōscere, cōgnōvī, cōgnitum;** supine **cōgnitum,** p. p. p. **cōgnitus,** *having been found out.*

258. Adjectives used as substantives.—The *adjective* in the *masculine plural* is often used as a noun, meaning *men, soldiers, friends,* etc.; as, **ad eōs,** *to those* (*men*); **prīmōrum,** *of the foremost* (*men*); **reliquī,** *the rest;* **ad suōs,** *to his or their* (*friends*);—so **noster** in the masculine plural: **nostrī,** *our men.*

The *adjective* in the *neuter plural,* as a substantive, means *things* or *possessions;* as, **ea,** *those* (*things*); **haec,** *these* (*things*); **sua omnia,** *all his* or *their* (*possessions*).

259.   **EXERCISES.**

I.—1. Multa Gallōrum castella ā nostrīs quī conlocātī erant in hībernīs in Galliā occupāta sunt. 2. Proelium ab eīs quōs Caesar in Sēquanōrum fīnīs mīsit redintegrātum est. 3. Lēgātī Rōmānī in extrēmās Galliae partēs vēnērunt ut ea quae hostēs facerent[1] cōgnōscerent.

---
[1] *were doing:* for mood of **facerent** see (276)—'subjunctive by attraction.'

4. Omnia quae erant idōnea bellō ā Belgīs comparāta erant, quod adventum nostrī exercitūs exspectābant. 5. Eī quibus Galba loca in Galliā ad hiemandum dedit ā Gallīs fortibus facile prōturbātī sunt. 6. Gallī spē[1] pācis faciendae obsidēs dēdent.

II.—1. All who handed over arms and (que) gave hostages were spared by our general and called friends of the Roman people. 2. About the middle of the night Caesar will send scouts into those territories, in which the camp of the Germans has been placed, to find out those things which the enemy are doing.[2] 3. The rest of the Gauls (*nom.*) from whom Caesar had received hostages were incited by the enemies of the Roman people. 4. When (ubi) the ambassador of the Belgians came into our camp, Caesar ordered him to surrender to the Roman people all the fields on this side of the river Rhine. 5. The Gauls surround their towns with high walls that they may not be overcome by the Romans.

LESSON XLIX.
SECOND CONJUGATION. PASSIVE OF DĒLEŌ.

260. The present system of *dēleō* continued in the passive.

Present Indicative.	Imperfect Indicative.	Future Indicative.
am being destroyed.	was being destroyed.	shall be destroyed.
SINGULAR.	SINGULAR.	SINGULAR.
1. dēleor	dēlēbar	dēlēbor
2. dēlēris (-re)	dēlēbāris (-re)	dēlēberis (-re)
3. dēlētur	dēlēbātur	dēlēbitur
PLURAL.	PLURAL.	PLURAL.
1. dēlēmur	dēlēbāmur	dēlēbimur
2. dēlēminī	dēlēbāminī	dēlēbiminī
3. dēlentur	dēlēbantur	dēlēbuntur

[1] Abl. of cause: *because of their hopes.*   [2] faciant; see (276).

The *present stem* is **dēlē**, as in the *active*. The *personal endings* are the *same* as in the *corresponding* tenses of the *first-conjugation verb*. Avoid putting in an extra syllable in the second person singular, present indicative; it is **dē-lē-ris**, *not* dē-lē-e-ris.

261. *Compare carefully the following tenses:*

First conjugation, present subjunctive.		Second conjugation, present indicative.	
SINGULAR.	PLURAL.	SINGULAR.	PLURAL.
1. porter	portēmur	dēleor	dēlēmur
2. portēris (-re)	portēminī	dēlēris (-re)	dēlēminī
3. portētur	portentur	dēlētur	dēlentur

When the verb ends in **ētur**, **entur**, etc., it is *present subjunctive* in the *first* conjugation, *present indicative* in the *second* conjugation.

262.   VOCABULARY.

Verbs 42–48 (450).

sagittārius, sagittāriī, *mas.*	*bowman*
funditor, funditōris, *mas.*	*slinger*
quīnque, *indecl. num. adj.*	*five*
circiter, *adv.*	*about*
cum, *conj.*	*after*
trādūcō, trādūcere, trādūxī, trāductum,	*to lead across*
perveniō, pervenīre, pervēnī, perventum,	*to arrive at*
pellō, pellere, pepulī, pulsum,	*to drive*
tum, *adv.*	*then*

263. *Cum* + pluperfect subjunctive (208, 359).—*Cum, when,* in the sense of '*after,*' takes the pluperfect subjunctive, translated like the *pluperfect indicative*; as,

Cum Caesar in Galliam iter fēcisset, multae cīvitātēs ad eum lēgātōs dē pāce mīsērunt,   *After Caesar had marched into Gaul, many states sent ambassadors to him with respect to peace*

264.   EXERCISES.

I.—1. Exercitus noster in Galliā distinētur, nē rēgnum ā Caesaris hostibus occupētur. 2. Fossae quae oppidum circumdant corporibus eōrum quī peditum Rōmānōrum impetum nōn sustinuērunt complentur. 3. Cum Caesar eō vēnisset, Rēmī quōrum cīvitātēs proximae Belgīs sunt ad eum prīncipēs lēgātōs, ut eī¹ sua omnia trādant, mittunt. 4. Caesar māgnō numerō cōpiārum fortium collem in quō hostēs sua castra mūniēbant circumdedit praefectīsque, ut in eōs māgnā cum virtūte impetum ācriter facerent, imperāvit.

II.—1. Unless Caesar leads² the bowmen and (que) slingers across the bridge and prevents² the departure of the enemy, he will not receive the hostages which he had demanded. 2. That state, from (ā) which auxiliaries came so that they might aid our army, will not be attacked by the Roman soldiers. 3. Because the Remi are ready to give hostages and receive him in their towns, Caesar will command his generals not to lead the army through that state. 4. After the Remi had surrendered all their (possessions), Caesar ordered them to inhabit that part of Gaul from which he had driven (**expellō**) the bands of the enemy.

LESSON L.

SECOND CONJUGATION. PASSIVE OF DĒLEŌ, CONTINUED.

265. The present system of *dēleō* completed in the passive.

Decline **ūnus, duo,** and **trēs (468).**

Present subjunctive.		Imperfect subjunctive.	
may be destroyed.		*might be destroyed.*	
SINGULAR.	PLURAL.	SINGULAR.	PLURAL.
1. dēlear	dēleāmur	dēlērer	dēlērēmur
2. dēleāris (-re)	dēleāminī	dēlērēris (-re)	dēlērēminī
3. dēleātur	dēleantur	dēlērētur	dēlērentur

---

¹ Dative. ² Future or future-perfect indicative.

Imperative.		Present Infinitive.
be thou destroyed, etc.		dēlērī, *to be destroyed*
SINGULAR.	PLURAL.	
2. { dēlēre	dēlēminī	Gerundive.
{ dēlētor		dēlendus, -a, -um, (*worthy*) *to*
3. dēlētor	dēlentor	*be destroyed*

The *stem* is **dēlē**: this completes the *present system* of *eight* forms based upon **dēlē**.

266. *Compare carefully the following tenses:*

First conjugation, present indicative, stem *portā*.		Second conjugation, present subjunctive, stem *dēlē*.	
SINGULAR.	PLURAL.	SINGULAR.	PLURAL.
1. portor	portāmur	dēlear	dēleāmur
2. portāris (-re)	portāminī	dēleāris (-re)	dēleāminī
3. portātur	portantur	dēleātur	dēleantur

Thus when a verb ends in **ātur, antur**, etc., it is *present indicative* in the *first* conjugation, *present subjunctive* in the *second* conjugation.

267.   VOCABULARY.

Verbs 49-55 (450).

ūnus, ūna, ūnum, *num. adj.* one
quantus, quanta, quantum, *adj.* how great
neque ... neque, *conj.* neither ... nor
celeriter, *adv.* quickly
ipse, ipsa, ipsum, *emphatic pron.* he, self
quaerō, quaerere, quaesīvī, quaesītum, to inquire
palūs, palūdis, *fem.* swamp
coniungō, coniungere, coniūnxī, coniūnctum, to join

268.   EXERCISES.

I.—1. Omnēs reliquī Belgae in armīs sunt Germānīque quī cis Rhēnum incolunt sē cum hīs coniūnxērunt, nē sua oppida ā nostrīs dēleantur. 2. Cum Germānī suās cōpiās trāns Rhēnum trādūxissent, ibi cōnsēdērunt Gallōsque quī ea loca incolēbant armīs expulērunt. 3. Cum ab hīs

Caesar quaereret quantae cīvitātēs in armīs essent[1] atque quantum exercitum hostēs cōgere possent,[2] haec reperiēbat. 4. Palūs erat nōn māgna inter nostrum atque hostium exercitum et hostēs trāns hanc suās cōpiās trādūcere parābant. 5. Hostēs prōtinus ex eō locō ad flūmen quod esse post nostra castra dēmōnstrātum est contendērunt.

II.—1. Caesar leads out all the army and prepares to storm the walls so that the town may be destroyed and many weapons may be seized. 2. After Caesar had come into those parts in which he had placed (pōnō) his camp, many states joined themselves with our army so that their children might not be reduced into slavery. 3. While Caesar was inquiring of (ab) the scouts with respect to the number of the enemy, ambassadors of the Germans came into our camp and surrendered themselves and (que) all their (possessions) to Caesar (*dative*). 4. After Caesar had driven the enemy out of these boundaries and had received a suitable number of hostages, he led his soldiers back into camp.

LESSON LI.

SECOND CONJUGATION. PASSIVE OF DĒLEŌ, CONTINUED.

269. Principal parts of *dēleō* **in the passive:** *dēleor, dēlērī, dēlētus sum.*

For the tense names of these forms, see (249).

Perfect system of *dēleō* **in the passive.**—Stem dēlēt.

Perfect Indicative.

have been—was—destroyed.

SINGULAR.	PLURAL.
1. dēlētus, -a, -um sum	dēlētī, -ae, -a sumus
2. " " " es	" " " estis
3. " " " est	" " " sunt

---

[1] *were.* [2] *were able ;* for mood in both, see (313), '*indirect question.*'

Pluperfect indicative.
had been destroyed.

SINGULAR.
1. dēlētus, -a, -um eram
2. "   "   "   erās
3. "   "   "   erat

PLURAL.
1. dēlētī, -ae, -a erāmus
2. "   "   " erātis
3. "   "   " erant

Future-perfect indicative.
shall have been destroyed.

SINGULAR.
1. dēlētus, -a, -um erō
2. "   "   "   eris
3. "   "   "   erit

PLURAL.
1. dēlētī, -ae, -a erimus
2. "   "   " eritis
3. "   "   " erunt

Perfect subjunctive.
may have been destroyed.

SINGULAR.
1. dēlētus, -a, -um sim
2. "   "   "   sīs
3. "   "   "   sit

PLURAL.
1. dēlētī, -ae, -a sīmus
2. "   "   " sītis
3. "   "   " sint

Pluperfect subjunctive.
might have been destroyed.

SINGULAR.
1. dēlētus, -a, -um essem
2. "   "   "   essēs
3. "   "   "   esset

PLURAL.
1. dēlētī, -ae, -a essēmus
2. "   "   " essētis
3. "   "   " essent

Perfect infinitive.
dēlētum, -am, -um esse, *to have been destroyed*

Future infinitive.
dēlētum īrī, *to be about to be destroyed*

Perfect participle.
dēlētus, -a, -um, *having been destroyed*

SECOND CONJUGATION.

270. Synopsis, present system, passive.—*Present stem* dēlē.

1. *Present indicative*	dēleor
2. *Imperfect indicative*	dēlēbar
3. *Future indicative*	dēlēbor
4. *Present subjunctive*	dēlear
5. *Imperfect subjunctive*	dēlērer
6. *Imperative*	dēlēre
7. *Present infinitive*	dēlērī
8. *Gerundive*	dēlendus

Perfect system, passive.—*Stem* dēlēt, *seen in the perfect participle,* dēlētus.

1. *Perfect indicative*	dēlētus sum
2. *Pluperfect indicative*	dēlētus eram
3. *Future-perfect indicative*	dēlētus erō
4. *Perfect subjunctive*	dēlētus sim
5. *Pluperfect subjunctive*	dēlētus essem
6. *Perfect infinitive*	dēlētum esse
7. *Future infinitive*	dēlētum īrī
8. *Perfect participle*	dēlētus, -a, -um

271.   **VOCABULARY.**

Verbs 56–64 (450).

272.   **EXERCISES.**

I.—1. Cīvitātēs multae, quod cōpiae superātae erant atque sua oppida ā nostrīs occupāta et dēlēta erant, in fidem Caesaris sē suaque omnia permīsērunt. 2. Caesar, ubi eae cōpiae quās Germānī trāns Rhēnum trādūxerant in summō monte ā Caesare vīsae sunt, mīlitibus legiōnis prīmae ut in eās impetum facerent imperāvit. 3. Nisi legiōnēs novae cōnscrībentur[1] ac castra nostra ex eō locō movēbuntur,[2] imperātōrēs Rōmānī neque in Galliā agrōs lātōs possidēre neque nōmen populī Rōmānī amplificāre poterunt. 4. Caesar suīs peditibus nē inīquō locō proelium

---
[1] cōnscrībentur or cōnscrīptae erunt; see (223, *a*, *b*).
[2] What other form may be used ?

committant mandat. 5. Galba in servitūtem Belgās quōrum oppida frūmentō commeātibusque complentur rediget.

II.—1. While Caesar was enrolling a new legion in that state which had been overcome, the Germans were preparing to make an attack upon him with a large army. 2. After the Aedui had entrusted themselves and (que) all their (possessions) to (in + acc.) the power and protection of the Roman people, Caesar ordered them to settle in farthest Gaul. 3. By collecting[1] a large army and fortifying[1] their towns with new ramparts the enemy were able to cut off (prohibeō) our men from[2] their supplies and withstand the attacks of the Roman legions. 4. Caesar directs his commanders to separate their forces and drive the enemy out of the boundaries of Gaul. 5. When (ubi) the first baggage of our army was seen by those who were concealed in the forests, the generals of the enemy ordered all their forces to rush forth and seize our baggage.

LESSON LII.
THIRD CONJUGATION. PASSIVE OF PŌNŌ.

273. The present system of *pōnō* in the passive.

Decline vis, milia, and insigne (458, 459).

Present indicative. am being placed.	Imperfect indicative. was being placed.	Future indicative. shall be placed.
SINGULAR.	SINGULAR.	SINGULAR.
1. pōnor	pōnēbar	pōnar
2. pōneris (-re)	pōnēbāris (-re)	pōnēris (-re)
3. pōnitur	pōnēbātur	pōnētur
PLURAL.	PLURAL.	PLURAL.
1. pōnimur	pōnēbāmur	pōnēmur
2. pōniminī	pōnēbāminī	pōnēminī
3. pōnuntur	pōnēbantur	pōnentur

---

[1] '*Gerundive construction*'; see (253).
[2] Abl. *without prep.* to denote *separation*; see (221).

THIRD CONJUGATION.

Conjugate **mittō, cōgō,** and **expellō** in the above tenses.
The *present stem* is **pōne**; for change in *stem-vowel*, see (180).

274. Table of endings.

PRESENT INDICATIVE.		FUTURE INDICATIVE.	
-or	-imur	-ar	-ēmur
-eris (-re)	-iminī	-ēris (-re)	-ēminī
-itur	-untur	-ētur	-entur

A verb ending in **ētur, entur,** etc., is *present subjunctive* in the *first* conjugation, *present indicative* in the *second* conjugation, *future indicative* in the *third* conjugation.

275.   **VOCABULARY.**

Verbs 65-70 (450).

iter facere,   *to march*
sēcum = (cum sē),   *with himself* or *themselves*
poscō (see vocab. for princ. parts), *to demand*
repellō " " " " " *to drive back*
aut, *conj.*   *or*

276. Intermediate clauses—mood.—Quī clause: a simple *relative clause*, introducing only a descriptive fact, has its verb in the *indicative*. **Quod clause:** *causal* clauses introduced by **quod, quia,** and **quoniam** have the verb in the *indicative*, when the reason given is vouched for by the writer or speaker; *subjunctive*, when the reason is given on the authority of another. These clauses take the verb in the *subjunctive*, in *Indirect Discourse*[1]—that is, when they express the thought of some other person than the speaker or writer—or *by attraction*, when they form a necessary part of a *subjunctive clause* or an *infinitive* upon which they depend.

Example of a *relative clause* the verb of which is in the *subjunctive by attraction:*

---

[1] See (301), (302), (305), (306).

Nostrī in Galliam contendunt ut oppidum quod commeātibus armīsque compleātur oppūgnent,   *Our men hasten into Gaul to attack a town which is being filled with arms and supplies*

Here the *verb* in the *relative clause*, quod ... compleātur, which is within an ut *clause* forming an essential part of it, is *drawn into the subjunctive*.

277.   EXERCISES.

I.—1. Sī obsidēs Caesarī dabuntur (datī erunt) ā Gallīs, omnēs Germānī ex fīnibus Galliae expellentur. 2. Germānī, cum in prōvinciam nostram et Ītaliam iter facerent, ea impedīmenta quae sēcum nōn portāre poterant cis Rhēnum flūmen relīquērunt. 3. Caesar Sēquanīs fīnitimīsque imperābit nē Rēmōs ā quibus auxilium multum accēperit[1] exagitent. 4. Belgae, ā quibus proelium redintegrātum est cum nostrī sua castra mūnīrent, facile celeriterque ab equitātū repulsī sunt. 5. Spē imperiī dēlendī populī Rōmānī, māgnus exercitus ab eīs cīvitātibus quae adventū legiōnum Rōmānārum perterritae sunt cōgitur.

II.—1. Caesar will make peace with those from whom he has received corn and supplies. 2. Because of the courage[2] of our infantry the enemy were alarmed and fled into the nearest fortifications. 3. The Aedui whose forces joined themselves with the rest of the enemy will be quickly defeated (prōturbō) and reduced to[3] subjection by Caesar's brave generals. 4. Scouts will be sent forward by Caesar to find out those (things) which are being carried[4] on in the enemies' camp.

---

[1] Subjunctive *by attraction* (276); *perfect* by 'rule of sequence' (185).
[2] Because of the courage: virtūte, *abl. of cause*.
[3] in + *acc.*   [4] Why subjunctive ? What tense ?

LESSON LIII.

THIRD CONJUGATION. PASSIVE OF PŌNŌ, CONTINUED.

278. The present system of *pōnō* completed in the passive.—*Stem* pōne.

Present subjunctive.		Imperfect subjunctive.	
may be placed.		*might be placed.*	
SINGULAR.	PLURAL.	SINGULAR.	PLURAL.
1. pōnar	pōnāmur	pōnerer	pōnerēmur
2. pōnāris (-re)	pōnāminī	pōnerēris (-re)	pōnerēminī
3. pōnātur	pōnantur	pōnerētur	pōnerentur

Imperative.

be thou placed, etc.

SINGULAR.	PLURAL.
2. { pōnere	pōniminī
{ pōnitor	
3. pōnitor	pōnuntor

Present Infinitive.	Gerundive.
pōnī, *to be placed*	pōnendus, (*worthy*) *to be placed*

279. To form the *present infinitive passive* of a verb of the *third conjugation*, change **ere** of the present infinitive active to **ī**. **cōgō**: present infinitive *active* **cōgere**, present infinitive *passive* **cōgī**. **mittō**: present infinitive *active* **mittere**, present infinitive *passive* **mittī**. **gerō**: present infinitive *active* **gerere**, present infinitive *passive* **gerī**. When a verb ends in **ātur, antur**, etc., it is *present indicative* in the *first* conjugation, *present subjunctive* in the *other* conjugations.

280.   **VOCABULARY.**

Verbs 71–75 (450).

dexter, dextra, dextrum, *adj.*	right
ā dextrō cornū,	on the right wing
paene, *adv.*	almost
aut . . . aut, *conj.*	either . . . or
tōtus, tōta, tōtum, *adj.*	entire
sē recipere,	[to retreat to betake one's self or

281. Synopsis of the present system, passive, of pōnō.— *Present stem* **pōne.**

1. *Present indicative*	pōnor
2. *Imperfect indicative*	pōnēbar
3. *Future indicative*	pōnar
4. *Present subjunctive*	pōnar
5. *Imperfect subjunctive*	pōnerer
6. *Imperative*	pōnere
7. *Present infinitive*	pōnī
8. *Gerundive*	pōnendus

Give synopsis, *present system, passive,* of dūcō, mittō, dēdō, and incendō.

282. Comparative table of endings.

First and second conjugations.

FUTURE INDICATIVE.

Active.		Passive.	
SINGULAR.	PLURAL.	SINGULAR.	PLURAL.
1. -bō	-bimus	-bor	-bimur
2. -bis	-bitis	-beris (-re)	-biminī
3. -bit	-bunt	-bitur	-buntur

Third and fourth conjugations.

FUTURE INDICATIVE.

Active.		Passive.	
SINGULAR.	PLURAL.	SINGULAR.	PLURAL.
1. -am	-ēmus	-ar	-ēmur
2. -ēs	-ētis	-ēris (-re)	-ēminī
3. -et	-ent	-ētur	-entur

283. **EXERCISES.**

I.—1. Cum Caesar hōc bellum cōnfēcisset, inter eās cīvitātēs quās pepulerat (**pellō**) in hībernīs omnīs cohortēs prīmae atque secundae legiōnis posuit. 2. Cum imperātōrēs hostium aut vulnerātī aut concīsī essent, omnēs mīlitēs perterritī sunt et ad Germānōs, fīnitimōs, sē recēpērunt. 3. Caesar cum omnibus cōpiīs in Belgārum fīnīs iter facit ut hostēs expellantur aut in servitūtem redigantur; adventū hōrum hostēs in oppidum māgnum quod mūrō altō mūnīverant sē recipiunt. 4. Mūnītiōnēs multae ā Gallīs in suīs fīnibus exstruentur nē sua castella aedificiaque adventū (*upon the arrival*) exercitūs nostrī incendantur.

II.—1. After all the cavalry had been summoned out of camp, Caesar's forces surrounded the enemies' winter-quarters on all sides in order that they might not be able to depart in the night. 2. Brave soldiers are placed (**pōnō**) in the foremost line,[1] because the enemy have a great multitude of men and will make a fierce[2] attack upon our men. 3. While Caesar was marching thither, scouts were sent forward by the Gauls to find out the plans of our commanders and to cut off our men from supplies.

LESSON LIV.

PASSIVE OF PŌNŌ, CONTINUED. ABLATIVE ABSOLUTE

284. Principal parts of *pōnō*.

Active, pōnō   pōnere   posuī   positum
Passive, pōnor   pōnī   positus sum

---

[1] in prīmā aciē.   [2] Adverb.

Synopsis of the perfect system, passive, of pōnō.—*Stem* posit, *seen in the perfect passive participle,* positus.

1. *Perfect indicative* — positus sum
2. *Pluperfect indicative* — positus eram
3. *Future-perfect indicative* — positus erō
4. *Perfect subjunctive* — positus sim
5. *Pluperfect subjunctive* — positus essem
6. *Perfect infinitive* — positum esse
7. *Future infinitive* — positum īrī
8. *Perfect participle* — positus, -a, -um

Conjugate the entire verb pōnō *in both voices*, as given in (478, 479).

285.   VOCABULARY.

Verbs 76–86 (450).

inde, *adv.* — *thence* or *then*
nam, *conj.* — *for*
proximē, *adv.* — *lately*
expedītus, -a, -um, *adj.* — *light-armed*
cōnsuētūdō, -dinis, *fem.* — *custom* or *habit*

286. Adjectives with the genitive in īus and the dative in ī.—The following adjectives (o-stems) have the *genitive singular* in īus and the *dative* in ī:

ūnus, *one*   alius, *other* or *another*
ūllus, *any*   uter, *which* (of two)
nūllus, *no, none*   neuter, *neither*
sōlus, *alone, only*   alter, *the other* (of two)
tōtus, *whole, entire*

These words are declined regularly in the plural, like altus. The vocative is lacking in all save sōlus and ūnus. The i of the genitive singular ending īus is usually long.

Tōtus *is thus declined in the singular:*

	Mas.	Fem.	Neuter.
Nom.	tōtus	tōta	tōtum
Gen.	tōtīus	tōtīus	tōtīus
Dat.	tōtī	tōtī	tōtī
Acc.	tōtum	tōtam	tōtum
Abl.	tōtō	tōtā	tōtō

287. Ablative absolute.—A noun or pronoun in the *ablative* may be used with a *participle* in agreement to define the *time* or *circumstances* of an action; such a phrase is called an *ablative absolute* and serves in the place of a *subordinate clause*.

Examples of the ablative absolute:

1. Pāce factā,
2. Obsidibus datīs,
3. Obsidibus acceptīs Caesar suum exercitum ex hostium fīnibus ēdūxit,

Peace having been made
Hostages having been given
Hostages having been received,[1] *Caesar led his army out of the enemies' territories*

288. The noun and participle in the *ablative absolute* may each have one or more modifiers; as,

Tōtō exercitū in aciē īnstrūctō, Caesar sīgnum proeliī dedit,

The whole army having been drawn up in line of battle, Caesar gave the signal for battle

Tōtō, the adjective, limits exercitū in the *ablative singular masculine;* the adverbial phrase in aciē modifies īnstrūctō; the ablative absolute tōtō . . . īnstrūctō represents a subordinate clause *defining the time of the action of the verb* dedit.

In the above *ablative absolute* exercitū, the *basis* or *principal* word, takes the participle īnstrūctō into agreement with it; in rendering the *ablative absolute* by a *subordinate clause* the *basis* (noun or pronoun in the ablative) becomes the *subject*, and the *participle* a *finite verb;* thus, exercitū īnstrūctō, *when* or *after the army had been* or *was* drawn up.

289. **EXERCISE.**

1. Caesar necessāriīs rēbus imperātīs ad cohortandōs mīlitēs dēcucurrit et ad legiōnem decimam dēvēnit. 2. Nostrī propter propīnquitātem et celeritātem hostium nihil

---
[1] That is, *after, when, because* hostages had been received.

iam Caesaris imperium exspectābant, sed per sē¹ quae²
vidēbantur administrābant. 3. Temporis brevitās et successus hostium māgnam hārum rērum partem impediēbat;
sed nostrī, quod superiōribus (*former*) proeliīs exercitātī
erant, nōn minus (*less*) commodē sibi³ praescrībere quam
(*than*) ab aliīs docērī poterant.

LESSON LV.

THIRD CONJUGATION PASSIVE, THE 'IŌ' VERB— ACCIPIŌ.

290. Principal parts of *accipiō* in the passive: *accipior, accipī, acceptus sum.*

Passive voice of accipiō, *I receive.*—The *present stem* **accipe** is found by dropping **re** from the *present infinitive active,* **accipere.** The *perfect stem* **accēp** is not used in the passive. In the passive of **accipiō** eight forms are based upon the present stem **accipe,** eight upon the supine stem **accept** (*seen in the perfect passive participle,* [acceptus). For the occurrence and omission of i in the 'iō' verbs, see (213) and foot-note.

The second person singular of the present indicative is pronounced, *not* ac-ci-pi-e-ris, but ac-ci'-pe-ris.

291. Present system, passive, of *accipiō.*—*Stem* accipe.

Present indicative.		Imperfect indicative.
am being received.		*was being received.*
SINGULAR.	PLURAL.	SINGULAR.
1. accipior	accipimur	accipiēbar
2. acciperis (-re)	accipiminī	accipiēbāris (-re)
3. accipitur	accipiuntur	accipiēbātur, etc.

---
¹ *Of themselves.*
² Nominative plural neuter, subject of **vidēbantur,** *seemed best;* the antecedent of **quae = ea,** object of **administrābant.**
³ Dative with the *compound verb* **praescrībere;** see (337).

THIRD CONJUGATION PASSIVE.

Future indicative.
shall be received.
SINGULAR.
1. accipiar
2. accipiēris (-re)
3. accipiētur, etc.

Imperfect subjunctive.
might be received.
SINGULAR.
1. acciperer
2. accipererēris (-re)
3. acciperētur, etc.

Present subjunctive.
may be received.
SINGULAR.
accipiar
accipiāris (-re)
accipiātur, etc.

Imperative.
be thou received, etc.
SINGULAR.   PLURAL.
2. { accipere   accipiminī
   { accipitor
3. accipitor   accipiuntor

Present infinitive.
accipī, *to be received*

Gerundive.
accipiendus, -a, -um, (*worthy*) *to be received*

292. Synopsis of the perfect system.—*Stem* accept, *seen in the perfect passive participle,* acceptus.

1. acceptus sum
2. acceptus eram
3. acceptus erō
4. acceptus sim
5. acceptus essem
6. acceptum esse
7. acceptum īrī
8. acceptus, -a, -um

293. VOCABULARY.
Verbs 87-96 (450).

ubi, *adv.*   *where*
aciēs, aciēī, *fem.*   *line of battle, army*
sub, *prep. with abl.*   *under*
sub monte,   *at the foot of the mountain*
equester, equestris, equestre, *adj.*   *of cavalry*
proeliō equestrī,   *in a cavalry skirmish*
summus mōns,   *the top of the mountain*

294. **EXERCISES.**

I.—1. Hōc bellō factō hostēs castra prōmōvērunt ac sub monte in Rēmōrum fīnibus cis Rhēnum cōnsēdērunt. 2. Omnibus aedificiīs vīcīsque in Galliā incēnsīs Caesar trāns flūmen contendit ut hostium cōpiās frūmentō commeātibusque prohibēret. 3. Fortēs peditēs legiōnis prīmae in Galliam ā Caesare mīssī sunt ut exercitum cōgerent et castra in eīs cīvitātibus quae Caesarī sē suaque omnia dēdidissent pōnerent. 4. Cohortibus reliquīs ē castrīs ēductīs Galba suīs praefectīs, ut aciem triplicem īnstruerent atque ā dextrō cornū in hostēs impetum facerent, imperāvit. 5. Triplicī aciē factā imperātōrēs nostrī ē castrīs suōs peditēs ēdūxērunt atque ad eum locum, ubi hostium explōrātōrēs vīderant, mātūrāvērunt. 6. Quod hostēs in castrīs quae sub monte salūtis causā posuerant sē continēbant neque peditēs ad proelium ēdūcēbant, Caesar Galbae ut in aciē equitātum omnem īnstrueret mandāvit et ipse suō mōre ad portās hostium castrōrum peditēs fortīs dūxit.

II.—1. After their fields had been laid waste,[1] the enemy sent ambassadors to Caesar to ask for peace. 2. When the camp had been fortified[2] on all sides, Caesar commanded the Remi to give his (men) corn and supplies. 3. If the enemy surrender[3] hostages, Caesar will command his generals not to destroy the town into which they carried[4] all their arms.

---

[1] Two ways: by *ablative absolute* and by a *cum clause*.
[2] By *ablative absolute* and the *ubi clause*.
[3] See (223).
[4] Mood ? (276), '*intermediate clauses.*' Tense ? (185).

LESSON LVI.

FOURTH CONJUGATION PASSIVE. COMPARISON OF ADJECTIVES.

295. Principal parts of *mūniō, I fortify.*

Active, mūniō   mūnīre   mūnīvī   mūnītum
Passive, mūnior mūnīrī   mūnītus sum

In the *passive two stems* are used: **mūnī** and **mūnīt**, upon each of which eight forms are based.

Present system of *mūniō* **in the passive.**—*Present stem* **mūnī.** *For the tense forms complete*, see (**488**).

Present Indicative.
am being fortified.

SINGULAR.   PLURAL.
1. mūnior   mūnīmur
2. mūnīris (-re) mūnīminī
3. mūnītur   mūniuntur

Present subjunctive.
may be fortified.

SINGULAR.
mūniar
mūniāris (-re)
mūniātur, etc.

Imperfect Indicative.
was being fortified.

SINGULAR.
1. mūniēbar
2. mūniēbāris (-re), etc.

Imperfect subjunctive.
might be fortified.

SINGULAR.
mūnīrer
mūnīrēris (-re), etc.

Future Indicative.
shall be fortified.

SINGULAR.
1. mūniar
2. mūniēris (-re)
3. mūniētur, etc.

Imperative.
mūnīre, *be thou fortified*
mūnītor, *thou shalt be fortified,*
                                    etc.

Present Infinitive.
mūnīrī, *to be fortified*

Gerundive.

mūniendus, -a, -um, (*worthy*) *to be fortified*

296. Synopsis of the perfect system, passive.—*Stem* mūnit.

1. *Perfect indicative*   mūnītus sum
2. *Pluperfect indicative*   mūnītus eram
3. *Future-perfect indicative*   mūnītus erō
4. *Perfect subjunctive*   mūnītus sim
5. *Pluperfect subjunctive*   mūnītus essem
6. *Perfect infinitive*   mūnītum esse
7. *Future infinitive*   mūnītum īrī
8. *Perfect participle*   mūnītus, -a, -um

Conjugate *each tense* of cōnsentiō in both voices; repeat mūniō entire as given in (482, 483).

297.   VOCABULARY.

Verbs 97–106 (450).

tumultus, -ūs, *mas.*   *uproar*
īnsidiae, -ārum, *fem.*   *ambush*
lūx, lūcis, *fem.*   *light*
prīmā lūce,   *at early dawn*
lēgātus, -ī, *mas.*   *lieutenant*
prīmō, *adv.*   *at first*

298. Comparison of adjectives.—There are three degrees of comparison: the *positive, comparative,* and *superlative.* The *comparative* is regularly formed by adding ior (*masculine* and *feminine*) and ius (*neuter*) to the *stem* of the positive, which loses its final vowel; the *superlative* is formed by adding issimus, -a, -um, to the *stem* of the positive. Adjectives of the *first* and *second* declensions, like nouns, form the *stem* in o or a. For the stem of altus, altum (alto), see (18); for the stem of alta (alta), see (2). Third-declension adjectives, like nouns, are *vowel* or *consonant stems;* fortis (*stem* forti), see collis (131) · potēns (*stem* potent), see mīles (113) and pūgnāns (467).

FOURTH CONJUGATION PASSIVE.

POSITIVE.	COMPARATIVE.	SUPERLATIVE.
altus, -a, -um	altior, -ior, -ius	altissimus, -a, -um
fortis, -is, -e	fortior, -ior, -ius	fortissimus, -a, -um
potēns, -ēns, -ēns	potentior, -ior, -ius	potentissimus, -a, -um

The meanings of the above are:

altus, *tall*	altior, *taller*	altissimus, *tallest* or *very tall*
fortis, *brave*	fortior, *braver*	fortissimus, *bravest* or *very brave*
potēns, *powerful*	potentior, *more powerful*	potentissimus, *most* or *very powerful*

299.   EXERCISES.

I.—1. Eā rē cōnstitūtā hostēs secundā vigiliā tumultū māgnō ē castrīs contendērunt et in extrēmās Galliae partēs, ubi exercitūs nostrī adventum nōn timuērunt, fūgērunt. 2. Hāc rē ab explōrātōribus cōgnitā Caesar prīmā lūce equitātum omnem ut in novissimum agmen hostium impetum faceret praemīsit. 3. Quod vīcī omnēs ā nostrīs incēnsī erant, Sēquanī in Aeduōrum fīnīs sē recēpērunt, ubi in amīcitiam acceptī sunt agrōsque multōs possēdērunt. 4. Castra sub monte ab hostibus posita sunt ac prō mūnītiōnibus aciēs īnstrūcta est, nē nostrī in eōs impetum facere possent, cum fīnitimōrum lēgātōs acciperent. 5. Caesar, ubi hostium fugam audīvit (*heard of*), in castra peditēs equitātumque redūxit et, quod īnsidiās timēbat, iussit suōs nōn eō diē hostēs subsequī.

II.—1. The enemy at first fought (**contendō**) in a cavalry skirmish; then (**inde**), after our cavalry had been driven back, they suddenly led out their infantry which had been concealed in the forests next to the river. 2. After Caesar had determined (**cōnstituō**) to spare the rest of the enemy, towns were given to them in Gaul and their neighbours were commanded not to make an attack upon them. 3. A triple line of battle having been drawn up, Caesar directs his lieutenants to begin battle on the right wing and to fight bravely for the sake of their commander.

LESSON LVII.

ŌRĀTIŌ OBLĪQUA, OR INDIRECT DISCOURSE.

300. Irregular verb *eō, I go.* **Principal parts:** *eō, īre, īvī (iī) itum.*

Learn the indicative mood of **eō** (*six tenses*), (**486**).

301. Direct and indirect discourse.—In *direct discourse* (Ōrātiō rēcta) the exact words of the speaker or writer are given. In *indirect discourse* (Ōrātiō oblīqua) certain forms of words may be altered to suit the point of view of the new speaker, viz.: moods, tenses, persons. The more regular of such changes will be stated. *Indirect discourse* depends upon some verb of *seeing, knowing, thinking, perceiving,* etc., the verb of the *main (declarative)* clause being put in the *infinitive* with its *subject* in the *accusative*, the verb of the *subordinate* clause becoming *subjunctive*.

302. Statement in indirect discourse.—In the following sentences, this much of the principle of 'indirect discourse' is employed, viz.: *verbs of saying, thinking,* etc., are followed by the *accusative + infinitive*, to describe a *fact*. [See (**392**), 'mood in indirect discourse.']

The *infinitive* in *indirect discourse*, though representing a *finite verb* of *direct discourse*, does not admit of *number* and *person*.

1. **Caesar dīcit lēgātum discēdere,** — *Caesar says that the ambassador is departing* [*the ambassador to depart*]
2. **Labiēnus exīstimat hostīs discēdere,** — *Labienus thinks that the enemy are departing* [*the enemy to depart*]

ŌRĀTIŌ OBLĪQUA, OR INDIRECT DISCOURSE.

The infinitive **discēdere**, with no form to distinguish *number*, has a *singular subject* in (1) and a *plural subject* in (2): before the accusative and infinitive supply (in translation) '*that*,' for which the Latin *has no word* in the sense of the English idiom, and change the *accusative subject* to the *nominative*, making the *infinitive* a *finite* (*declarative*) verb.

3. **Caesar vīdit lēgātōs pācem   *Caesar saw that the ambassa-*
   petere,   *dors were seeking peace***

Were seeking = **petere**, *present infinitive*. The *time* of the action of the verb **petere** is *present* relative to the *time* of the action of the verb **vīdit**; that is, the action (of seeking) *was going on* at the *time* when Caesar *saw* the ambassadors, hence the *present infinitive* **petere** represents time *relatively present* with respect to the time of the verb of seeing (**vīdit**) upon which it depends.

803.   VOCABULARY.

opus, operis, *neut.*	*work*
interim, *adv.*	*meanwhile*
item, *adv.*	*likewise*
cursus, -ūs, *mas.*	*speed*
inter sē,	*to one another*
inter sē dare,	*to exchange*
opportūnus, -a, -um, *adj.*	*convenient*
Labiēnus, -ī, *mas.*	*Labienus*
citerior, -ior, -ius, *adj.*	*hither, nearer*
superior, -ior, -ius, *adj.*	*former, higher*
ex superiōre locō,	*from a higher place*

804.   EXERCISES.

I.—1. Prīmā legiōne quam proximē cōnscrīpserat in castrīs relictā Caesar prō castrīs in aciē quīnque legiōnēs reliquās īnstrūxit.   2. Caesar Belgās contrā populum Rōmānum coniūrāre obsidēsque inter sē dare audit.   3. Caesar, ubi hostēs in legiōnem prīmam impetum facere vīdit, ex castrīs exercitum omnem ēdūxit.   4. Galba, cum Belgās in fidem potestātemque populī Rōmānī sē suaque omnia permittere vīdisset, iussit Gallōs (*accusative subject*) frūmentō commeātibusque Belgās iuvāre et in Ītaliam exercitum tōtum redūxit. 5. Caesar sub monte altissimō proeliō locum dēlēgit, nē hostēs, cum aciem suam īnstrūxisset, ab latere in legiōnēs Rōmānās impetum facere possent.

II.—1. The general sees that the enemy are collecting all their bands into one place and are fortifying a camp. 2. When Caesar saw that the Germans were joining (*present*) themselves with these and were cutting off Galba's soldiers from supplies, he himself at once led his army thither. 3. While Caesar was collecting corn and supplies for the entire army, he saw that the Germans were leading (*present*) cavalry across the river. 4. When peace had been made, Caesar placed the legions in winter-quarters among the Belgians who were the bravest of all the Gauls.

LESSON LVIII.

INDIRECT DISCOURSE, CONTINUED.

305. Learn the remainder of the verb *eō* (486).

The perfect infinitive in indirect discourse.—The *perfect infinitive* shows time *absolutely past*, that is, time *completed* in the past.

The *present infinitive* denotes time *contemporaneous*, the *perfect infinitive* time *antecedent*.

1. **Caesar cōgnōscit lēgātum iisse,**   *Caesar finds out that the ambassador has gone* (action finished *before* he finds it out)

2. Caesar cōgnōvit hostīs dis- | Caesar found out that the
cessisse, | enemy had departed (action completed before he found it out)

806. Subordinate clause in indirect discourse.—After verbs of *saying, thinking, hearing,* etc., the verb of the principal clause is put in the infinitive, *that of the subordinate clause in the subjunctive.*

1. Caesar intellegit Germānōs exagitāre Belgās quī cis Rhēnum incolant, | *Caesar learns that the Germans are harassing the Belgians who live on this side of the Rhine*
2. Explōrātōrēs nūntiāvērunt Sēquanōs quōs nostrī pepulissent cum omnibus impedīmentīs discēdere, | *Scouts announced that the Sequani whom our men had defeated were departing with all their baggage*

In (1) **incolant** is *present* subjunctive, denoting time *contemporaneous* relative to the *time (tense)* of **intellegit**; see 'rule of sequence' (135). In (2) **pepulissent** (from **pellō**), the *pluperfect*, denotes time *antecedent (completed)* with reference to the *time (tense)* of **nūntiāvērunt.**

807. **VOCABULARY.**

Verbs 107–116 (**450**).

sinister, -tra, -trum, *adj.* *left*
ab sinistrā parte, *on the left side*
ipse, -a, -um, *emphatic pron.* *he, self*
trānseō, -īre, -īvī -iī, -itum, *to cross*
senātus, -ūs, *mas.* *senate*
septimus, -a, -um, *num. adj.* *seventh*

808. Adjectives ending in er.—Adjectives in **er** form the *superlative* by adding **rimus** to the nominative singular masculine of the *positive.* The comparative is *regular.*

miser, -era, -erum,   miserior, -ior, -ius   miserrimus, -a, -um
   wretched
ācer, ācris, ācre,   ācrior, -ior, -ius   ācerrimus, -a, -um
   sharp

309.   **EXERCISES.**

I.—1. Hostēs, ubi nostrōs proeliō equestrī ā dextrō cornū contendere vident, celeritāte māgnā in oppidum sē recipiunt atque oppidō undique mūnītō ad[1] impetum nostrōrum sustinendum parant. 2. Hīs rēbus ab explōrātōribus cōgnitīs aciēs triplex prō castrīs īnstrūcta est et omnēs cōpiae nostrae ēductae sunt; sed, quod hostēs flūmen trānsīre et in suōs fīnīs revertī (*were returning*) vīdit, Caesar in eōs impetum nōn fēcit ac cōpiās in castra redūxit. 3. Legiōne novā in citeriōre Galliā cōnscrīptā locō idōneō castrīs dēlēctō Caesar ipse cum secundā legiōne per agrōs Aeduōrum contendit et prō oppidō hostium cōpiās triplicī aciē īnstrūxit.

II.—1. The chiefs of the Aedui will go into the territories of the Sequani to exchange hostages and cut off our men from supplies which[2] are being sent into our camp by the Remi. 2. After Caesar had seen (that) the enemy were leading a part of their forces across the bridge and were leaving a part on this side of the river, he determined to attack that part which had not yet crossed the river. 3. On account of the large number and the courage of the enemy the bravest soldiers are drawn up in the foremost (**prīmus**) line of battle by Caesar, in order that the enemy may not surround and take (**capiō**) our camp.

---

[1] Ad + gerundive, '*to withstand.*'
[2] Intermediate clause, subjunctive by *attraction*; see (267).

LESSON LIX.

RELATIVE OF PURPOSE. INDIRECT QUESTION.

810. Learn the entire passive of *faciō*, *I do* or *make* (498). Principal parts:

Active,	faciō	facere	fēcī	factum
Passive,	fīō	fierī	factus sum	

811. **Relative clause of purpose.**—When quī = ut is (*so that he*, etc.) or ut eī (*so that they*, etc.), the verb in the relative clause is put in the *subjunctive* to denote *affirmative purpose*. The antecedent of the relative is expressed or implied in the main clause.

1. Mittunt lēgātum quī pācem petat,[1] *They send an ambassador to ask for peace*
2. Lēgātī vēnērunt quī obsidēs dēderent, *Ambassadors came to surrender hostages*

Apply '*rule of sequence*' (185).

812.   VOCABULARY.

Verbs 117–124 (450).

cōnspectus, -ūs, *mas.*   *sight*
littera, -ae, *fem.*   *letter*
tribūnus, -ī, *mas.*   *tribune*
Pedius, -ī, *mas.*   *Pedius*
dīversus, -a, -um, *adj.*   *different, separate*
commūnis, -is, -e, *adj.*   *common*
et . . . et, *conj.*   *both . . . and*
interior, -ior, -ius, *adj.* *interior*

---

[1] Who may—*so that he may*—ask for peace.

313. Indirect question.—See declension of **quis** (465). A *direct question* takes the *indicative;* as,

Quid (quae) hostēs gerunt?   *What are the enemy doing?*

An *indirect question*, giving the interrogative (inquiry) in a dependent form, takes the *subjunctive;* as,

Caesar reperit quid (quae) hostēs gerant (*sequence*),   *Caesar finds out what the enemy are doing*
Caesar repperit quid (quae) hostēs gererent (*sequence*),   *Caesar found out what the enemy were doing*
Caesar reperiet quid (quae) hostēs gesserint (*sequence*),   *Caesar will find out what the enemy did (have done)*
Caesar repperit quid (quae) hostēs gessissent (*sequence*),   *Caesar found out what the enemy did (had done)*

314. Adjectives in *ilis*.—*Six* adjectives in **ilis** form the *superlative* by adding **limus** to the stem stripped of its final vowel; they are: **facilis**, *easy;* **difficilis**, *hard;* **similis** and **dissimilis**, *like* and *unlike;* **gracilis**, *slender;* **humilis**, *low*. **Facilis** is thus compared:

facilis, -is, -e   facilior, -ior, -ius   facillimus, -a, -um

315.   EXERCISES.

I.—1. Caesar hīs litterīs nūntiīsque commōtus est et in citeriōre Galliā legiōnēs duās novās cōnscrīpsit atque Pedium lēgātum, quī eās dēdūceret in interiōrem Galliam, mīsit. 2. Cum Caesar eō vēnisset, Rēmī quī proximī Belgīs sunt ad eum lēgātōs prīmōs cīvitātis mīsērunt, quī sē suaque omnia in fidem populī Rōmānī trādere [1] dīcerent. 3. Lēgātī in nostra castra vēnērunt, quī sē cum Belgīs reliquīs nōn cōnsēnsisse parātōsque esse obsidēs dare et Caesaris imperāta facere dīcerent. 4. Caesar, cum per

---
[1] In the sense of future time, *would hand over*.

Rēmōrum fīnēs iter faceret, omnēs reliquōs Gallōs in armīs esse Germānōsque cum hīs coniūrāvisse audīvit.

II.—1. An attack will be made upon the Germans in the sight of Caesar and the entire army, unless they surrender[1] themselves and all their (possessions) to our commanders. 2. The baggage having been left in camp, Caesar at early dawn sent forward scouts to find out those (things) which were being done[2] in the enemies' camp. 3. When the scouts returned and announced that the enemy had moved their camp and were hastening out of Gaul, Caesar commanded the tribunes of the soldiers not to lead their (men) out of camp.

LESSON LX.

AGREEMENT OF THE PARTICIPLE.

316. Use and agreement of the perfect passive participle (p. p. p.).—A common Latin construction is the *perfect passive participle*, which is used in preference to *relative clauses* or *conjunctions* + *indicative* or *subjunctive*. The perfect passive participle often modifies the *subject* or *object*, agreeing with the same in *gender*, *number*, and *case*.

1. **Dux commōtus discessit,** — *Having been alarmed* (= *because he was alarmed*), *the general withdrew*
2. **Nostrī hostēs circumventōs undique interfēcērunt,** — *Our men killed the enemy surrounded* (= *who were surrounded* or *after they were surrounded*) *on all sides*

---

[1] Write in two *different* tenses, explaining the *time-relation*; see (228).
[2] *Intermediate clause;* see (276).

3. Caesar in aciē suās cōpiās ē castrīs ēductās īnstrūxit,
Caesar drew up in line of battle his forces (who were, after they were) led out of camp

4. Hostēs (*nom.*) omnibus hīs rēbus adductī (*nom.*) ad Caesarem lēgātōs mīsērunt,
Influenced (=because they were influenced) by all these things, the enemy sent ambassadors to Caesar

817. VOCABULARY.

Verbs 125–135 (450).

gēns, gentis, *fem.*   tribe
aestuārium, -ī, *neut.*   marsh
puerī, -ōrum, *mas.*   children
nōnnūllus, -a, -um, *adj.* some
frūmentārius, -a, -um, *adj.* of corn
rēs frūmentāria,   supply of corn

818. **Tenses of the infinitive mood in indirect discourse.** For further treatment of such infinitives, see (301, 302, 805).

1. Explōrātōrēs nūntiant hostēs ad nostra castra iter facere,
Scouts announce that the enemy are marching towards our camp

2. Caesar intellēxit Germānōs Rhēnum trānsiisse,
Caesar learned that the Germans had crossed the Rhine

3. Caesar crēdit legiōnēs suās Gallōs victūrās esse,
Caesar believes that his legions will conquer the Gauls

4. Galba audīvit hostīs prīmā lūce castra mōtūrōs esse,
Galba heard that the enemy would break camp at early dawn

In (1) **iter facere** denotes action *going on at the time* of the action in **nūntiant**; in (2) **trānsiisse** denotes action *completed before the time* of the action in **intellēxit**; in (3) and (4) **victūrās** and **mōtūrōs esse** denote action *which is to occur in the future* at a time *subsequent* to the time of the action in **crēdit** and **audīvit**.

819. EXERCISES.

I.—1. Germānī trāns Rhēnum trāductī in interiōre Galliā cōnsēdērunt et agrōs lātissimōs possidēbant. 2. Hostēs Caesarī sē suaque omnia dēdere iussī,[1] quod sē nostrum exercitum sustinēre nōn posse vīdērunt, ex oppidō statim tēla armaque omnia trādidērunt. 3. Prīncipēs ad Caesarem ab cīvitāte mīssī[2] suam cīvitātem cum reliquīs Gallīs nōn cōnsēnsisse atque parātam[3] esse et (both) obsidēs dare et in oppidīs eum accipere dīxērunt. 4. Hōc proeliō factō Caesar intellegit multās cīvitātēs līberōs prīncipum obsidēs mīssūrās esse et exercituī nostrō frūmentum commeātūsque datūrās esse. 5. Hīs rēbus commōtus Caesar cum parte septimae legiōnis eīsque cōpiīs quae proximē cōnscrīptae erant in summum montem Labiēnum lēgātum, quī hostium adventum exspectāret, praemīsit. 6. Caesar, cum vīdisset hostēs aciem īnstruere nostrāsque mūnītiōnēs sine morā oppūgnātūrōs esse, praefectōs legiōnēs distinēre, ut in hostēs undique impetum ūnō tempore facerent, iussit.

II.—1. Influenced by the power of Caesar, those states into whose boundaries the Roman army was preparing to march determined to seek peace and do the commands of the senate. 2. Alarmed by Caesar's arrival, the Belgians send ambassadors to say[4] (that) they have collected corn and (que) supplies for our army and will surrender hostages. 3. When Caesar found out (that) the enemy had collected large forces and were marching into Italy, he immediately led all his legions out of camp.

---

[1] p. p. p. modifies hostēs, the *subject* of the sentence.
[2] Modifies the *subject* prīncipēs.
[3] *Predicate adjective* limiting cīvitātem.
[4] *Not infinitive* in Latin; note the *sequence*.

LESSON LXI.

PURPOSE AND RESULT CLAUSES.

820. Affirmative and negative purpose.—As previously stated, clauses denoting *affirmative purpose* take **ut** + *subjunctive;* clauses of *negative purpose*, **nē** + *subjunctive*.

1. Caesar legiōnēs cōnscrībit, *Caesar enrolls the legions to*
   ut Galliam vincat (*affirma-* *conquer Gaul*
   tive purpose),
2. Gallī māgnās cōpiās coēgē- *The Gauls gathered large forces,*
   runt, nē ā Caesare pelle- *that they might not (lest they*
   rentur (*negative purpose*), *should) be defeated by Caesar*

The *relative clause* may denote *affirmative purpose* (811).

821. Affirmative and negative result.—Affirmative result is expressed by **ut** + *subjunctive*, negative result by **ut . . . nōn** + *subjunctive*.

1. Nostrī tam fortiter pū- *Our men fight so bravely that*
   gnant, ut Gallōs expellant *(as a result) they drive out*
   (*affirmative result*), *the Gauls*
2. Nostrī in hostīs impetum *Our men made so fierce an at-*
   tam ācriter fēcērunt, ut *tack upon the enemy, that*
   sustinēre diūtius nōn pos- *they could not withstand any*
   sent (*negative result—note* *longer*
   the sequence),

822.   VOCABULARY.

Verbs 136–146 (**450**).

spīritus, -ūs, *mas.*   breath, (plur.) *arrogance*
etiam, *adv.*   *even*
māximē, *adv.*   *especially* or *very much*
memoria, -ae, *fem.*   *memory*
lātitūdō, -dinis, *fem.*   *width*

828. Distinguish ablative absolute from participle agreeing with the subject or object.—1. The enemy, *defeated* in many battles, surrendered hostages. In this sentence taken literally, *defeated*, the *past participle passive*, modifying the *subject, enemy*, becomes **pulsī** (*p. p. p.*), *nominative plural*, agreeing with the subject **hostēs**, and the sentence is written: **Hostēs multīs proeliīs pulsī obsidēs dēdidērunt.** By converting the participle into a *relative clause*, '*who had been defeated*,' it is seen that *defeated* limits and describes the *subject, enemy*. Change the sentence to this form: 2. The enemy having been defeated, Caesar demanded hostages. The phrase '*the enemy having been defeated*' contains an idea equivalent to that expressed by a subordinate clause, such as, '*after* or *because* the enemy had been defeated,' but the *noun* in such a phrase cannot be the *same* as the *subject* or *object* of the main sentence, is placed in the *ablative case* with the participle *in agreement with it*, and such a phrase, called the *Ablative Absolute*, modifies the verb.

824.   EXERCISE.

1. Aeduī sibi tantōs spīritūs sūmēbant ut Caesar contrā eōs suum exercitum dūcere cōnstitueret. 2. Imperātōrēs nostrī tam multās cīvitātēs pepulērunt ut in Galliā maximē imperium Rōmānum amplificārent. 3. Germānī ā potentiōribus Rōmānīs multīs proeliīs repulsī sē ex Galliā cōpiās omnīs mīsisse nūntiāvērunt. 4. Omnibus suīs agrīs vāstātīs oppidīsque incēnsīs ut commeātibus exercitum nostrum prohibērent, hostēs in extrēmās Galliae partēs sē recēpērunt. 5. Turrēs tantae altitūdinis prō mūrīs oppidī ā nostrīs positae sunt ut oppidānī maximē commōtī sē nostrīs ducibus obsidēs datūrōs esse suaque omnia Caesarī trāditūrōs esse nūntiārent. 6. Hōc bellō in Galliā cōnfectō omnēs nostrae cōpiae trāns Rhēnum

trāductae sunt atque impetus in rēgem potentissimum ibi ab omnibus legiōnibus factus est, quod etiam nostrā memoriā Rēmōs, populī Rōmānī amīcōs, māximē vexāverat et oppida multa incenderat.

LESSON LXII.
DEPONENT VERB, FIRST CONJUGATION.

825. The deponent verb *populor*, *I plunder*.—The deponent verb has *passive forms* with *active meanings*.

Principal parts: **populor populārī populātus sum**

Each tense is conjugated *exactly like* the corresponding tenses of **portō** in the *passive*. For conjugation of forms, see (494).

826. Synopsis of the present system.—*Present stem,* **populā.**

1. populor,   *I plunder*
2. populābar,   *was plundering*
3. populābor,   *shall plunder*
4. populer,   *may plunder*
5. populārer,   *might plunder*
6. populāre,   *plunder thou*
7. populārī.   *to plunder*
8. populandus, (*worthy*) *to be plundered*

To these are added the *active forms:*

9. populāns.   *plundering*
10. populandī, *of plundering*

827. Synopsis of the perfect system.—*Supine stem,* **populāt.**

1. populātus sum,   *I plundered*
2. populātus eram,   *had plundered*
3. populātus erō,   *shall have plundered*
4. populātus sim,   *may have plundered*
5. populātus essem,   *might have plundered*
6. populātum esse,   *to have plundered*
7. populātus, -a, -um, *having plundered*

To these are added *four active forms:*
8. populātum, *to plunder* (first supine)
9. populātū, *in the plundering* (second supine)
10. populātūrus, -a, -um, *being about to plunder*
11. populātūrum, -am, -um esse, *to be about to plunder*

828. The *future infinitive* **populātum īrī**, corresponding to **amātum īrī**, is not found in the deponent verb; in its place a form like the *future infinitive active* is used (see 11).

The deponent verb has *six active forms,* two based upon the *present stem* (see 9, 10, *present system*); *four* upon the *supine* or *perfect-participle stem* (see 8, 9, 10, 11, *perfect system*).

829.   VOCABULARY.

Verbs 147-157 **(450).**

cum prīmum, *adv.*	*as soon as*
pābulum, pābulī, *neut.*	*fodder*
negōtium, negōtiī, *neut.*	*business*
negōtium dare,	*to employ*
certus, -a, -um, *adj.*	*certain*
certiōrem facere,	*to inform*

830. Use of *negōtium dare, to employ.*

Negōtium dare, *to employ,* takes the *indirect object* in the *dative,* denoting the person or persons employed. Like **imperō** and **mandō** it is followed by a *subjunctive clause* to denote what one is employed to do, the *subjunctive* verb being translated by the *present infinitive;* the rule of sequence prevails in the choice of tense.

1. **Explōrātōribus negōtium**   *He employs scouts to find out*
   dat, ut hostium cōnsilia   *the plans of the enemy*
   cōgnōscant,
2. **Gallīs negōtium dedit, ut**   *He employed the Gauls to cut*
   pontem interscinderent,   *down the bridge*

831.   EXERCISES.

I.—1. Castrīs mūnītīs et rē frūmentāriā comparātā Caesar Sēquanīs negōtium dedit, ut in Belgārum fīnēs īrent atque ea quae hostēs facerent cōgnōscerent. 2. Caesar, cum cōpiās in triplicī aciē prō castrīs īnstrūxisset, omnēs suōs ut ācriter in hostēs impetum faciant cohortātur et ipse sīgnō datō ā dextrō cornū proelium committit. 3. Hāc rē statim ab explōrātōribus cōgnitā omnibus cohortibus prīmā lūce ēductīs ac prō castrīs īnstrūctīs Caesar omnem equitātum, quī in novissimum agmen hostium impetum faceret, praemīsit, atque T. Labiēnum cum quīnque cohortibus subsequī iussit. 4. Proelium ā dextrō cornū tam ācriter gestum est, ut equitātus[1] hostium sub monte īnstrūctus prīmō nostrōrum impetū[2] fugā salūtem peteret. 5. Cīvitātēs Rēmōrum et Aeduōrum multīs proeliīs repulsae[3] ad Caesarem suōs prīmōs, quī sibi pācem salūtemque peterent, mīsērunt.

II.—1. When this war was finished, Caesar ordered the remaining states to give a supply of corn to those forces for which he had chosen winter-quarters in Gaul. 2. Because the royal power (*plural of* **rēgnum**) in Gaul was seized by the more powerful, who had many opportunities for inciting (**ad + *gerundive***) men, Caesar led the army thither and ordered hostages to be sent to him. 3. Those whom Caesar employed to plunder the enemies' camp returned in about five days and announced (that) they had not been able to take the redoubts. 4. When scouts announced (that) the enemy were fortifying[4] a camp and would not surrender[5] hostages, Caesar directed his commanders to surround the camp on all sides.

---

[1] Nominative. [2] *At the first attack.* [3] p. p. p limiting cīvitātēs.
[4] For mood and tense, see (818), 1. [5] See (818), 4.

332. REVIEW VOCABULARY.

LESSONS XLI–LXII.

1. circiter (adv.), *about*
2. dē mediā nocte, *about midnight*
3. cum (conj.), *while* or *after*
4. post (prep. with the acc.), *after* or *behind*
5. paene (adv.), *almost*
6. īnsidiae, īnsidiārum, *ambush*
7. que, atque (conj.), *and*
8. aciēs, aciēī (fem.), *army* or *line of battle*
9. adventus, adventūs (mas.), *arrival*
10. perveniō, pervenīre, pervēnī, perventum, *arrive (at)*
11. spīritus, spīritūs (mas.),*breath;* (in the plur.) *arrogance*
12. prīmā lūce, *at early dawn*
13. prīmō (adv.), *at first*
14. sub monte, *at the foot of the mountain*
15. auxilia, auxiliōrum (neut.), *auxiliaries*
16. proelium committere, *begin battle*
17. sē recipere, *betake one's self*
18. inter (prep. with the acc.), *between*
19. et ... et (conj.), *both ... and*
20. sagittārius, sagittāriī (mas.), *bowman*
21. puerī, puerōrum (mas.), *children*
22. veniō, venīre, vēnī, ventum, *come*
23. commūnis, commūnis, commūne (adj.), *common*
24. fidēs, fideī (fem.), *confidence*
25. opportūnus, opportūna, opportūnum (adj.), *convenient*
26. concilium, conciliī (neut.), *council of war*
27. trānseō, trānsīre, trānsīvī or transiī, trānsitum, *cross*
28. cōnsuētūdō, cōnsuētūdinis (fem.), *custom* or *habit*
29. diēs, diēī (mas.), *day*
30. pellō, pellere, pepulī, pulsum, *drive* or *defeat*
31. poscō, poscere, poposcī, [no supine], *demand*

32. dīversus, dīversa, dīversum (adj.), *different*
33. moneō, monēre, monuī, monitum, *direct* or *advise*
34. repellō, repellere, repulī, repulsum, *drive back*
35. aut . . . aut (conj.), *either* . . . *or*
36. tōtus, tōta, tōtum (adj.), *entire*
37. māximē (adv.), *especially* or *very much*
38. etiam (conj.), *even*
39. inter sē obsidēs dare, *exchange hostages*
40. quīnque (indeclin. num. adj.), *five*
41. longē (adv.), *far*
42. vadum, vadī (neut.), *ford*
43. superior, superior, superius (adj.), *former* or *higher*
44. mūniō, mūnīre, mūnīvī, mūnītum, *fortify*
45. ē superiōre locō, *from a higher place*
46. eō, īre, īvī or iī, itum, *go*
47. dēfēnsiō, dēfēnsiōnis (fem.), *defence*
48. contendō, contendere, contendī, contentum, *hasten*
49. audiō, audīre, audīvī, audītum, *hear*
50. is, ea, id (personal pron. third person), *he* or *that*
51. ipse, ipsa, ipsum (intensive pron.), *he* or *self*
52. sē (reflexive pron. third person), *himself* or *themselves*
53. impediō, impedīre, impedīvī, impedītum, *hinder*
54. citerior, citerior, citerius (adj.), *hither*
55. spēs, speī (fem.), *hope*
56. quantus, -a, -um (adj.), *how great* or *how many*
57. prōtinus (adv.), *immediately*
58. (in) proeliō equestrī, *in a cavalry skirmish*
59. interior, interior, interius (adj.), *interior*
60. quaerō, quaerere, quaesīvī, quaesītum, *inquire*
61. coniungō, coniungere, coniūnxī, coniūnctum, *join*
62. Labiēnus, Labiēnī (mas.), *Labienus*
63. proximē (adv.), *lately*
64. trādūcō, trādūcere, trādūxī, trāductum, *lead across*
65. sinister, sinistra, sinistrum (adj.), *left*
66. littera, litterae (fem.), *letter*
67. lēgātus, lēgātī (mas.), *lieutenant*
68. lūx, lūcis (fem.), *light*
69. expedītus, expedīta, expedītum (adj.), *light-armed*

70. **item** (adv.), *likewise*
71. **vulgō** (abl. as adv.), *commonly* or *generally*
72. **iter, itineris** (neut.), *march*
73. **iter facere**, *to march*
74. **aestuārium, aestuāriī** (neut.), *marsh*
75. **interim** (adv.), *meanwhile*
76. **memoria, memoriae** (fem.), *memory*
77. **medius, media, medium** (adj.), *middle of*
78. **propīnquitās, propīnquitātis** (fem.), *nearness*
79. **neque . . . neque** (conj.), *neither . . . nor*
80. **inde** (adv.), *after that, thence* or *then*
81. **equester, equestris, equestre** (adj.), *of cavalry*
82. **frūmentārius, frūmentāria, frūmentārium** (adj.), *of corn* or *grain*
83. **ūnus, ūna, ūnum** (num. adj.), *one*
84. **ā sinistrā parte**, *on the left side*
85. **ā dextrō cornū**, *on the right wing*
86. **in summō colle**, *on the top of the hill*
87. **Pedius, Pediī** (mas.), *Pedius*
88. **populor, populārī, populātus sum**, *plunder*
89. **potēns, potēns, potēns** (adj.), *powerful*
90. **celeriter** (adv.), *quickly*
91. **dexter, dextra, dextrum** (adj.), *right*
92. **senātus, senātūs** (mas.), *senate*
93. **septimus, septima, septimum** (num. adj.), *seventh*
94. **exiguitās, exiguitātis** (fem.), *shortness*
95. **cōnspectus, cōnspectūs** (mas.), *sight*
96. **funditor, funditōris** (mas.), *slinger*
97. **nōnnūllus, -a, -um** (adj.), *some*, (plur. as noun)
98. **cursus, cursūs** (mas.), *speed*
99. **rēs frūmentāria, reī frūmentāriae** (fem.), *supply of corn* or *grain*
100. **palūs, palūdis** (fem.), *swamp*
101. **suus, sua, suum** (possessive adj. pron. third person), *his* or *their*, with *reflexive* force
102. **tum** (adv.), *then*
103. **rēs, reī** (fem.), *thing*
104. **hīc, haec, hōc** (adj.), *this*

105. eō (adv.), *thither* or *there*
106. ad eum. ad sē, *to him*
107. ad eōs. ad sē, *to them*
108. summus, summa, summum (adj.), *top of*
109. gēns, gentis (fem.), *tribe*
110. tribūnus, tribūnī (mas.), *tribune*
111. triplex, triplex, triplex (adj.), *triple*
112. duo, duae. duo, *two*
113. sub (prep. with the *acc.* and *abl.*), *under*
114. cōnsentiō, cōnsentīre, cōnsēnsī, cōnsēnsum, *unite*
115. nisi (conj.), *unless*
116. tumultus, tumultūs (mas.), *uproar*
117. lātitūdō, lātitūdinis (fem.), *width*
118. sēcum, *with themselves* or *himself*
119. ubi (adv.), *where*
120. opus, operis (neut.), *work*
121. vulnus, vulneris (neut.), *wound*
122. eōrum, eārum (possessive pron. third person), *their*, without *reflexive* force: compare no. (101)

LESSON LXIII.

THE PHRASE CERTIŌREM FACERE, *TO INFORM.*

333. *Certiōrem facere.*—When the verb **facere** (any form) is *active*, the adjective **certior** modifies the *direct object*; as,

1. **Lēgātus Galbam certiōrem facit,**   *The ambassador informs Galba [makes Galba more certain]*
2. **Caesar nūntiōs certiōrēs fēcit,**   *Caesar informed the messengers*

As a verb of '*saying*,' **certiōrem facere** is followed by the *accusative* and *infinitive* to describe a *fact.*

THE PHRASE 'CERTIŌREM FACERE,' TO INFORM.

1. Caesar lēgātum certiōrem facit sē pācem factūrum esse — *Caesar informs the ambassador that he will make peace*
2. Hostēs nostrōs praefectōs certiōrēs fēcērunt sē suōs fīnīs dēfēnsūrōs esse — *The enemy informed our generals that they would defend their territories*

334. VOCABULARY.

Review words 1–62 in 'review vocabulary' (332).

dē imprōvīsō — *unexpectedly*
regiō -ōnis, *fem.* — *region*
diūtius, *adv.* — *longer*
passus -ūs, *mas.* — *pace*
longē, *adv.* — *far*
ad, apud, prep. with the *acc.* — *near*
paulisper, *adv.* — *for a little while*
quantus, -a, -um, *adj.* — *how great, how many*

335. Conditionals. Less vivid future.—In the *more vivid* future condition (223) the supposition of a future case is *positive* and *distinct*, the *apodosis* stating what *will be* the result; the mood in both clauses is *indicative*. In a *less vivid* future condition the supposition (in the *protasis*) is in suspense and is *less distinct*, the *apodosis* stating what *would be* the result: in both protasis and apodosis the *present* (rarely the *perfect*) *subjunctive* is used. The verb in the *protasis* is usually translated '*should*' or '*were to*,' that in the apodosis '*would*.' Example of the *less vivid* future condition:

Caesar cīvitātem cōnservet, sī hostēs sē dēdant, — *Caesar would spare the state, if the enemy should* or *were to surrender*

336. EXERCISES.

I.—1. Sī Germānī vīcōs agrōsque Aeduōrum populentur, Caesar in eōrum fīnēs omnibus cōpiīs iter faciat.

2. Cum Caesar eō dē imprōvīsō pervēnisset, explōrātōrēs eum certiōrem fēcērunt hostēs (*accusative subject*) ē castrīs discessisse et in (*upon*) proximum montem omnēs cōpiās impedīmentaque cōgere. 3. Sēquanī erant sōlī quibus Gallī negōtium dedērunt ut ex hīs regiōnibus cōpiās ēdūcerent atque contrā populum Rōmānum cōnsentīrent. 4. Caesar dīxit sē hostēs cōnservātūrum esse neque eōrum oppida dēlētūrum esse, quod prīmōs cīvitātis ad sē lēgātōs, quī peterent pācem, mīsissent (**mīsissent**, why subjunctive?). 5. Caesar ubi vīdit quantō in perīculō mīlitēs septimae legiōnis essent,¹ ipse ad eōs cum parte peditum fortissimōrum contendit.

II.—1. Scouts inform our generals (that) the Aedui will conspire with the rest of (*not genitive*) the Gauls so as to² plunder those towns which have been left³ by our men. 2. Caesar will employ the chiefs of many states to collect fresh cavalry and choose places suitable for winter-quarters. 3. When these facts (**rēs**) had been found out,⁴ Caesar commanded his generals not to lead their men⁵ out of camp on that day. 4. At early dawn Caesar drew up in line of battle all the legions, after they were led forth⁶ from camp.

LESSON LXIV.

COMPOUND VERBS WITH THE DATIVE.

837. Learn the deponent verb *vereor*, second conjugation (495).

Dative with compound verbs.—Many verbs compounded

---

¹ *Were*, see (818), '*indirect question.*'
² '*So as to*,' etc. = **ut** + *subjunctive* denoting *affirmative purpose.*
³ Subjunctive by *attraction*, see (276).
⁴ Render clause by the *ablative absolute.*
⁵ '*Their men*' = **suōs**: see (258).
⁶ '*After they were led forth*'—render by *one word* in Latin (p. p. p.).

with **ad, ante, con, in, inter, ob, post, prae, sub,** and **super** take the *dative* of the *indirect object*; if transitive, these verbs may take a *direct object* in the *accusative*.

Titūrius castellō (*dative*) **praeerat,**	*Titurius was in command of the redoubt*

Praeficiō, *to place* (*one*) *in command of,* takes the *person* placed in command *in the accusative*.

Caesar novīs mūnītiōnibus Galbam praeficiet,	*Caesar will place Galba in command of the new fortifications*

388. *Certior factus* (**passive**).—When the form of **facere** is *passive,* **certior** agrees with the *subject* of the verb, and is placed in the *nominative*; as,

1. **Caesar per explōrātōrēs certior fīēbat (factus est),**	*Caesar was informed by means of scouts*
2. **Lēgātī certiōrēs fīunt Caesarem pācem nōn factūrum esse,**	*The ambassadors are informed that Caesar will not make peace*

889.   **VOCABULARY.**

Review words 63–122 in 'review vocabulary' (**382**).

passus, -a, -um, *adj.*	*outstretched*
manus, -ūs, *fem.*	*hand*
plūrimum posse, ⎱	*to be very powerful,* or
plūrimum valēre, ⎰	*to have very great influence*
mīlle, indeclin. num. *adj.*	*a thousand*
octō, indeclin. num. *adj.*	*eight*

840. Perfect participle of the deponent.—As Latin has no perfect *active* participle, the perfect participle of a *deponent verb,* which has an *active* meaning, serves in its place; as,

1. Caesar veritus īnsidiās in castrīs suōs continuit, — Having feared—fearing—an ambush, Caesar kept his men in camp

2. Hostēs paulisper ad Caesaris castra morātī sē in suōs fīnīs recēpērunt, — Having delayed a little while near Caesar's camp, the enemy retreated into their own boundaries

If the verb is *not* a *deponent*, the clause containing the *perfect active participle* may be recast and expressed by the *ablative absolute* or by a *subordinate clause*. See (372).

341. EXERCISES.

I.—1. Hīs rēbus per[1] explōrātōrēs cōgnitīs equitātus, cui Caesar Labiēnum praefēcerat, ā dextrō cornū īnstrūctus est atque sīgnō datō impetus in hostium aciēs ab omnibus nostrīs ācriter factus est. 2. Item cum Caesar ad oppidum accessisset castraque ibi pōneret, hostēs ex mūrō passīs manibus suō mōre ab Rōmānīs pācem petīvērunt. 3. Aeduī ab latere nostrōs peditēs fortissimōs circumvenīre cōnātī multīs vulneribus acceptīs pulsī sunt ac sē in cīvitātēs proximās recēpērunt. 4. Rēmī quī auxiliō ad nostra castra veniēbant hāc pūgnā nūntiātā coepērunt revertī in suōs fīnēs ē quibus ā Germānīs expulsī erant. 5. Caesar Sēquanīs nē per nostram prōvinciam in Galliam iter faciant imperat atque sē eōs, sī cōnentur,[2] prohibitūrum esse nūntiat.

II.—1. Scouts are sent forward to find out the plans of the enemy and to inform Caesar with respect to these things. 2. Galba directed the tribunes of the soldiers not to begin battle on the right wing, because he saw (that) the enemy had drawn up their bravest infantry in that place and had[3]

---

[1] per = *by means of.*   [2] *If they try* (to do so).   [3] Pres. Infin.

very great power there. 3. An attack will not be made, unless Caesar places Galba in command of the infantry of the first legion. 4. Having attempted to destroy our new fortifications, the brave forces of the enemy were quickly driven back and some, surrounded by our cavalry, were brought (**addūcō**) to Caesar.

LESSON LXV.

ACCUSATIVE OF EXTENT IN SPACE OR TIME.

842. Learn *ūtor*, *I use*, **deponent of the third conjugation (496).**

Accusative of extent in space or time.—Extent in space and duration of time are expressed by the *accusative without a preposition;* as,

1. **Caesar ab oppidō duo mīlia passuum cōnsēdit,**   *Caesar encamped two thousand of paces (two miles) from the town*
2. **Hostēs cis Rhēnum multōs diēs morābantur,**   *The enemy delayed many days on this side of the Rhine*

843. Verbs of fearing.—Verbs of fearing are followed by a *subjunctive* clause introduced by **ut** = *that not* and **nē** = *that* or *lest*. Note *sequence of tense* in the following:

1. **Hostēs verentur nē Caesar ad eōs suum exercitum addūcat,**   *The enemy fear that Caesar will lead his army against them*
2. **Caesar verēbātur ut Aeduī sustinēre Germānōs possent**   *Caesar feared that the Aedui would not be able to withstand the Germans*

344.   **VOCABULARY.**

Irregular verbs 1–8 (452).

parvulus, -a, -um, *adj.*	*slight*
excursiō, -ōnis, *fem.*	*sally*
crēber, -bra, -brum, *adj.*	*frequent*
vadum, -ī, *neut.*	*ford*
tegimentum, -ī, *neut.*	*covering*
necessārius, -a, -um, *adj.*	*necessary*
decimus, -a, -um, *num. adj.*	*tenth*
vesper, -perī, *mas.*	*evening*
sub vesperum	*towards evening*
magistrātus, -ūs, *mas.*	*officer*

345. Construction with *persuādeō, I persuade.*—Persuādeō takes its object in the *dative* (like **imperō** and **mandō**) and is followed by an **ut** or **nē** *clause*, translated by an *infinitive*. Note *sequence* in the following:

1. **Belgae Gallīs reliquīs ut coniūrent contrā populum Rōmānum persuādent,**   *The Belgians persuade the remaining Gauls to conspire against the Roman people*
2. **Caesar Rēmīs persuāsit nē Senōnibus auxilium darent,**   *Caesar persuaded the Remi not to give aid to the Senones*

346.   **EXERCISE.**

1. Cum Caesar ab potentissimō Rēmōrum oppidō octō mīlia passuum abesset, lēgātī ad eum vēnērunt, quī pācem peterent obsidēsque trāderent. 2. Caesar, cum auxiliīs Q. Titūrium praefēcisset, suō mōre ē castrīs expedītōs mīlitēs ēdūxit. 3. Cum prīma legiō pervēnisset ac castra mūnīre coepisset atque legiōnēs reliquae circiter duo mīlia passuum abessent, hostēs triplicī aciē īnstrūctā magnō cum tumultū ad nostrās mūnītiōnēs accessērunt. 4. Aeduī

VERBS OF COMMANDING. CAUSAL CUM.

adventū nostrōrum commōtī māgnō exercitū coāctō mīsērunt ad Caesarem lēgātōs, quī sē neque obsidēs datūrōs neque ab eō (*of him*) pācem petītūrōs esse nūntiārent. 5. Hostēs vadīs ibi repertīs partem suārum cōpiārum trādūcere cōnātī sunt eō cōnsiliō, ut, sī possent, castellum cui Q. Titūrius lēgātus praeerat expūgnārent. 6. Nostrī oppidum expūgnāre cōnātī, quod audīvērunt facilem aditum habēre, ad mūrōs oppidī accēdere propter aestuāria palūdēsque nōn poterant. 7. Caesar amīcitiae causā sē in fidem eōs receptūrum et cōnservātūrum esse dīxit; sed quod erat cīvitās māgnā[1] inter Belgās auctōritāte atque multitūdine hominum plūrimum valēbat, multōs obsidēs poposcit: hīs trāditīs omnibusque armīs ex oppidīs collātīs (*from* cōnferō) Caesar ab eō locō in fīnīs Suessiōnum quī sē suaque omnia sine morā dēdidērunt pervēnit.

LESSON LXVI.

VERBS OF COMMANDING. CAUSAL CUM.

847. Learn *potior* **(497).**

Use of *cohortor*, *I urge, encourage.*—Cohortor takes the *accusative* of direct object and an **ut** *or* **nē** *clause;* as,

1. **Caesar suōs cohortātur ut fortiter impetum hostium sustineant,** *Caesar encourages his men to withstand bravely the enemies' attack*
2. **Caesar suōs cohortātus nē animō perturbārentur sīgnum proeliī dedit,** *Having urged his men not to become discouraged at heart, Caesar gave the signal for battle*

---

[1] **māgnā auctōritāte** = *of great influence;* **see (376),** '*ablative of quality*' and example.

348. Dative with special verbs.—Most verbs signifying to *yield* and *resist*, *bid* and *forbid*, *please* and *displease*, *desire*, *favor*, *trust*, *persuade*, *obey*, *command*, *serve*, *envy*, *harm*, *threaten*, and *pardon*, apparently transitive in English, are *intransitive in Latin* and take an *indirect object in the dative;* so with many phrases having similar meanings.

As previously stated in exercises, **imperō**, **mandō**, and **persuādeō** take the *dative* and an **ut** or a **nē** *clause;* **iubeō**, the *accusative and infinitive;* **cohortor**, the *accusative* and an **ut** or a **nē** *clause.*

349.   VOCABULARY.

Verbs 9–16 (**452**).

mercātor, -ōris, *mas.*	*merchant*
condiciō, -ōnis, *fem.*	*terms*
captīvus, -ī, *mas.*	*captive*
centuriō, -ōnis, *mas.*	*centurion*
complūrēs, -rēs, -r(i)a, *adj.*	*very many*
iniūria, -ae, *fem.*	*injury*
dēfēnsor, -ōris, *mas.*	*defender*
ita . . . utī, *adverbs*	*thus, accordingly . . . as*
suprā, *adv.*	*above*

350. Causal and concessive *cum.*—**Cum** meaning *since* or *although* takes the *subjunctive:* choice of *tense* is regulated by the *rule of sequence.*

Causal **cum:**

Caesar cum hostēs trānsīre flūmen cōnārentur (*time contemporaneous*), imperāvit suīs ut pontem interscinderent,   *Since the enemy were attempting to cross the river, Caesar commanded his men to cut down the bridge*

Concessive **cum:**

Cum legiōnēs Rōmānae fortissimae sint, Gallī nōn dubitābunt cum eīs proelium committere,   *Although the Roman legions are very brave, the Gauls will not hesitate to begin battle with them*

351. EXERCISES.

I.—1. Nostrī hostēs in flūmine impedītōs (*modifies* hostēs) aggressī māgnum eōrum numerum interfēcērunt. 2. Caesar id oppidum quod sine dēfēnsōribus esse audiēbat oppūgnāre cōnātus propter lātitūdinem fossae mūrīque altitūdinem expūgnāre nōn potuit. 3. Caesar, quod verētur nē cīvitātēs Galliae contrā sē cōnsentiant, suōs imperātōrēs certiōrēs facit sē prīmā lūce castra mōtūrum et eō iter factūrum esse. 4. Conciliō commūnī convocātō Germānī exercitūs nostrī adventum veritī pontem interscindere cōnstituērunt, nē nostrī in suōs fīnīs trādūcerentur. 5. Gallī, cum verērentur nē Caesar in Galliam omnīs legiōnēs dūceret, fīnitimīs persuādēre cōnātī sunt, nē exercituī Rōmānō frūmentum aut commeātūs darent.

II.—1. Our men killed the foremost who had crossed after they had been surrounded[1] by the cavalry. 2. When the matter had been investigated[2] by means[3] of scouts at early dawn, Caesar sent forward all the cavalry to delay[4] the rear of the enemy. 3. Fearing (having feared) that they could not withstand the attack of our men, the enemy, after burning[5] all their towns and villages, retreated into the territories next to the Germans. 4. Since his infantry could not approach the enemies' camp on account of swamps, Caesar sent forward scouts to find out the plans of the enemy and to inform him with respect to those matters.

---

[1] Render the entire clause by *one* Latin word.
[3] per + acc.
[5] Recast in the passive, *having been burned*.
[2] *Ablative absolute.*
[4] *Deponent.*

LESSON LXVII.
DOUBLE DATIVE. AFFIRMATIVE PURPOSE.

852. Learn the active voice of *ferō*, *I bear* **(490).**

Double dative.—A dative of *purpose, end,* or *service* often accompanies the dative of the *person* or *thing interested* or *concerned* ; as,

1. **Haec ūsuī nostrīs sunt,**   *These things are useful (for a use) to our men*

Here **ūsuī** is the *dative* of *purpose, end,* or *service,* **nostrīs** the *dative* of the *persons interested.*

2. **Caesar subsidiō nostrīs decimam legiōnem mīsit,**   *Caesar sent the tenth legion as a help (for a help) to our men*

853. Deponent verbs governing the ablative.—The following deponent verbs take the *ablative :* **ūtor,** *to use ;* **abūtor,** *misuse ;* **fruor,** *enjoy ;* **fungor,** *perform ;* **potior,** *capture ;* **vescor,** *eat.*

Labiēnus impedīmentīs hostium potītus in castra suōs redūxit,   *Having captured the enemies' baggage, Labienus led his men back into camp*

854.   **VOCABULARY.**

Verbs 17-26 (452).

deinde, *adv.*	*then*
rūrsus, *adv.*	*again*
nōn modo	*not only*
sed etiam	*but also*
īnsīgne, -is, *neut.*	*badge*
minus, *adv.*	*less*
minus facile	*less easily*
posteā, *adv.*	*afterwards*
ūsus, -ūs, *mas.*	*use*

DOUBLE DATIVE.

355. How to express affirmative purpose.—1. Ut + *subjunctive*. 2. Quī + *subjunctive*. 3. Ad + *gerundive*, agreeing with a noun in the *accusative*. 4. *First supine*, with verbs of motion.

Example of ad + *gerundive*:

Hostēs ad suōs fīnēs dēfendendōs conveniunt, — *The enemy assemble to defend their territories*

First supine:

Caesar vēnit postulātum obsidēs, — *Caesar came to demand hostages*

356. EXERCISES.

I.—1. Duābus legiōnibus praesidiō castrīs (*dat.*) relictīs Caesar reliquās, quae in hostium cōpiās impetum facerent, praemīsit. 2. Temporis fuit tanta brevitās hostiumque animus ad dīmicandum tam parātus, ut nōn modo ad īnsīgnia accommodanda sed etiam ad galeās induendās scūtīsque (*from their shields*) tegimenta dētrūdenda tempus deesset. 3. Caesar mīlitēs (*acc. obj.*) cohortātus ut suae prīstinae virtūtis memoriam retinērent, quod hostēs nōn longē aberant, proeliī committendī signum dedit. 4. In alteram partem item cohortandī causā profectus (*from proficīscor*) Caesar intellēxit fortissimōs mīlitēs secundae legiōnis vīribus (*from vīs*) redintegrātīs in prīmā aciē fortiter pūgnāre. 5. Duābus cohortibus in castrīs relictīs praesidiō impedīmentīs Caesar cum equitātū omnī prīmā lūce profectus in fīnēs Aeduōrum quōrum agrōs Germānī populābantur dē imprōvīsō pervēnit.

II.—1. Since[1] the enemy feared (*imperf. subjunc.*) that their infantry might be defeated by our men, they ordered their commanders to close all the gates and restrain their soldiers from battle. 2. Dumnorix employed scouts to go

---

[1] Order: '*the enemy, since*,' etc.

(*imperf. subjunc.*) to the nearest states and inform the chiefs that Caesar was collecting large bands and would march into their territories on the next day. 3. While our infantry were making an attack upon the enemies' forces on the opposite hill, Caesar ran down to the river with slingers and (**que**) bowmen and drove back those who were trying[1] to cross.

LESSON LXVIII.
DATIVE OF POSSESSION.

857. Learn *ferō* in the passive (491).

Dative of possession.—The *dative* is used with forms of **sum** to denote possession. Instead of saying '*the boy has a horse*' the Romans frequently expressed the idea thus: '*a horse is to the boy*,' **equus est puerō**. The *thing* possessed is put in the *nominative* (*accusative* in *indirect discourse*), and the *possessor* in the *dative*.

Proelium cum hostibus erit nostrīs, *Our men will have a battle with the enemy*

Which word denotes the *thing possessed*, which the *possessor?* Observe that the forms of **sum** are translated by the *corresponding tenses of the verb 'have.'*

858. Temporal clauses with the indicative.—**Ubi** and **postquam**, *when;* **ut**, *when* or *as;* **ut semel**, *as soon as;* **simulac, simulatque**, *as soon as*, usually take the *perfect* or *historical present in the indicative* (208).

859. *Cum* clauses.—**Cum** temporal, *when*, takes the *indicative* (like **ubi**, etc.) merely to *define the time of the action.*

Cum historical, *when* (in the sense of '*while*'), takes the

---

[1] Render '*who were trying*' by the *present participle*.

imperfect subjunctive to describe the circumstances of the action.

Cum historical, *when* (in the sense of '*after*'), takes the *pluperfect subjunctive to describe the circumstances of the action.*

Cum causal, *since*, takes the *subjunctive, any tense.*

Cum concessive, *although*, takes the *subjunctive, any tense.*

860. EXERCISES.

I.—1. Quod oppidō sunt altissimī mūrī, Caesar ad oppidum multōs diēs morābitur et commeātibus oppidānōs prohibēre cōnābitur. 2. Nam cum tanta multitūdō lapidēs ac tēla cōnicerent, in mūrō cōnsistendī potestās erat nūllī (*possession*). 3. Eō dē mediā nocte Caesar servīs[1] ducibus (*apposition*) ūsus (*participle*) sagittāriōs et funditōrēs subsidiō oppidānīs mīsit. 4. Prīmō adventū exercitūs nostrī hostēs crēbrās ex oppidō excursiōnēs faciēbant[2] parvulīsque proeliīs cum nostrīs contendēbant; posteā vallō māgnō crēbrīsque castellīs mūnītī in oppidō sē continēbant. 5. Ibi vadīs repertīs partem suārum cōpiārum trāns flūmen trādūcere cōnātī, ut castellum cui praeesset[3] Q. Titūrius lēgātus expūgnārent, omnēs hostēs ā nostrō equitātū circumventī (*participle*) interficiēbantur.

II.—1. Having feared an ambush, Caesar decided to keep all of his infantry[4] and cavalry in camp. 2. The enemy were informed by scouts that Caesar's army was advancing towards their camp and was then about five thousand paces distant. 3. Having set out from camp in the second watch, Caesar hastened with the auxiliaries, which were of great use to our men, and cut down the bridge

---
[1] *Ablative object of* ūsus ; see (853).
[2] *Kept making ;* [see (101), *meanings of the imperfect.*]
[3] See (276).   [4] *Not genitive.*

that the enemy might not be able to cross the river.
4. Since the Belgians are attempting to drive Galba's men out of winter-quarters, Caesar will command Titurius to march into their borders at once with two new legions.

LESSON LXIX.

PERIPHRASTIC CONJUGATION. IMPERSONAL VERBS.

861. Periphrastic conjugation.—Learn the periphrastic conjugation of *amō*, both voices (498, 499).

The *active periphrastic* is formed by annexing parts of **sum** to the *future participle*, and is used to express what *is likely—is going*—to happen; as,

1. Caesar hīs in regiōnibus   *Caesar is going to wage war in*
  bellum gestūrus est,   *these regions*
2. Hostēs impetum factūrī   *The enemy were about to make*
  erant in nostrōs,   *an attack upon our men*

The *passive periphrastic* is composed of the *gerundive* and parts of **sum**, and implies *obligation* or *necessity;* as,

1. Karthāgō dēlenda est,   *Carthage must be (has to be, ought to be) destroyed*
2. Omnia ūnō tempore facienda   *All things had to be done at one*
  erant,   *time*

862. Dative of personal agent.—The *dative* is used with the *gerundive* (*periphrastic passive*) to denote the *personal agent;* as, **hōc faciendum est mihi**, (literally) *this must be done by me;* it is better to recast the English sentence in the *active voice*, changing the *personal agent* to the *nominative subject;* thus, 'I *must* do this.' The idea of *necessity, duty*, or *obligation*, conveyed usually in English in the *active voice*, is expressed by the Latin *periphrastic passive* with the *agent* in the *dative*.

863. Examples of the periphrastic verb. (See Caesar's text, Book II, Chapter XX.)

1. **Caesarī omnia ūnō tempore erant agenda,** *Caesar had to attend to everything at one time*
2. (Again in line 3:) **Caesarī ab opere revocandī (erant) mīlitēs,** *Caesar had to recall the soldiers from their work*
3. (Chapter XVII, last sentence—*see text.*) *Since the advance (march) of our column was checked (would be checked) by these circumstances, the Nervii concluded that they* (**sibi**) *ought not to disregard the advice* [literally, *that the advice ought not to be disregarded* (**omittendum esse,** indirect discourse) *by them*]

864. Ablative absolute.—The *ablative absolute* may be expressed by (1) a *noun* or *pronoun* and the *perfect passive participle* (previously stated); (2) by a *noun* and an *adjective;* as, **locō idōneō,** *since the place was suitable;* (3) by a *noun* and the *present participle;* as, **nostrīs pūgnantibus,** *while* or *although our men were fighting;* (4) by *two nouns;* as, **duce Caesare,** *under Caesar's leadership* (literally, *Caesar being the leader*).

865. Impersonal verbs.—These are so called, as they have no subject separately expressed, the word *it* being used as the subject in the translation.

Examples of the *impersonal* verb in the *passive, third singular:*

1. **Ācriter eō locō pūgnātum est,**	*A fierce battle occurred in that place* (literally, *it was fought fiercely,* etc.)
2. **Hostēs, ad quōs ventum erat, cōnstitērunt,**	*The enemy, whom we* (*they*) *overtook, halted* (literally, *the enemy to whom it had been come,* etc.)
3. **Eō ex proximīs castellīs celeriter concursum est,**	(*Our men*) *rushed thither quickly from the nearest redoubts* (*it was rushed thither,* etc.)

366.   **EXERCISES.**

I.—1. Sēquanī, quod Caesarem cum exercitū ad sē iter facere audiēbant, omne frūmentum praeter (*except*) id quod sēcum portātūrī erant incendērunt et ex suīs fīnibus discessērunt. 2. Caesar vult (*wishes*) manūs hostium distinērī nē cum tantā multitūdine sibi ūnō tempore cōnflīgendum sit (*impersonal*). 3. Ubi neutrī (*nom. plur.*) flūminis trānseundī initium faciunt, secundiōre¹ equitum proeliō¹ nostrīs, Caesar suōs in castra redūxit. 4. Oppidum oppūgnāre cōnātus quod vacuum ab dēfēnsōribus esse audiēbat, propter lātitūdinem fossae mūrīque altitūdinem paucīs dēfendentibus² expūgnāre nōn potuit. 5. Caesar equitātū praemīssō omnibus cōpiīs subsequēbātur et, quod ad hostēs appropīnquābat, suā cōnsuētūdine ipse sex legiōnēs expedītās dūcēbat; post eās tōtīus exercitūs impedīmenta conlocāvit atque duae legiōnēs quae proximē cōnscrīptae erant tōtum agmen claudēbant praesidiōque impedīmentīs erant.

II.—1. Greatly alarmed³ by the approach of our army, the Suessiones sent ambassadors to Caesar to ask for⁴ peace. 2. Caesar placed Galba in command of (those) forces which had been sent⁵ to him by the Aedui and he himself, after encouraging⁶ his men, drew up a triple line of battle. 3. After the enemies' camp had been burned and their army routed, Caesar concluded that he ought⁷ to demand many hostages.

---

¹ See *ablative absolute*, example (2).   ³ See *ablative absolute* (3).
² *Modifies the subject.*   ⁴ See (355), '*how to express purpose.*'
⁵ Not *relative clause*, but p. p. p.   ⁶ = '*having encouraged.*'
⁷ See '*dative of agent*,' example (3)—literally '*that many hostages ought to be demanded by him.*'

LESSON LXX.

THE RELATIVE PRONOUN AS AN INTRODUCTORY WORD.

367. Learn the verb *volō*, *I wish* (487).
Learn the comparison of *'irregular adjectives and adverbs'* (472, 473).
Relative as a connective.—Frequently in Latin independent sentences are connected by the *relative*, which is usually translated by a conjunction (*and, now*, etc.) + a *demonstrative pronoun;* as,

1. **Quae omnia ab hīs dīligenter ad diem facta sunt** (*Caesar*, Book II, chapt. v, line 3),
   Now all these things were done by the latter carefully to the day

2. **Quī cum sē suaque omnia in oppidum Bratuspantium contulissent** (chapt. xiii, line 4),
   Now after they (those) had taken refuge with all their possessions in the town of Bratuspantium

3. **Cāius adventū spē illātā** (*from* **Inferō**) **mīlitibus ... paulum hostium impetus tardātus est** (chapt. xxv, last sentence),
   And hope being inspired in the soldiers on account of his arrival (the arrival of that one), the charge of the enemy was checked a little

368. Relative of cause or concession.—When **quī** = **cum is, cum eī** (*since* or *although he, they*), expressing *cause* or *concession*, the verb in the relative clause is in the *subjunctive*; as,

Aduatucī dīxērunt: nōn exīstimāre Rōmānōs sine ope dīvīnā bellum gerere, quī tantās māchinātiōnēs prōmovēre possent,
The Aduatuci said they did not think the Romans waged war without divine assistance, since (causal **quī***) they could move forward such machines of war*

In the *direct discourse* this relative clause takes the *subjunctive*.

369. Ablative with the comparative.—The comparative degree is followed by the *ablative*, signifying *than;* as,

Rōmānī erant fortiōrēs Gallīs, *The Romans were braver than the Gauls*

The comparative may be followed by **quam,** '*than*,' the following noun taking the case required by the context. After **minus, amplius,** and the like, **quam** is often omitted without affecting the construction.

370. Verbs of hindering.—Verbs of *hindering, preventing,* and the like, *when negatived,* are followed by **quīn or quōminus** and the *subjunctive;* by **nē** (sometimes **quōminus**) *when not negatived.* **Prohibēre** usually has *accusative + infinitive.* **quīn,** etc. + *subjunctive* may be translated by '*from*' and the *gerund* (ending in '*ing*'); as,

Nōn poterant dēterrēre Aeduōs   *They were not able to prevent*
  quīn cum Belgīs cōnsentīrent   *the Aedui from conspiring with the Belgians*

371.   **EXERCISE.**

1. When Caesar learned that all the states had been subdued, he decided to place his men in winter-quarters: [write *two verb-forms,* one with **cum** and one with **ubi**—see **(208, 358, 359)**—and explain *difference in meaning.*] 2. Unless Caesar sends help to the Remi, they will not be able to hold out against the Gauls: [write '*sends*' in *two tenses,* see **(223)**, and explain relation of the *time of its action* to the *time* of the action of the *principal verb* '*will not be able.*'] 3. If the enemy should attempt to cross, our men would attack **(aggredior)** and drive them back: [see **(335).**] 4. The enemy fear that Caesar will not accept hostages. Caesar feared that the enemy would capture **(potior)** Galba's

camp: ['*verbs of fearing,*' see (**848**); for case of the *object* of potior, see (**858**).] 5. Since the Roman soldiers excel (praestō) all in courage, they will easily conquer many tribes: [**cum**, '*since,*' see (**850**); '*all,*' for use and meaning of, see (**458**); for its *case*, see (**887**).]

LESSON LXXI.
ADVERBIAL ACCUSATIVE. ABLATIVE OF QUALITY.

872. Learn the verb nōlō, *I am unwilling* (**488**).

Substitutions for the perfect active participle.—In place of the *perfect active participle* (lacking in Latin) the *perfect participle of a deponent verb* may be used; in case the Latin verb is *not a deponent*, the participial clause may be *recast* in the *passive* and expressed by the *Ablative Absolute*; thus, *having killed a large number of the enemy the cavalry retreated into camp.* Since interficiō is *not a deponent*, recast in the *passive:* '*a large number . . . having been killed,*' etc.; **māgnō hostium numerō interfectō nostri in castra sē recēpērunt.**

The ablative absolute may be translated like a *subordinate clause* introduced by **cum, quod, ubi,** etc.; as, **cum māgnus hostium numerus interfectus esset, nostri in castra sē recēpērunt,** *when (after) a large number . . . had been killed,* etc.

873. Relative pronoun agreeing with a predicate word.—Sometimes the relative agrees with a *word in the predicate* instead of its *antecedent;* as,

Rōma quod est caput¹ Ītaliae, *Rome which is the capital of Italy*

874. Adverbial accusative.—A neuter pronoun or adjective is often used in the accusative with an adverbial force;

---
¹ **Caput,** genitive **capitis,** literally '*head,*' is a *neuter* noun of the third declension.

as, **quid possum**, *what can I? what power or strength do I possess?* **hōc tē moneō.** *I give you this advice.*

375. Perfect participle passive with *habeō* or *teneō.*— The p. p. p. (with **habeō** or **teneō**) modifying a noun in a predicate sense denotes *the continued effect of the action of its verb* and is translated with an *active meaning;* as, **Caesar habuit māgnum exercitum coāctum,** *Caesar had collected a large army.* Here **habuit coāctum** almost equals **coēgerat.**

376. Ablative of quality.—*Quality* is expressed by the *ablative* accompanied by an adjective or an equivalent; this is often called the '*Descriptive Ablative.*' **Vir, homō,** or some such word is sometimes to be supplied with this ablative: **est māgnā auctōritāte,** *he is (a man) of great influence.*

377.   **EXERCISE.**

1. The chiefs knew how great a calamity they had brought upon their state: ['*had brought*'; see **(313)** for mood of '*indirect question*'; see **(337)** for the case of '*state.*'] 2. Caesar informs the Gauls that he will not make war upon those states that give hostages: ['*informs,*' **certiōrem facere,** see **(333)**; '*will make,*' see **(318)**, *example* 3; '*give,*' see **(276)**, '*intermediate clauses in indirect discourse.*'] 3. The enemy came to Caesar to excuse (**excūsō**) themselves: [write the purpose clause in *four ways* as given in **(355)**]. 4. Although the Germans were departing from (**ex**) Gaul, Caesar decided that he ought to check (**impediō**) their departure: ['*although,*' concessive **cum,** see **(350)**; '*that he ought,*' see **(362, 363)**, '*dative of personal agent,*' and *example* **(3)** *of periphrastic verb.*] 5. The Belgians will persuade the Germans to cross the Rhine: [**persuādeō,** see **(345)**.]

LESSON LXXII.

PARTITIVE GENITIVE. ABLATIVE WITH OPUS AND ŪSUS.

878. Learn *mālō, I prefer* (489).

Partitive genitive.—Words denoting a *part* are followed by a *genitive of the whole* from which the part is taken; as, **nihil vīnī**, *no wine* (*nothing of wine*). *Exceptions:* Cardinal numerals (one, two, three, etc.) regularly take ē (ex) or dē + *ablative* instead of the *partitive genitive;* so usually **quīdam** (*certain*); as, **ūnus ex iīs**, *one of those;* **quīdam ex mīlitibus**, *certain* (*some*) *of the soldiers*.

879. Ablative with *opus* and *ūsus*.—Opus and ūsus, meaning *need*, take the *ablative* of the *thing needed* or *wanted* and the *dative of the person* who needs; as, **mihi est opus virtūte**, *I have need of courage*. Opus is sometimes in the *predicate* with the *thing needed* as *nominative subject:* **sī quid opus est**, *if there is any need*.

880. *Persuādeō* **in the passive construction.**— Intransitive verbs governing the *dative* (see **848**) are used *impersonally* in the *passive* and *retain the dative*. The *dative* of the *active* does *not* become the *subject of the passive;* as,

Active:

Hīs (*dative*) **persuādēre nōn poterant,**   *They could not persuade these* (*people*)

Passive:

Hīs (*dative*) **persuādērī** (*passive*) **nōn poterat,**[1]   *These* (*people*) *could not be persuaded*

881. Perfect participle passive translated as a finite (coordinate) verb.—The p. p. p. limiting and describing a

---

[1] Literally, *it was not able to be* (*could not be*) *persuaded—made sweet—to these*.

noun is often used in Latin, where English would make use of a *co-ordinate verb;* as,

Caesar suās cōpiās ē castrīs ēductās īnstrūxit,	*Caesar led his forces out of camp and drew them up (in battle array)*
Nostrī hostēs circumventōs interfēcērunt,[1]	*Our men surrounded and killed the enemy*

882. Substitution for the future infinitive.—The *future infinitive* in supineless verbs and usually in the *passive voice* of any verb is expressed by the periphrasis **futūrum esse** (or **fore**) **ut** + *subjunctive.* This periphrasis is sometimes used in the *active voice* of a regular verb. When the sentence *Caesar said that he would demand hostages* is written in Latin, '*would demand*' is placed in the *infinitive* according to the rule of *indirect discourse,* since it depends upon '*said*'; but **poscō**, which has no supine, lacks the *future infinitive.* The sentence, therefore, must be turned thus: *Caesar said it would be that he would demand hostages.*

In the following sentences notice carefully *sequence of tenses* in the periphrases:

1. **Caesar dīxit futūrum esse ut obsidēs posceret,**	*Caesar said it would be that he would demand hostages*
2. **Caesar exīstimat futūrum esse ut hostēs vincantur,**	*Caesar thinks the enemy will be conquered*
3. **Dīxērunt futūrum esse ut reliquae legiōnēs contrā cōnsistere nōn audērent,**	*They declared that the rest of the legions would not dare to stand against them*

883. **EXERCISE.**

1. Having delayed near the town a few days and (*omit*) having destroyed many fortifications, Caesar decided to lead his army against the Bellovaci: ['*having delayed,*' see (**340**); '*having destroyed,*' see (**872**).] 2. The Nervii who

---

[1] See (**816**), '*use and agreement of participle,*' example 2.

had been sent as an aid to Caesar could not be deterred by the Gauls from marching into Italy: ['*who had been sent*,' render by one Latin word (p. p. p.), see (816); '*as an aid*' = *for an aid*, see (852); '*from marching*,' see (870).] 3. Because Caesar kept hearing that the enemies' forces had been collected and were coming towards him, he decided that he ought to begin battle on the next day: [*Order:* '*Caesar because he kept*,' etc.; '*had been collected*,' render by the p. p. p., see (881), and omit '*and*'; '*he ought to begin*,' recast in the passive, see (862) and (868), example 3.]

LESSON LXXIII.

RELATIVE CLAUSE OF RESULT.

884. Review words 1-42 (899).

The ablative quō (= ut eō) with the comparative. —The ablative quō (ut eō, *so that thereby, by it*) is used to introduce *purpose clauses containing a comparative*; as,

Tenerīs arbŏribus incīsīs atque inflexīs, quō facilius fīnitimōrum equitātum impedīrent, (see chapt. xvii, line 16,)	*Young trees being notched and bent down so that they could thereby (by it) more easily check the cavalry of their neighbours*
Caesar manipulōs laxāre iussit, quō facilius gladiīs ūtī possent,(chapt. xxv, *ad finem*,)	*Caesar ordered them to open out their ranks so as to handle their swords with better effect*

885. How to express 'ought' or 'must.'

I ought to do this may be rendered:

1. By dēbeō + *infinitive:* hōc facere dēbeō.
2. By oportet (*impersonal verb*): (*a*) With *accusative* + *infinitive:* mē hōc facere oportet; ['*it behooves me to do this.*'] (*b*) With *subjunctive:* hōc faciam oportet; [note *sequence;* compare (*c*) below.]

3. By *gerundive* (*periphrastic passive*): **hōc faciendum est mihi**; [what *literally?* see (862), '*dative of personal agent.*']

Past action of these verbs may be expressed by placing **dēbeō** or **oportet** in the *tense required, the infinitive remaining present;* as,

(*a*) **Hōc facere dēbuī,**
(*b*) **Mē hōc facere oportuit (oportēbat),** } *I ought to have done this*
(*c*) **Hōc facerem**[1] **oportuit,**

386. Place to which (end of motion); place from which.— The place to which is expressed by **ad** or **in** + *accusative;* but the names of *towns* or *small islands* together with **domum** (*home*) and **rūs** (*country*) are put in the *accusative without a preposition;* as, **domum revertit,** *he returned home;* **rūs** (*neut.*) **ibit,** *he will go to the country.* The place *from which* is denoted by **ab, dē,** or **ex** + *ablative;* but with the names of *towns* or *small islands*, and also **domō** and **rūre,** *the ablative is used without a preposition;* as, **Romā abiit,** *he went from Rome;* **domō profectī sunt,** *they set out from home.*

387. Relative clauses of result.—*Relative clauses of result* are introduced by the relative **quī** or the adverbs **unde, ubi, quō,** etc., with the antecedent expressed or implied in the main clause; as,

Effēcerant ut īnstar mūrī hae saepēs mūnīmenta praebērent, quō nōn modo nōn intrārī sed nē perspicī quidem posset, (chapt. xvii, *ad fīnem*,)	*They had caused these hedges to furnish fortifications like a wall into which (whither, as a result) one could not only not enter, but not even see*

---

[1] Observe that *facerem* is *imperfect*, depending upon **oportuit**, a verb of *past time.*

388. EXERCISE.

1. Our men with the cavalry surrounded and killed the foremost (men) who had crossed the river: ['*surrounded*,' render by the p. p. p., see (381), and omit '*and*'; '*foremost*,' see (258).] 2. If the enemy should not surrender, Caesar would not prevent his (men) from burning their town: [The 'less vivid future condition,' see (385); '*would prevent*,' write in two ways with **impediō** and **prohibeō**; see (370).] 3. If hostages are given to Caesar so that he may know that the enemy will do those (things) which they are promising, he will make peace with them: ['*are given*,' write in two tenses; see (223); what kind of a condition is this? '*will do*,' future infinitive; '*those things*,' see (258); '*are promising*,' subjunctive by attraction; see (276). Observe the *sequence of tenses.*]

LESSON LXXIV.
COMMANDS AND EXHORTATIONS IN INDIRECT DISCOURSE.

389. Review words 43-84 (399).

See *imperative of* **nōlō** (488).

Commands and exhortations are put in the imperative, negative *nē* (never *nōn*); as,

1. Affirmative command: **Ad Belgās adī et in officiō continē**, *Go to the Belgians and keep them in allegiance.*
2. Negative command: **Nōlī hōc facere**, *Do not do this*, (literally, '*be unwilling to do this*'). **Nōlī** + infinitive is preferred to **nē** + *present imperative*, **nē** being generally used with the *perfect subjunctive* in a direct address or command; as, **nē hōc fēceris**, *thou shalt not do this.* When the phrase **nōlī facere**, '*do not do this*,' is changed to *indirect discourse*, as, *he told him not to do this*, the *nega-*

tive adverb **nē** *must be used* in place of **nōlī** (*see following rule*).

890. Commands and exhortations in indirect discourse.— The imperative of the *direct* becomes *subjunctive of the indirect, negative* **nē**. The application of the *rule of sequence* may be aided by a study of the following tables:

PAST.

Indicative mood.		Subjunctive mood.
Imperfect		*Imperfect* or *pluperfect*
Perfect	followed by	" " "
Pluperfect		" " "

NOT PAST.

Present		*Present* or *perfect*
Future	followed by	" " "
Future-perfect		" " "

891. The *imperfect subjunctive* represents time that is *not past*, the *pluperfect subjunctive* time that *is past*, according as the time indicated is *past* or is *not past* with reference to the *time* of the tense in the opposite column. In the second table the *present* and *perfect subjunctive* (in view of *relative time*) bear the *same relation* to the tenses in the opposite column, as is indicated by the *imperfect* and *pluperfect* in the first table.

892. Mood in Ōrātiō Oblīqua. [See 301, 302, 805, 806.]— In changing from *direct* to *indirect discourse*, if the main clause contains a *statement* (*indicative*), the verb of this clause is turned into an *infinitive;* if the main clause contains an *imperative* or *its equivalent*, the verb is turned into a *subjunctive; all subordinate* verbs are put in the *subjunctive;* as,

1. (*a*) Statement in O. R.:

Caesar dīcit: 'In officiō Gallōs continēbō,'   *Caesar says: 'I will keep the Gauls in allegiance'*

(b) Statement in O. O.:
Caesar dīcit sē in officiō Gallōs   Caesar says that he will keep,
contentūrum esse,   etc.

(c) Statement in O. O.:
Caesar dīxit sē in officiō Gallōs   Caesar said that he would keep,
contentūrum esse,   etc.

2. (a) Affirmative command in O. R.:
Caesar respondet: 'Continēte   Caesar replies: 'Keep the Gauls
Gallōs in officiō.'   in allegiance'

(b) Affirmative command in O. O.:
Caesar respondet in officiō   Caesar replies that they must [1]
Gallōs contineant,   keep the Gauls in allegiance

(c) Affirmative command in O. O.:
Caesar respondit in officiō   Caesar replied that they should
Gallōs continērent,   keep, etc.

3. (a) Negative command in O. R.:
'Nōlīte īnferre quam iniūriam   'Do not inflict any harm upon
hīs,'   these people'

(b) Negative command in O. O.:
Caesar dīcit nē hīs quam in-   Caesar says that they must not
iūriam īnferant,   inflict, etc.

(c) Negative command in O. O.:
Caesar dīxit nē hīs quam in-   Caesar said that they must not,
iūriam īnferrent,   etc.

393. Compare (1) *a* and *b*: the *first person*, 'I,' becomes *third person*, 'he'; the *indicative* becomes *infinitive*, time remaining *future*. Compare (2) *a*, *b*, and *c*: when *a* is changed to *b*, the *mood* of the *verb* changes, but the *tense* remains *present*; when *a* becomes *c*, though both *mood* and *tense* are changed, the imperfect **continērent** denotes the *same* time (in its new relation) as is indicated by the verb *keep* in *a*. (See *table* and *rule of sequence*.)

---

[1] should.

894. **EXERCISE.**

1. Caesar says: 'I cannot (present indicative of **possum**) cross the river because the enemy have destroyed the bridge': [write again in O. O. *twice: first* after 'Caesar *says*,' and *second* after 'Caesar *said*.'] 2. 'Give me a large number of hostages': [write again in O. O. *two ways:* first, Caesar informs the enemy that they must give *him*, etc.; second, Caesar *informed*, etc.] 3. 'Do not deprive the Aedui of their arms' (*ablative* of separation): [put in O. O.: Caesar *tells* and *told* his generals *not to*, etc.]

LESSON LXXV.
HORTATORY SUBJUNCTIVE.

895. Hortatory subjunctive.—The simple *subjunctive of exhortation* or *command*, called the 'Hortatory (from hortor) Subjunctive,' is used in the *present tense* and in the *first* or *third persons*. It is usually translated by '*let*' placed before the meaning of the verb; as, **contendāmus**, *let us hasten;* **retineant memoriam virtūtis**, *let them retain the memory of* (*keep in mind*) *their courage*.

When turned into O. O. (indirect discourse) the hortatory subjunctive *remains subjunctive*, being *present* in form after a verb of saying, etc., whose tense does *not* indicate *past time*, but *imperfect* when the tense of the verb of saying *does* indicate *past time;* as,

'Hostēs congrediantur!'	'*Let the enemy engage!*'
Caesar dīcit hostēs congrediantur,	*Caesar says, let the enemy engage*
Caesar dīxit hostēs congrederentur,	*Caesar said, let the enemy engage*

896. Conditionals in indirect discourse.—In O. O. all difference in form between the *more vivid* and the *less*

vivid future condition is effaced, the verb of the apodosis in both being rendered by the *future infinitive*, and that of the protasis going into the *subjunctive*.

1. O. R. *If hostages are given to me, I will make peace.* This (the more vivid future) is written in *two ways:* see (228).

(a) Sī obsidēs mihi dabuntur, pācem faciam; [dabuntur = future, *unfinished* time.]

(b) Sī obsidēs mihi datī erunt, pācem faciam; [datī erunt = future-perfect, time *finished* in the *future before another future action.*]

When written after dīcit, (a) becomes [O. O.]:

(c) Caesar dīcit, sī obsidēs sibi dentur, sē pācem factūrum esse.

Written after dīxit, (a) becomes [O. O.]:

(d) Caesar dīxit, sī obsidēs sibi darentur, sē pācem factūrum esse.

Written after dīcit, (b) becomes [O. O.]:

(e) Caesar dīcit, sī obsidēs sibi datī sint, sē pācem factūrum esse.

Written after dīxit, (b) becomes [O. O.]:

(f) Caesar dīxit, sī obsidēs sibi datī essent, sē pācem factūrum esse.

2. O. R. *If hostages should be given to me, I would make peace* (less vivid future): see (335).

(a) Sī obsidēs mihi dentur, pācem faciam (*present subjunctive*).

Written after dīcit, it is:

(b) Caesar dīcit, sī obsidēs sibi dentur, sē pācem factūrum esse.

Written after dīxit, it is:

(c) Caesar dīxit, sī obsidēs sibi darentur, sē pācem factūrum esse.

Compare (b) and (c) in the *less vivid* with (c) and (d) in the *more vivid*.

397. Subordinate clauses depending upon *infinitive verbs* in *indirect discourse* get their *sequence* usually from the *main verb of saying, telling*, etc., rather than from the *infinitive;* as,

Caesar dīcit sē fīnitimīs imperātūrum nē Aeduīs iniūriam īnferant (*present*).
Caesar says that he will command—Caesar said that he would command—their neighbours not to do violence to the Aedui

Caesar dīxit sē fīnitimīs imperātūrum nē Aeduīs iniūriam īnferrent (*imperfect*),

898. **EXERCISE.**

1. If the scouts sent forward during (in) the first watch inform Caesar in what direction the enemy are fleeing, Caesar will pursue without delay with all his forces: ['*sent forward*,' p. p. p. agreeing with the *subject;* '*inform*,' render by *future indicative;* '*in what direction*,' **quam in partem**; '*are fleeing*,' subjunctive, see (**318**).] 2. Write the above sentence after **Caesar dīxit** thus: Caesar said that, if the scouts . . . *informed him* in what direction . . . *were* fleeing, *he would* pursue . . ., etc.

899. REVIEW VOCABULARY.

Lessons LXIII—LXXV.

1. **suprā** (adv.), *above*
2. **successus, successūs** (mas.), *advance*
3. **posteā** (adv.), *afterwards*
4. **rūrsus** (adv.), *again*
5. **sōlus, sōla, sōlum** (adj.), *alone* or *only*
6. **in** (prep. with the *abl.*), *among*
7. **diūtius** (adv.), *longer*
8. **ut (utī)** (conj.), *as* or *so that*
9. **cum prīmum**, *as soon as*
10. **ūnō tempore**, *at one and the same time*
11. **īnsīgne, īnsīgnis** (neut.), *badge*
12. **praesum, praeesse, praefuī**, *be in command of*

REVIEW VOCABULARY.

13. ferō, ferre, tulī, lātum, *bear*
14. coepī, coepisse, coeptus sum (defective verb), *begin*
15. post (prep. with the acc.), *behind* or *after*
16. audācter (adv.), *boldly*
17. addūcō, addūcere, addūxī, adductum, *bring (to)*
18. negōtium, negōtiī (neut.), *business*
19. sed etiam (conj.), *but also*
20. captīvus, captīvī (mas.), *captive*
21. potior, potīrī, potītus sum *capture*
22. centuriō, centuriōnis (mas.), *centurion*
23. certus, certa, certum (adj.), *certain*
24. tegimentum, tegimentī (neut.), *covering*
25. dēfēnsor, dēfēnsōris (mas.), *defender*
26. dēspērō, dēspērāre, dēspērāvī, dēspērātum, *despair, cease to hope*
27. octō (indeclin. num. adj.), *eight*
28. negōtium dare, *employ*
29. cohortor, cohortārī, cohortātus sum (depon.), *encourage*
30. hostis, hostis (mas.), *enemy*
31. longē (adv.), *far*
32. vereor, verērī, veritus sum (depon.), *fear*
33. pābulum, pābulī (neut.), *fodder*
34. nam (conj.), *for*
35. vīs, vīs (fem.), *force* or *vigor*
36. vadum, vadī (neut.), *ford*
37. superior, superior, superius (adj.), *former*
38. crēber, crēbra, crēbrum (adj.), *frequent*
39. manus, manūs (fem.), *hand* or *band*
40. plūrimum posse, plūrimum valēre, *have very great power*
41. prōgressus, -a, -um (perf. particip. of prōgredior), *having advanced*
42. adortus, -a, -um (perf. particip. of adorior), *having attacked*
43. collātus, -a, -um (perf. particip. of cōnferō), *having been collected*
44. subsecūtus (perf. particip. of subsequor), *having followed after, having pursued*

45. impedītus, -a, -um (perf. particip. of impediō), *hindered*
46. ego (personal pron. first person), *I*
47. auctōritās, auctōritātis (fem.), *influence*
48. certiōrem facere (followed by the *acc.* and *infin.*), *inform*
49. iniūria, iniūriae (fem.), *injury*
50. ita utī (adv.), *just as*
51. minus (adv.), *less*
52. minus facile (adv.), *less easily*
53. mercātor, mercātōris, *merchant*
54. ad (prep. with the *acc.*), *near*
55. necessārius, necessāria, necessārium (adj.), *necessary*
56. nōn modo (conj.), *not only*
57. magistrātus, magistrātūs (mas.), *officer*
58. adversus, adversa, adversum (adj.), *opposite*
59. passus, passa, passum (adj.), *outstretched*
60. passus, passūs (mas.), *pace*
61. persuādeō, persuādēre, persuāsī, persuāsum, *persuade*
62. praeficere (with *acc.* and *dat.*), *place in command over*
63. populor, populārī, populātus sum (depon.), *plunder*
64. regiō, regiōnis (fem.), *region*
65. opīniō, opīniōnis (fem.), *report*
66. cēterī, cēterae, cētera (adj.), *the rest*
67. excursiō, excursiōnis (fem.), *sally*
68. videō, vidēre, vīdī, vīsum, *see*
69. ipse, ipsa, ipsum (intensive pron.), *he or self*
70. brevitās, brevitātis (fem.), *shortness*
71. cum (conj.), *since*
72. parvulus, parvula, parvulum (adj.), *slight*
73. tam (adv.), *so, such*
74. Suessiōnēs, Suessiōnum (mas.), *Suessiones*
75. decimus, decima, decimum (num. adj.), *tenth*
76. condiciō, condiciōnis (fem.), *terms*
77. tum, inde, deinde (adverbs), *then*
78. mīlle (indecl. adj.; noun in plur.), mīlia, mīlium, *thousand*
79. sub vesperum, *towards evening*
80. dē imprōvīsō, *unexpectedly*

81. ūsus, ūsūs (mas.), *use*
82. ūtor, ūtī, ūsus sum, *to use*
83. complūrēs, complūrēs, complūra (-ia) (adj.), *very many*
84. incrēdibilis, incrēdibilis, incrēdibile (adj.), *incredible*

SPECIMENS OF INDIRECT DISCOURSE.

400. O. O. (Caesar, Book II, Chapt. 32.)—Ad haec Caesar respondit: 'Sē magis cōnsuētūdine suā quam meritō eōrum cīvitātem cōnservātūrum, sī, prius quam mūrum ariēs attigisset, sē dēdidissent; sed dēditiōnis nūllam esse condiciōnem nisi armīs trāditīs. Sē id quod in Nerviīs fēcisset factūrum, fīnitimīsque imperātūrum nē quam dēditīciīs populī Rōmānī iniūriam īnferrent.'

401. O. R.—'Magis cōnsuētūdine *meā* quam meritō *vestrō* cīvitātem *cōnservābō*, sī, prius quam mūrum ariēs *attigerit, vōs dēdideritis;* sed dēditiōnis *nūlla est condiciō* nisi armīs trāditīs. Id quod in Nerviīs *fēcī faciam*, fīnitimīsque *imperābō* nē quam dēditīciīs populī Rōmānī iniūriam *īnferant.*'

402. O. O. (Caesar, Book I, Chapt. 13.)—Is respondit: 'Sī pācem populus Rōmānus cum Helvētiīs faceret, in eam partem itūrōs atque ibi futūrōs Helvētiōs, ubi eōs Caesar cōnstituisset atque esse voluisset: sīn bellō persequī persevērāret, reminīscerētur et veteris incommodī populī Rōmānī et prīstinae virtūtis Helvētiōrum. Quod imprōvīsō ūnum pāgum adortus esset, cum eī quī flūmen trānsīssent suīs auxilium ferre nōn possent, nē ob eam rem aut suae māgnopere virtūtī tribueret aut ipsōs dēspiceret: sē ita ā patribus māiōribusque suīs didicisse ut magis virtūte contenderent quam dolō aut īnsidiīs nīterentur. Quā rē nē committeret ut is locus ubi cōnstitissent ex calamitāte populī Rōmānī et interneciōne exercitūs nōmen caperet aut memoriam prōderet.'

403. O. R.—'Sī pācem populus Rōmānus cum Helvētiīs *faciet*, in eam partem *ībunt* atque ibi *erunt Helvētiī*, ubi eōs *cōnstitueris*¹ atque esse *volueris:* sīn bellō persequī *persevērābit, reminīscere* (*imperative*) et veteris incommodī populī Rōmānī et prīstinae virtūtis Helvētiōrum. Quod imprōvīsō ūnum pāgum adortus *es*, cum eī quī flūmen *trānsierant* suīs auxilium ferre nōn possent, *nōlī* ob eam rem aut *tuae* māgnopere virtūtī *tribuere* [*nē tribueris*], aut *nōs dēspicere: nōs* ita ā patribus māiōribusque *nostrīs didicimus* ut magis virtūte *contendāmus* quam dolō aut īnsidiīs *nītāmur*. Quā rē *nōlī committere* ut is locus ubi *cōnstitimus* ex calamitāte populī Rōmānī et internecīōne exercitūs nōmen *capiat* aut memoriam *prōdat.'*

404. O. O. (Caesar, Book I, Chapt. 35.)—Hīs respōnsīs ad Caesarem relātīs, iterum ad Ariovistum Caesar lēgātōs cum hīs mandātīs mittit: (line 7) 'haec esse quae ab eō postulāret : prīmum, nē quam multitūdinem hominum amplius trāns Rhēnum in Galliam trādūceret; deinde, obsidēs quōs habēret ab Aeduīs redderet, Sēquanīsque permitteret ut quōs illī habērent voluntāte ēius reddere illīs licēret ; nēve Aeduōs iniūriā lacesseret, nēve hīs sociīsque eōrum bellum īnferret. Sī id ita fēcisset, sibi populōque Rōmānō perpetuam grātiam atque amīcitiam cum eō futūram; sī nōn impetrāret, sēsē (..... line 25) Aeduōrum iniūriās nōn neglēctūrum.'

405. O. R.—'Haec *sunt* quae ab eō *postulō:* prīmum, nē quam multitūdinem hominum amplius trāns Rhēnum trādūcat; ['*let* him *not* lead across'—hortatory subjunc.] deinde, obsidēs quōs *habet* ab Aeduīs *reddat*, ['let him

---

¹ In the treatment of this passage in direct discourse, we regard Caesar as addressed in person and place the main verbs in the second pers. sing.; thus, 'Where thou, O Caesar, shalt place us,' etc. In order to retain the second person of the verb, the form **reminīscere** is given, rather than **reminīscat**.

return,'] Sēquanīsque *permittat* ut quōs illī *habeant* voluntāte ēius reddere illīs *liceat;* nēve Aeduōs iniūriā *lacessat*, nēve hīs sociīsque eōrum bellum *īnferat*. Sī id ita *fēcerit*, *mihi* populōque Rōmānō *perpetua grātia* atque *amīcitia* cum eō *erit;* sī nōn *impetrābō*, *ego* . . . . . Aeduōrum iniūriās nōn *neglegam*.'

406. O. O. (Caesar, Book II, Chapt. 14.)—Prō hīs Dīvitiācus . . . facit verba: 'Bellovacōs omnī tempore in fidē atque amīcitiā cīvitātis Aeduae fuisse : impulsōs ā suīs prīncipibus, quī dīcerent Aeduōs ā Caesare in servitūtem redāctōs omnīs indīgnitātēs contumēliāsque perferre, et ab Aeduīs dēfēcisse et populō Rōmānō bellum intulisse. Quī ēius cōnsiliī prīncipēs fuissent, quod intellegerent quantam calamitātem cīvitātī intulissent, in Britanniam profūgisse. Petere nōn sōlum Bellovacōs sed etiam prō hīs Aeduōs ut suā clēmentiā ac mānsuētūdine in eōs ūtātur. Quod sī fēcerit, Aeduōrum auctōritātem apud omnēs Belgās amplificātūrum, quōrum auxiliīs atque opibus, sī qua bella inciderint, sustentāre cōnsuērint.'

407. O. R.—'*Bellovacī* omnī tempore in fidē atque amīcitiā cīvitātis Aeduae *fuērunt: impulsī* ā suīs prīncipibus, quī *dīcēbant* Aeduōs ā Caesare in servitūtem redāctōs omnīs indīgnitātēs contumēliāsque perferre, et ab Aeduīs *dēfēcērunt* et populō Rōmānō bellum *intulērunt*. (Eī) quī ēius cōnsiliī prīncipēs *fuerant*, quod *intellegēbant* quantam calamitātem cīvitātī intulissent, in Britanniam *profūgērunt. Petunt* nōn sōlum *Bellovacī* sed etiam prō hīs *Aeduī* ut *tuā* clēmentiā ac mānsuētūdine in eōs *ūtāris*. Quod sī *fēceris*, Aeduōrum auctōritātem apud omnēs Belgās *amplificābis*, quōrum auxiliīs atque opibus, sī qua bella *incidērunt*, sustentāre *cōnsuērunt*.'

LESSON LXXVI.

CAESAR, BOOK II. CHAPTER I, ADAPTED AND SIMPLIFIED.

The Belgae conspire against Caesar.

408.—Cum esset Caesar in citeriōre Galliā¹ in hībernīs,¹ ita utī² suprā dēmōnstrāvimus, litterīs³ Labiēnī certior⁴ fīēbat omnēs Belgās⁵ contrā populum Rōmānum coniūrāre obsidēsque inter sē⁶ dare. Belgae coniūrābant prīmum, quod verēbantur nē⁷ omnī Galliā pācātā⁸ ad⁹ eōs exercitus noster addūcerētur; deinde,¹⁰ quod sollicitābantur ab¹¹ nōnnūllīs Gallīs quī, ut nōluerant¹³ Germānōs¹³ diūtius in Galliā versārī, ita¹⁴ exercitum¹⁵ populī Rōmānī hiemāre atque inveterāscere in Galliā nōlēbant.

409.—After Caesar had come¹ into hither Gaul, Labienus informed² him that all the Belgians had been incited³ by the Gauls⁴ and had conspired⁵ against the Roman people. Some Gauls who feared that⁶ all Gaul would be subdued⁷ by our army⁸ incited the Belgians with whom⁹ they conspired against Caesar.

408.—¹ Adverbial phrases, modifying esset. ² ita uti, 'just as.' ³ 'Abl. of *means*'; see (43). ⁴ certior + pass. (see 338): notice the force of the *imperf.*, 'he was being informed.' ⁵ Acc. subj. (indir. disc.) of coniurare and dare; see (301, 302, 318). ⁶ inter se dare, 'were exchanging.' ⁷ With verb of *fear*; see (343). ⁸ Abl. absol. ⁹ 'against them.' ¹⁰ Mod. coniurabant; 'in the second place they *kept conspiring.*' ¹¹ Pers. agent; see (237). ¹² ut + indic. = 'as'; note the force of the pluperf., 'as they *had been* unwilling.' ¹³ Acc. subj. of versari ; 'that the Germans should remain.' ¹⁴ ita nolebant; see the force of the *imperf.*, 'were unwilling.' ¹⁵ Acc. subj. of the two following infinitives, 'that the army of . . . should winter,' etc.

409.—¹ cum +*pluperf.* subjunc.; see (265). ² certiorem+*act.*; see (338): why eum, not se ? see (214). ³ Notice that the voice is *pass.*; indir. disc.; see (301, 302, 305, 318). ⁴ Pers. agent; see (237). ⁵ The *active* voice, *indir. disc.* ⁶ Verb of *fear* ; see (343). ⁷ Sequence of tense; see (185). ⁸ Abl. of means without a preposition; see (43). ⁹ cum, 'with,' is post-positive with the *personal pronouns* and the *relative* ; quibuscum.

LESSON LXXVII.

CHAPTER I, CONTINUED.

Additional reasons for the conspiracy. Caesar's preparations.

410.—Belgae sollicitābantur partim ab eīs quī mōbilitāte¹ et levitāte¹ animī novīs imperiīs² studēbant: partim ab nōnnūllīs etiam, quod³ in Galliā vulgō rēgna⁴ ā potentiōribus⁵ atque eīs⁵ quī ad condūcendōs⁶ hominēs facultātēs habēbant occupābantur. Hīs nūntiīs litterīsque commōtus⁷ Caesar duās legiōnēs novās in citeriōre Galliā cōnscrīpsit et Pedium lēgātum quī⁸ initā⁹ aestāte eās legiōnēs in interiōrem Galliam dēdūceret¹⁰ mīsit.

411.—Those¹ by² whom the Belgians were incited desired a revolution.³ By hiring⁴ men the more powerful⁵ generally seized sovereignty⁶ in Gaul. These messages alarmed Caesar, by⁷ whom two new legions were quickly enrolled. Pedius his lieutenant *is sent*⁸ to lead⁹ those legions into Gaul.

LESSON LXXVIII.

CHAPTER II.

Caesar leads his army into the country of the Belgae.

412.—Caesar ipse, cum prīmum¹ cōpia pābulī esse inciperet,² ad exercitum vēnit. Dat³ negōtium Senonibus⁴

410.—¹ Ablatives of *cause*; see (210): 'on account of fickleness,' etc. ² Dat. indir. obj. of **studēbant** ; see ' dat. with special verbs ' (848). ³ Goes with **occupābantur**. ⁴ Neut. plur. subj. of **occupābantur**; 'sovereignty was being seized.' ⁵ 'Adjs. as substantives'; see (258). ⁶ ' Gerundive construction '; see (258). ⁷ See (316) : begin the translation with this word, ' alarmed greatly by . . . Caesar enrolled.' ⁸ ' Rel. clause of purpose '; see (811). ⁹ From **ineo**, p. p. p. abl. absol. with **aestate**. ¹⁰ Sequence ? see (185).

411.—¹ ' Adjectives used as substantives '; see (258). ² n. ³ **novīs imperiīs**; see note 2, (410). ⁴ Gerundive construction; see (253). ⁵ See note 4, (410). ⁶ Note the change of tense. ⁷ ' Rel. clause of purpose '; see (811) and (355).

412.—¹ ' as soon as.' ² ' began ': copia the subj. ³ Historical present. ⁴ See **negotium do** (880).

reliquīsque Gallīs quī erant fīnitimī² Belgīs, utī³ ea⁴ quae apud eōs gerantur⁵ cōgnōscant sēque⁶ dē hīs rēbus certiōrem faciant. Rē frūmentāriā comparātā¹⁰ castra movet diēbusque¹¹ circiter quīndecim ad fīnēs Belgārum pervenit.

413.—Caesar himself¹ will come to the army because there² is a supply of fodder. He *employed* the Senones to find out³ those things which the Belgians were doing.⁴ Caesar informed his⁵ men that he would obtain⁶ a supply of corn and would break camp within five days.⁷

LESSON LXXIX.

CHAPTER III.

The Remi refuse to enter the league against Caesar.

414.—Eō¹ cum Caesar vēnisset, Rēmī quī proximī Galliae² ex Belgīs sunt ad eum lēgātōs prīmōs³ cīvitātis mīsērunt, quī dīcerent:⁴ 'sē⁵ suaque omnia in fidem atque in potestātem populī Rōmānī permittere,⁶ neque⁷ sē cum Belgīs reliquīs cōnsēnsisse neque contrā populum Rōmānum coniūrāvisse.⁷ Lēgātī,⁸ cum pervēnissent, nūntiāvērunt cīvitātem parātam⁹ esse et¹⁰ obsidēs dare et imperāta

² Nom. predicate. ³ utī ... cognōscant, faciant following dat negotium; see (880); note the sequence. ⁷ Obj. of cognōscant; see (258). ⁸ 'Intermediate rel. clause, subjunc. by *attraction*'; see (276). ⁹ Reflexive; refers to the subj. of the main verb dat (negotium). ¹⁰ Abl. absol. ¹¹ Abl. of time within which; see (65).

413.—¹ Intensive pron. ipse. ² Omit. ³ Be careful as to *sequence*; 'employed' is *past*; see notes 4 and 6, (412). ⁴ Subjunc. by *attraction*; notice that this verb is in the *active voice*. ⁵ Omit 'men' and use the proper form of suus. ⁶ Fut. infin. act., with subj. se ('he'); see (318), example 3. ⁷ Abl. of time within which; see (65).

414.—¹ 'thither.' ² See 'dat. with adjs.'; (126). ³ See (258): 'the foremost men.' ⁴ Not 'who said,' but '*who should (were to) say*'; see (311). ⁵ Acc. obj. of permittere; the subj. of permittere is se understood. ⁶ Equivalent to a *fut.*; 'that they would place themselves ... under the protection,' etc. ⁷ 'and not,' 'and that they had not united ... nor (neque) had they conspired.' ⁸ 'After (cum) the ambassadors had arrived, *they* announced.' ⁹ Acc. pred. after esse. ¹⁰ 'Both.'

facere et oppidīs eum accipere ac frūmentō cēterīsque rēbus iuvāre.

415.—The foremost¹ men of their state will be sent to Caesar as ambassadors² by the Remi to say³ that they⁴ will receive him⁵ in their towns. Because⁶ they had not conspired and were⁶ ready to give up themselves and all their possessions,⁷ the Remi aided Caesar with the corn⁸ which they had brought from⁹ the fields of the Sequani.

LESSON LXXX.

CHAPTER III, CONTINUED.

The Remi inform Caesar concerning the number of the enemies' forces.

416.—Rēmī dīxērunt reliquōs¹ omnēs in armīs esse,² Germānōsque³ quī cis Rhēnum incolant⁴ sēsē cum hīs coniūnxisse, tantumque⁵ esse eōrum omnium furōrem, ut⁶ nē Suessiōnēs quidem,⁷ frātrēs cōnsanguineōsque suōs, dēterrēre potuerint quīn cum hīs cōnsentīrent.⁸ Cum Caesar ab⁹ hīs quaereret quae cīvitātēs quantaeque in armīs essent et quid¹⁰ in bellō possent,¹⁰ sīc reperiēbat.

417.—When¹ the Germans united² with the Belgians, the Remi sent ambassadors to Caesar, who said³ that they were

---

415.—¹ See (258) and note 3. (414). ² Appositive. ³ Affirmative purpose. ⁴ ne. ⁵ eum. ⁶ *Imperf. indic.* ⁷ Omit. ⁸ Abl. of *means*; see (43). ⁹ ex.

416.—¹ Used as a substantive, subj. of *esse*. ² 'were.' ³ Acc. subj. of coniunxisse; 'and that the Germans ... had united.' ⁴ Subjunc. because a subord. verb in *indir. disc.*; incolunt in the *direct*; see (306). ⁵ Connects coniunxisse and the *esse* following. ⁶ ut ... potuerint, affirmative result; in clauses of result, the *perf. subjunc.* is very often used after *past tenses:* 'that they (the Remi) could *not* hinder even the Suessiones.' ⁷ ne ... quidem, 'not even'; emphasize the word *between them.* ⁸ quin + *subjunc.* (clause of result) following deterrere; see (370). ⁹ 'of these.' ¹⁰ essent, possent; subjunctives of *indir. quest.*; see (313): essent = 'were.' ¹¹ quid; adverbial accusative with possent; see (374): quid ... possent = 'what they could do,' or 'how much power they had.'

417.—¹ Use ubi; see (208, 358). ² se coniungo. ³ dixerunt.

not able⁴ to prevent their own brothers and kinsmen from conspiring.⁵ Caesar finds out⁶ what and how great states are⁷ under arms and what⁸ they can do⁹ in war.

LESSON LXXXI.

CHAPTER IV.

The origin and power of the Belgae.

418.—Caesar reperiēbat plērōsque¹ Belgās ab Germānīs ortōs esse² Rhēnumque³ antīquitus trāductōs⁴ propter locī fertilitātem ibi cōnsēdisse Gallōs'que⁵ quī ea loca incolerent⁷ expulisse. Caesar reperiēbat Belgās sōlōs⁸ esse quī patrum nostrōrum memoriā, omnī Galliā vexātā, Teutonōs Cimbrōsque intrā suōs fīnīs ingredī⁹ prohibuerint.¹⁰

419.—The Gauls were driven¹ out of those places which² they were inhabiting by the Belgians³ whose fathers were descended from⁴ the Germans. The Belgians were led across⁵ the Rhine in olden times and⁶ drove out the Gauls who could not prevent⁷ them from seizing⁸ a large part of Gaul.

---

⁴ 'they were not able' = **se non posse**. ⁵ **quin** + *impf. subjunc.*; see (370). ⁶ Pres. indic. of **reperio**. ⁷ Indir. quest.: for mood, see (313); for tense, see (135). ⁸ **quid**; see note 12 (416): note the change in the *tense*.

418 —¹ 'that most of the Belgians.' ² 'were descended.' ³ Connects **ortos esse** and **consedisse**, with **Belgas** as the subj. ⁴ p. p. p. mod. **Belgas**; see (316). ⁵ Dir. obj. of **expulisse**. ⁶ Connects **consedisse** and **expulisse**, having **Belgas** as the subj. ⁷ Subord. verb in O. O.; see (306). ⁸ 'were the only ones': after **solus sum**, even in O. R., the mood of the relative clause is generally *subjunc*. ⁹ 'from entering'; see (370). ¹⁰ *Subjunc*.; subord. clause in indir. disc.: strictly speaking it is a *rel. clause* of *characteristic*, which takes the *subjunc*.; see note 8. Observe that the *perf*. subjunc. is here used after the *past tense*; see (416), note 6.

419.—¹ Perf. indic. pass. ² For *gend. of the rel.* see (39), foot-note 1. ³ Person. agent; see (237). ⁴ a or ab. ⁵ Change to p. p. p.; see (381), and text above. ⁶ Omit. ⁷ 'could not prevent,' **impedire non poterant**. ⁸ **quin** + subjunc.; see (370) and text.

LESSON LXXXII.

CHAPTER V.

The Remi surrender hostages and give aid to Caesar.

420.—Caesar Rēmōs cohortātus¹ līberāliterque² ōrātiōne prōsecūtus³ omnem senātum⁴ ad sē convenīre principumque līberōs⁵ obsidēs⁶ ad sē addūcī iussit. Quae⁷ omnia ab hīs dīligenter ad diem facta sunt. Ipse⁷ Dīvitiācum Aeduum māgnopere cohortātus docet⁸ sē manūs hostium distentūrum⁹ esse, nē¹⁰ cum tantā multitūdine ūnō tempore cōnflīgendum sit.¹¹

421.—Caesar urged¹ the Remi to bring² their children as hostages and to do³ all those⁴ things which they had promised.⁵ After⁶ Caesar had addressed the Remi kindly, all their senate was ordered⁶ to gather together before⁷ him. Caesar will not join⁸ in battle, unless the bands of the enemy are kept apart.⁹

420.—¹ Depon. perf. participles mod. Caesar; see (340) prosecutus = 'having addressed.' ² Connects cohortatus and prosecutus. ³ Acc. subj. of convenire, clause depending upon iussit; 'he ordered their whole senate to assemble before him.' ⁴ Acc. subj. of adduci. ⁵ Apposition with liberos. ⁶ Relative at the beginning of the sent.; 'now (and) all of these things'; see (367). ⁷ Intensive pron., 'Caesar himself.' ⁸ 'states,' verb of saying or declaring followed by *acc.* + *infin.* ⁹ Subject is se, 'that he will keep apart.' ¹⁰ Neg. purpose clause; see (320) ¹¹ Pres. subjunc. *pass.* of the periphrastic conjugation; see (361); here an *impersonal verb*, see (305): 'so that it may not have to be fought '; more freely, ' that he may not have to fight.'

421.—¹ Perf. indic. of cohortor; see (347). ² Be careful as to the sequence; at the *time* he urged them, the *action* implied in 'bringing the children' and 'doing the things' was *incomplete*, *unfinished* and as yet in the *future*. ³ See (258) ⁴ Subjunc. by *attraction*; note the sequence, the action in 'had promised' being completed; see (276). ⁵ Historical cum; see (203, 259, 268). ⁶ Perf. indic. pass. of iubeo. ⁷ ad + *acc.* ⁸ Use the phrase proelium committere, proelium being *accus*. ⁹ 'are kept apart,' verb in the *protasis* of a *more viv. fut. condition*; write this in *two* tenses; see (228).

LESSON LXXXIII.

CHAPTER V, CONTINUED.

Caesar hastens forward to meet the Belgae.

422.—Sī Aeduī in fīnēs Bellovacōrum suās cōpiās intrōdūxerint¹ et eōrum agrōs populārī coepcrint,¹ id fierī poterit. Caesar postquam² omnīs³ Belgārum cōpiās in ūnum locum coāctās⁴ ad sē venīre vīdit, et ab⁵ eīs explōrātōribus quōs mīserat et ab⁶ Rēmīs eās cōpiās iam nōn longē abesse⁶ cōgnōvit, flūmen Axonam quod est in extrēmīs Rēmōrum fīnibus exercitum trādūcere mātūrāvit.

423.—If the forces of the Aedui are led¹ into the boundaries of the Bellovaci, these² things will be done.³ When⁴ scouts informed⁵ Caesar that the forces of the Belgians were being collected,⁶ he prepared to cross the river. While the Belgians were gathering all their forces into one place, Caesar led his army across the river. After⁷ all the forces of the Belgians had been gathered together, Caesar led his army into the farthest territories of the Remi.

422.—¹ *More vivid fut.;* see (223). ² Introduces vīdit and cognovit, joined by et; see (358): 'when C. saw that... and found out that...' ³ omnīs: acc. plur. = omnes. ⁴ p. p. p. mod. copias, translated by a *finite verb*, 'had been collected* and were coming; see (381). ⁵ Adverbial phrases mod. cognovit; 'when he found out from those scouts,' etc. ⁶ Indir. disc. depend upon cognovit: 'that those forces were now ... distant.' ⁷ Does quod refer to and agree with Axonam or flumen, and why?

423.—¹ Place in two tenses; see (223). ² Neut. plur. as noun, omit *things*. ³ The *pass.* of **facio** is **fio**: place in the fut. indic. ⁴ ubī + *indic.;* see (203). ⁵ certiorem + *act.;* see (333). ⁶ Indir. disc. (main verb) after certiorem fecerunt, which is taken as a verb of *saying;* what *voice* and *time* are indicated? ⁷ Render by abl. absol.; see (287), example 3.

LESSON LXXXIV.

CHAPTER VI.

The Belgae attack a town of the Remi. Mode of attack.

424.—Ab hīs[1] castrīs oppidum Rēmōrum nōmine Bibrax aberat mīlia[2] passuum octō. Id ex itinere[3] māgnō impetū[4] Belgae oppūgnāre coepērunt. Aegrē eō diē sustentātum est.[5] Ubi, multitūdine[6] hominum tōtīs moenibus[7] circumiectā,[8] undique in mūrum lapidēs iacī[9] coeptī sunt mūrusque dēfēnsōribus[9] nūdātus est, testūdine[10] factā portās succēdunt mūrumque subruunt. Quod[11] tum facile fīēbat. Nam cum tanta multitūdō lapidēs ac tēla cōnicerent,[12] in mūrō cōnsistendī potestās erat nūllī.[13]

425. — While the Belgians were attacking the town which[1] had[2] tall fortifications, a testudo was made so that they might draw near[3] the wall. After stones and javelins had been thrown[4] from all sides upon the wall and the wall had been stripped[4] of defenders, the townsmen[5] did not have[6] the power of holding out any longer. Since[6] the townsmen saw (were seeing) that so great a multitude were throwing stones and javelins upon the wall and[7] that they[8] could not[7] hold out longer, they surrendered themselves and all their possessions[9] to the Belgians.[10]

424.—[1] ' from *this* camp '; adverbial phrase limits **aberat**. [2] Acc. of extent in space; see (342). [3] **ex itinere**, 'turning aside from the march'; making an attack immediately after a march without preparation. [4] Abl. of *manner*, mod. **oppugnare coeperunt**; see (210). [5] Impers. verb; see (365). [6] Abl. absol., 'a multitude of men being thrown around all the walls.' [7] Dat. indir. obj. of **circumiecta**. [8] Pres. pass. infin. of **facio**; with a *pass.* infin. **coepi** is put in the pass. [9] Abl. of sep. mod. **nudatus est**; 'of defenders'; see (221). [10] Abl. absol.: a testudo was a covering for the soldiers' heads made by overlapping the shields like shingles on a roof, and used in approaching and storming walls. [11] See (307): 'and *this* thing.' [12] Plur., agreeing with **multitudo** taken collectively. [13] See (357) : ' power was to no one '—' no one had the power.'

425.—[1] Dat. of possession; see (357). [2] **erant**. [3] Observe the *sequence*. [4] Render both clauses by *abl. absol.*; see (287). [5] **erat**. [6] See 'causal cum,' (350). [7] 'and not ' = **neque**. [8] **se**, acc. subj. [9] Omit. [10] Dat.

LESSON LXXXV.

CHAPTERS VI AND VII.

The Remi ask aid from Caesar, who sends relief.

426.—Cum fīnem oppūgnandī nox fēcisset, Iccius Rēmus summā nōbilitāte¹ et grātiā¹ inter suōs,² quī tum oppidō³ praefuerat, ūnus⁴ ex eīs quī lēgātī dē pāce ad Caesarem vēnerant, ad eum nūntium quī⁵ auxilium peteret mīsit. Eō dē mediā nocte Caesar īsdem⁶ ducibus⁷ ūsus quī nūntiī ab Icciō vēnerant, sagittāriōs et funditōrēs subsidiō⁸ oppidānīs⁸ mittit; quōrum adventū⁹ et¹⁰ Rēmīs¹¹ cum spē dēfēnsiōnis studium prōpūgnandī accessit, et hostibus¹² eādem dē causā spēs potiundī¹³ oppidī discessit.

427.—Because of the hope¹ of driving² the Belgians out of their territories, the Remi ordered Iccius to go³ to Caesar as an ambassador and to ask for help. Because Iccius whom⁴ the Remi had put in command of their town⁵ was friendly to the Roman people,⁶ Caesar said he would send⁷ archers and slingers as a relief⁷ to the town.⁵ Now⁸ upon the arrival of these⁸ the townsmen fought with great courage⁹ and¹⁰ the enemy could not¹⁰ storm their town.

426.—¹ Ablatives of *quality* ; supply **vir** (a man) and translate the *abl.* like the *gen.*; see (376). ² Adj. used as noun; see (258). ³ See 'dat. with compound verbs'; (387). ⁴ See (378), 'partitive genitive—exceptions.' ⁵ Rel. clause of purpose; see (311). ⁶ Adj. used as noun, obj. (*abl.*) of **usus**; 'using (making use of) the same men'; see (353). ⁷ Apposition: 'as guides.' ⁸ Doub. dat.; see (352). ⁹ Abl. of *cause* mod. **accessit** and **discessit**; 'on account of whose arrival.' ¹⁰ 'both.' ¹¹ Dat. indir. obj. of **accessit**; 'eagerness to fight was inspired in the Remi.' ¹² Dat. with a verb of *taking away* (**discessit**) instead of the abl. of separation; 'from the enemy.' ¹³ **potiundī** = **potiendī**: gerundive construction; see (258).

427.—¹ **spe**, an abl. of *cause*. ² Use **de** and the *abl.* of the gerundive; see (253). ³ 'Iccius to go' = acc. + infin., if **iubeo** is used; *what*, if **impero**? ⁴ **praeficio** takes *acc.* and *dat.*: 'whom' to be turned into the *acc.*, 'town' into the *dat.*; see (337). ⁵ See 'dat. with adjs.'; (126). ⁶ Indir. disc.; what *time* is indicated ? ⁷ Doub. dat.; see (352). ⁸ 'now these'; render both words by the relative pron.; see (307). ⁹ Abl. of *manner ;* see (210). ¹⁰ 'and not' = **neque**.

LESSON LXXXVI.

CHAPTER VII, CONTINUED.

The Belgae abandon the siege and turn against Caesar.

428.—Itaque paulisper apud¹ oppidum morātī² agrōsque Rēmōrum dēpopulātī,³ omnibus⁴ vīcīs aedificiīsque quōs⁴ adīre potuerant incēnsīs, ad castra Caesaris omnibus cōpiīs contendērunt et ab⁵ mīlibus passuum minus duōbus castra posuērunt. Quae⁶ castra, ut⁷ fūmō atque īgnibus sīgnificābātur, amplius⁸ mīlibus⁸ passuum octō in lātitūdinem patēbant. Caesar prīmō et propter multitūdinem hostium et propter eximiam opīniōnem virtūtis¹⁰ proeliō¹¹ supersedēre statuit; cotīdiē tamen equestribus proeliīs¹² hostium virtūtem perīclitābātur.

429.—The Belgians will delay¹ many days² near the town whose³ walls they cannot storm so as to lay waste⁴ the fields of the Remi and burn⁴ their buildings. Because he saw⁵ that the multitude of the enemy was so great,⁶ Caesar commanded the generals⁷ of the infantry to refrain⁷ from battle. Fearing⁸ the power and courage of the

---

428.—¹ 'near.' ² Depon. perf. participles mod. **hostes**, the subj. implied in **contenderunt**; see (840). ³ **omnibus... incensis**: abl. absol. of *time*, mod. **contenderunt**. ⁴ **quos**: has two antecedents, **vicis** and **aedificiis**. When the gender of two or more antecedents is different, the relative takes the gender sometimes of the *strongest* or *most important* word, sometimes that of the *nearest* word; **quos** in this sentence takes the gender of **vicis**, the more important noun. ⁵ **ab... duobus**: **ab** is used adverbially, 'off,' i.e., distant from the Roman camp. **milibus duobus**: abl. of *degree of difference*, 'by two thousand,' the abl. being used without reference to the comparative **minus**, which does not affect the construction; the force of **minus** is seen in the translation, 'by two thousand [and] less.' The entire phrase is best translated 'less than two miles off.' ⁶ 'now this'; see (807). ⁷ **ut**, 'as.' ⁸ Accus. of extent in space; see (842). ⁹ Abl. with the comparative **amplius**; see (869). See the other construction for these neuter comparatives, note 5 above (**minus**). ¹⁰ 'for valor.' ¹¹ 'from battle.' ¹² Abl. of means mod. **periclitabatur**.

429.—¹ Deponent verb. ² See (842). ³ Why *gen. sing. neut.?* ⁴ See (820, 855). ⁵ Imperf. indic. ⁶ Pred. adj. after **esse**. ⁷ See (184, 135, 145). ⁸ Perf. particip. (depon.).

Belgians who⁹ had large forces, Caesar ordered his generals not to begin battle on that day.

LESSON LXXXVII.
CHAPTER VIII.
Caesar protects his camp with strong defences.

480.—Is collis,¹ ubi² castra Caesaris posita erant, paululum ex plānitiē ēditus³ in lātitūdinem tantum⁴ locī⁵ patēbat quantum aciēs īnstrūcta⁶ occupāre poterat. Caesar⁷ ubi nostrōs nōn esse īnferiōrēs⁸ intellēxit, locō⁹ prō castrīs ad aciem īnstruendam¹⁰ nātūrā opportūnō atque idōneō, ab¹¹ utrōque latere ēius collis¹² trānsversam fossam obdūxit. Ad extrēmās fossās¹³ castella cōnstituit ibique tormenta collocāvit, nē,¹⁴ cum aciem īnstrūxisset, hostēs ab lateribus suōs¹⁵ pūgnantēs circumvenīre possent.

481.—A place suitable for¹ setting up² redoubts and engines of war is chosen by³ those scouts whom Caesar sent forward during the second watch.⁴ Unless Caesar should dig⁵ a ditch, the enemy would surround⁶ our infantry on their flanks and kill them while (as) they were fighting.⁷

---

⁹ Dat. of possession: see (357).
480.—¹ Is collis: 'that hill,' subj. of patebat. ² 'where.' ³ Limits collis; 'sloping upward gradually from the plain.' ⁴ Accus. of extent in space; see (342). ⁵ Partitive gen. with tantum; 'as much ground as (quantum).' ⁶ Mod. acies; 'an army drawn up for battle.' ⁷ Order: 'when Caesar perceived... he dug,' etc. ⁸ Adj. in the pred. accus. after esse; 'that our men were not inferior (in courage).' ⁹ loco... idoneo: see (364), example 2. ¹⁰ See (253). ¹¹ ab... latere: adverbial phrase (latus, lateris), mod. obduxit. ¹² Gen. depend. upon latere. ¹³ 'at the ends of the ditches.' ¹⁴ ne... possent: neg. purpose; see (320). ¹⁵ suos: adj. used as a substantive modified by pugnantes (pres. particip.): pugnans is declined in (467). Translate, 'his men while (as) they were fighting.' The pres. particip. is translated, 'as (while) they are or were fighting.'
481.—¹ ad. ² Gerundive in agreement with the acc.; see (258). ³ Pers. agent; see (237). ⁴ Abl. of time, without prep. ⁵ See 'less viv. fut. condition' (335). ⁶ 'while they were fighting': render by the pres. particip.; why acc.?

Caesar drew up his line of battle upon a hill ' fortified by nature, in order that⁸ his infantry as they were fighting⁹ might not⁸ be surrounded by the enemy.

LESSON LXXXVIII.

CHAPTERS VIII AND IX.

The Belgae encamp opposite Caesar's camp across a marsh.

482.—Hōc factō duābus legiōnibus quās¹ proximē cōnscrīpserat in castrīs relictīs, ut² sī quō³ opus esset⁴ subsidiō⁵ dūcī possent, reliquās sex legiōnēs prō castrīs in aciē cōnstituit. Hostēs item suās cōpiās ē castrīs ēductās⁶ īnstrūxerant. Palūs erat nōn⁷ māgna inter nostrum⁸ atque hostium exercitum. Hostēs exspectābant sī⁹ hanc nostrī trānsīrent; nostrī autem in armīs erant parātī ut impedītōs¹⁰ aggrederentur, sī ab illīs trānseundī initium fieret.¹¹ Interim proeliō equestrī inter duās aciēs contendēbātur.¹² Ubi neutrī initium trānseundī faciunt proeliō¹³ equitum nostrīs secundiōre¹⁴ Caesar in castra suōs redūxit.

483.—If Caesar leaves¹ the two legions, which² were

---

⁷ Abl. of *place where* with **in**. ⁸ 'In order that ... not': neg. purpose; see (820). ⁹ 'as they were fighting'; render by the pres. particip.; why *nom* ?
482.—¹ Why 'which he *had enrolled*,' and not 'which *had been enrolled*'? ² ut ... possent: shows the *purpose of* and derives its *sequence* from relictīs. ³ quo = adv., 'anywhere'; translate the clause, 'if they were needed anywhere.' ⁴ subjunc. by attraction; see (276). ⁵ Dat. of purpose, end or service; 'as (for) a relief.' ⁶ 'had led out ... and arranged in order'; see (881). ⁷ A negative with *large* = 'small.' ⁸ Mod. *exercitum*. ⁹ Indir. quest. introduced by **sī**, 'whether'; 'kept waiting to see (**exspectābant**) whether our men would cross'; for mood in 'indir. quest.' see (813). ¹⁰ p. p. p. mod. **eos** (**hostes**), obj. of **aggrederentur**; 'to attack them placed at a disadvantage.' ¹¹ sī ... fīeret: depends upon **aggrederentur**, hence subjunc. (see note 4); bear in mind that **fīeret** is the *passive* of **facio**. ¹² Impersonal; see (865). ¹³ Abl. absol.; see (864), example 2.

483.—¹ Fut. or fut. pf. indic. (228, 335). ² Why *nominative?* Compare this with note 1 (482).

recently enrolled, as a defence⁸ to the camp,⁵ the enemy will not lead out their forces. If the enemy should try⁴ to cross the swamp, our cavalry would surround⁵ them on all sides and attack⁶ (them). After drawing up⁶ all their forces in front of their camp the enemy sent forward cavalry who were to⁷ attack the two legions that were left⁸ in our camp.

LESSON LXXXIX.

CHAPTER IX, CONTINUED.

The enemy attempt to cross the river and surprise Titurius.

484.—Hostēs prōtinus ex eō locō ad flūmen Axonam contendērunt, quod¹ esse post nostra castra dēmōnstrātum est. Ibi vadīs repertīs partem suārum cōpiārum trādūcere cōnātī sunt, eō cōnsiliō,² ut³ sī possent⁴ castellum cui⁵ praeerat Titūrius lēgātus expūgnārent pontemque interscinderent; sī minus⁶ potuissent,⁷ (ut) agrōs Rēmōrum populārentur⁸ quī ad⁹ bellum gerendum māgnō ūsuī¹⁰ nōbīs¹⁰ erant commeātūque¹¹ nostrōs prohibērent.⁸ Caesar ab Titūriō certior factus¹² omnem equitātum et levis armātūrae¹³ Numidās,

---

³ Doub. dat.; see (352). ⁴ Pres. subjunc. in a less viv. fut. condition; see (335). ⁵ ' would surround '; change to p. p. p., omit *and*, and make *attack* the verb of the apodosis; order, ' would attack (them) surrounded on all sides'; see text (482) and note 10. ⁶ Render by abl. absol.: ' all their forces having been.' etc.; see (287). ⁷ ' who were to attack ': *rel. clause of purpose*; be careful about the *sequence*; see (311). ⁸ ' that were left '; render by the p. p. p.

484.—¹ Nom. subj. of **demonstratum est;** ' which has been shown to be in the rear of.' ² ' with this design (in view).' ³ **ut . . . expugnarent, interscinderent:** affirmative purpose and explanatory of **eo consilio:** ' with this design, viz., to storm,' etc. ⁴ Subjunc. by attraction, time *unfinished* (see **potuissent,** note 7). ⁵ Dat. with comp. verb. ⁶ **minus = non.** ⁷ ' if (having made the attempt) they should not have been (should not be) able '; **potuissent** is *pluperf.* to show time finished; since **conati sunt traducere** denotes *past time,* the depend. subjunctives appear in either the *imperf.* or *pluperf.* ⁸ Introduced by **ut,** explaining **eo consilio** (see note 3). ⁹ ' for.' ¹⁰ Doub. dat.; ' were very useful to us.' ¹¹ Abl. of *separation.* ¹² ' Upon being informed (as to this) by Titurius, Caesar leads.' ¹³ Gen. depend. upon **Numidas;** ' of light equipment.'

funditōrēs sagittāriōsque pontem trādūcit atque ad eōs contendit.

485.—After¹ the enemy had reached² that river on whose banks³ our camp had been pitched, they attempted to find⁴ fords so that they might lead across a part of their forces. By destroying⁵ the bridge and storming the redoubts over which⁶ Caesar had placed his lieutenant Titurius in command, the enemy will be able to cut off⁷ our men from supplies. The enemy will try to cross the river so as to storm the redoubt and cut down the bridge, if they can.⁸

LESSON XC.

CHAPTER X.

The Belgae are defeated in a fierce battle.

486.—Ācriter in eō locō pūgnātum est.¹ Hostēs² in flūmine impedītōs³ nostrī aggressī⁴ māgnum eōrum numerum occīdērunt; reliquōs⁵ per eōrum corpora audācissimē trānsīre cōnantēs⁶ nostrī multitūdine tēlōrum reppulērunt; prīmōs,⁷ quī trānsierant, equitātū circumventōs⁸ interfēcērunt. Hostēs ubi⁹ et dē expūgnandō oppidō et dē flūmine trānseundō spem¹⁰ sē fefellisse intellēxērunt, neque¹¹

485.—¹ cum. Order: 'the enemy, after they had reached,' etc. ² pervenio ad + acc. ³ in + abl. ⁴ Complementary infin. following *attempted;* verbs which imply another action of the same subject to complete their meaning take the complementary infin. without a subj. acc. ⁵ Gerundive; see (258). ⁶ Dat.; why? ⁷ Pres. infin. act. of prohibeo. ⁸ Subjunc. by attraction.

486.—¹ Impersonal; see (365). ² Acc. obj. of aggressi. ³ Mod. hostes; 'the enemy placed at a disadvantage in the river.' ⁴ Mod. the subj. nostri: 'having attacked ... our men slew.' ⁵ Acc. obj. of reppulerunt, whose subj. is nostri. ⁶ Pres. particip. acc. plur. mod. reliquos (used as noun); 'the rest as they were trying.' ⁷ Acc. obj. of interfecerunt. ⁸ Mod. primos, but translated by a coordinate verb; see (881). ⁹ ubi: see (208, 858); ubi introduces intellexerunt, viderunt, and coepit. ¹⁰ Acc. subj. of fefellisse. ¹¹ '*and* that our men were *not* advancing' (progredi).

nostrōs iu locum inīquiōrem prōgredī pūgnandī causā vīdērunt, atque ipsōs[12] rēs frūmentāria dēficere coepit, concilium convocāvērunt.

487.—The enemy hindered in the river were driven back by our men and the foremost were surrounded[1] by the cavalry and killed by the darts of our men. Because[2] hope with respect to crossing the river kept failing[3] the enemy, they decided after calling[4] a council of war to surrender themselves and all their possessions to Caesar. Since[5] the enemy saw[6] that our men had killed[7] the foremost, who had tried[8] very boldly to cross, and were driving back[9] the rest, they sent ambassadors to Caesar with respect to peace.

LESSON XCI.

CHAPTER X, CONTINUED.

The Belgae decide to return home.

438.—Conciliō convocātō Belgae cōnstituērunt optimum[1] esse quemque[2] domum[3] suam revertī et undique convenīre ad[4] eōs dēfendendōs quōrum in fīnīs prīmum Rōmānī[5] exercitum intrōdūxissent,[6] ut potius in suīs quam in aliēnīs

---

[12] 'themselves,' as distinguished from our men; it is the object of *deficere*.
487.—[1] Change thus: 'the foremost surrounded . . . were killed.' [2] See (276). [3] Imperfect. [4] Recast and render by abl. absol.: 'a council having been called, they decided.' [5] Causal cum; see (350). [6] viderent. [7] For 'tenses of the infin. in indir. disc.,' see (301, 302, 305, 318). [8] Subord. verb. in indir. disc.; see (306).
438.—[1] Superlative of bonus; see (472), acc. sing. neut. pred. adj. with esse limiting the *verbal phrase*, **quemque . . . revertī et convenīre**, which phrase is the subject of esse : 'An infin. may have another verb or a verbal phrase for its subject being *neuter*.' Translate: 'that it was best for each one to return.'
[2] From quisque; subj. of revertī and convenīre. [3] Acc. of end or limit of motion *without* ad. [4] 'to defend;' see (355) and example. [5] Subj. of introduxissent. [6] Subjunc. mood because it is a subordinate verb in indir. disc., depending indirectly upon constituerunt ; notice the sequence. This pluperf. subjunc. was *fut. perf. indic.* in the original sentence, conveying the same *time relation* as that of a verb in the protasis of a more vivid fut. condition; see (223).

fīnibus dēcertārent; praetereā' cōgnōverant Dīvitiācum atque Aeduōs fīnibus Bellovacōrum appropīnquāre.⁸ Hīs⁹ persuādērī ut diūtius morārentur¹⁰ neque¹¹ suīs¹² auxilium ferrent nōn poterat.

489.—The Belgians will assemble from all sides to defend¹ those² states into which³ the Romans first lead⁴ an army. [Ōrātiō Rēcta]. Scouts inform Caesar that the Belgians will assemble⁴ from all sides to defend those states into which the Romans first lead⁵ an army. [Ōrātiō Oblīqua].

LESSON XCII.

CHAPTER XI.

The Romans pursue and kill many Belgae.

440.—Eā rē cōnstitūtā, secundā vigiliā māgnō cum strepitū ac tumultū castrīs ēgressī,¹ cum² sibi quisque prīmum itineris locum peteret et domum pervenīre properāret, fēcērunt³ ut profectiō cōnsimilis fugae⁴ vidērētur. Hāc rē per⁵ speculātōrēs statim cōgnitā, Caesar īnsidiās

---
⁷ 'and besides.' ⁸ 'were drawing near to.' ⁹ *his;* explained in (880). ¹⁰ ut ... morarentur: 'to delay.' ¹¹ 'and not.' ¹² Indir. object, 'to their friends.'

489.—¹ ad + *gerundive;* why does the *ending* of this gerundive differ from that of the gerundive in the text above ? ² Why feminine ? ³ Fut. perf. indic. representing action *completed in the future* before another fut. action; see (223), for tense required to express such time relation in the protasis. If considered an indir. quest., the mood would be subjunc.; what tense (subjunc.) would here represent the fut. perf. indic. ? Why not the *pluperf.*, as in the text (488)? ⁴ Principal verb in O. O. following 'inform'; see (806). ⁵ Subordinate verb in O. O.; this verb is *fut. perf* (indic.) in the direct disc.; to what tense is it changed in the indir.? see (806).

440.—¹ Depon. particip.; mod. the *subj.* hostes contained in **fecerunt**; see (840). ² Causal cum; with peteret and properaret (subj. quisque); these clauses mod. fecerunt; 'since each man sought for himself;' see (350). ³ fecerunt ut profectio videretur; '(the enemy) made their departure seem; literally, 'caused it so that,' etc. ⁴ See 'dat. with adjs.'; (126). ⁵ 'by means of.'

veritus,⁶ quod ⁷ nōndum perspēxerat quā dē causā hostēs discēderent,⁸ exercitum equitātumque castrīs continuit. Rē ab explōrātōribus cōgnitā, prīmā lūce omnem equitātum quī novissimum agmen morārētur mīsit. Hīs Q. Pedium et L. Cottam lēgātōs praefēcit. T. Labiēnum lēgātum cum legiōnibus tribus subsequī iussit. Hī⁹ novissimōs adortī et multa mīlia passuum prōsecūtī māgnam multitūdinem eōrum fugientium¹⁰ concīdērunt, cum¹¹ ab extrēmō agmine,¹² ad quōs ventum erat,¹³ cōnsisterent fortiterque impetum nostrōrum mīlitum sustinērent.

441.—Because Caesar did not know¹ for what reason the enemy had departed,² he decided that he ought³ to keep his army in camp. By seeking⁴ the foremost place on (of) the road they will make their departure seem⁵ very much like flight. Caesar informed Labienus that scouts would be sent forward⁶ at early dawn.

LESSON XCIII.

CHAPTER XII.

Caesar attacks Noviodunum, which surrenders.

442.—Postrīdiē Caesar in fīnēs Suessiōnum quī proximī¹ Rēmīs erant exercitum dūxit et māgnō itinere cōnfectō ² ad

---

⁶ 'fearing.' ⁷ The quod clause mod continuit. ⁸ Indir. question; 'for [what reason the enemy *were departing*.' ⁹ 'the latter;' meaning Labienus and his troops. ¹⁰ Pres particip. mod. eorum, 'of them as they were fleeing.' ¹¹ Causal cum with consisterent and sustinerent. ¹² 'those in (from) the extreme rear.' ¹³ Impersonal: 'whom they (our men) overtook,' literally, 'to whom it had been come'; sec (365), example 2.

441.—¹ Imperf. indic. ² Why a *different tense* from that in the text? ³ Recast in the *pass.*, ' that his army ought to be kept by him'; this is explained *fully* in (361, 362, 363): look up the Latin text for example 3 under, 'dat. of personal agent.' ⁴ Gerundive; see (253). ⁵ Why a *different tense* from that in the text ? ⁶ This fut. infin. *pass.* (in O. O.) is expressed by the periphrasis 'it would be that scouts would be sent'; see (382).

442.—¹ Adj. in the pred. nom. followed by the *dat.*; see (126). ² 'by making a *forced march.*'

oppidum Noviodūnum contendit. Id³ ex itinere oppūgnāre cōnātus, quod⁴ vacuum ab dēfēnsōribus esse audiēbat, propter lātitūdinem fossae mūrīque altitūdinem paucīs⁵ dēfendentibus expūgnāre nōn potuit. Castrīs mūnītīs vīneās agere⁶ quae'que ad oppūgnandum ūsuī⁸ erant comparāre coepit. Iuterim omnis ex fugā⁹ Suessiōnum multitūdō in oppidum proximā nocte convēnit. Celeriter vīneīs ad oppidum āctīs,¹⁰ aggere¹¹ iactō turribusque cōnstitūtīs, māgnitūdine¹² operum quae Gallī neque vīderant ante neque audierant et celeritāte Rōmānōrum permōtī¹³ lēgātōs ad Caesarem dē dēditiōne mittunt.

443.—Although¹ Caesar had heard that the town² had³ a few defenders, the townsmen were able to prevent⁴ him from taking⁵ it by storm. When⁶ the Suessiones came into the town on the next night and⁷ saw the agger and the towers, they were greatly alarmed and decided that they ought to⁸ ask for peace. Certain of⁹ the Gauls said they feared¹⁰ that they could not persuade¹¹ Caesar to make peace.

---

³ id (oppidum): obj. of oppugnare, 'having tried to attack that town immediately after the march.' ⁴ Acc. subj. of esse, 'which he heard was free.' ⁵ See 'abl. absol.'; (864), example 3; 'although (only) a few were defending it.' ⁶ agere and comparare joined by que, follow coepit: 'he began to bring up the vineae and to procure.' ⁷ Subj. of erant; its anteced. is ea, the obj. of comparare. ⁸ Dat. of purpose; 'useful' ('for a use'). ⁹ ex fuga: 'in their flight.' ¹⁰ 'after the vineae had been quickly brought up.' ¹¹ Noun from agger; abl. absol. with iacto (from iacio). ¹² magnitudine et celeritate : abls. of cause mod. permoti; 'being greatly alarmed by the greatness of the works and by the speed.' ¹³ P. p. p. mod. the subject implied in mittunt.

443.—¹ Concessive cum; see (350). ² Dat. of possession; see (357). ³ erant. ⁴ deterrere. ⁵ See (870): will you use ne or quin ? 'taking (it) by storm' = one word, expugno. ⁶ postquam; see (358). ⁷ Position of que ? ⁸ Recast in the pass., 'peace ought to be asked for by them'; see (861, 362, 368). ⁹ See (378), 'partitive gen., exceptions.' ¹⁰ se vereri. ¹¹ 'that not—after verbs of fear'; see (343) (sequence following dixerunt): 'could persuade', use proper mood and tense of possum with the infin. persuadere; also see (845).

LESSON XCIV.
CHAPTER XIII.

Hearing of Caesar's approach, the Bellovaci surrender.

444.—Caesar obsidibus' acceptīs prīmīs cīvitātis atque ipsīus² Galbae rēgis duōbus fīliīs, armīsque omnibus ex oppidō trāditīs, in dēditiōnem Suessiōnēs accēpit exercitumque in³ Bellovacōs dūcit. Quī⁴ cum sē suaque omnia in oppidum Bratuspantium contulissent atque ab eō oppidō Caesar cum exercitū circiter mīlia⁵ passuum quīnque abesset, omnēs māiōrēs⁶ nātū ex oppidō ēgressī⁷ manūs ad Caesarem tendere et vōce sīgnificāre⁸ coepērunt, sēsē in ēius fidem ac potestātem venīre⁹ neque¹⁰ contrā populum Rōmānum armīs contendere. Item cum¹¹ ad oppidum accessisset castraque ibi pōneret, puerī mulierēsque ex mūrō passīs manibus suō mōre pācem ab Rōmānīs¹² petiērunt.

445.—Caesar received the foremost men of the state as hostages and did not put to death¹ the people. Then he started² for³ the territories of the Bellovaci, who, having learned⁴ that Caesar was coming, gathered⁵ in the town (of)

444.—¹ Apposition with primis and filiis, the two main words forming the basis of the abl. absol., 'the foremost ... and two sons ... having been received'; translate, 'after receiving as hostages the foremost men of,' etc. ² Intensive pron. emphasizing Galbae, 'of King Galba himself.' ³ 'against.' ⁴ Rel. at the begin. of the sent. as a *connective*; incorporate qui in the cum clause. '*now* after these had carried ... and while Caesar was distant.' ⁵ 'Acc. of extent in space,' see (842). ⁶ maiores natu, literally, 'greater by birth,' 'all the elders (older men).' ⁷ Although modifying maiores (*nom. subj.*), it is translated by a co-ordinate verb, 'came forth and began.' ⁸ voce significare : 'to declare.' ⁹ In a fut. sense: 'that they would put themselves under his protection,' etc. ¹⁰ 'and not.' ¹¹ '*after* he had come near ... and *while* he was pitching;' see note 4. ¹² ab Romanis petierunt, 'asked the Romans for peace,' 'begged peace of the Romans.'

445.—¹ 'put to death' = interficio : 'and not' = *one word* in Latin. ² proficiscor. ³ in + acc. ⁴ Recast (why?) in the pass.; 'the arrival of C. having been learned of.' ⁵ confero + se.

Bratuspantium. The older men came[6] out of the town and placed their state under[7] Caesar's protection; likewise the women and children[8] extended[9] their hands from (off) the wall and begged peace *of* him.

LESSON XCV.

CHAPTER XIV.

Divitiacus pleads in behalf of the Bellovaci.

446.—Prō[1] hīs Dīvitiācus dīcit: 'Bellovacī omnī tempore[2] in fidē atque amīcitiā cīvitātis Aeduae fuērunt; impulsī[3] ā suīs prīncipibus, quī dīcēbant[4] Aeduōs omnīs indīgnitātēs contumēliāsque perferre,[5] et[6] ab Aeduīs dēfēcērunt et populō Rōmānō[7] bellum intulērunt. Eī quī ēius cōnsiliī prīncipēs fuērunt, quod cīvitātī māgnam calamitātem intulerant, in Britanniam profūgērunt. Petunt[8] nōn sōlum Bellovacī sed etiam prō hīs Aeduī ut[9] tuā clēmentiā,[10] ac mānsuētūdine in eōs ūtāris. Quod[11] sī fēceris,[12] Aeduōrum auctōritātem apud omnēs Belgās amplificābis, quōrum auxiliīs[13] atque opibus, sī quā[14] bella incidērunt, sustentāre cōnsuērunt.'

447.—The Bellovaci had been urged[1] on by their chiefs to make[2] war upon the Roman people. Those who were

---

[6] Turn into a particip. (see text) and omit 'and.' [7] in + acc. [8] pueri. [9] Perf. indic. act. of tendo.

446.—[1] 'in behalf of.' [2] 'always.' [3] P. p. p. *nom. plur.*; mod. the subject contained in defecerunt and intulerunt; 'being urged on, they (the Bellovaci) both revolted.' [4] 'kept saying.' [5] 'that the Aedui *were enduring*.' [6] 'both.' [7] See (337). [8] Note the emphatic position of the verb. [9] ut . . . utaris; following petunt; 'not only the Bellovaci beg . . . *you to exercise*.' [10] Abl. with the depon. utor; see (353). [11] quod: obj. of feceris; 'now . . . this,' see (367). [12] Fut. perf. in a more viv. fut. condition; 'if you do (will have done), see (228). [13] Abl. of means, mod. sustentare; 'by whose aid and assistance.' [14] quis (465) is used as the indef. pron. 'any—some,' *after* si, nisi, ne, num.

447.—[1] impello. [2] ut + subjunc. (sequence?): inferre bellum + dat.

the chiefs in (of) this design brought³ great disaster upon their state. Divitiacus informed Caesar that those who were⁴ the leaders in this design had brought great disaster upon the state. Because Caesar knew for what reason⁵ they had done⁶ these things, he exercised⁷ his usual clemency toward⁸ the Bellovaci.

---

³ Again inferre, which takes the *acc.* and *dat.* ⁴ In a *past* sense = 'had been'; the subord. verb in O. O. goes in what mood? see (806). ⁵ 'for what reason,' qua de causa. ⁶ 'indir. quest.'; verb in what mood? see (818); sequence? ⁷ utor + abl. ⁸ in + acc.

C. IULĪ CAESARIS
DĒ BELLŌ GALLICŌ.

LIBER SECUNDUS.

Formation by the Belgae of a league against Caesar.

I. Cum esset Caesar in citeriōre Galliā in hībernīs, ita utī suprā dēmōnstrāvimus, crēbrī ad eum rūmōrēs afferēbantur, litterīsque item Labiēnī certior fīēbat omnēs Belgās, quam tertiam esse Galliae partem dīxerāmus, contrā populum Rōmānum coniūrāre obsidēsque inter sē dare. 5 Coniūrandī hās esse causās: prīmum quod verērentur nē omnī pācātā Galliā ad eōs exercitus noster addūcerētur; deinde quod ab nōnnūllīs Gallīs sollicitārentur, partim quī, ut Germānōs diūtius in Galliā versārī nōluerant, ita populī Rōmānī exercitum hiemāre atque inveterāscere in Galliā 10 molestē ferēbant, partim quī mōbilitāte et levitāte animī novīs imperiīs studēbant; ab nōnnūllīs etiam, quod in Galliā ā potentiōribus atque eīs quī ad condūcendōs hominēs facultātēs habēbant vulgō rēgna occupābantur, quī minus facile eam rem imperiō nostrō cōnsequī poterant. 15

Caesar strengthens his force by the addition of two legions and marches against them.

II. Hīs nūntiīs litterīsque commōtus Caesar duās legiōnēs in citeriōre Galliā novās cōnscrīpsit et initā aestāte, in interiōrem Galliam quī dēdūceret, Quintum Pedium lēgātum mīsit. Ipse, cum prīmum pābulī cōpia esse inciperet,

5 ad exercitum vēnit. Dat negōtium Senonibus reliquīsque Gallīs quī fīnitimī Belgīs erant, utī ea quae apud eōs gerantur cōgnōscant sēque dē hīs rēbus certiōrem faciant. Hī cōnstanter omnēs nūntiāvērunt manūs cōgī, exercitum in ūnum locum condūcī. Tum vērō dubitandum nōn 10 exīstimāvit quīn ad eōs proficīscerētur. Rē frūmentāriā comparātā castra movet diēbusque circiter quīndecim ad fīnēs Belgārum pervenit.

The Remi refuse to enter the league against the Romans and surrender to Caesar.

III. Eō cum dē imprōvīsō celeriusque omnī opīniōne vēnisset, Rēmī quī proximī Galliae ex Belgīs sunt ad eum lēgātōs Iccium et Andecumborium, prīmōs cīvitātis, mīsērunt, quī dīcerent sē suaque omnia in fidem atque in pote-
5 stātem populī Rōmānī permittere; neque sē cum Belgīs reliquīs cōnsēnsisse neque contrā populum Rōmānum coniūrāsse, parātōsque esse et obsidēs dare et imperāta facere et oppidīs recipere et frūmentō cēterīsque rēbus iuvāre; reliquōs omnēs Belgās in armīs esse, Germānōsque quī cis
10 Rhēnum incolant sēsē cum hīs coniūnxisse, tantumque esse eōrum omnium furōrem, ut nē Suessiōnēs quidem, frātrēs cōnsanguineōsque suōs, quī eōdem iūre et īsdem lēgibus ūtantur, ūnum imperium ūnumque magistrātum cum ipsīs habeant, dēterrēre potuerint quīn cum hīs cōnsen-
15 tīrent.

Through the Remi Caesar obtains information as to the number, etc., of the enemies' forces.

IV. Cum ab hīs quaereret quae cīvitātēs quantaeque in armīs essent et quid in bellō possent, sīc reperiēbat: plērōsque Belgās esse ortōs ab Germānīs, Rhēnumque antīquitus trāductōs propter locī fertilitātem ibi cōnsēdisse, Gallōs-

que quī eu loca incolerent expulisse, sōlōsque esse quī 5
patrum nostrōrum memoriā, omnī Galliā vexātā, Teutonōs
Cimbrōsque intrā fīnīs suōs ingredī prohibuerint; quā ex
rē fierī ūtī eārum rērum memoriā māgnam sibi auctōritātem māgnōsque spīritūs in rē mīlitārī sūmerent. Dē
numerō eōrum omnia sē habēre explōrāta Rēmī dīcēbant, 10
proptereā quod propīnquitātibus affīnitātibusque coniūnctī,
quantam quisque multitūdinem in commūnī Belgārum
conciliō ad id bellum pollicitus sit, cōgnōverint. Plūrimum inter eōs Bellovacōs et virtūte et auctōritāte et hominum numerō valēre; hōs posse cōnficere armāta mīlia cen- 15
tum, pollicitōs ex eō numerō ēlēcta sexāgintā, tōtīusque
bellī imperium sibi postulāre. Suessiōnēs suōs esse fīnitimōs; fīnīs lātissimōs ferācissimōsque agrōs possidēre.
Apud eōs fuisse rēgem nostrā etiam memoriā Dīvitiācum,
tōtīus Galliae potentissimum, quī cum māgnae partis 20
hārum regiōnum tum etiam Britanniae imperium obtinuerit; nunc esse rēgem Galbam: ad hunc propter iūstitiam
prūdentiamque suam summam tōtīus bellī omnium voluntāte dēferrī; oppida habēre numerō XII, pollicērī mīlia
armāta quīnquāgintā; totidem Nerviōs, quī māximē ferī 25
inter ipsōs habeantur longissimēque absint; quīndecim
mīlia Atrebātēs, Ambiānōs decem mīlia, Morinōs XXV
mīlia, Menapiōs VII mīlia, Caletōs X mīlia, Veliocassēs et
Viromanduōs totidem, Aduatucōs decem et novem mīlia;
Condrūsōs, Eburōnēs, Caeroesōs, Paemānōs, quī ūnō 30
nōmine Germānī appellantur, arbitrārī ad XL mīlia

After receiving hostages from the Remi Caesar crosses the Axona on his way to meet the Belgae.

V. Caesar Rēmōs cohortātus līberāliterque ōrātiōne prō-
secūtus, omnem senātum ad sē convenīre prīncipumque
līberōs obsidēs ad sē addūcī iussit. Quae omnia ab hīs

dīligenter ad diem facta sunt. Ipse Dīvitiācum Aeduum
5 māgnopere cohortātus docet quantō opere reī pūblicae
commūnisque salūtis intersit manūs hostium distinērī, nē
cum tantā multitūdine ūnō tempore cōnflīgendum sit. Id
fierī posse, sī suās cōpiās Aeduī in fīnēs Bellovacōrum
intrōdūxerint et eōrum agrōs populārī coeperint. Hīs
10 mandātīs eum ā sē dīmittit. Postquam omnīs Belgārum
cōpiās in ūnum locum coāctās ad sē venīre vīdit, neque
iam longē abesse ab eīs quōs mīserat explōrātōribus et ab
Rēmīs cōgnōvit, flūmen Axonam, quod est in extrēmīs Rēmōrum fīnibus, exercitum trādūcere mātūrāvit atque ibi
15 castra posuit. Quae rēs et latus ūnum castrōrum rīpīs
flūminis mūniēbat et post eum quae essent tūta ab hostibus
reddēbat, et commeātūs ab Rēmīs reliquīsque cīvitātibus
ut sine perīculō ad eum portārī possent efficiēbat. In eō
flūmine pōns erat. Ibi praesidium pōnit et in alterā parte
20 flūminis Quintum Titūrium Sabīnum lēgātum cum sex
cohortibus relinquit; castra in altitūdinem pedum duodecim vāllō fossāque duodēvīgintī pedum mūnīre iubet.

*The Belgae attack Bibrax. The way in which the Belgae
lay siege to a town.*

VI. Ab hīs castrīs oppidum Rēmōrum nōmine Bibrax
aberat mīlia passuum octō. Id ex itinere māgnō impetū
Belgae oppūgnāre coepērunt. Aegrē eō diē sustentātum
est. Gallōrum eadem atque Belgārum oppūgnātiō est
5 haec. Ubi circumiectā multitūdine hominum tōtīs moenibus undique in mūrum lapidēs iacī coeptī sunt mūrusque
dēfēnsōribus nūdātus est, testūdine factā portās succēdunt
mūrumque subruunt. Quod tum facile fīēbat. Nam cum
tanta multitūdō lapidēs āc tēla cōnicerent, in mūrō cōn-
10 sistendī potestās erat nūllī. Cum fīnem oppūgnandī nox
fēcisset, Iccius Rēmus summā nōbilitāte et grātiā inter

suōs, quī tum oppidō praefuerat, ūnus ex eīs quī lēgātī dē pāce ad Caesarem vēnerant, nūntium ad eum mittit: nisi subsidium sibi submittātur, sēsē diūtius sustinēre nōn posse. 15

When Caesar sends aid to the Remi, the Belgae abandon the siege and turn against him.

VII. Eō dē mediā nocte Caesar īsdem ducibus ūsus quī nūntiī ab Icciō vēnerant, Numidās et Crētās sagittāriōs et funditōrēs Baleārēs subsidiō oppidānīs mittit; quōrum adventū et Rēmīs cum spē dēfēnsiōnis studium prōpūgnandī accessit, et hostibus eādem dē causā spēs potiundī 5 oppidī discessit. Itaque paulisper apud oppidum morātī agrōsque Rēmōrum dēpopulātī, omnibus vīcīs aedificiīsque quōs adīre potuerant incēnsīs, ad castra Caesaris omnibus cōpiīs contendērunt et ab mīlibus passuum minus duōbus castra posuērunt; quae castra, ut fūmō atque īgnibus 10 sīgnificābātur, amplius mīlibus passuum octō in lātitūdinem patēbant.

Caesar prepares strong defences upon a hill near the Axona and awaits the enemies' attack.

VIII. Caesar prīmō et propter multitūdinem hostium et propter eximiam opīniōnem virtūtis proeliō supersedēre statuit : cotīdiē tamen equestribus proeliīs quid hostis virtūte posset et quid nostrī audērent perīclitābātur. Ubi nostrōs nōn esse īnferiōrēs intellēxit, locō prō castrīs ad 5 aciem īnstruendam nātūrā opportūnō atque idōneō,—quod is collis, ubi castra posita erant, paululum ex plānitiē ēditus tantum adversus in lātitūdinem patēbat, quantum locī aciēs īnstrūcta occupāre poterat, atque ex utrāque parte lateris dēiectūs habēbat et in frontem lēniter fastīgā- 10 tus paulātim ad plānitiem redībat,—ab utrōque latere eius

collis trānsversam fossam obdūxit circiter passuum quadringentōrum et ad extrēmās fossās castella cōnstituit ibique tormenta collocāvit, nē, cum aciem īnstrūxisset, hostēs,
15 quod tantum multitūdine poterant, ab lateribus pūgnantēs suōs circumvenīre possent. Hōc factō duābus legiōnibus quās proximē cōnscrīpserat in castrīs relictīs, ut, sī quō opus esset, subsidiō dūcī possent, reliquās sex legiōnēs prō castrīs in aciē cōnstituit. Hostēs item suās cōpiās ex
20 castrīs ēductās īnstrūxerant.

The enemy attempt to cross the river in an effort to surprise Titurius.

IX. Palūs erat nōn māgna inter nostrum atque hostium exercitum. Hanc sī nostrī trānsīrent hostēs exspectābant; nostrī autem, sī ab illīs initium trānseundī fieret, ut impedītōs aggrederentur parātī in armīs erant. Interim
5 proeliō equestrī inter duās aciēs contendēbātur. Ubi neutrī trānseundī initium faciunt, secuudiōre equitum proeliō nostrīs Caesar suōs in castra redūxit. Hostēs prōtinus ex eō locō ad flūmen Axonam contendērunt, quod esse post nostra castra dēmōnstrātum est. Ibi vadīs
10 repertīs partem suārum cōpiārum trādūcere cōnātī sunt, eō cōnsiliō ut, sī possent, castellum cui praeerat Quintus Titūrius lēgātus expūgnārent pontemque interscinderent; sī minus potuissent, agrōs Rēmōrum populārentur, quī māgnō nōbīs ūsuī ad bellum gerendum erant, commeātūque
15 nostrōs prohibērent.

A fierce battle ensues in which the Belgae are defeated and dispersed.

X. Caesar certior factus ab Titūriō omnem equitātum et levis armātūrae Numidās, funditōrēs sagittāriōsque pontem trādūcit atque ad eōs contendit. Ācriter in eō locō pūgnātum est. Hostēs impedītōs nostrī in flūmine aggressī māgnum cōrum numerum occīdērunt; per eōrum corpora reliquōs audācissimē trānsīre cōnantēs multitūdine tēlōrum reppulērunt; prīmōs, quī trānsierant, equitātū circumventōs interfēcērunt. Hostēs ubi et dē expūgnandō oppidō et dē flūmine trānseundō spem sē fefellisse intellēxērunt, neque nostrōs in locum inīquiōrem prōgredī pūgnandī causā vīdērunt, atque ipsōs rēs frūmentāria dēficere coepit, conciliō convocātō cōnstituērunt optimum esse domum suam quemque revertī, et, quōrum in fīnēs prīmum Rōmānī exercitum intrōdūxissent, ad eōs dēfendendōs undique convenīrent, ut potius in suīs quam in aliēnīs fīnibus dēcertārent et domesticīs cōpiīs reī frūmentāriae ūterentur. Ad eam sententiam cum reliquīs causīs haec quoque ratiō eōs dēdūxit, quod Dīvitiācum atque Aeduōs fīnibus Bellovacōrum appropīnquāre cōgnōverant. Hīs persuādērī ut diūtius morārentur neque suīs auxilium ferrent nōn poterat.

The Romans pursue and slaughter large numbers of the Belgae.

XI. Eā rē cōnstitūtā secundā vigiliā māgnō cum strepitū ac tumultū castrīs ēgressī nūllō certō ōrdine neque imperiō, cum sibi quisque prīmum itineris locum peteret et domum pervenīre properāret, fēcērunt ut cōnsimilis fugae profectiō vidērētur. Hāc rē statim Caesar per speculātōrēs cōgnitā, īnsidiās veritus, quod quā dē causā discēderent nōndum perspēxerat, exercitum equitātumque castrīs continuit. Prīmā lūce cōnfīrmātā rē ab explōrātōribus, omnem equitātum quī novissimum agmen morārētur praemīsit. Hīs Quintum Pedium et Lucium Aurunculēium Cottam lēgātōs praefēcit; Titum Labiēnum lēgātum cum legiōnibus tribus subsequī iussit. Hī novissimōs adortī et multa mīlia passuum prōsecūtī māgnam multitūdinem eōrum fugientium concīdērunt, cum ab extrēmō agmine, ad quōs ventum erat, cōnsisterent fortiterque impetum nostrōrum mīlitum sustinērent, priōrēs, quod abesse ā perīculō vidērentur neque ūllā necessitāte neque imperiō continērentur, exaudītō clāmōre perturbātīs ōrdinibus omnēs in fugā sibi praesidium pōnerent. Ita sine ūllō perīculō tantam eōrum multitūdinem nostrī interfēcērunt, quantum fuit diēī spatium, sub occāsumque sōlis sequī dēstitērunt, sēque in castra, ut erat imperātum, recēpērunt.

After a forced march Caesar attacks Noviodunum and the town surrenders.

XII. Postrīdiē ēius diēī Caesar, priusquam sē hostēs ex terrōre ac fugā reciperent, in fīnīs Suessiōnum quī proximī Rēmīs erant exercitum dūxit et māgnō itinere cōnfectō ad oppidum Noviodūnum contendit. Id ex itinere oppūgnāre cōnātus, quod vacuum ab dēfēnsōribus esse audiēbat, propter lātitūdinem fossae mūrīque altitūdinem paucīs dēfendentibus expūgnāre nōn potuit. Castrīs mūnītīs vīneās agere quaeque ad oppūgnandum ūsuī erant comparāre coepit. Interim omnis ex fugā Suessiōnum multitūdō in oppidum proximā nocte convēnit. Celeriter vīneīs ad oppidum āctīs, aggere iactō turribusque cōnstitūtīs, māgnitūdine operum, quae neque vīderant ante Gallī neque audierant, et celeritāte Rōmānōrum permōtī, lēgātōs ad Caesarem dē dēditiōne mittunt et petentibus Rēmīs ut cōnservārentur impetrant.

When the Bellovaci learn of Caesar's approach, they too submit.

XIII. Caesar obsidibus acceptīs prīmīs cīvitātis atque ipsīus Galbae rēgis duōbus fīliīs, armīsque omnibus ex oppidō trāditīs, in dēditiōnem Suessiōnēs accēpit exercitumque in Bellovacōs dūcit. Quī cum sē suaque omnia in oppidum Bratuspantium contulissent, atque ab eō oppidō Caesar cum exercitū circiter mīlia passuum quīnque abesset, omnēs māiōrēs nātū ex oppidō ēgressī manūs ad Caesarem tendere et vōce sīgnificāre coepērunt sēsē in ēius fidem et potestātem venīre neque contrā populum Rōmānum armīs contendere. Item, cum ad oppidum accessisset castraque ibi pōneret, puerī mulierēsque ex mūrō passīs manibus suō mōre pācem ab Rōmānīs petiērunt.

Divitiacus pleads in behalf of the Bellovaci.

XIV. Prō hīs Dīvitiācus (nam post discessum Belgārum dīmīssīs Aeduōrum cōpiīs ad eum reverterat) facit verba: Bellovacōs omnī tempore in fidē atque amīcitiā cīvitātis Aeduae fuisse; impulsōs ab suīs prīncipibus, quī dīcerent Aeduōs ā Caesare in servitūtem redāctōs omnīs indīgnitātēs contumēliāsque perferre, et ab Aeduīs dēfēcisse et populō Rōmānō bellum intulisse. Quī ēius cōnsiliī prīncipēs fuissent, quod intellegerent quantam calamitātem cīvitātī intulissent, in Britanniam profūgisse. Petere nōn sōlum Bellovacōs sed etiam prō hīs Aeduōs ut suā clēmentiā ac mānsuētūdine in eōs ūtātur. Quod sī fēcerit, Aeduōrum auctōritātem apud omnēs Belgās amplificātūrum, quōrum auxiliīs atque opibus, sī qua bella inciderint, sustentāre cōnsuērint.

Caesar spares the Bellovaci and demands hostages.
Character and habits of the Nervii.

XV. Caesar honōris Dīvitiācī atque Aeduōrum causā sēsē eōs in fidem receptūrum et cōnservātūrum dīxit; quod erat cīvitās māgnā inter Belgās auctōritāte atque

hominum multitūdine praestābat, sexcentōs obsidēs popo-
5 scit. Hīs trāditīs omnibusque armīs ex oppidō collātīs,
ab eō locō in fīnīs Ambiānōrum pervēnit, quī sē suaque
omnia sine morā dēdidērunt. Eōrum fīnīs Nerviī attin-
gēbant ; quōrum dē nātūrā mōribusque Caesar cum quaereret, sīc reperiēbat: Nūllum aditum esse ad eōs mercā-
10 tōribus ; nihil patī vīnī reliquārumque rērum ad lūxuriam
pertinentium īnferrī, quod eīs rēbus relanguēscere animōs
et remittī virtūtem exīstimārent; esse hominēs ferōs mā-
gnaeque virtūtis ; increpitāre atque incūsāre reliquōs
Belgās, quī sē populō Rōmānō dēdidissent patriamque vir-
15 tūtem prōiēcissent; cōnfīrmāre sēsē neque lēgātōs mīssūrōs
neque ūllam condiciōnem pācis acceptūrōs.

*The Nervii encamp on the Sabis and await the approach
of Caesar.*

XVI. Cum per eōrum fīnēs trīduum iter fēcisset, inve-
niēbat ex captīvīs Sabim flūmen ab castrīs suīs nōn amplius
mīlia passuum x abesse: trāns id flūmen omnēs Nerviōs
cōnsēdisse adventumque ibi Rōmānōrum exspectāre ūnā
5 cum Atrebātibus et Viromanduīs, fīnitimīs suīs (nam hīs
utrīsque persuāserant utī eandem bellī fortūnam experī-
rentur); exspectārī etiam ab hīs Aduatucōrum cōpiās
atque esse in itinere: mulierēs quīque per aetātem ad
pūgnam inūtilēs vidērentur in eum locum coniēcisse, quō
10 propter palūdēs exercituī aditus nōn esset.

*Urged on by deserters from the Roman army the Nervii
plan to attack Caesar's advanced guard.*

XVII. Hīs rēbus cōgnitīs explōrātōrēs centuriōnēsque
praemittit quī locum idōneum castrīs dēligant. Cum ex
dēditīciīs Belgīs reliquīsque Gallīs complūrēs Caesarem

secūtī ūnā iter facerent, quīdam ex hīs, ut posteā ex captīvīs cōgnitum est, eōrum diērum cōnsuētūdine itineris nostrī exercitūs perspectā, nocte ad Nerviōs pervēnērunt atque hīs dēmōnstrārunt inter singulās legiōnēs impedīmentōrum māgnum numerum intercēdere, neque esse quicquam negōtiī, cum prīma legiō in castra vēnisset reliquaeque legiōnēs māgnum spatium abessent, hanc sub sarcinīs adorīrī; quā pulsā impedīmentīsque dīreptīs futūrum ut reliquae contrā cōnsistere nōn audērent. Adiuvābat etiam eōrum cōnsilium quī rem dēferēbant, quod Nerviī antīquitus, cum equitātū nihil possent (neque enim ad hōc tempus eī reī student, sed quicquid possunt, pedestribus valent cōpiīs), quō facilius fīnitimōrum equitātum, sī praedandī causā ad eōs vēnissent, impedīrent, teneris arboribus incīsīs atque īnflexīs crēbrīsque in lātitūdinem rāmīs ēnātīs et rubīs sentibusque interiectīs effēcerant, ut īnstar mūrī hae saepēs mūnīmenta praebērent, quō nōn modo nōn intrārī sed nē perspicī quidem posset. Hīs rēbus cum iter agminis nostrī impedīrētur, nōn omittendum sibi cōnsilium Nerviī exīstimāvērunt.

Location of Caesar's camp. Position of the two armies.

XVIII. Locī nātūra erat haec quem locum nostrī castrīs dēlēgerant. Collis ab summō aequāliter dēclīvis ad flūmen Sabim, quod suprā nōmināvimus, vergēbat. Ab eō flūmine parī acclīvitāte collis nāscēbātur adversus huic et contrārius, passūs circiter ducentōs īnfimus apertus, ab superiōre parte silvestris, ut nōn facile intrōrsus perspicī posset. Intrā eās silvās hostēs in occultō sēsē continēbant; in apertō locō secundum flūmen paucae statiōnēs equitum vidēbantur. Flūminis erat altitūdō circiter pedum trium.

The Romans surprised by the unexpected attack skilfully carried out by the Nervii.

XIX. Caesar equitātū praemīssō subsequēbātur omnibus cōpiīs; sed ratiō ōrdōque agminis aliter sē habēbat ac Belgae ad Nerviōs dētulerant. Nam quod ad hostīs appropīnquābat, cōnsuētūdine suā Caesar sex legiōnēs expedītās ducēbat; post eās tōtīus exercitūs impedīmenta collocārat; inde duae legiōnēs quae proximē cōnscrīptae erant tōtum agmen claudēbant praesidiōque impedīmentīs erant. Equitēs nostrī cum funditōribus sagittāriīsque flūmen trānsgressī cum hostium equitātū proelium commīsērunt. Cum sē illī identidem in silvās ad suōs reciperent et rūrsus ex silvā in nostrōs impetum facerent, neque nostrī longius quam quem ad fīnem porrēcta loca aperta pertinēbant cēdentēs īnsequī audērent. interim legiōnēs sex quae prīmae vēnerant opere dīmēnsō castra mūnīre coepērunt. Ubi prīma impedīmenta nostrī exercitūs ab eīs, quī in silvīs abditī latēbant, vīsa sunt, quod tempus inter eōs committendī proeliī convēnerat, ut intrā silvās aciem ōrdinēsque cōnstituerant atque ipsī sēsē cōnfīrmāverant, subitō omnibus cōpiīs prōvolāvērunt impetumque in nostrōs equitēs fēcērunt. Hīs facile pulsīs et prōturbātīs, incrēdibilī celeritāte ad flūmen dēcucurrērunt, ut paene ūnō tempore et ad silvās et in flūmine et iam in manibus nostrīs hostēs vidērentur. Eādem autem celeritāte adversō colle ad nostra castra atque eōs quī in opere occupātī erant contendērunt.

Conduct of Caesar's soldiers and lieutenants in an emergency.

XX. Caesarī omnia ūnō tempore erant agenda: vēxillum prōpōnendum, quod erat īnsīgne cum ad arma concurrī oportēret, sīgnum tubā dandum, ab opere revocandī milites, qui paulō longius aggeris petendī causā prōcesserant arcessendī, aciēs īnstruenda, milites cohortandī, signum daudum. Quārum rērum māgnam partem temporis brevitās et successus hostium impediēbat. Hīs difficultātibus duae rēs erant subsidiō, scientia atque ūsus mīlitum, quod superiōribus proeliīs exercitātī quid fierī oportēret nōn minus commodē ipsī sibi praescrībere quam ab aliīs docērī poterant, et quod ab opere singulīsque legiōnibus singulōs lēgātōs Caesar discēdere nisi mūnītīs castrīs vetuerat. Hī propter propinquitātem et celeritātem hostium nihil iam Caesaris imperium exspectābant, sed per sē quae vidēbantur administrābant.

So sudden the attack, the soldiers are compelled to begin fighting before they can arm themselves.

XXI. Caesar necessāriīs rēbus imperātīs ad cohortandōs milites quam in partem fors obtulit dēcucurrit, et ad legiōnem decimam dēvēnit. Mīlitēs nōn longiōre ōrātiōne cohortātus quam utī suae prīstinae virtūtis memoriam retinērent neu perturbārentur animō hostiumque impetum fortiter sustinērent, quod nōn longius hostēs aberant quam quō tēlum adigī posset, proeliī committendī signum dedit. Atque in alteram partem item cohortandī causā profectus pūgnantibus occurrit. Temporis tanta fuit exiguitās hostiumque tam parātus ad dīmicandum animus ut nōn modo ad īnsīgnia accommodanda, sed etiam ad galeās induendās scūtīsque tegimenta dētrūdenda tempus dēfuerit. Quam quisque ab opere in partem cāsū dēvēnit quaeque prīma sīgna cōnspēxit, ad haec cōnstitit, nē in quaerendīs suīs pūgnandī tempus dīmitteret.

Confusion on the part of the soldiers. Difficulties encountered by the commander.

XXII. Īnstrūctō exercitū magis ut locī nātūra dēiectusque collis et necessitās temporis quam ut reī mīlitāris ratiō atque ōrdō postulābat, cum dīversae legiōnēs aliae aliā in parte hostibus resisterent, saepibusque dēnsissimīs (ut ante 5 dēmōnstrāvimus) interiectīs prōspectus impedīrētur, neque certa subsidia collocūrī neque quid in quāque parte opus esset prōvidērī neque ab ūnō omnia imperia administrārī poterant. Itaque in tantā rērum inīquitāte fortūnae quoque ēventūs variī sequēbantur.

In one quarter the Romans win; in another they lose.

XXIII. Legiōnis nōnae et decimae mīlitēs, ut in sinistrā parte aciē cōnstiterant, pīlīs ēmīssīs cursū ac lassitūdine exanimātōs vulneribusque cōnfectōs Atrebātēs (nam hīs ea pars obvēnerat) celeriter ex locō superiōre in flūmen com- 5 pulērunt, et trānsīre cōnantēs īnsecūtī gladiīs magnam partem eōrum impedītam interfēcērunt. Ipsī trānsīre flūmen nōn dubitāvērunt et in locum inīquum prōgressī rūrsus resistentēs hostēs redintegrātō proeliō in fugam coniēcērunt. Item aliā in parte dīversae duae legiōnēs, 10 ūndecima et octāva, prōflīgātīs Viromanduīs, quibuscum erant congressī, ex locō superiōre in ipsīs flūminis rīpīs proeliābantur. At tōtīs ferē ā fronte et ab sinistrā parte nūdātīs castrīs, cum in dextrō cornū legiō duodecima et nōn māgnō ab eā intervāllō septima cōnstitisset, omnēs 15 Nerviī cōnfertissimō agmine duce Boduōgnātō, quī summam imperiī tenēbat, ad eum locum contendērunt; quōrum pars apertō latere legiōnēs circumvenīre, pars summum castrōrum locum petere coepit.

The day seems to be going against the Romans. The Nervii gain Caesar's camp.

XXIV. Eōdem tempore equitēs nostrī levisque armātūrae peditēs, quī cum eīs ūnā fuerant, quōs prīmō hostium impetū pulsōs dīxeram, cum sē in castra reciperent, adversīs hostibus occurrēbant ac rūrsus aliam in partem fugam petēbant; et cālōnēs, quī ab decumānā portā et 5 summō iugō collis nostrōs victōrēs flūmen trānsīsse cōnspēxerant, praedandī causā ēgressī, cum respēxissent et hostēs in nostrīs castrīs versārī vīdissent, praecipitēs fugae sēsē mandābant. Simul eōrum quī cum impedīmentīs veniēbant clāmor fremitusque oriēbātur, aliīque aliam in 10 partem perterritī ferēbantur. Quibus omnibus rēbus permōtī equitēs Treverī, quōrum inter Gallōs virtūtis opīniō est singulāris, quī auxiliī causā ab cīvitāte ad Caesarem mīssī vēnerant, cum multitūdine hostium castra complērī nostra, legiōnēs premī et paene circumventās tenērī, 15 cālōnēs, equitēs, funditōrēs, Numidās dīversōs dissipātōsque in omnēs partēs fugere vīdissent, dēspērātīs nostrīs rēbus domum contendērunt; Rōmānōs pulsōs superātōsque, castrīs impedīmentīsque eōrum hostēs potītōs, cīvitātī renūntiāvērunt. 20

Caesar seizes a shield and takes part in the fight in the foremost ranks.

XXV. Caesar ab decimae legiōnis cohortātiōne ad dextrum cornū profectus, ubi suōs urgērī sīgnīsque in ūnum locum collātīs duodecimae legiōnis cōnfertōs mīlitēs sibi ipsōs ad pūgnam esse impedīmentō vīdit, quartae cohortis omnibus centuriōnibus occīsīs sīgniferōque interfectō, 5 sīgnō āmīssō, reliquārum cohortium omnibus ferē centu-

riōnibus aut vulnerātīs aut occīsīs, in hīs prīmipīlō P. Sextiō Baculō, fortissimō virō, multīs gravibusque vulneribus cōnfectō, ut iam sē sustinēre nōn posset; reliquōs esse
10 tardiōrēs et nōnnūllōs ab novissimīs dēsertō proeliō excēdere ac tēla vītāre, hostīs neque ā fronte ex īnferiōre locō subeuntēs intermittere et ab utrōque latere īnstāre, et rem esse in angustō vīdit neque ūllum esse subsidium quod summittī posset; scūtō ab novissimīs ūnī mīlitī dētrāctō,
15 quod ipse eō sine scūtō vēnerat, in prīmam aciem prōcessit centuriōnibusque nōminātim appellātīs reliquōs cohortātus mīlitēs sīgna īnferre et manipulōs laxāre iussit, quō facilius gladiīs ūtī possent. Cūius adventū spē illātā mīlitibus et redintegrātō animō, cum prō sē quisque in cōnspectū im-
20 perātōris etiam in extrēmīs suīs rēbus operam nāvāre cuperet, paulum hostium impetus tardātus est.

Caesar reinforced by the arrival of two legions. The scene begins to change.

XXVI. Caesar cum septimam legiōnem, quae iūxtā cōnstiterat, item urgērī ab hoste vīdisset, tribūnōs mīlitum monuit ut paulātim sēsē legiōnēs coniungerent et conversa sīgna in hostēs īnferrent. Quō factō, cum alius aliī sub-
5 sidium ferret neque timēreut nē āversī ab hoste circumvenīrentur, audācius resistere ac fortius pūgnāre coepērunt. Interim mīlitēs legiōnum duārum quae in novissimō agmine praesidiō impedīmentīs fuerant, proeliō nūntiātō, cursū incitātō in summō colle ab hostibus cōnspiciēbantur, et
10 Titus Labiēnus castrīs hostium potītus et ex locō superiōre quae rēs in nostrīs castrīs gererentur cōnspicātus, decimam legiōnem subsidiō nostrīs mīsit. Quī, cum ex equitum et cālōnum fugā quō in locō rēs esset quantōque in perīculō et castra et legiōnēs et imperātor versārētur cōgnōvissent,
15 nihil ad celeritātem sibi reliquī fēcērunt.

A desperate encounter in which the Romans win.

XXVII. Hōrum adventū tanta rērum commūtātiō est facta ut nostrī, etiam quī vulneribus cōnfectī prōcubuissent, scūtīs innīxī proelium redintegrārent. Tum cālōnēs perterritōs hostēs cōnspicātī etiam inermēs armātīs occurrērunt; equitēs vērō, ut turpitūdinem fugae virtūte dēlē- 5
rent, omnibus in locīs pūgnārunt, quō sē legiōnāriīs mīlitibus praeferrent. At hostēs etiam in extrēmā spē salūtis tantam virtūtem praestitērunt ut, cum prīmī eōrum cecidissent, proximī iacentibus īnsisterent atque ex eōrum corporibus pūgnārent; hīs dēiectīs et coacervātīs cadūveribus, 10
quī superessent ut ex tumulō tēla in nostrōs cōnicerent et pīla intercepta remitterent: ut nōn nēquīquam tantae virtūtis hominēs iūdicārī dēbēret ausōs esse trānsīre lātissimum flūmen, ascendere altissimās rīpās, subīre inīquissimum locum ; quae facilia ex difficillimīs animī māgnitūdō 15
redēgerat.

Terrible fate of the Nervii. Pardon for the few that survive.

XXVIII. Hōc proeliō factō et prope ad internecionem gente ac nōmine Nerviōrum redāctō, māiōrēs nātū, quōs ūnā cum puerīs mulieribusque in aestuāria et palūdēs coniectōs dīxerāmus, hāc pūgnā nūntiātā, cum victōribus nihil impedītum, victīs nihil tūtum arbitrārentur, omnium 5
quī supererant cōnsēnsū lēgātōs ad Caesarem mīsērunt sēque eī dēdidērunt ; et, in commemorandā cīvitātis calamitāte, ex sexcentīs ad trēs senātōrēs, ex hominum mīlibus LX vix ad quīngentōs quī arma ferre possent sēsē redāctōs esse dīxērunt. Quōs Caesar, ut in miserōs ac 10
supplicēs ūsus misericordiā vidērētur, dīligentissimē cōnservāvit, suīsque fīnibus atque oppidīs ūtī iussit, et

fīnitimīs imperāvit ut ab iniūriā et maleficiō sē suōsque prohibērent.

Caesar next lays siege to a stronghold in which the Aduatuci have gathered.

XXIX. Aduatucī, dē quibus suprā scrīpsimus, cum omnibus cōpiīs auxiliō Nerviīs venīrent, hāc pūgnā nūntiātā ex itinere domum revertērunt; cūnctīs oppidīs castellīsque dēsertīs sua omnia in ūnum oppidum ēgregiē 5 nātūrā mūnītum contulērunt. Quod cum ex omnibus in circuitū partibus altissimās rūpēs dēspectūsque habēret, ūnā ex parte lēniter acclīvis aditus in lātitūdinem nōn amplius ducentōrum pedum relinquēbātur; quem locum duplicī altissimō mūrō mūnierant tum māgnī ponderis 10 saxa et praeacūtās trabēs in mūrō collocābant. Ipsī erant ex Cimbrīs Teutonīsque prōgnātī, quī, cum iter in prōvinciam nostram atque Ītaliam facerent, eīs impedīmentīs quae sēcum agere et portāre nōn poterant citrā flūmen Rhēnum dēpositīs, custōdiam ex suīs ac praesidium sex mīlia homi- 15 num ūnā relīquērunt. Hī post eōrum obitum multōs annōs ā fīnitimīs exagitātī, cum aliās bellum īnferrent aliās illātum dēfenderent, cōnsēnsū eōrum omnium pāce factā hunc sibi domiciliō locum dēlēgērunt.

From the walls they taunt the Romans in their preparations for an attack.

XXX. Ac prīmō adventū exercitūs nostrī crēbrās ex oppidō excursiōnēs faciēbant parvulīsque proeliīs cum nostrīs contendēbant; posteā vāllō passuum in circuitū xv mīlium crēbrīsque castellīs circummūnītī oppidō sēsē con- 5 tinēbant. Ubi vīneīs āctīs aggere exstrūctō turrim procul cōnstituī vīdērunt, prīmum irrīdēre ex mūrō atque increpitāre vōcibus, quod tanta māchinātiō ab tantō spatiō īnstruerētur: quibusnam manibus aut quibus vīribus praesertim hominēs tantulae statūrae (nam plērumque omnibus Gallīs prae māgnitūdine corporum suōrum brevi- 10 tās nostra contemptuī est) tantī oneris turrim mōtūrōs sēsē cōnfīderent?

Soon they lose heart and ask of Caesar his terms of surrender.

XXXI. Ubi vērō movērī et appropinquāre moenibus vīdērunt, novā atque inūsitātā speciē commōtī lēgātōs ad Caesarem dē pāce mīsērunt, quī ad hunc modum locūtī: nōn exīstimāre Rōmānōs sine ope dīvīnā bellum gerere, quī tantae altitūdinis māchinātiōnēs tantā celeritāte prō- 5 movēre possent, sē suaque omnia eōrum potestātī permittere dīxērunt. Ūnum petere et dēprecārī: sī forte prō suā clēmentiā ac mānsuētūdine, quam ipsī ab aliīs audīrent, statuisset Aduatucōs esse cōnservandōs, nē sē armīs dēspoliāret. Sibi omnēs ferē fīnitimōs esse inimīcōs 10 ac suae virtūtī invidēre; ā quibus sē dēfendere trāditīs armīs nōn possent. Sibi praestāre, sī in eum cāsum dēdūcerentur, quamvīs fortūnam ā populō Rōmānō patī quam ab hīs per cruciātum interficī inter quōs domināri cōnsuēssent. 15

They are promised protection if they disarm. Treachery on the side of the Nervii.

XXXII. Ad haec Caesar respondit: Sē magis cōnsuētūdine suā quam meritō eōrum cīvitātem cōnservātūrum, sī prius, quam mūrum ariēs attigisset, sē dēdidissent; sed dēditiōnis nūllam esse condiciōnem nisi armīs trāditīs. Sē

5 id quod in Nerviīs fēcisset factūrum, fīnitimīsque imperātūrum nē quam dēditīciīs populī Rōmānī iniūriam īnferrent. Rē nūntiātā ad suōs, quae imperārentur facere dīxērunt. Armōrum māgnā multitūdine dē mūrō in fossam quae erat ante oppidum iactā, sīc ut prope summam
10 mūrī aggerisque altitūdinem acervī armōrum adaequārent, et tamen circiter parte tertiā, ut posteā perspectum est, cēlātā atque in oppidō retentā, portīs patefactīs eō diē pāce sunt ūsī.

The enemies' plans fail to carry and they meet a terrible fate.

XXXIII. Sub vesperum Caesar portās claudī mīlitēsque ex oppidō exīre iussit, nē quam noctū oppidānī ab mīlitibus iniūriam acciperent. Illī, ante initō (ut intellēctum est) cōnsiliō, quod dēditiōne factā nostrōs praesidia dēduc-
5 tūrōs aut dēnique indīligentius servātūrōs crēdiderant, partim cum eīs quae retinuerant et cēlāverant armīs, partim scūtīs ex cortice factīs aut vīminibus intextīs, quae subitō, ut temporis exiguitās postulābat, pellibus indūxerant, tertiā vigiliā, quā minimē arduus ad nostrās mūnī-
10 tiōnēs ascēnsus vidēbātur, omnibus cōpiīs repentīnō ex oppidō ēruptiōnem fēcērunt. Celeriter, ut ante Caesar imperārat, īgnibus sīgnificātiōne factā, ex proximīs castellīs eō concursum est, pūgnātumque ab hostibus ita ācriter est, ut ā virīs fortibus in extrēmā spē salūtis, inīquō locō,
15 contrā eōs quī ex vāllō turribusque tēla iacerent, pūgnārī dēbuit, cum in ūnā virtūte omnis spēs salūtis cōnsisteret. Occīsīs ad hominum mīlibus quattuor reliquī in oppidum reiectī sunt. Postrīdiē ēius diēī refrāctīs portīs, cum iam dēfenderet nēmō, atque intrōmīssīs mīlitibus nostrīs, sec-
20 tiōnem ēius oppidī ūniversam Caesar vēndidit. Ab eīs

quī ēmerant capitum numerus ad eum relātus est mīlium
quīnquāgintā trium.

The maritime nations submit to the Romans.

XXXIV. Eōdem tempore ā Publiō Crassō, quem cum
legiōne ūnā mīserat ad Venetōs, Venellōs, Osismōs, Curio-
solitas, Esubiōs, Aulercōs, Redonēs, quae sunt maritimae
cīvitātēs Ōceanumque attingunt, certior factus est omnīs
eās cīvitātēs in diciōnem potestātemque populī Rōmānī 5
esse redāctās.

*Ambassadors come to Caesar from across the Rhine. The
army goes into winter quarters and a thanksgiving is
decreed at Rome.*

XXXV. Hīs rēbus gestīs, omnī Galliā pācātā, tanta
hūius bellī ad barbarōs opīniō perlāta est, utī ab eīs
nātiōnibus quae trāns Rhēnum incolerent lēgātī ad
Caesarem mitterentur, quī sē obsidēs datūrās, imperāta
factūrās pollicērentur. Quās lēgātiōnēs Caesar, quod in 5
Italiam Illyricumque properābat, initā proximā aestāte ad
sē revertī iussit. Ipse in Carnutēs, Andēs, Turonēs, quaeque cīvitātēs propīnquae hīs locīs erant ubi bellum gesse
rat, legiōnibus in hībernācula dēductīs, in Italiam profectus est. Ob eāsque rēs ex litterīs Caesaris in diēs quīn- 10
decim supplicātiō dēcrēta est, quod ante id tempus accidit
nūllī.

TABLE OF ABBREVIATIONS.

abl. absol.	= ablative absolute	lim.	= limit
affirm.	= affirmative	mod.	= modify
agreem.	= agreement	neg.	= negative
appos.	= apposition	p. p.	= perfect participle
condit.	= condition	p. p. p.	= perfect pass. participle
depen.	= depend		
depon.	= deponent	quest.	= question
dir.	= direct	sep.	= separation
disc.	= discourse	subj.	= subject
doub.	= double	subjunc.	= subjunctive
i.e.	= that is	subord.	= subordinate
impers.	= impersonal	substan.	= substantive
indir.	= indirect	syst.	= system
lit.	= literally	viv.	= vivid

NOTES.

BOOK II.

THE CAMPAIGNS OF CAESAR IN GAUL.

Gallia, 'Gaul', as used in Caesar, included the vast region which comprises all of France, the greater part of Switzerland, and the western portion of Germany, with Holland and Belgium.

The campaigns of Caesar in Gaul lasted through eight years (B.C. 58–51), and are described in eight books—each book giving an account of the operations of one year.

In Book I (B.C. 58), after a general description of Gaul, Caesar describes the war with the Helvetians, a tribe of Northern Switzerland numbering over 300,000, who attempted to reach Western Gaul by an armed emigration through central Gaul. Their attempt to pass was checked by Caesar, who, after several skirmishes and two bloody battles, forced the Helvetians to return into their territories with the loss of 200,000 lives. He also tells of an engagement with a powerful tribe of Germans under their chief, Ariovistus, who had settled in Eastern Gaul. These were repulsed and driven back across the Rhine.

Book II (B.C. 57) contains an account of the conspiracy and defeat of the Belgians, a people in Northern Gaul. The Belgians were a fierce and barbarous people living amid forests and swamps far remote from any country reached by the Roman arms. They appear to have formed a powerful confederacy and to have offered to Caesar a most desperate resistance. In a battle, perhaps the most desperate of all that Caesar ever fought, the enemy was defeated and the confederacy of Northern Gaul suppressed, with the almost complete annihilation of the Nervii, the bravest of the Belgian tribe. In this campaign Publius Crassus reduced the maritime states to submission.

CHAPTER I.—1. **cum esset**: 'while Caesar was,' see (128, 203); note the emphatic position of the *verb* **citeriore Gallia**: that is, northern Italy. **ita uti**: 'just as.' 2. **demonstravimus**: the rhetorical *we*. Caesar speaks of himself as the general in the *third* person, as the writer in the *first*. 3. **litteris**: abl. of means, see (43), mod. **certior fiebat**; 'by letters from (of) Labienus.' **que**: joins **afferebantur** and **certior fiebat**, imperf. of *repeated action*, see (102); 'kept coming in and he was informed (from day to day).' **certior**: with *pass.*, see (338). **Belgas**: acc. subj. of **coniurare** and **dare**, depend upon **certior fiebat**; 'that all the Belgians *were* conspiring ;' for the *tense of the infin.*, see (301, 302, 305, 318). **quam**: acc. subj. of **esse**, agreeing with the *pred acc.* **partem**, rather than with **Belgas**, see (373); 'who, we had said, constitute (**esse**) a third part of Gaul.' 4. **esse**: indir. disc. depen. on **dixeramus**, see (301, 302, 318). **dixeramus**: pluperf. denoting what took place before the time of **demonstravimus**. 5. **inter se dare**: 'were exchanging.' **coniurandi**: gen. of the gerund dep. upon **causas**. In the sight of the Romans any war against Rome was a 'conspiracy.' But this uprising of the Belgians was in reality the effort of a spirited people to protect their rights. 6. **esse**: following **certior fiebat**, 'that the reasons for (of) conspiring were *as follows* (has)' **quod vererentur, sollicitarentur**: subjunc. because subord. clau es in indir. disc., see (306); the two **quod** clauses are preceded b primum, 'in the first place,' and **deinde**, 'in the second place'; for the *sequence* of tense, see (135); these subjunctives are dependent upon a *past* verb, **fiebat**. **ne**: 'that' or 'lest,' see (343), *verbs of fear*, etc. 7. **ad eos**: 'against them.' **sollicitarentur**: 'because they were being incited.' 8. **ab Gallis**: pers. agent, see (237). **partim qui**: 'some of whom.' **ut**: introduces **noluerant** (*indic. mood*); the indic. verbs in the remaining part of the chapt. indicate that this is not regarded as part of Labienus's report (which would make the verbs *subjunc. in indir. disc.*), but as explanatory remarks made by Caesar. **ut noluerant**: 'as they had been unwilling.' note the force of the *pluperf*. **Germanos**: acc. subj. of **versari**, following **noluerant**, 'that the Germans should remain.' 9. **ita ferebant moleste**: literally, 'were bearing with trouble ;' freely, 'took it hard.' **populi**: gen. sing. dep. upon **exercitum**. 10. **hiemare, inveterascere**: with the subj. acc. **exercitum** in indir. disc. depending upon **moleste ferebant**; 'that an army of the Roman people was wintering and getting a foothold in Gaul.' 11. **partim qui**: anteced. of **qui** is **Gallis** (line 8); 'some of whom

NOTES TO CAESAR, BOOK II, CH. I, II.   223

were always desiring.' **mobilitate, levitate** : abl. of cause, see **210**) 'on account of inconstancy and fickleness'; the ablatives mod. **studebant. imperiis** : dat. with **studebant**, for which construction see (**348**); 'a new government,' literally, 'new ruling powers.' 12. **ab nonnullis** : pers. agent, mod. **sollicitabantur**, 'they were incited by some *also* (**etiam**),' see (**237**). **quod** : with **occupabantur**, a causal clause, mod. **sollicitabantur** ; 'they were incited also *because* royal power was being (constantly) usurped.' **a potentioribus** : adj. as substan , see (**258**); 'by the more powerful and by those who.' 13. **ad conducendos** : gerundive, see (**253**); 'for hiring.' **facultates** : 'opportunities,' 'means.' 14. **regna** : plur., literally, 'kingdoms'— see translation above as the subj. of **occupabantur**, beginning with **quod. minus** : adv. mod. another adv. **facile**, 'less easily.' **rem** : obj. of **consequi. imperio nostro** : 'under our rule,' abl. absol. implying condition ; the idea is, 'the government being ours,' see (**364**)—2. 15. **consequi poterant** : 'who could secure that or such *power* (**rem**).'

CHAPTER II.—1. **nuntiis, litteris** : abl. of cause, mod. and in the translation *following* **commotus** ; '(being) greatly alarmed by these messages and letters.' **duas legiones** : XIIIth and XIVth. Caesar had now eight legions, numbered VII to XIV, inclusive, amounting to perhaps 60,000 men including auxiliaries. 2 **inita** : p. p. p. of **ineo**, forming an abl. absol of *time* with **aestate**, 'at the beginning of summer'; what literally? see (**287**). **in interiorem Galliam** : see (**35**); 'into the Central part of Gaul.' 3. **qui deduceret** : anteced. is **Q. Pedium**, rel. clause of purpose (**qui = ut is**), see (**311**); sequence derived from **misit**, see (**135**). Pedius, nephew of Caesar and one of his heirs. 4. **ipse** : intensive pron., placed first for special emphasis. 'Caesar himself.' **cum primum** : 'as soon as;' in the early part of May or June ; when grass and young grain began to be plentiful for the numerous beasts of burden carrying military stores as well as for the horses of the cavalry and officers. **inciperet** : ' began ' —subj. is **copia**. 5. **dat** : historical pres., used for the historical perfect to enliven the narrative. **Senonibus, Gallis** : why dat.? see (**330**). 6. **Belgis** : see ' dat. with adjs.,' (**126**). **uti (ut) cognoscant, faciant** : substantive clauses of *purpose* in apposition with, or defining, **negotium** ; observe the *sequence, pres. + pres.* **gerantur** : subjunc. by *attraction*, see (**276**); 'to find out those things which are being 'transacted.' 7. **se** : ' and to inform him (Caesar) ;' if the *subord.* clause expresses the words or thought of the *main* clause, the *reflexive* is used to refer to the subject of the latter. **constanter**: 'uniformly,' without disagreement in the reports. 8. **manus**: acc. subj. of **cogi** (pres. pass. infin.); 'that bands (forces) were being collected.' in **locum**: not *abl.*, but *acc.*, see (35); mod. a verb of *motion*—**conduci**; 'was being gathered.' 9. **tum vero**: observe the emphatic position, 'then indeed.' **dubitandum** (esse sibi): periphrastic *pres. infin. pass.* used impersonally, depen. upon **existimavit**; see (361, 362, 363); literally, 'he thought it ought not to be hesitated by him;' freely, 'he thought he ought not to hesitate.' 10. **quin proficisceretur**: 'to set out' (lit., 'but that he should,' etc.); in the sense of '*hesitate*,' dubito regularly takes the *infin.*, this being an exception; dubito, 'to doubt,' takes quin + *subjunc.* 11. **diebus**: abl. of time within which, see (65); 'in about fifteen days.' **ad fines**: Caesar marched from Vesontio to the Belgian frontier (northwest), about 145 miles, in 15 days.

CHAPTER III.—1. **eo**: 'thither' = **ad fines Belgarum. de improviso**: 'unexpectedly.' **opinione**: abl. after the comparative **celerius**, see (369); 'than any one expected,' lit. 'than all opinion.' 2. **Remi**: they were next to the Aedui in power and were friendly to the Romans. These people were impressed by the decision of Caesar's movements, and, not having committed themselves to the Belgian confederacy, they were free to give Caesar information of the enemies' designs. **ex Belgis**: for the partitive gen. **Belgarum**, see (378); 'who are the nearest *of the Belgians* to Gaul.' 3. **legatos**: predicate apposition; observe that **legatus** sometimes means 'lieutenant,' and sometimes, as here, 'ambassador.' **primos**: adj. used as substant., see (259), in apposition with the proper names preceding it; 'the foremost men.' 4. **qui dicerent**: not 'who said,' but 'who *were to say*' (or simply 'to say'), rel. clause of purpose, see (311). The rest of the chapt. is given in *indir. disc.* Notice that the *principal clauses* have the verbs in the *infin.* with a *subj. acc.*, and all *subord.* or *depend. clauses* take the *subjunc.;* see (301, 302, 306, 318, 392). **se in fidem permittere**: 'that they placed themselves and all their possessions under the protection;' **se** is here the acc. obj. of **permittere**, while the *subj. acc* (**se**) is omitted to prevent awkward repetition; *regularly the subj. acc. is expressed* in *indir. disc.* 5. **neque**: '*and* that they had *not* united (conspired).' **cum Belgis**: see (43). 6. **neque**: '*nor* had they conspired against.' 7. **paratos**: pred. adj. in the *acc.* to agree with the *subj.* of **esse** (**se** understood). **et . . . et**: 'both . . . and.' **oppidis**: sometimes *place where* is put in the abl. *without a prep.*, as with **loco** and castris. 8. frumento, rebus: see (43). 9. esse: indir. disc., 'that all the rest of the Belgians *were* under arms.' Germanos: acc. subj. of coniunxisse. cis Rhenum; i.e. the west side of the Rhine; Caesar writes from the standpoint of the Roman Province. incolant: 'who dwell'—in the *dir. disc.* it is incolunt. 10. his: = Belgis. tantum esse furorem: 'and that the madness of all these *was* so great that (ut).' eorum omnium: i.e. Belgarum et Germanorum. 11. ut . . . potuerint: affirmative result clause, 'that they could prevent'; see (321); observe the *perf. tense,* and note that in clauses of result, the *perf. subjunc.* is very often used after secondary (past) tenses. ne . . . quidem: make emphatic the word between them, '(could prevent) *not even the Suessiones.*' The Suessiones occupied territory west of the Remi. 12. qui utantur, habeant: subjunc. for two reasons; subord. clause in indir. disc., see (306, 392); or by *attraction,* being within the ut clause, see (276). iure, legibus ; abl. with depon. verb utantur, see (353). ius: = 'principles of justice,' lex: = the enacted 'law'; 'who enjoyed the same rights and laws.' 13. cum ipsis: i. e. the Remi; in indir. disc. se is regularly used to refer to the speaker, but the oblique cases of ipse may be used instead, especially for *emphasis.* 14. quin consentirent : 'from uniting;' for construction with quin, see (370).

CHAPTER IV.—1. cum . . . quaereret: 'when Caesar inquired of these' or 'asked these men.' quae, etc.: 'what and how great states *were.*' 2. essent: subjunc. of indir. quest., see (313). quid: 'adverbial acc.,' see (374). reperiebat: imperf. to denote repeated action. plerosque : indir. disc. to the end of the chapt., except the words Remi dicebant (line 10); 'that most of the Belgians were descended from (ab).' These were especially the Nervii and Treveri, who claimed descent from the Germans—a proud and heroic ancestry. 3. que: joins ortos esse and consedisse ; Belgas is the subj. of both verbs. 4. traductos: p. p. p. mod. Belgas; this construction is fully explained in (316). propter . . . fertilitatem: limits consedisse. que: connects consedisse and expulisse, which have the same subj. Gallos: obj. of expulisse ; 'and had driven out the Gauls who inhabited.' 5. incolerent : subord. clause in indir. disc., see (276, 306, 392). solos: acc. pred. adj. with esse, limiting Belgas ; solos is an adj. used as a noun, see (258). qui . . . prohibuerint : subord. clause in indir. disc.; observe the use of the *perf. tense;* see chapt. 3, note 11. ut . . . potuerint. In the dir. disc., solus est, etc., takes a rel. clause with the verb in the *subjunc.,* called the 'characteristic relative clause.' Translate solosque, etc.; 'that they (the Belgians) were the only men who could prevent.' 6. **memoria**: abl. of time when, mod. **prohibuerint**, 'in (during) the memory—remembrance—of our fathers.' **omni**, etc.: translate by a 'when' clause. 7. **ingredi**: depen. upon **prohibuerint**, see (370); 'from entering.' **qua ex re**: 'and in consequence of this fact;' see (367). **fieri**: pass. infin. of **facio**, depen. upon **reperiebat**; 'he found out that it was coming to pass.' 8. **uti ... sumerent**: this clause is the *subj.* of **fieri**; that *what* was coming to pass? viz., 'that they were assuming.' **memoria**: abl. of cause (compare note 6 above), mod. **sumerent**; 'in consequence of their remembrance.' 9. **in re militari**: 'in the art of war.' **de numero**: i.e. the numerical strength of the Belgian soldiery; (the rest of the chapt. depends upon **Remi dicebant**). 10. **omnia ... explorata**: almost = **omnia se exploravisse**, 'that they had found out all *about* (de); agreem. of this particip. and its use with **habere** is fully explained in (375). **propterea quod**: 'on account of the fact that' = 'because,' introducing **cognoverint**, again the *perf. tense*, as in note 5 above. The perf. is very often retained in indir. disc., and a statement is made more vivid by putting it in the tense that the speaker used. The speaker's word was '**cognovimus**,' 'we know' (lit. 'have found out'). 11. **coniuncti**: p. p. p. mod. the subj. of **cognoverint**, see (316); 'because, being closely connected by blood and marriage relationships.' **quantam ... pollicitus sit**: subjunc. of indir. quest., see (313); depen. upon **cognoverint**; 'how great a multitude *each one* (quisque) had promised.' **quisque**: i.e. each representative of the war council. 13. **plurimum valere**: follows **Remi dicebant**; 'that the Bellovaci were the most powerful.' 15. **hos posse**, etc.: 'that the latter (these) could muster.' **armata milia centum** = armatorum hominum milia centum; as here used, **milia** is the noun with which the adj. armata agrees. **pollicitos esse**: 'that they had promised.' 16. **sexaginta (milia) electa**: 'sixty thousand picked men.' **postulare**: '*were* demanding.' **sibi**: refers to **Bellovacos**. 17. **suos**: refers to the **Remi**. **latissimos**: 'very wide.' 18. **possidere**: subj. is **eos (Suessiones)** understood. **fuisse**: 'had been;' in the direct disc. **fuisse** becomes **fuit**. 19. **totius Galliae**, etc.: 'the most influential man in entire Gaul;' **totius** is declined in (286). **qui ... imperium obtinuerit**: 'who *had had* control of.' 20. **cum ... tum**: 'not only ... but also.' **Britanniae**: This is the first notice of Britain in Latin literature. 21. **esse**: 'they said that Galba *was now* king;' the speaker's words (dir. disc.) were '**nunc est rex Galba**'—compare note **fuisse** (line 18) above. **ad hunc**: 'upon this one.' 22. **summam**: *noun*, acc. subj. of **deferri**; 'that the management (conduct) of . . . was being conferred.' 23. **voluntate**: abl. of manner, see (210). **habere**: subj. is **Suessiones** **polliceri**: 'that they were promising.' 24. **milia**: see note, line 15. **Nervios**: acc. subj. of **polliceri**. **maxime feri**: *adv.* and *adj.* = the superl. degree of the adj., 'very fierce.' 26. **habeantur**: 'are considered;' observe the use of the *pres. subjunc.* where the *imperf.* would have been more regular; see note, lines 5 and 10, above. 27. **Atrebates**: for this and the following proper names (of tribes), ending with **Aduatucos**, supply **polliceri**. 30. **Condrusos**, etc.: acc. subjects of **polliceri** or **conficere posse** understood, the infin. clause depending upon (**se**) **arbitrari**; 'the Remi said *they* (**se**) believed that the Condrusi, etc., could muster.' **qui . . . appellantur**: the indic. indicates that this is an explanatory note made by Caesar and not included in the address of the Remi; not so with **qui . . . habeantur, absint**, line 25, which is treated as a subord. clause in indir. disc.

CHAPTER V.—1. **cohortatus, prosecutus**: 'having encouraged the Remi and having addressed them kindly;' both particips. mod. *Caesar*. 2. **senatum**: a Roman term used to describe a Gallic institution. **liberos**: acc. subj. of **adduci**, depend. upon **iussit**; 'he ordered the children of . . . to be brought to him;' see **iubeo** (155). 3. **obsides**: pred. apposition, 'as hostages.' The boys would probably be sold into captivity, if these chiefs were to break their faith. 3. **Quae**: for use and meaning of the rel. pron. at the beginning of a sentence, see (367); 'now all these things;' see also (258). 4. **ad diem**: 'to the day;' as we say, 'to the minute'—promptly. **ipse**: intensive force; 'Caesar in person.' 5. **cohortatus**: p. p. depon. mod. **ipse**, but best rendered by a *co-ordinate verb*; 'encourages Divitiacus very earnestly and explains *how greatly it concerns*.' **reipublicae, salutis**: gen. depen. upon **intersit**; the impersonal verbs **interest** and **refert** ('it interests,' 'it concerns'); take the gen. of the *person*, rarely of the *thing*, affected; 'the republic and their common safety.' This Divitiacus was one of the leading men among the Aedui who were now in alliance with the Romans. 6. **intersit**: indir. quest., see (313). **manus**: acc. subj. of **distineri**; this infin. clause is the subj. of **intersit**, 'that the bands (forces) of the enemy be kept apart.' **ne . . . confligendum sit**: neg. purpose, see (211, 320); **confligendum sit**, *pres.* subjunc. pass. periphrastic, used impersonally; lit., 'that it may not have to be fought (by them),' better, 'lest they should have to fight'; see (361, 362, 363). 8. **id fieri posse**: depen. upon **docet**; 'he explains that this (**id**) can be done.' **suas copias**: notice the emphatic position. 9. **introduxerint, coeperint**: more viv. fut. condit. turned into indir. disc.; both verbs were *fut. perf. indic.* in the dir. disc.; see (223, 396). **eorum = Bellovacorum**. The Bellovaci were already disaffected in that they had not secured the leadership of the league and the ravaging of their lands would probably lead them from their homes. 10. **post quam**: with **vidit** and **cognovit**; see (358). **coactas**: p. p. p. mod. **copias**, but best turned into a finite verb; see (381). 11. **neque = et ... non**: '*and* when he found out from ... that they (**eas copias**) were *not* far distant now (by this time).' 15. **quae res**: see (387); 'now this position.' Caesar's camp was protected in the rear by the Axona, and in front by a small marshy stream. Traces of Caesar's works at this place were discovered in 1862, on a hill called **Mauchamp**, about eighty feet above the river, with gentle slopes, well suited for a camp. **latus**: noun, acc. obj. of **muniebat**. 16. **muniebat, reddebat**: for the force of the imperf., see (102); 'both kept one side of ... fortified and rendered secure (**tuta**) from the enemy (those places) which were behind him.' **essent**: subjunc. in a characteristic rel. clause. **tuta**: acc. plur. neut. mod. **ea loca** (understood), the anteced. of **quae**. 18. **efficiebat**: subj. is **quae res**; the order is **et efficiebat ut commeatus possent portari**; literally, 'and caused (it) so that supplies could be brought'; better, 'and made it possible for supplies to be brought.' 19. **in altera parte**: 'on the other side.' 21. **pedum duodecim**: gen. of measure or quality with **vallo**. 22. **duodeviginti pedum**: 'eighteen feet in width'—the depth being about ten feet. **munire**: subj. is **eum**, (**Sabinum**).

CHAPTER VI.—1. **ab his castris**: adverbial phrase mod. **aberat**; '[from this camp.' **Bibrax**: in apposition with **oppidum**. 2. **milia**: acc. of extent in space, see (342). **id**: with **oppidum** understood, *obj.* of **oppugnare**. **ex itinere**: 'on the march'—that is, turning aside from their course without making any formal disposition of their troops. **impetu**: see (210). 3. **sustentatum est**: 'impersonal verb,' see (365); 'it was with difficulty that they held out.' 4. **eadem atque**: 'the same as,' with **oppugnatio**; 'the mode of attack (**oppugnatio**) of the Gauls (which is) the same as (that) of the Belgians is *as follows* (**haec**).' **ubi**: with **coepti sunt** and **nudatus est**; see (358). 5. **circumiecta multitudine**: abl. absol. mod. **coepti sunt iaci. moenibus**: dat. indir. obj. of **circumiecta**, 'a multitude of men being thrown round all the walls.' 6. **iaci**: pres. infin. pass. (complementary infin.) with **coepti sunt**, which is always *pass.* when accompanied by a *pass. infin.* ; 'when (ubi) stones began to be thrown.' que : connects coepti sunt and nudatus est. defensoribus : abl. of separation, mod. nudatus est ; 'was stripped of defenders.' 7. testudine : 'having formed a testudo,' by lapping their shields above their heads as was their custom in storming a town. 8. quod : rel. pron. at the beginning of the paragraph, see (367); 'now this was easily done *in the present instance* (tum).' cum . . . conicerent : historical cum, see (128, 203, 359); conicerent is plur. from the individuals composing the *subj.* multitudo. 10. nulli : 'dat. of possession,' see (357); 'no one had the power to stand (could stand) upon the wall ;' what literally? 11. summa nobilitate et gratia : 'abl. of quality or description,' see (376); supply vir, '(a man) of the highest nobility and influence.' inter suos : 'among his (own people),' see (258). oppido : dat., see (337); 'who was then in command of the town.' 12. unus : adj. used as a noun, in apposition with Iccius ; 'one of those who had come as ambassadors'; see (376), 'partitive gen., *exceptions*.' 13. mittit : a verb of *saying* to be supplied, 'sends a message to him (saying)'; hence the principal verbal phrase posse non sustinere is *infin.*, and the subord. verb submittatur is *subjunc.* Notice that the princ. verb of *saying* is *pres. tense*, as is seen in mittit : this requires that the depen. subjunc. verb shall be in either the *pres.* or *perf.* subjunc., the *pres.* to denote *unfinished;* the *perf., finished* time. This is a more viv. fut. condit. in *indir. disc.:* is the verb in the protasis (of the dir. disc.) *fut. indic.* submittetur or *fut. perf.* submissum erit? see (223, 396). se non posse = ego non possum, in the *direct disc.*

CHAPTER VII.—1. 'thither,' i.e. to Bibrax. isdem = eisdem · abl. obj. of usus (from utor); see (353); 'employing as guides the same persons who had come as messengers.' 2. Numidas, Cretas : 'Numidian and Cretan bowmen.' 3. Baleares : 'and Balearic slingers.' The Numidians and especially the people of Crete were famous archers, and, together with the celebrated slingers from the Balearic Islands, they were valuable auxiliaries of the Romans, serving as light-armed troops. subsidio, oppidanis : doub. dat., see (352). quorum adventu : 'and because of (upon) their arrival.' 4. Remis : dat. indir. obj. of accessit (*subj.* studium); 'there both came (was added) to the Remi along with the hope of (making a successful) defence, a desire for making sallies (against the enemy).' 5. et hostibus discessit : hostibus is dat. with discessit (as a verb of *taking away*) instead of the abl. of separation ; 'and from the enemy there was taken away . . . the hope of.' **potiundi = potiendi**: see (**253**) 6. **itaque**: 'and so.' **apud**: 'near.' **morati, depopulati**: mod. the subj. of **contenderunt**; observe that these are particips. of depon. verbs; 'having delayed—having ravaged.' 7. **omnibus vicis . . . incensis**: 'having burnt all the villages,' etc.: why translate **incensis**, a *pass.* particip. (not a *depon.*) with an act. meaning? see (**372**). **quos**: has two antecedents, **vicis** and **aedificiis**, which are of different genders; in such instances the relative takes the gender sometimes of the *strongest* or *most important* word, sometimes that of the *nearest*. Here the rel. has the gender of **vicis**. 8. **potuerant**: pluperf., 'had been able.' 9. **ab . . . duobus**: 'less than two miles away (off);' **ab** is used adverbially, 'off,' i.e. distant from Caesar's camp; **milibus** is the abl. of degree of difference, 'by two thousands,' being used independently of **minus**, '(and) less,' which does not affect the construction. 10. **quae castra**: see (**367**), 'and this camp.' **ut significabatur**: 'as was indicated,' a clause used parenthetically. 11. **amplius milibus**: **amplius** is the accus. of extent in space, see (**342**); **milibus** is abl. after the comparative **amplius**, see (**369**). For the other construction allowable with these neuter accusatives see note 9 above.

CHAPTER VIII.—2. **eximiam . . . virtutis**: 'remarkable reputation for valor;' **virtutis** = objective genitive, that is, a gen. which denotes the object of an action or feeling: as, **matris amor pueri**, 'a mother's love *for her boy*'; boy (**pueri**) is here the object of the feeling of love implied in the noun **amor**. **proelio**: abl. of separation; 'to refrain from an engagement.' 3. **equestribus proeliis**: 'in cavalry skirmishes.' **quid possent, quid auderent**: subjunctives of indir. quest., see (**313**); **quid** = adverbial acc., see (**374**); 'what prowess the enemy had,' literally, '*what* the enemy *could* (do) from the standpoint of courage.' 4. **periclitabatur**: *imperf.* 'kept trying to ascertain by experiment.' 5. **inferiores**: acc. pred. with **esse**, 'that our men were not inferior' (in courage); i.e. were not losing heart. **loco . . . idoneo**: abl. absol. composed of *noun + adj.*; see (**364**), example 2; this abl. absol. shows *cause* and mod. **obduxit** (line 12). 6. **natura**: 'by nature.' **quod is collis**: taken with **patebat, habebat, redibat**, these clauses explaining **loco idoneo** and also, indirectly, modifying **obduxit**. **ubi**: 'where.' 8. **editus**, etc.: mod. **collis**; 'elevated a very little from (above) the level ground.' **tantum**: acc. of extent in space, mod. **patebat; loci** in the next line (a *partitive gen.*) is to be translated with **tantum**; 'extended in width (over) as much ground (**loci**).' **adversus**:

NOTES TO CAESAR, BOOK II, CH. VIII, IX. 281

mod. collis, 'right in front.' quantum: obj. of occupare, 'as an army arranged in battle order could cover.' 9. instructa: p. p. p. mod. acies. ex utraque parte: 'on each side.' 10. lateris delectus: delectus is a noun, acc. plur.; 'it had a steep slope' (lit. 'slopes of the side'). 10. fastigatus: mod. collis, 'falling with an easy slope in front sank gently to the plain.' 11. ab utroque latere: 'on each side.' 12. transversam: '(a ditch) at right angles.' passuum: gen. of measure, 'about 400 feet (long).' 13. ad extremas: 'at the ends of the ditches.' 14. tormenta: 'engines of war.' ne ... possent: neg. purpose, see (211, 320); 'so that the enemy could *not* surround.' eum: 'after' 15. quod ... poterant: parenthetical clause and hence not *subjunc.*, 'because they were so (thus) strong in numbers'—tantum is the adverbial accus.; see note 8 above. ab lateribus: 'on their flanks.' pugnantes: pres. particip. mod. suos (referring to *Caesar*); 'his men while they were fighting.' 17. ut ... possent: affirm. purpose; 'so that they could *be led out* (duci).' quo: adv., 'if they should be needed anywhere.' 18. subsidio = dat. of purpose or service. 20. eductas: p. p. p. mod. the *obj.* of the verb; see (381); '*had led out and* drawn up.'

CHAPTER IX.—1. non magna: = parva, 'there was a small marsh.' nostrum: mod. exercitum. 2. si transirent: indir. quest., see (313); 'the enemy kept waiting to see whether our men would cross.' 3. autem: 'on the other hand.' si ... fieret: a part of the ut clause, hence subjunc. by attraction, see (276); 'if a beginning of ... should be made.' ut ... aggrederentur: affirmative purpose with parati erant; 'our men were ready under arms to *attack*.' impeditos: mod. (hostes), 'as they struggled in the river.' 5. contendebatur: impersonal, see (365); 'the two armies engaged.' 6. neutri: nom. plur. subj. of faciunt. secundiore: adj. with proelio, forming an abl. absol.; see (364); 'as the battle of cavalry was rather favorable to our men.' nostris: dat. with adj. (secundiore); see (126). 9. quod: rel. pron. nom. subj. of demonstratum est; 'which has been shown to be in the rear of.' 10. conati sunt: depon., 'they attempted to lead a part across.' 11. eo consilio: 'with this design.' ut: with expugnarent, interscinderent, popularentur, and prohiberent, explaining eo consilio; viz., 'to storm, if they could,' etc. possent: subjunc. by attraction; *sequence?* cui: dat. with comp. verb (praeerat); see (337) 13. si potuissent: subjunc. by attraction, being within the ut popularentur clause; 'if (having made the attempt) they should have been unable': in these two si clauses, possent = *fut.* indic., potuissent = *fut. perf.*

indic. of a more viv. fut. condition, see (223); thus 'we will storm, if we are (*shall be*) able,' and 'we will ravage, if we are not (shall not have been) able (to storm)': for *mood* of condition in indir. disc., see (396). 14. **nobis usui**: doub. dat., see (352); 'who were very useful (for a great use) to us.' **commeatu**: abl. of separation, 'from supplies.'

CHAPTER X.—1. **certior factus**: see (338), '(on) being informed by Titurius.' The lieutenant was about a mile nearer the fords where the Belgians were crossing than Caesar was. 2. **levis armaturae**: gen. depen. upon **Numidas**, 'Numidians of light equipment'; these light-armed troops were swift runners and could arrive at the ford more quickly than the rest, where they were to stop the passage of the Belgians. 4. **pugnatum est**: impers. verb, see (365), 'a fierce engagement occurred.' **hostes**: acc. obj. of **aggressi**. **impeditos**: p. p. p. mod. **hostes**; 'having attacked the enemy who were hindered in the river.' 5. **aggressi**: limits **nostri**. **reliquos**: adj. used as noun, acc. obj. of **reppulerunt**, and modified by **conantes**, the pres. particip. of **conor**; 'our men drove back ... the rest of the enemy as they were trying very boldly to cross over (per)'. 6. **multitudine**: abl. of means mod. **reppulerunt**. 7. **primos**: adj. as noun, dir. obj. of **interfecerunt**. 8. **circumventos**: p. p. p. mod. **primos**; see (381)-**hostes**: stands at the head of the sent. and belongs to the principal clause in Latin, but is incorporated in the **ubi** clause when translated: 'when the enemy perceived that hope had failed them.' **et de expugnando**: 'both with respect to storming.' 9. **neque progredi viderunt**: 'and when they say that our men were not advancing.' 11. **atque**: still using **ubi**, 'and when corn supplies began.' **ipsos**: i.e. the enemy. On account of a lack of provisions the enemy could not carry on a long campaign with such a large army as Caesar's. 12. **optimum**: acc. *neut.* pred. adj. with **esse**, whose subj. is the **domum ... reverti** clause: 'decided that it was best for each one (**quemque**) to return to his own home.' 13. **domum**; see (386). **et convenirent**: after **constituerunt**, 'and (they decided) *to assemble*.' **constituo** is followed sometimes by the *acc. + infin.*, sometimes by **ut** + *subjunc.*; rarely, as *here*, by both in the *same sentence*. **quorum**: anteced. **eos**; order, **ad defendendos eos quorum in fines Romani introduxissent**, 'with a view toward defending those into whose borders the Romans should lead (should have led).' 14. **introduxissent**: subjunc. as being a part of the **ut convenirent** clause following a *past* verb, **constituerunt**; it stands for the fut. perf. indic. of the *direct;* see (223, 396). **ad ... defendendos**: gerundive of purpose, see (253, 355). 15. **ut decertarent**, uterentur: affirm. purpose depen. upon convenirent, '(to assemble, etc.) so that they might contend and use.' potius quam: 'rather than.' 16. alienis = aliorum, 'of others,' as opposed to domesticis, that is, *their own*. copiis: 'supplies.' rei frumentariae: 'of grain.' 17. ad eam sententiam: 'to this determination.' 18. ratio: order, haec ratio quoque cum reliquis causis deduxit; 'this consideration too, together with other reasons, brought them.' quod: 'namely, the fact that.' 19. cognoverant: 'they knew.' appropinquare: has two subjects, 'were drawing near to.' finibus: dat. after comp. verb (ad + propinquo), see (337). 20. his persuaderi: this idiom is fully explained in (380). ut morarentur neque ferrent: 'to delay *and not* to offer.' suis: indir. obj.; adj. used as noun, 'to their friends.'

CHAPTER XI.—1. ea re: 'after this matter had been agreed upon,' that is, for each one to return to his home. strepitu, tumultu: abl. of manner, mod. egressi; see (210). 2. egressi: mod. subj. contained in fecerunt; see (340). nullo . . . imperio: abl. of manner, as though explaining or adding to magno . . . tumultu; '(that is) without orderly array and without an officer in command.' 3. cum peteret, properaret: 'causal cum,' see (350); this clause in turn explains nullo . . . imperio; 'since each soldier was seeking for himself . . . and was hastening.' domum: see (386). 4. ut . . . videretur: affirmative *result* clause, object of fecerunt; 'they made their departure seem,' lit. 'they caused it so that their departure seemed.' fugae: dat. with (adj.) consimilis, see (126). 5. videretur: in the *pres.* syst. pass. used as a depon. 'to seem.' hac . . . cognita: abl. absol. mod. continuit, of which 'Caesar' is the subj.; re = the departure of the enemy. per speculatores: 'by means of spies'; difference betw. ab and per? ab + abl. = direct (voluntary) agency; per + acc. = indirect agency, the agent being considered the instrument or means. speculatores = spies who mingled in disguise with the enemy to obtain information; exploratores = scouts or squads of regular cavalry detailed to range the country in the vicinity of the enemy. 6. veritus: 'fearing.' quod . . . perspexerat: causal clause mod. continuit, see (276). discederent: 'indir. quest.,' see (313); sequence from perspexerat; the *imperf.* tense shows that the *action* of the verb (discederent) *is going on* at the *time* of the action of the verb upon which it depends, 'he had not yet found out (did not know) for what reason the enemy *were departing*.' 8. prima luce: 'at early dawn.' re = the fact of the enemies' departure. qui . . . moraretur: rel. clause of purpose, 'to delay the rear' (of the Belgians); sequence from praemisit; the *imperf.* tense denotes that the *action* of the verb (**moraretur**) is to take place at some time in the *future*, *subsequent to the time* of the action in **praemisit**; hence this *imperf. subjunc.* = time *fut.* (*subsequent*); the *imperf. subjunc.* (**discederent**, just above) denotes time *pres.* (*contemporaneous*). 10. **his . . . praefecit**: 'over these he placed in command;' see (337). 12. **hi**: 'the latter,' i. e. Labienus and his men. **novissimos**: supply **hostes**, 'the rear.' **adorti, prosecuti**: mod **hi**. 13. **eorum fugientium**: 'of them as they fled;' **fugientium** = pres. particip. gen. plur. mod. **eorum**. 14. **cum**: causal, see (350); introduces **consisterent, sustinerent,** and **ponerent**; 'since those in the rear (ab, etc.) whom the Romans had overtaken were making a stand.' **ventum erat** = impers., see (365); lit., '(to whom) it had been come.' 16. **priores**: adj. used as noun (**prior, -ior, -ius**), subj. of ponerent, see (258); 'and since those in front,' that is, those at the head of the retreating column. 17. **quod viderentur, continerentur**: subjunc. by attraction, as being part of the **cum ponerent** clause; 'because they seemed to be out of danger and were not restrained.' 18. **omnes**: mod. **priores**. 19. **tantam . . . spatium**: 'as great a number as the length of the day permitted.' 21. **sub occasum**: 'about the setting.' 22. **ut**: parenthetical, 'as they were commanded.'

CHAPTER XII.—1. **postridie eius diei**: 'on the next day,' lit., 'on the after day of that day.' **prius quam**: takes the subjunc. when the action is expected, intended or in suspense; 'before the enemy could recover (themselves).' Caesar now proceeded to subdue the enemy tribe by tribe, since his plans for separating them had been successful. 3. **magno**: 'by making a forced march.' 4. **Noviodunum**: about 20 miles west of Bibrax. **id** (**oppidum**): obj. of oppugnare. **ex itinere**: as we say, 'on the fly,' without stopping to invest or besiege. 5. **quod**: acc. subj. of **esse**, 'which he kept hearing was.' 6. **paucis defendentibus**: abl. absol., denoting concession, see (364), example 3; 'although few were defending it.' 7. **vineas**: 'to bring up the vineae.' Movable sheds (**vineae**), with roofs and sides of wickerwork or planks covered with skins, were placed end to end, forming galleries through which the men passed back and forth when they were besieging a strongly fortified town. 8. **quae**: anteced. is **ea**, the dir. obj. of **comparare**, 'and to prepare those things which were useful.' **usui**: dat. of purpose, end, or service. 9. **ex fuga**: 'in their flight.' 10. **veneis . . . actis**: 'when the vineae were brought up.' 11. **iacto**: p. p. p. (from **iacio**), forming an abl. absol. with **aggere** (from **agger**). **magnitudine**: abl. of

NOTES TO CAESAR, BOOK II, CH. XII-XIV. 235

cause, mod. **permoti**; 'being greatly alarmed on account of the extent of the works,' i.e. by the extent of these offensive operations. 12. **quae**: refers to **operum**, hence neut. plur.; it is dir. obj. of **viderant** and **audierant**, 'which (such as) the Gauls had neither seen nor heard of.' 13. **celeritate**: abl. of cause with **permoti**. 14. **petentibus Remis**: abl. absol., see (364), 'at the request of the Remi.' **ut conservarentur**: affirm. result clause, obj. of **impetrant**, 'they obtain the request that they should be spared.'

CHAPTER XIII.—1. **obsidibus**: apposition with **primis** and **filiis**, which are the principal words—the basis—of the abl. absol. with **acceptis**, 'after he had received as hostages the chief men of the state and the two sons.' **ipsius**: adds emphasis to **Galbae**. 4. **in Bellovacos**: 'against the Bellovaci;' their territory lay west of the Suessiones. **qui**: the rel. pron. at the beginning of a paragraph, see (367); **qui** is translated after **cum**, 'now when these.' 5. **contulissent**: 'had betaken themselves with all their possessions;' **omnia** modifies **sua**, which is used as a *noun;* see (258). **atque**: joins **contulissent** and **abesset**, both following **cum**; 'and while Caesar was distant.' 7. **maiores**: comparative of **magnus**, used as a noun, subj. of **cooperant**, etc.; 'all the older men,' lit., 'all the greater by birth.' **egressi**: mod. **maiores**. 8. **voce significare**: 'to declare,' what literally? They uttered cries of supplication in a tongue different from Latin. **sese ... contendere**: indir. disc., **venire** and **contendere** being used in a *fut.* sense: 'that they would place themselves under his protection ... and would not contend;' **sese** refers to the speakers (*reflexive*), **eius** to Caesar—the person addressed. 10. **cum accessisset, poneret**: 'after he had approached (time *antecedent*) and while he was pitching (time *contemporaneous*) his camp.' 11. **pueri**· 'the children.' **ex muro**: '(standing) on.' **passis manibus**: 'with outstretched hands,' abl. of manner. 12. **ab Romanis**: 'of the Romans.'

CHAPTER XIV.—1. **pro his**: 'in behalf of these'; i.e. the Bellovaci. **discessum**: noun, 'after the departure.' 2. **dimissis**: 'when the forces of the Aedui had been dismissed.' **reverterat**: notice the tense, 'he *had* come back.' **facit verba** = **dicit**. The rest of the chapter is in *indir. disc.;* for the 'Oratio Recta' form of this chapter, see (407). 3. **Bellovacos**: 'he said that the Bellovaci had been.' **omni tempore**: 'always.' 4. **impulsos**: p. p. p. mod. (**eos**) the subj. of **defecisse** and **intulisse**; notice the emphatic position of **impulsos**, 'he said that they (the Bellovaci), urged on (being urged on) by their chiefs... had both revolted and brought war.' **qui dicerent**: 'who kept saying;' subord. clause in indir. disc., hence *subjunc.*, see (306). Following **dicerent** (a verb of 'saying') there is an infin. proposition, **Aeduos... perferre**; this makes indir. disc. *within* indir. disc. 5. **redactos**: p. p. p. mod. **Aeduos**, lit. 'having been (being) reduced,' but best rendered by a *finite verb*, see (381) 'who kept saying that the Aedui *had been reduced*... and were suffering (**perferre**). 6. **et... et**: see note 4 above, 'both... and.' **defecisse, intulisse**: princ. verbs (infin.) in the indir. disc.; for the *time relation of tense*, see (305). **populo**: dat. with comp. verb, **intulisse**, see (337). 7. **qui**: anteced. is (**eos**), acc. subj. of **profugisse**; see O. R. (407); follows **facit verba**: 'he said that those, who had been (were) the leaders in (of) this scheme.' **fuissent**: subord. clause in O. O., see (306); what tense in O. R.? see (407). It is *pluperf.* in the indir. disc. (for *past* time) since it follows **facit verba** (*historical pres.*) which is regarded as a *past tense* rather by its *meaning* than its form. 8. **quod... intellegerent**: subord. in O. O., 'because they knew'; what in the direct? **civitati**: dat. with comp. verb. **intulissent**; indir. quest. remains subjunc. in O. R., see (407); its sequence is from **intellegerent** and it denotes action *completed;* 'because they realized how great a disaster they *had* brought upon.' 9. **profugisse**: see note 7, first part. **petere**: princ. verb in O. O.; notice that it denotes action *going on at the time of the action of* **facit verba** and that **facit verba** is treated, in the rest of the chapt., as a *pres.* tense, by its *form* rather than its meaning: 'he says that not only the Bellovaci *are pleading.*' 10. **Aeduos**: also subj. of **petere**. **ut... utatur**: depends upon **petere**, 'that he should exercise'— freely with **petere**, 'are begging him to exercise': direct, 'the Bellovaci beg *you to exercise*,' see (407). **in eos**: 'toward them'; **se** would have appeared here, but for the interposition of **Aeduos**. 11. **Quod si fecerit**: 'and (he says) that if he (Caesar) does this'; **fecerit** = *perf. subjunc.*, sequence from **facit verba** (**dicit**). 12. **amplificaturum esse**: subj. is (**eum**), 'that he will increase': for this condit. in O. R., see (223, 407); for change of mood and tense, in O. R., see (396). **auxiliis**, etc.: 'by whose aid and assistance,' abl. of *means*, mod. **sustentare**. 13. **si qua**, etc.: 'if any wars (whatever wars) arose.' **consuerint**: perf. subjunc., 'they were (had become) accustomed to hold out.' See (407), for construction in O. R.

CHAPTER XV.—1. **honoris**: gen. depen. upon **causa**, see (7), 'for the sake of his regard.' **Divitiaci, Aeduorum**: objective genitives,

NOTES TO CAESAR, BOOK II, CH. XV, XVI. 237

depen. upon honoris, 'for Divitiacus and the Aedui'; see chapter 8, note 2, '**virtutis.**' **sese recepturum esse**: depen. upon **dixit**; see (318), 3 and 4. 3. **magna auctoritate**: 'abl. of quality,' see (376), 'because the state was (one) of great influence.' **his ... collatis** (from **confero**): two abls. absol. of time, mod. **pervenit**; translate by an '*after*' clause, 'after these were handed over,' etc. 6. **Ambianorum**: north of the Bellovaci; Caesar's route lay to the north, probably by way of Amiens. 7. **finis**: obj. of **attingebant**; observe the emphatic position of **finis eorum**. **Nervii**: considered the most savage of all the Belgae, occupying the basin of the Sambre river. **quorum de natura**: adv. phrase mod. **quaereret**, 'when Caesar inquired about their nature and customs.' 9. **nullum aditum**: acc. of thing possessed. **mercatoribus**: dat. of possessor. **esse** = 'have', see (357); indir. disc. to the end of the chapter; 'he found out that merchants *have* no access to them,' lit. 'that no access to them is to merchants'; direct, '**nullus aditus** (*nom.*) **ad eos est mercatoribus.**' **pati**: pres. infin. of **patior**, princ. verb (infin.) depen. upon **reperiebat**; the subj. of **pati** is (**eos**); 'that they allowed (were allowing) no wine to be imported (**inferri**).' **vini**: partitive gen., see (378). 11. **pertinentium**: pres. particip. gen. plur. mod. **rerum**. **inferri**: complementary infin. depen. upon **pati**. **quod ... existimarent**: subjunc. because a subord. clause in indir. disc.; though modifying **pati** (a *pres.* tense), it derives its sequence from **reperiebat**, *the main verb of saying.* **rebus**: abl. of means, mod. the *two following infins.* which depend upon **existimarent**, 'because they believe that by these things.' **animos**: 'spirit,' as a quality of character. **virtutem**: 'valor,' as a manifestation of courage in deeds; 'their spirit is (would be) weakened and their valor given up.' 12. **esse**: follows **reperiebat**, 'he found out that the men were fierce.' **que** connects **feros** (adj.) and **virtutis** (*gen. of quality*), the latter being used in the *sense* of an *adj.;* 'fierce and of great courage.' **increpitare, incusare**: princ. verbs in indir. disc., subj. (**eos**); 'he found out that they kept chiding and blaming.' 14. **qui**, etc.: would have a subjunc. verb in the direct disc. also, since it is a rel. causal clause; **qui** = **cum ei**, see (350, 366); 'since they had surrendered.' 15. **confirmare**: depen. upon **reperiebat**, and has as its subj. (**se**); 'that they declare.' **se missuros esse**: infin. in indir. disc. with **confirmare**, 'that they will neither send ambassadors nor accept.'

CHAPTER XVI.—1. **eorum**: i.e. of the Nervii. **triduum**: acc. of extent in time, 'for three days'; see (342). **inveniebat**: 'he continued to find out (further).' 2. non amplius: adv. 'not more (than).' milia: acc. of extent of space, mod. abesse; see (342). 4. consedisse, exspectare: note the difference in time, with reference to the time of inveniebat; 'that all the Nervii *had encamped* and *were awaiting*.' 4. una cum: 'along with.' 6. utrisque: from uterque, dat. plur. mod. his: for declension of uter, see (286); for the case of his, see (345); 'for they had persuaded each of these (tribes).' uti (ut) ... experirentur: clause of purpose depen. upon persuaserant (see preced. note and reference), 'to try.' 7. exspectari: infin. in indir. disc. depen. upon reperiebat; 'that the forces of the Aduatuci *were* also *being waited for*.' 8. esse: 'were.' in itinere: 'on the march.' mulieres: acc. dir. obj. of coniecisse, whose subj. is (Nervios), the infin. clause depen. upon reperiebat; 'that (the Nervii) had hurriedly placed the women.' qui: anteced. is (eos), which is to be supplied as a second dir. obj. of coniecisse, 'and those (men) who.' per aetatem: 'by reason of old age.' 9. viderentur: as depon., 'seemed.' quo: rel. adv. = ad quem, 'to which,' 'where.' 10. exercitui, aditus: dat. of possessor, and nom. of thing possessed, see (357); 'the army could not (did not) have access.' esset: introduced by quo, a rel. clause of *characteristic*, which takes the *subjunc.*, even in the direct disc.

CHAPTER XVII.—2. qui ... deligant: see (311); in what *four* ways may affirmative purpose be expressed? see (355). ex dediticiis: with complures, in place of the partitive gen., see (378), 'exceptions'; 'while several of the surrendered Belgians': i.e. the Ambiani, Suessiones, and Bellovaci. 4. secuti: depon. particip. mod. complures, rendered by a finite verb, see (381), 'were following Caesar and were marching along (with him).' quidam ex his: 'certain of these'—see note 2 above. ut ... cognitum est: ut + indic. = 'as'; parenthetical and verb impersonal, see (365); 'as he afterwards found out'—what literally? 5. consuetudine perspecta: abl. absol. mod. pervenerunt; notice the accumulation of genitives; dierum and exercitus limit itineris, which in turn depends upon consuetudine, 'after observing the army's usual marching order during those days.' 7. atque his: 'and announced to the latter (the Nervii).' Inter singulas legiones: indir. disc. through auderent (line 12) depen. upon demonstra(ve)runt; 'that between every two legions.' 8. intercedere: depen. upon demonstrarunt, subj. numerum, 'a great number of baggage (animals) passed (as a usual thing).' neque: continues indir. disc., 'and that it was not any trouble.' negotii: partitive

NOTES TO CAESAR, BOOK II, CH. XVII, XVIII. 239

gen. depen. upon **quicquam** (for **quidquam**) acc. neut. in the predicate with **esse**. 9. **venisset**: 'after the first legion had come.' 10. **abessent**: 'and while the rest of . . . were quite a good distance off.' **adoriri**: infin. used as *subj.* of **esse**; *what* was no trouble ? '*to attack* this legion.' **qua pulsa** (from **pello**): abl. absol. rendered by a conditional, 'and that, if this should be routed;' see (**364**). 12. **futurum (esse)**: with **demonstrarunt**, 'that it would be,' or 'the result would be.' **ut non auderent**: neg. result clause, 'that the rest of the legions would not dare;' see (**321**). **futurum esse ut** + *subjunc.* = periphrasis or substitution for the *fut. infin.*; see (**382**). 13. **adiuvabat**: used impersonally, with the **quod . . . effecerant** clause as its subj.; 'the fact that (**quod**) the Nervii . . . helped the plan of those who reported the matter.' 14. **Nervii**: subj. of **effecerant**; 'the fact that the Nervii had caused these hedges to furnish,' lit. 'had made it so that (**ut**) these hedges furnished (**praeberent**).' **cum . . . possent**: 'since they could do nothing with cavalry.' 15. **neque enim**: 'and in fact . . . not.' **ei rei**: dat. obj. of *studeni*, 'do they care for this kind of service,' i.e. use of cavalry. **quic(d)quid**: adverbial accus., see (**374**); **quicquid . . . copiis**, freely translated, 'all the strength they possess lies in infantry.' 16. **quo = ut eo** (accompanied by the comparative **facilius**) introducing **impedirent**: translated and explained in (**384**). 17. **si . . . venissent**: for the *fut. perf. indic.* in the *direct*, see (**223**, **396**); 'if they should come against them.' 18. **crebrisque . . . interiectis**: 'and, when their numerous branches had grown out *on the sides* (in **latitudinem**) and when brambles and thornbushes had been *thrown into* (**interiectis**) the spaces between the trees.' The trees were notched and bent when young and the branches were trained to grow out on the sides. In the spaces left between the trees and not covered up were placed brambles and bushes which made an impregnable hedge. 21. **quo . . . posset**: rel. clause of result, **quo** = rel. adv.; see (**387**). **ne . . . quidem**: give emphasis to the word between them, 'but not even *be seen*.' **cum**: *causal*, see (**350**); 'since the march (advance) of our line would be checked.' 23. **omittendum sibi**: see (**361**, **362**, **363**).

CHAPTER XVIII.—2. **delegerant**: note the force of the pluperf. **collis**: the hill upon which the Roman camp was laid out. **ab summo**: 'from the top,' mod. **declivis**. **declivis**: 'sloping down uniformly.' 3. **vergebat**: 'inclined.' 4. **pari acclivitate**: 'of equal steepness,' with **collis**. **pari** = adj. of third declens. (one ending), from **par**. **nascebatur**, etc.: 'rose up facing this and on the other side (of the stream).' 5. **ducentos passus**: acc. extent of space, mod. **apertus**; see (342). **infimus, apertus**: mod. **collis**, 'open (bare of trees) for about 200 feet at the foot (**infimus**)': the hill was bare of trees for 200 feet up the slope from the bank of the river. **ab superiore parte**: abl. with **ab**, giving the point of view from which; 'along the upper part.' 6. **silvestris**: mod. **collis**, 'covered with trees.' **ut non** ... **posset**: neg. result clause, see (321); recast in the *act.*, 'so that one could not easily see within.' 7. **continebant**: imperf. of continued action, see (102). 8. **secundum**: prep. + acc. **videbantur**: 'there appeared a few squads.' 9. **pedum**: gen. of measure used in the predicate.

CHAPTER XIX.—1. **praemisso**: 'after sending forward.' 2. **copiis**: abl. of attendance or accompaniment; this abl. often omits **cum** in military phrases. **ratio ordoque**: since the two phrases convey a single idea, the verb is singular. **aliter ac**: 'otherwise than;' **atque, ac**, after words of likeness and unlikeness mean 'than'; translate, 'was different from what the Belgae had reported.' 5. **post eas (legiones)**: 'behind these (legions).' **totius**: gen.; declined in (286). **colloca(ve)rat**: 'he had placed (for safety).' 7. **praesidioque impedimentis erant**. doub. dat., see (352), 'and guarded the baggage.' 9. **transgressi**: particip. (perf.) depon., see (340), mod. **equites**, the subj. of the sent.; 'having crossed.' 10. **cum**: with **reciperent, facerent, auderent**, the clauses describing the situation and mod. **coeperunt munire**. **illi**: subj. of **reciperent** and **facerent**. **ad suos**: 'adj. used as noun,' see (258); refers to the *subj.*, 'while they (the enemy) would retreat ... and would make an attack again.' 11. **neque** = **et** ... **non**; **nostri**: subj. of **auderent**. **longius**: adv. compar. degree (followed by **quam** = 'than'), mod. **insequi**; 'and while our men did not dare to pursue them as they were retreating farther than.' 12. **quem ad finem** = **ad finem ad quem**, 'to the limit where.' **perrecta, aperta**: adjs. mod. **loca**; 'the level (clear) open ground extended.' 13. **cedentes**. pres particip. acc. plur. mod. (**eos**), obj. of **insequi**. 14. **quae ... venerant**: 'which had been the first to arrive.' **dimenso** (from **dimetior**): in *pass.* sense, abl. absol. 15. **ubi**: introduces a purely temporal clause: compare this with **cum** (line 10); see (203). **ubi ... visa sunt**· 'when the foremost (part of the) baggage of our army was seen.' 16. **quod ... convenerat**: 'which had been agreed upon as the time.' 17. **committendi**: see gerundive, (253). **ut ... confirmaverant**· 'just as they had arranged their line ... and (as) they had resolved (to do)'—**sese confirmaverant** = 'had resolved.' 20. **his**: abl. absol., 'as these (our cavalry) were easily defeated.' 21.

decucurrerunt: 'they ran down.' ut... viderentur: affirm. result, see (321); 'so that the enemy seemed (to be).' paene uno 'almost at one and the same time.' 22. et ad silvas: 'both near the woods.' iam in manibus nostris: 'and now close at hand.' Perhaps about twenty minutes, as the Roman camp was three-quarters of a mile from the river, in fording which there was no doubt some delay. It is a surprise that Caesar did not have troops ready to repel the enemies' charge. 23. adverso colle: 'up the hill (facing them).' 24. eos: with ad; 'and to those who were engaged;' occupati has the force of a pred. adj. opere: i.e. fortifying the camp.

CHAPTER XX.—1. Caesari: dat. of pers. agent, mod. agenda erant; see (361, 362, 363); 'Caesar had to do everything at once,' lit. 'all things had to be done by Caesar.' 2. proponendum erat: 'had to be raised;' supply erat or erant with each of the following verbs (periphrastic). The vexillum was the large banner hoisted to announce an intended engagement. cum... oporteret: lit., 'when it ought to be hurried,' freely, 'when the soldiers ought to hasten;' see (385). 3. tuba: 'the call had to be sounded with the trumpet;' the call to take their places in the line. ab opere: 'from their work.' 4. qui: its anteced. is the *subj.* contained in arcessendi erant, '*those* who had proceeded.' These soldiers would need a special messenger since they were out of hearing of the usual signals. paulo longius: 'a little farther (than usual).' aggeris, etc.: 'for the sake of procuring material for the rampart;' see gerundive (253). 5. cohortandi erant: the *gerundive* of a *depon.* always has a *passive* meaning; 'had to be encouraged;' this was always done if possible. 6. signum dandum (erat): here a signal for the attack made by horns and trumpets. quarum rerum: gen. depen. upon partem; quarum = '*but these*,' see (367); '*but* the shortness of the time and the approach of... prevented a great part of *these* things.' 7. impediebat: sing. agreeing with the nearer subj. difficultatibus, subsidio: doub. dat., see (352); 'in (to) these difficulties two things were (for) a help;' first, the previous training of the soldiers; second, putting a lieutenant over each legion. 8. scientia atque usus: apposition with duae res. quod ... poterant: 'because they themselves (ipsi) could.' 9. exercitati: p. p. p. mod. ipsi, the *subj.* of the quod clause; see (316). quid: acc. subj. of fieri, depen. upon the impersonal verb oporteret—a subjunc. of *indir. quest.*, see (313); oporteret gets its sequence from poterant praescribere; 'could give directions to themselves (sibi) as to *what* ought to be done.' 10. non minus: 'no less.' quam: 'than.' 11.

doceri (poterant): 'could be directed by others.' **12. singulis legionibus**: 'from (ab) the several legions.' **singulos legatos**: acc. subj. of **discedere**, depen. upon **vetuerat** (from **veto**); 'had forbidden the several lieutenants to withdraw.' **13. nisi castris munitis**: idiom, 'until the camp had been fortified.' **14. nihil imperium**: 'no command whatever;' 'not at all.' **15. per se**: 'of their own efforts.' **quae**: anteced. is (**ea**), obj. of **administrabant**, 'attended to what (= those things which) seemed best.'

CHAPTER XXI.—1. **necessariis**, etc.: 'after giving (only) the necessary commands.' **ad cohortandos**: see (355), 'four ways to express *purpose*;' see (253), 'gerundive construction.' 2. **quam in partem = in eam partem in quam**: 'into that quarter where fortune led him.' 3. **decimam**: Caesar's favorite legion; it was at the extreme left of the line; next came the IXth, then the XIth, VIIIth, XIIth, and lastly the VIIth. **milites**: acc. dir. obj. of **cohortatus**, which mod. *Caesar;* 'having encouraged his soldiers.' **non longiore quam ut**: 'with no longer an address than (to tell them) that.' 4. **suae**: refers to the subj. of **retinerent**; see (189, 214); 'of their usual.' 5. **neu**: negatives are continued by **neve** or **neu**, 'and that they should not.' 6. **sustinerent**: with **ut** understood depen. upon **cohortatus**. **quod ... aberant**: mod. **dedit**. **non longius quam**: 'no farther than (the distance)' 7. **quo**: adverbial relative; 'to which a dart could be hurled.' **posset**: introduced by **quo**, a characteristic relative, taking the verb in the *subjunc.* 8. **profectus**: 'depon. perf. participle,' see (340); mod. the subj. of **occurrit**; 'having advanced into another quarter.' 9. **pugnantibus**: pres. particip. dat. plur. mod. (**suis**), the dat. obj. of **occurrit** (comp. verb—**ob-curro**); see (337); 'he came upon his men (already) fighting.' **tanta exiguitas**: 'such was the want of time.' 10. **hostium**: with **animus**; 'and the spirit of ... so determined upon a battle.' **ut ... defuerit** (from **desum**): affirm. result, 'that time was lacking;' note the use again of the *perf. subj.* (of result) after **fuit**, a verb of *past* time. 11. **ad insignia**: 'for putting on their decorations': to distinguish the different legions and officers. 12. **scutis**: mod. **detrudenda**, 'from their shields': for agreem. of these gerundives, see (253). 13. **quam in partem**: 'to whatever place each man from his work came.' **quaeque**, etc.: 'and whatever standards he first saw.' 14. **ad haec**: 'near these.' **ne ... dimitteret**: neg. purpose, see (320); 'lest he should lose the opportunity (**tempus**).' **in quaerendis suis (signis)**: gerundive, 'in searching for his own standards.'

CHAPTER XXII.—1. **magis ut, quam ut**: 'rather as,' 'than as,' take the *indic* **postulabat. natura, delectus, necessitas**: subjects of **postulabat**. in the **magis ut** clause, the verb (singular) being in agreement with the nearest subj. 2. **ratio, ordo**: subj. in the **quam ut** clause, 'than as the arrangement and order of military science.' 3. **cum**... **resisterent**: 'since the legions were resisting the enemy separately, some in one place and some in another'; this clause and the next, **cum ... impediretur**, modify **poterant collocari** in the main clause. **cliae**: with **legiones** understood. 4. **hostibus**: dat. indir. obj. of **resisterent**; for case, see (343). **saepibus interiectis**: abl. absol. of *means* mod. **impediretur**; 'by the interposition of very thick hedges.' **tu**: 'as.' 5. **impediretur**: causal subjunc. introduced by **cum** (line 8), 'since the view was cut off.' **neque**: beginning of the main clause whose verb is **poterant**. 6. **subsidia**: subj. of **poterant collocari**; 'neither could reserves be stationed regularly.' **quid ... esset**: indir. quest. *subj. of* **poterat provideri**; 'nor could whatever was needed in each quarter be provided—for.' 7. **administrari**: complementary infin. with **poterant**, 'could all commands be executed by a single man'—notice the emphatic position of **ab uno**. 8. **itaque**: 'and so.' **tanta**: mod. **iniquitate. fortunae**: gen. depen. upon **eventus**, the subj. of **sequebantur**, 'various issues of fortune also.'

CHAPTER XXIII.—1. **milites**: subj. of **compulerunt et interfecerunt**, 'the soldiers of the ninth,' etc., who were commanded by Labienus. **ut ... constiterant**: 'as they had taken their stand.' 2. **acie = aciei** (gen.). **pilis emissis**: abl. absol. of *means* mod. **compulerunt**; best translated, 'by throwing pikes.' **pilum** = an offensive weapon, a strong and heavy pike six feet long and weighing ten or eleven pounds. This was the principal weapon of the legion soldiers, being thrown only at close range. **cursu ac lassitudine**: abl. of means mod. **exanimatos**, 'made breathless by speed and fatigue.' They had run about a mile and forded the river. 3. **exanimatos, confectos**: mod. **Atrebates**, the obj. of **compulerunt**; 'drove the Atrebates, made breathless ... and exhausted with wounds.' **his** = Atrebates; dat. after comp. verb **obvenerat**; see (337). **ea pars**: on the Roman side; 'for that part (the Roman left wing) had encountered these (the latter).' 5. **conantes**: pres. particip. (*act. form*) of depon., acc. plur. mod. **eos**, i.e. Atrebates, to be supplied as the dir. object of **insecuti**; 'and pursuing (them) as they were trying.' 6. **impeditam**: mod. **partem**, 'embarrassed (in the attempt to cross).' **ipsi**: emphatic; the soldiers of the IXth and Xth legions. 8. **resistentes**: pres. particip. mod.

244   NOTES TO CAESAR, BOOK II, CH. XXIII, XXIV.

hostes, the obj. of **conieoerunt**, 'put to flight the enemy when they again offered resistance.' 10. **profligatis**: p. p. p. abl. absol.; 'after routing the Viromandui with whom they had been engaged.' 11. **in ipsis ripis**: 'on the very banks.' 12. **proeliabantur**: for the force of the impf. see (102); 'kept up the fight.' **at**: 'but.' **totis**...**castris**: abl. absol. of *time* or *cause* mod. **contenderunt** (line 16). Notice the emphatic position of **totis** modified by **fere**, 'almost'; 'now that the camp was almost *entirely* laid bare along the front and on the left side.' The VIIIth and XIth had left the front of the camp, and the IXth and Xth the left, in pursuit of the enemy. 13. **cum**...**constitisset**: see causal **cum** (350)—'since the twelfth legion had taken its stand...and at no great distance from it.' 14. **ab ea**: **ea** refers to **duodecima legio**. **intervallo**: abl. of degree (measure) of difference. 15. **duce Boduognato**: abl. absol. composed of *two nouns*; see (364). 16. **summam**: noun, with limiting gen. **imperii** = 'the chief command.' 17. **aperto latere**: 'on the unprotected flank.' **circumvenire**: depen. upon **coepit**, which has the *first* pars as its subj., 'a part of whom began to surround.' 18. **summum castrorum locum**: 'the main point occupied by the camp.'

CHAPTER XXIV.—1. **levis armaturae**: 'of light equipment' = 'light-armed,' limiting **pedites**. 2. **cum eis una**: 'along with them'; **una** = adv. **quos**: acc. subj. of **pulsos esse**, indir. disc. depen. upon **dixeram**, 'who (not *whom*) I had said (before) were routed at the first assault.' **eis** = **equites**, **quos** = **equites et pedites**. 3. **cum ... se reciperent**: historical **cum**, (see 128, 203, 359); 'as they were retreating.' **adversis hostibus**: dat. indir. obj. of the comp. verb, **occurrebant**, see (337); 'met the enemy face to face.' 4. **aliam in partem**: 'in another direction.' 5. **fugam petebant**: 'took flight.' Observe the *descriptive* force of the *imperfects* in this chapter. Just as the Nervii entered the Roman camp from the right, the Roman cavalry and auxiliaries (**pedites levis armaturae**) who had returned by a circuitous route poured into the camp from the left side, face to face with the enemy. **ab decumana porta**: 'from the rear gate.' abl. of the point of view from which. 6. **summo**, etc.; 'and from the uppermost ridge of the hill.' The rear of the camp was higher than the front and the **calones**, stationed here, could see the legions at the left cross the stream. They started to follow, but on looking back saw the Nervii rushing into the Roman camp from the right. **victores**: in the predicate with **nostros**. **transisse** (from **transeo**): infin. of indir. disc. with **conspexerant**; the subj. is **nostros**; for meanings of the *perf. infin.* in O. O., see (305), 'that our men *had crossed the river as victors.*' 7. egressi: depon. perf. particip., see (340); mod. calones, 'having gone forth.' cum respexissent et vidissent : histor. cum, see (359): compare the *time* of the action in *these verbs*, with that of reciperent, note 3 (line 3): these clauses mod. mandabant, 'on looking back and seeing.' 8. hostes ... versari: depen. upon vidissent, 'that the enemy were (versari).' praecipites: adj. nom. plur. mod. calones, but with an adverbial force, 'in haste.' 9. eorum : the drivers, etc., in charge of the baggage-train behind which the XIIIth and XIVth legions had been placed ; it is gen. depen. upon clamor fremitusque, 'the din and noise of those who were coming.' 10. oriebatur: sing., as clamor and fremitus contain one idea, 'arose.' 11. perterriti : p. p. p. mod. the subj. alii, see (316); 'and in great terror (thoroughly frightened) they fled (were borne), *some* in one direction, *some* in another.' quibus: see (367); mod. rebus, which in turn limits permoti (as an abl. of *means*) ; '*and* thoroughly frightened by all *these* happenings.' 12. permoti : p. p. p. mod. equites Treveri, the subj. of contenderunt and renuntiaverunt. virtutis opinio : 'reputation for valor.' 14. missi : p. p. p. mod. qui, 'who had come being sent,' etc. cum : with vidissent, denoting time or cause, 'when or since they saw.' The infinitives (indir. disc.) depending upon vidissent, are: compleri, premi, teneri, and fugere; notice that these infin. are in the *pres. tense*, denoting action *going on* at the *time* of (*contemporaneous with*) the action of vidissent ; see (301, 302, 392). castra : acc. subj. of compleri: 'that our camp was filling (was being filled).' 15. legiones: acc. subj. of premi and teneri. circumventas: p. p. p. mod. legiones, 'and that they *were being held* (teneri) almost surrounded.' 16. calones, etc.: acc. subj. of fugere, 'that the slaves, etc., were fleeing.' diversos dissipatosque : 'separated and scattered.' 17. desperatis ... rebus : 'giving up our affairs as hopeless.' 18. Romanos : acc. subj. of pulsos, superatos(esse), indir. disc. with renuntiaverunt ; 'that the Romans had been defeated,' etc. 19. castris impedimentisque : abl. obj. of potitos esse, see (353). hostes : acc. subj. of potitos esse, indir. disc., 'that the enemy had captured their camp,' etc.

CHAPTER XXV.—1. ab cohortatione : 'from the cheering of the tenth legion'; abl. of place from which, mod. profectus. 2. profectus : depon. mod. Caesar, 'having proceeded.' ubi ... vidit : translate Caesar as the subj. of this clause, though in the Latin it is the subj. of processit (line 15)—the first principal verb : 'when Caesar saw that his men were hard pressed.' signis ... collatis (from confero) : abl.

absol. 'the standards being brought together'; better rendered as a clause of statement, 'and that the standards were brought together.' 3. **confertos milites**: acc. subj. of **esse**, with **vidit**. **sibi, ipsos**: reciprocally emphasizing, these words are kept together: **ipsos** mod. **milites**; **sibi** with **impedimento** = doub. dat., see (352), lit. 'for a hindrance to themselves'; translate, 'and (when he saw) that the crowded soldiers of . . . were in one another's way for fighting (in the fight).' 4. **cohortis**: gen. depen. upon **centurionibus**. 5. **occisis**: abl. absol. with **centurionibus**, 'after all the centurions of . . . had been cut down.' 6. **amisso**: abl. absol., '(and) after the standard was lost.' These ablatives absol. denote *time* and mod. **processit**, **fere**; adv. mod. **omnibus** (another abl. absol.), 'after nearly all the centurions of . . . had been either killed or wounded.' 7. **in his**: 'among these.' **primipilo . . . confecto**: abl. absol. 'the chief centurion, P. Baculus, a very brave man, being disabled by many severe wounds.' The chief ambition of the centurions was to become a **primipilus**, the highest in rank of all the centurions who stood in regular gradation. He had charge of the standard and was a member of the council of war. 9. **ut non posset**: neg. result; see (321); 'so that he could no longer stand up'; the sequence of **posset** is from **confecto**, which denotes *past time;* the *imperf.* (**posset sustinere** = **sustineret**) denotes action *going on* at the time of (contemporaneous with) the action of **confecto**. **reliquos**: adj. used as noun, see (258); acc. subj. of e:se with **vidit**, which is repeated in line 13 because of the length of the sentence; 'that the rest were *losing spirit* (tardiores).' 10. **nonnullos ab novissimis**: acc. subj. of **excedere** and **vitare**, 'and that some of those in the rear were withdrawing.' 11. **vitare**: 'were avoiding'; for the meaning of the *pres. infin.* in O. O., see (301, 302). **hostis** = **hostes**, acc. subj. of **intermittere** and **instare**. **neque**: 'and . . . not.' 12. **subeuntes**: pres. particip. of **subeo**, acc. plur. mod. **hostis**; 'and (when he saw) that the enemy did not cease coming up along the front from.' **instare**: 'and were pressing forward.' 13. **rem esse in augusto**: 'and that the matter had reached a crisis.' **neque subsidium**: 'and that there was no reserve force.' 14. **quod . . . posset**: characteristic rel. clause, 'that could be brought up.' **scuto . . . detracto**: abl. absol., 'jerking a shield.' **uni militi**: dat. with a verb of *taking away;* see construction of **hostibus**, chap. 7, note 5; 'from *a* soldier.' **ab novissimis**: '(among those) in the rear.' 16. **appellatis**: abl. absol., 'addressing the centurions by name.' **cohortatus**: mod. Caesar, 'and encouraging the rest.' 17. **signa inferre**: 'to advance,' infin. with

NOTES TO CAESAR, BOOK II, CH. XXV, XXVI. 247

iussit. By advancing they would increase the space between the ranks and obtain more room for the use of their swords. 18. quo ... possent : affirm. purpose ; quo = ut eo + comparative (facilius), see (384); 'so that they could use their swords to more advantage.' uti : from utor. cuius adventu : see (367), 'now upon the arrival of this one.' 18. spe illata (from infero): 'hope being inspired.' militibus : dat. with comp. verb, see (337) ; 'in the soldiers.' 19. cum ... cuperet : causal clause, mod. tardatus est; see (350); 'since each man on his own account ... even (etiam) in the greatest peril to himself desired to do his best.' 21. paulum : adv., 'a little.'

CHAPTER XXVI.—1. cum ... vidisset : although *Caesar* (in the Latin sent.) is the subj. of monuit, it is to be read as the subj. of the cum clause ; 'when Caesar saw that the seventh legion was likewise hard pressed.' 2. tribunos : dir. obj. of monuit, which is followed by the ut clause as a secondary object, 'he advised the tribunes ... that the legions should gradually draw together.' 3. conversa : p. p. p. acc. plur. mod. signa, the acc. obj. of inferrent ; lit., 'the turned standards,' but best translated by a co-ordinate verb; see (381); 'that they should face about and advance upon the enemy.' 4. quo : see (367); abl. absol., 'now when this was done.' cum alius, etc. : 'since one rendered assistance to one, another to another.' alii : dat., see (348). 5. neque, etc. : 'and since they did not fear (were not fearing).' ne : see (343), 'verbs of *fearing*' ; 'that (lest) they would be surrounded.' aversi : p. p. p. nom. plur. mod. the subj. of circumvenirentur ; 'in the rear' : i.e. with their backs turned towards the enemy. 8. praesidio, impedimentis : doub. dat., see (352); translate (with fuerant), 'which had guarded the baggage in the rear.' proelio nuntiato : 'on hearing a report of the battle.' cursu incitato : 'having quickened their pace.' 10. Labienus : modified by two depon. participles, potitus and conspicatus, 'and Labienus having captured ... and having observed from his higher position.' He, with the IXth and Xth legions, had been pursuing the Atrebates. 10. castris : abl. obj. of potitus, see (353). 11. quae res ... gererentur : indir. quest., see (313); sequence from conspicatus; 'having observed what things were going on (lit. 'were being waged') in our camp.' 12. qui : i.e. the soldiers of the Xth legion. Translate *within the* cum *clause*, '*now* when *these* had found out.' 13. quo ... esset : quo, from interrog. quis, introducing an indir. quest. ; sequence from cognovissent, 'in what condition the affair was.' quanto ... versaretur : indir. quest. (interrog. quantus), 'and in how great danger both the camp

... etc., *were* (**versaretur**).' 14. **versaretur**: sing. agreeing with the *nearest* of the *three* subjects. 15. **nihil... fecerunt**: 'they came up with the utmost possible speed.' **reliqui**: partitive gen. depen. upon **nihil**, lit. 'they made nothing of the rest as to (**ad**) quickness.'

CHAPTER XXVII.—1. **adventu**: abl. of cause, see (210), mod. **facta est**; 'upon (on account of) the arrival of these.' **rerum**: gen. with **commutatio**, 'change in things.' 2. **ut... redintegrarent**: affirm. result, see (321), sequence from **facta est**. **etiam qui**, etc.: 'even those who had fallen, exhausted with wounds.' **confecti**: p. p. p. mod. **qui**, see (316), and also (for *different* translation) see (381). 3. **scutis**: abl. known as the *locative ablative* (place where), mod. **innixi**. **innixi**: depon. perf. particip. mod. **nostri** (**qui**), 'leaning upon their shields.' **calones**: subj. of **occurrerunt**. 4. **perterritos**: p. p. p. mod. **hostes**, obj. of **conspicati**, which agrees with **calones**; 'then the slaves, seeing the enemy in utter confusion.' **inermes**: nom. plur. mod. **calones**, 'even though unarmed.' **armatis**: 'the armed'; p. p. p. of **armo**, mas. plur. *used as a substantive*, see (258); dat. with the compound verb **occurrerent**; see (337). 5. **equites vero**: 'and the cavalry too.' **ut... delerent**: affirm. purpose, 'so as to wipe out.' 6. **quo... praeferrent**: also affirm. purpose, **quo = ut eo**, rarely used without a comparative; 'so that thereby they might outdo.' **militibus**: dat. with a comp. verb, translated like an *accus.*; lit., 'place themselves before.' 7. **at**: 'but yet,' marks in an emphatic way a change in the point of view of the narrative, describing the maneuvers of the enemy. 8. **ut**: introduces **insisterent, pugnarent, conicerent, remitterent**, being repeated in line 12 (**ut non**) with **deberet**. **cum primi**, etc.; 'after their foremost men *had fallen*' (from **cado**). 9. **proximi**: adj. as noun, 'the next stood upon them as they lay prostrate.' **iacentibus**: pres. particip. dat. with **eis** understood after the comp. verb, **insisterent**. 10. **ex corporibus**: i.e. from the tops of the dead bodies; **ex = 'on.'** **his deiectis**: abl. absol., 'when these (**proximi**) were cut down.' 11. **qui superessent**: before this rel. clause supply **ut** going with **conicerent et remitterent**, the subj. of these verbs being the anteced. of **qui**; the **ut** clauses depend upon **praestiterunt**, in line 8; 'the enemy displayed such valor that those who survived hurled darts upon.' **ut ex tumulo**: 'as from a hill.' 12. **intercepta**: p. p. p. acc. plur. neut. mod. **pila**, but rendered by a verb co-ordinate with **remitterent**; 'picked up and threw back the pikes', or by a rel. clause, 'threw back the pikes which they picked up.' **ut non deberet**: neg. result, see (321), 'so that it ought not to be considered (iudicari).' 13. nequiquam ausos esse: the subj. of the infin. is homines; 'had vainly dared.' 15. quae: acc. plur. (mod. by facilia) obj. of redegerat; 'things (*bold deeds*) which their greatness of courage had made easy.' ex: 'from having been.' difficillimis: for comparison, see (314).

CHAPTER XXVIII.—1. facto: 'being finished.' 2. gente ac nomine redacto: 'the race and name of the Nervii being reduced almost to annihilation': redacto agrees with the *nearer* of the two nouns. maiores natu: 'the older men,' lit., 'the greater by birth': *subj.* of miserunt, dediderunt, and dixerunt. quos: acc. subj. of coniectos esse, depend. upon dixeramus; 'who (not *whom*) I had said were hastily placed.' 3. una cum: 'along with.' in: with *acc.*, because of the idea of *motion* that prevails in coniectos. 4. hac, etc.: abl. absol., rendered, 'upon hearing a report of this engagement.' cum ... arbitrarentur: causal clause, mod. miserunt, etc., see (350). arbitrarentur (a verb of *thinking*) governs two infn. propositions, nihil impeditum esse, and nihil tutum esse; 'that nothing was an obstacle to the victors and nothing secure for the conquered.' 5. victis: p. p. p. used as a noun, lit., 'for those having been conquered.' omnium: depen. upon consensu: 'with the consent of ... the older men (from line 2) sent ambassadors.' 7. ei: dat. indir. obj., 'to him.' in commemoranda calamitate: gerundive, see (253). 8. ex sexcentis, ex hominum milibus LX: adverbial phrases limiting redactos esse: so with the two ad phrases. 9. vix: adv. restricting ad quingentos, 'to barely 500.' qui ... possent: characteristic rel. clause and would take a subjunc. verb in the *direct.* sese redactos esse: for the *time relation* of this infin. with respect to the verb dixerunt, see (305); 'they said that they *had been* reduced.' 10. quos: obj. of conservavit, see (367); '*now* Caesar spared *these*.' 11. ut ... videretur: 'that he might appear to have shown (usus esse) mercy.' usus (esse): since the subj. of usus esse is the same as that of videretur, *a passive form*, the participial part of the *infin.* is retained in the *nom. case* (personal construction): here usus (nom. sing.) agrees with the subj. of videretur. in: 'toward.' 12. finibus, oppidis: abl. obj. of uti (from utor). 13. finitimis: dat. obj. of imperavit, see (145). What is the relation of the *time* expressed by prohiberent to that of imperavit? At the time he issued the command, were they not to execute it at some subsequent (fut.) time?

CHAPTER XXIX.—3. domum: acc. of limit of motion without ad, see (386). 4. desertis: 'after abandoning.' sua: adj. (neut. plur.)

as a noun mod. by **omnia**, obj. of **contulerunt** : for its reflex. force, see (189, 214); 'all their possessions.' **egregie munitum** : p. p. p. mod. **oppidum**, 'remarkably fortified.' Perhaps this **oppidum** (name not given) was placed upon the plateau in an angle formed by the confluence of the Chambre and Meuse, about 35 miles northeast of the battlefield. 5. **quod** . . . **haberet** : '*now* although *this* town had'; again the *relative* at the beginning of a paragraph, see (350, 367). **ex** . . . **partibus**: in brief, 'all round.' 7. **una ex parte** : 'on one side.' **leniter acclivis** : 'a gently sloping.' 8. **amplius**: acc. of ext. in space, used adverbially. **pedum** : the gen. (with numerals) is used to define measures of *length, width*, etc. 9. **duplici altissimo muro** : abl. of means, mod. **muni(v)erant**, 'with a very high double wall': meaning either two parallel walls, or a wall of double the usual thickness. **tum**: 'then,' i.e. at this particular time. **magni ponderis** : 'of great weight.' 10. **collocabant** : force of the imperfect ? **ipsi** : emphatic or intensive pron. 11. **ex Cimbris** : abl. of source. **erant prognati** : 'were descended.' **qui** : subj. of **reliquerunt**. 12. **eis impedimentis** : abl. absol. with **depositis**; 'having placed those incumbrances, which they could not take along': cattle as well as baggage. 14. **custodiam, praesidium**: in apposition with **milia**, 'left six thousand men as a guard and garrison.' **ex suis** : 'of their own.' 15 **una** : 'together with these'; i.e. with the **impedimentis**. **hi** : 'the latter,' i.e. the six thousand. 16. **exagitati** : 'being harassed.' **cum alias inferrent** : 'when at one time they were waging war.' 17. **alias**, etc.: supply **bellum sibi** with **illatum**, 'at another time they warded off (the war) *waged* (upon them).' 18. **pace facta** : abl. absol., mod. **delegerunt. delegerunt**: note the force of the perfect—time indefinitely past.

CHAPTER XXX.—**adventu** : abl. of time, 'and upon the first arrival of our army.' 2. **faciebant** : 'they kept making'; see (102). 3. **postea** : 'afterwards.' **vallo, castellis** : abl. of means, mod. **circummuniti**. 4. **circummuniti** : p. p. p. mod. the subj. of **continebant**; 'being protected by a rampart 15 miles around and by numerous strongholds.' **oppido** : supply in. 5. **vineis actis** : ·after the vineae were brought up.' **aggere exstructo** : '(and) after the agger had been made': **agger** = a long sloping mound of earth leading up to the height of the walls. **turrim** . . . **constitui** : indir. disc. with **viderunt** ; notice the *time* indicated by the tense of **constitui**, 'that a tower *was being* constructed,' see (301, 302). 6. **irridere, increpitare** : *historical infinitives;* the infin. is often used for the *impf. indic.*

NOTES TO CAESAR, BOOK II, CH. XXX, XXXI. 251

(descriptive impf.) and takes a subj. in the *nom.*; 'they at first began to laugh at us . . . and *to taunt*' (**increpitare vocibus**). 7. **quod . . . instrueretur**: subjunc. because the reason is given upon the authority of some one other than Caesar; see (**276**); 'because (as they stated) such an engine of war *was being erected*.' Notice the time of the action of **instrueretur**, as it relates to the time of the action in **irridere**; **irridere** = impf. indic. (a past tense), hence the subjunc. must be either impf. or plupf.; here impf. to denote *action* going on at the time of the action of **irridere** (contemporaneous action). **ab tanto spatio**: **ab** = adv., 'away.' **spatio** = abl. of degree of difference, 'at such a distance.' 8. **quibusnam manibus confiderent**: a question in the indirect disc., with the verb in the subjunc., 'by what hands, pray, or with what strength did they hope'? **viribus**: from **vis**. 9. **praesertim homines**: 'especially being men of such small stature,' spoken contemptuously. The Gauls expected the Romans to lift the tower and place it upon the wall—which seemed amusing. This indicates their utter lack of civilization. 10. **Gallis, contemptui**: doub. dat., see (**352**). 'for our shortness (of stature) is an object of ridicule with the Gauls.' 11. **tanti oneris**: 'of such weight.' **moturos (esse) sese**: indir. disc. with **confiderent**; for *time* indicated by **moturos esse**, see (**318**)—3 and 4; 'did they hope that they *would* move'? i.e. did they expect to move?

CHAPTER XXXI.—1. **ubi vero**: 'when indeed.' **moveri et appropinquare**: subj. **turrim** understood, 'was moving and approaching.' **moenibus**: dat. with a comp. verb. 2. **specie**: abl. of cause, mod. **commoti** (p. p. p.), which in turn mod. the subj. of **miserunt**; 'being greatly alarmed by the new and unusual sight.' 3. **locuti**: depon. perf. particip. mod. **qui**, the subj. of **dixerunt** (line 7); 'speaking after (**ad**) this fashion, said.' For use (mood and tense) of infin. and subjunc.—princip. and subord. clauses—in O. O., see (**301, 302, 305, 306, 318, 392**). 4. **existimare**: princip. verb depen. upon **dixerunt**; subj. **se** understood; 'that they did not believe (were not believing).' **Romanos . . . gerere**: is indir. disc. with **existimare**, like a wheel within a wheel; 'that the Romans waged (were waging)'; note the force of the pres. infin. in O. O., see (**302**)—example 3. 5. **qui . . . possent**: a rel. clause denoting cause, **qui** = **cum ei** (see **350**), which would take a subjunc. verb in the *direct*; 'since they could move forward.' 7. **permittere**: 'that they surrendered themselves,' etc. **unum**: 'one thing only,' acc. sing. neut. obj. of **petere**; notice the emphatic position of **unum**, which is explained by the **ne . . . despoliaret** clause; indir. disc. to the end of the chapt. **petere**, etc.: subj. is **se** understood, 'that they asked (were asking) and begged for one thing.' **si**: in this condition **si statuisset** is the protasis, **ne . . . despoliaret** the apodosis: in the *direct disc.* they were, **si statueris** (fut. perf. indic.) see (223), and **noli despoliare** (for **ne despolia**—imperative). For 'commands and exhortations,' see (389, 390). In changing this sent. to indir. disc., the princip. verb (**noli despoliare**) becomes *subjunc.* (neg. **ne**), *pres.* after **dicunt**, *imperf.* after **dixerunt** (*as in this instance*); the subord. verb, representing time *completed* (in the future), becomes *perf. subjunc.* after **dicunt**, *pluperf.* after **dixerunt** (*as in this instance*): observe that the person changes from the *second* to the *third;* 'if perchance Caesar resolved . . ., (they begged) that he would not (**ne**) deprive them of their arms.' 8. **pro sua**, etc.: 'in accordance with his usual.' **quam . . . audirent**: subord. clause in O. O., hence subjunc.; though depending upon the **si statuisset** clause, it obtains its sequence from **dixerunt**, the main verb of saying. Observe the *time* indicated by **audirent**, 'which they themselves *were* (constantly) *hearing of* through others.' 9. **conservandos esse**: periphras. pass. infin., indir. disc. with **statuisset**; 'that the Aduatuci ought to be spared.' How is the periphras. act. formed? how the pass.? how express the *person. agent* with this pass.? 10. **sibi**: dat. with **inimicos**, see (126), 'were hostile to them.' 11. **virtuti**: dat. indir. obj. of **invidere**, see (348), 'were jealous of their valor.' 12. **traditis armis**: abl. absol., translated by a conditional, 'if their arms were given up.' **sibi praestare**: indir. disc. with **dixerunt**; impersonal verb having the infin. clause, **quamvis fortunam . . . pati**, as the *subj.;* 'that it would be better for them . . . to suffer (**pati**),' etc. **si . . . deducerentur**: move viv. fut. in the direct; was this *fut.* or *fut. pf.* indic. in the direct? see (223). Does the imperf. subjunc. (O. O.) denote *finished* time, such as would be indicated by the fut. pf. indic. (O. R.)? Find answers to these questions in (396). 14. **quam interfici**: 'than to be put to death.' **consue(vi)ssent**: subord. clause in O. O., plupf. denoting completed time, 'had been in the habit of.'

CHAPTER XXXII.—1. **respondit**: perf., not *pres*. **se**: indir. disc. through **inferrent**. 2. **consuetudine, merito**: 'rather in accordance with his usual habit (of merciful treatment of a foe) than on account of any act of theirs'; the former = abl. of manner, the latter = abl. of cause; both mod. **conservaturum esse**. **conservaturum esse**: 'that

NOTES TO CAESAR, BOOK II, CH. XXXII. 253

he would spare': this is the *apodosis verb* of a more viv. fut. condition in indir. disc., the *protasis* verb being **dedidissent**. In the *direct* they are written, **ego conservabo, si dedideritis** (fut. perf. indic.): notice that there is a change of *mood, tense,* and *person* when turning direct into indir. disc., the principal verbs of *declarative statement* clauses becoming *infin.*, and all subord. verbs *subjunc.* In changing conservabo to the *infin.*, the *tense* remains the same (whether it follows *replies* or *replied*); but in changing **dedideritis** to the *subjunc.*, the *tense* must be changed (as there is no *fut. perf. subjunc.*); the representatives of *finished time* in the subjunc. (**dedideritis** = time *finished* in the fut. before another fut. action) are the *perf.* after *replies*, the *pluperf.* after *replied;* see rule of seq. (135), and condit. in indir. disc., (396); and specimens of indir. disc., (400, 401). 3. **prius quam**: introducing **attigisset**, subord. verb in O. O., 'before the battering ram touched (reached)': **attigisset** = **attigerit** (fut. perf. indic.) in the *direct;* why not *imperf.* subjunc.? 4. **nullam condicionem**: acc. subj. of **esse**, 'that there were (would be) no terms.' **nisi armis traditis**: idiom, translated, 'unless their arms were handed over.' Offers of submission must be made before the battering ram (**aries**) reached the wall, since a besieged place was looked upon as already captured when this stage of the siege was reached. 5. **id facturum esse**: id, obj. of **facturum**, and anteced. of **quod**, 'that he would do that thing.' **quod ... fecisset**: subord. verb in O. O., 'which he did (had done).' **fecisset** = what, in the *direct?* 6. **ne ... inferrent**: could non be used? see (228, 389, 390); 'that he would command them not to do any (**quam**) harm.' Although **ne ... inferrent** depends upon **imperaturum (esse)**, which is *fut.*, yet the *sequence of tense* is determined by **respondit** (*past* tense); see (397). 7. **ad suos**: 'to their own people.' **quae**: anteced. is (**ea**), obj. of **facere** ; **quae** = subj. of **imperarentur**. **facere** : infin. in indir. disc., subj. is (**se**); we should expect **facturos esse**, but the pres. tense is here used as an immediate future: 'they said that they would do those things which were being ordered.' 8. **magna multitudine ... iacta**: abl. absol. of *time* mod. **usi sunt**, 'after they had thrown a large number.' 9. **sic ut**: 'so that.' **summam**: noun, dir. obj. of **adaequarent** (subjunc. of affirm. result). 10. **acervi** : subj. of **adaequarent**, 'the heaps of arms were almost as high as the top of the wall and the agger.' The deep space (**fossa**) between the wall and the end of the mound (**agger**) which gradually rose to a height equal to that of the wall of the town was almost filled with the arms.

11. **et tamen tertia** . . . **celata, retenta**: 'and yet about a third part being concealed and kept.' 12. **portis patefactis**: abl. absol. mod. **usi sunt**; 'after throwing the gates wide open they enjoyed peace.' 13. **pace**: why abl.? see (353).

CHAPTER XXXIII.—1. **sub**: 'towards.' 2. **ne... acciperent**: neg. purpose; would non do? see (211, 320); 'lest they should receive.' **quam**: indefinite pron. after **si, nisi, ne, num**; 'any violence.' **ab**: 'at the hands of.' **illi**: subj. of **fecerunt**, line 11. **inito**: p. p. p. of **ineo**, forming abl. absol. with **consilio**, the phrase modifying **fecerunt**; 'according to a plan formerly arranged.' **ut**, etc.: parenthetical and impersonal, 'as it was learned (later on).' 4. **quod**... **crediderant**: mod. **fecerunt**, 'because they had supposed.' **deducturos esse**: indir. disc. with **crediderant**. 6. **partim cum**: 'partly with those arms... partly with shields,' adverbial phrases mod. **fecerunt**. 7. **ex... factis**, etc.: **factis** limits **scutis**, 'made out of bark or twigs woven together.' **quae**: antecod. is **scutis**; it is the dir. obj. of **induxerant**. 8. **ut**: 'as.' 9. **tertia vigilia**: abl. of time mod. **fecerunt**. **qua**: adv., 'where.' This passage indicates that the Roman lines were on high ground. **minime**: adv. mod. **arduus**, 'least difficult.' 10. **ascensus**: subj. of **videbatur**, 'the approach to (ad) ... seemed.' 11. **ut**, etc.: 'as Caesar had previously commanded'; **imperarat** = **imperaverat**. 12. **ignibus**: abl. of means mod. **facta**, which in turn limits **significatione** in the abl. sing. fem.; 'after fire-signals had been made.' 13. **eo concursum est**: impers., see (365). **pugnatum... est**: 'and the enemy fought,' what literally? **ita acriter ut**: 'just as bravely as.' 14. **ut**: goes with **pugnari debuit**, 'as it ought *to have been* fought.' For meaning of **pugnari** (pres. infin.), see (385), how ought and must are expressed, *past action*, example *a*. Translate freely 'as brave men ought to have fought.' **a viris**: pers. agent, see (240). 15. **qui... iacerent**: characteristic rel. clause which takes a *subjunc.* verb; 'who were casting.' 16. **cum... consisteret**: causal cum, see (350), 'since all hope depended (was depending)': the clause mod. **pugnari debuit**. **in una virtute**: 'upon valor alone.' 17. **ad**: adv. mod. **quattuor**, 'after about four thousand.' 18. **cum . . . defenderent**: causal clause mod. **refractis**, 'at a time when no one *any longer* (iam) defended them.' 20. **sectionem . . . universam**: i.e. the whole people with all their possessions. According to ancient ideas this procedure of selling into slavery the captured foe as a punishment for treachery was perfectly justifiable. **ab eis**: regular pers. agent, see (240), mod. **relatus est**; 'the number of souls reported to him by those who.' **milium**, etc.: pred. gen. of characteristic.

CHAPTER XXXIV.—1. **eodem tempore**: as the subjugation of the several tribes mentioned in this chapter was accomplished by the VIIth legion, which had been detached from the Roman army just after the battle of the Sambre, it would seem that the siege described in the few preceding chapters must have lasted a month or more. **a Crasso**: pers. agent mod. **certior factus est**. 2. **ad**: 'against.' 4. **certior factus est**: as a verb of hearing it takes the acc. + infin., **civitates ... redactas esse**.

CHAPTER XXXV.—1. **tanta opinio ... perlata est**: 'such a report of this war was spread.' Notice the emphasis given to the verb by the prefix **per**; the report went from tribe to tribe until it reached all of them. 2. **uti ... mitterentur**: affirm. result, 'that ambassadors were sent.' 3. **incolerent**: subjunc. by attraction, see (276). Why is **quae** *fem. plur.?* 4. **qui ... pollicerentur**: rel. clause of purpose, see (311). What is the *time* of the action of **pollicerentur** with respect to that of **mitterentur**, *present* (going on) at the *time of sending*, or *future* (subsequent to it)? **daturas (esse)**: why not **daturos**? To what does **se** refer? What is the gender of **nationibus**? 5. **quas Caesar iussit**: '*and* Caesar ordered *these*.' **legationes** = **legatos**. **in Italiam**: i.e. Cisalpine Gaul. Caesar's province extended to the Rubicon. **Illyricum**: east of the Adriatic, also a part of Caesar's 'province,' where he usually spent the winter season. 6. **inita**: from **ineo**, p. p. p. abl. absol. with **aestate**, 'at the beginning of the following summer,' 'early next summer.' 7. **in Carnutes**, etc.: adverbial phrases mod. **deductis**, which forms an abl. absol. with **legionibus**; 'after he had brought his legions into their winter-quarters among (in).' **quaeque civitates**: translate as if, **et civitates quae**, 'and among those states which were.' 8. **ubi**: 'where.' 10. **ob easque**: note the position of **que**. **ex litteris**: 'in accordance with letters from Caesar.' 11. **supplicatio**: a public thanksgiving, decreed by the Senate in honor of a victory, at first lasting only one day, then usually three or four. Caesar was granted a **supplicatio** which lasted for fifteen days, the longest time that had ever been granted. **quod**: = **id quod**, 'an honor (a thing) which.' 12. **nulli**: notice the emphatic position.

448. First-conjugation verbs.

For the principal parts of verbs marked *, see vocabulary at end of the book; those unmarked are regular, like portō, āınō, etc.

1. accommodō, *adjust*
2. adaequō, *equal*
3. adiuvō,* *aid*
4. administrō, *execute*
5. adpropīnquō, *draw near to*
6. aedificō, *build*
7. amplificō, *increase*
8. appellō, *call*
9. arbitror,[1] *think*
10. armō, *arm*
11. cēlō, *conceal*
12. circumdō,* *surround*
13. coacervō, *pile up*
14. cohortor,[1] *encourage*
15. commemorō, *relate*
16. comparō, *prepare*
17. cōnfīrmō, *establish*
18. coniūrō, *conspire*
19. conlocō, *place*
20. cōnor,[1] *attempt*
21. cōnservō, *spare*
22. convocō, *summon*
23. cōnspicor,* *see*
24. dēcertō, *contend*
25. dēmōnstrō, *explain*
26. dēpopulor,* *lay waste*
27. dēprecor,* *pray (for)*
28. dēspērō, *despair (of)*
29. dēspoliō, *deprive (of)*
30. dīmicō, *fight*
31. dissipō, *scatter*
32. dō,* *give*
33. dominor,* *rule*
34. dubitō, *hesitate, doubt*
35. exagitō, *harass*
36. exanimō, *make breathless*
37. exercitō, *train*
38. exīstimō, *think*
39. explōrō, *find out*
40. expūgnō, *storm*
41. exspectō, *await*
42. fugō, *rout*
43. hiemō, *winter*
44. imperō, *command*
45. impetrō, *obtain*
46. incitō, *quicken, excite*
47. increpitō, *taunt*
48. incūsō, *blame*
49. īnstō,* *press forward*
50. intrō, *enter*
51. iūdicō, *suppose*
52. iuvō,* *aid*
53. laxō, *spread out*
54. mandō, *direct, instruct*
55. mātūrō, *hasten*
56. moror,* *delay*
57. nāvō, *do with zeal* [operam nāvāre, *do one's best*]
58. nōminō, *name*
59. nūdō, *strip*
60. nūntiō, *announce*
61. occupō, *seize*
62. oppūgnō, *attack*
63. pācō, *subdue*
64. perīclitor,* *test, try* [order
65. perturbō, *throw into dis-*

---
[1] deponent verb; see (325) and vocabulary at end of the book.

FIRST- AND SECOND-CONJUGATION VERBS.

66. populor,* *plunder*
67. portō, *carry*
68. postulō, *demand*
69. praedor,* *plunder*
70. praestō,* *excel*
71. proelior,* *fight*
72. prōflīgō, *defeat*
73. properō, *hasten*
74. prōpūgnō, *fight*
75. prōturbō, *repulse*
76. prōvolō, *rush forth*
77. pūgnō, *fight*
78. redintegrō, *renew*
79. renūntiō, *announce*

80. revocō, *call back*
81. servō, *watch*
82. sīgnificō, *show*
83. sollicitō, *incite*
84. superō, *overcome*
85. sustentō, *hold out*
86. tardō, *check*
87. vāstō, *lay waste*
88. versor,* *remain, be*
89. vetō,* *forbid*
90. vexō, *harass*
91. vītō, *avoid*
92. vulnerō, *wound*

449. Second-conjugation verbs.

For the principal parts, see the vocabulary at end of the book.

1. audeō, *dare*
2. commoveō, *alarm*
3. compleō, *fill*
4. contineō, *keep, hold in*
5. dēbeō, *ought, owe*
6. dēleō, *destroy*
7. dēterreō, *prevent*
8. distineō, *separate, keep apart*
9. doceō, *explain*
10. habeō, *have*
11. iaceō, *lie prostrate*
12. invideō, *envy*
13. irrīdeō, *mock*
14. iubeō, *order*
15. lateō, *lie hid*
16. moneō, *direct, advise*
17. moveō, *move*
18. obtineō, *hold, maintain*
19. oportet, *ought, it behooves*
20. pateō, *extend*
21. permoveō, *excite*

22. persuādeō, *persuade*
23. perterreō, *frighten*
24. pertineō, *reach*
25. polliceor, *promise*
26. possideō, *possess, occupy*
27. praebeō, *furnish, display*
28. prohibeō, *prevent, cut off*
29. prōmoveō, *move forward*
30. prōvideō, *provide*
31. respondeō, *reply*
32. retineō, *restrain*
33. studeō, *desire*
34. supersedeō, *refrain from*
35. sustineō, *withstand*
36. teneō, *hold*
37. timeō, *fear*
38. urgeō, *press hard*
39. valeō, *have influence, be strong*
40. vereor, *fear*
41. videō, *see*
42. videor, *seem*

450. Third-conjugation verbs.

For the principal parts, see the vocabulary at end of the book.

1. abdō, *hide*
2. accēdō, *approach*
3. accidō, *happen*
4. accipiō, *receive*
5. addūcō, *bring, influence*
6. adiciō, *hurl*
7. aggredior, *attack*
8. agō, *do*
9. āmittō, *lose, let pass*
10. arcessō, *summon*
11. ascendō, *climb*
12. attingō, *border upon*
13. āvertō, *turn back* or *away*
14. cadō, *fall, be killed*
15. cēdō, *retreat*
16. circumiciō, *place around*
17. claudō, *close*
18. cōgnōscō, *find out*
19. cōgō, *collect, assemble*
20. committō, *begin*
21. compellō, *drive*
22. concīdō, *cut to pieces*
23. concurrō, *hurry, rush*
24. condūcō, *hire, collect*
25. cōnficiō, *exhaust, furnish, finish*
26. cōnfīdō, *trust, rely on*
27. cōnflīgō, *fight*
28. congredior, *fight*
29. cōniciō, *place, hurl, drive*
30. coniungō, *join*
31. cōnscrībō, *enroll*
32. cōnsequor, *pursue*
33. cōnsīdō, *settle, encamp*
34. cōnsistō, *make a stand, rally*
35. cōnspiciō, *see*
36. cōnstituō, *determine, arrange*
37. cōnsuēscō, *be accustomed*
38. contendō, *hasten, struggle*
39. convertō, *turn*
40. crēdō, *believe*
41. cupiō, *desire*
42. dēcernō, *decree*
43. dēcurrō, *run down*
44. dēdō, *surrender*
45. dēdūcō, *lead away*
46. dēfendō, *defend*
47. dēficiō, *revolt*
48. dēiciō, *hurl down*
49. dēligō, *choose*
50. dēpōnō, *set down*
51. dēserō, *desert*
52. dēsistō, *cease*
53. dētrahō, *jerk, snatch (away)*
54. dētrūdō, *remove, strip off*
55. dīcō, *say*
56. dīmittō, *dismiss*
57. dīripiō, *plunder*
58. discēdō, *depart*
59. dūcō, *lead*
60. ēdūcō, *lead out*
61. efficiō, *bring about, cause*
62. ēgredior, *depart*
63. ēligō, *choose*
64. ēmittō, *hurl*
65. emō, *buy*
66. ēnāscor, *grow out*
67. excēdō, *go away*
68. expellō, *drive out*

THIRD-CONJUGATION VERBS.

69. exstruō, *construct*
70. faciō, *make*
71. fallō, *disappoint*
72. fugiō, *flee*
73. gerō, *carry on*
74. iaciō, *hurl, construct*
75. impellō, *urge on*
76. incendō, *burn*
77. incidō, *happen*
78. incīdō, *notch, cut into*
79. incipiō, *begin*
80. incolō, *inhabit, live*
81. indūcō, *cover, draw on*
82. induō, *put on*
83. īnflectō, *bend*
84. ingredior, *enter*
85. innītor, *lean upon*
86. īnsequor, *pursue*
87. īnsistō, *stand upon*
88. īnstruō, *draw up, erect*
89. intellegō, *know* [tween
90. intercēdō, *be or move be-*
91. intercipiō, *pick up*
92. interficiō, *kill*
93. intericiō, *place between*
94. intermittō, *cease*
95. interscindō, *cut down*
96. intexō, *weave in*
97. intrōdūcō, *bring in*
98. intrōmittō, *let in*
99. inveterāscō, *grow old*
100. loquor, *speak*
101. mittō, *send*
102. nāscor, *rise, spring up*
103. obdūcō, *dig, construct*
104. occīdō, *slay*
105. occurrō, *meet*
106. omittō, *overlook*
107. patefaciō, *open wide*
108. patior, *allow*
109. pellō, *defeat, drive*
110. permittō, *give up, entrust*
111. perspiciō, *find out*
112. petō, *ask for, seek*
113. pōnō, *place*
114. poscō, *demand*
115. praeficiō, *place in command of*
116. praemittō, *send forward*
117. praescrībō, *give directions*
118. premō, *press hard*
119. prōcēdō, *advance*
120. prōcumbō, *fall*
121. proficīscor, *set out, go*
122. profugiō, *flee*
123. prōgredior, *advance*
124. prōiciō, *give up, abandon*
125. prōpōnō, *display*
126. prōsequor, *pursue*
127. quaerō, *inquire*
128. recipiō, *receive*
129. reddō, *give back, render*
130. redigō, *reduce*
131. redūcō, *lead back*
132. refringō, *break down*
133. rēiciō, *throw or drive back*
134. relanguēscō, *be weakened*
135. relinquō, *leave*
136. remittō, *hurl back, relax*
137. repellō, *drive back*
138. resistō, *resist*
139. respiciō, *look back*
140. revertō, *turn back*
141. revertor, *return*
142. scrībō, *write*
143. sequor, *follow*

144. statuō, *determine*
145. submittō, *send*
146. subruō, *undermine*
147. subsequor, *follow after*
148. succēdō, *approach*
149. sūmō, *claim, assume*
150. tendō, *stretch out*

151. trādō, *hand over*
152. trādūcō, *lead across*
153. trānsgredior, *cross*
154. ūtor, *use, employ*
155. vēndō, *sell*
156. vergō, *incline*
157. vincō, *conquer*

451. Fourth-conjugation verbs.

For the principal parts, see the vocabulary at end of the book.

1. adorior, *attack*
2. audiō, *hear*
3. circummūniō, *fortify strongly*
4. circumveniō, *surround*
5. cōnsentiō, *conspire*
6. conveniō, *assemble*
7. dēveniō, *come*
8. dīmētior, *measure off*
9. exaudiō, *hear distinctly*

10. experior, *try, risk*
11. impediō, *hinder*
12. inveniō, *come upon*
13. mūniō, *fortify*
14. obveniō, *meet*
15. orior, *descend, spring from*
16. perveniō, *arrive at*
17. potior, *capture*
18. reperiō, *find out*
19. veniō, *come*

452. Irregular verbs.

For the principal parts, see the vocabulary at end of the book.

1. absum, *be distant*
2. adeō, *approach*
3. adferō, *bring to*
4. coepī, *begin*
5. cōnferō, *collect*
6. dēferō, *report*
7. dēsum, *be lacking, wanting*
8. eō, *go*
9. exeō, *go out*
10. ferō, *bear*
11. fīō, *be made, happen*
12. ineō, *enter upon*
13. īnferō, *wage, bring upon*

14. intersum, impers., *it con-*
15. nōlō, *be unwilling* [*cerns*
16. offerō, *carry, bring*
17. perferō, *endure*
18. possum, *be able, can*
19. praeferō, *prefer*
20. praesum, *be in command of*
21. redeō, *go back, descend,*
22. referō, *report* [*slope*
23. subeō, *approach*
24. sum, *be*
25. supersum, *survive*
26. trānseō, *cross*

PARADIGMS OF DECLENSIONS.

453. First declension.—Most nouns are *feminine*. The stem ends in a.

Silva, *forest*.		Galea, *helmet*.	
SINGULAR.	PLURAL.	SINGULAR.	PLURAL.
silva	silvae	galea	galeae
silvae	silvārum	galeae	galeārum
silvae	silvīs	galeae	galeīs
silvam	silvās	galeam	galeās
silva	silvae	galea	galeae
silvā	silvīs	galeā	galeīs

454. Second declension.—Nouns in **us**, **er**, and **ir** are *masculine*, those in **um** *neuter*. The stem ends in o.

Gladius, *sword*.		Ager, *field*.	
SINGULAR.	PLURAL.	SINGULAR.	PLURAL.
gladius	gladiī	ager	agrī
gladiī	gladiōrum	agrī	agrōrum
gladiō	gladiīs	agrō	agrīs
gladium	gladiōs	agrum	agrōs
gladie	gladiī	ager	agrī
gladiō	gladiīs	agrō	agrīs

Vir, *man*.		Scūtum, *shield*.	
SINGULAR.	PLURAL.	SINGULAR.	PLURAL.
vir	virī	scūtum	scūta
virī	virōrum	scūtī	scūtōrum
virō	virīs	scūtō	scūtīs
virum	virōs	scūtum	scūta
vir	virī	scūtum	scūta
virō	virīs	scūtō	scūtīs

455. Classification of third-declension nouns by stems.— The stems are divided according to their last letter, called the *stem-characteristic*, into (1) *consonant stems* and (2) *vowel stems*.

Consonant stems are divided into—
1. *Liquid* stems, ending in l, m, n, r.
2. *Sibilant* stems, ending in s.
3. *Mute* stems
   { ending in *p-mute*, b, p.
   { " " *k-mute*, c, g.
   { " " *t-mute*, d, t.

456. Consonant stems.—A. *Liquid stems* in l or r form the nominative without terminations; as, **sōl, sōlis,** *sun*, stem **sōl; rūmor, rūmōris,** stem **rūmōr**.

In stems in **n** the nominative is formed without **s**; most masculine and feminine nouns drop the stem-characteristic and change a preceding vowel to **o**, while most neuter and a few masculine nouns retain the stem-characteristic and change preceding **i** to **e**:

homō, hominis, stem **homin**; **flūmen, flūminis,** stem **flūmin**.

B. *Sibilant stems* have no additional **s** in the nominative, masculines changing **e** to **i** before **s**, and neuters **e** or **o** to **u**; in the oblique cases the **s** of the stem changes to **r** between two vowels.

pulvis, pulveris (mas.), *powder*, stem **pulves**.
latus, lateris, stem **lates**; **corpus, corporis,** stem **corpos**.

C. *Mute stems*, masculines and feminines, have **s** in the nominative. Before **s**, a *p-mute* is retained, a *k-mute* unites with it as **x**, a *t-mute* is dropped. Most polysyllabic mute stems change the final vowel **i** to **e** in the nominative.

p-mute: **prīnceps, prīncipis,** stem **prīncip**.
k-mute: **lēx, lēgis,** stem **lēg**; **vōx, vōcis,** stem **vōc**.
t-mute: **mīles, mīlitis,** stem **mīlit**; **pēs, pedis,** stem **ped**.

PARADIGMS OF DECLENSIONS.

457. Vowel stems end in *i* or *u*.—Masculine and feminine nouns form the nominative in **s**, and have **ēs** and **īs** in the accusative plural; neuters end in **e**, **al**, **ar** and have **ia** in the nominative, accusative, and vocative plural, and **ī** in the ablative singular. Some masculine and feminine nouns also have **ī** in the ablative singular. A few feminines change the stem vowel i to **e** in the nominative before **s**, and neuters change the i to **e**, which is dropped in polysyllabics after l and r.

Vowel stems in i are *parisyllabic* and have **ium** in the genitive plural, masculines and feminines ending in **ēs**, **er, is**—neuters in **e, al, ar**.

  vātēs, vātis (mas. and fem.), *seer*, stem vāti.
  hostis, hostis (mas.), stem hosti.
  īnsīgne, īnsīgnis (neut.), stem īnsīgni.
  animal, animālis, *animal*, stem animāli.

458. Third declension.—General rules of gender for third-declension nouns, classed according to the nominative ending.

GROUP I.

Masculines are: (1) nouns in **es**, gen. **itis**: mīles, mīlitis;—(2) **es** or **is**, gen. **idis**: obsēs, obsidis; lapis, lapidis;—(3) **er** or **or**: frāter, rūmor;—(4) many *vowel stems* in i: fīnis, fīnis;—(5) some *monosyllables*: pēs, mōs, pōns;—(6) nouns in **ō** or **ōs**.

Mīles, *soldier.*   **Lapis**, *stone.*   **Frāter**, *brother.*

SINGULAR.	PLURAL.	SINGULAR.	PLURAL.	SINGULAR.	PLURAL.
mīles	mīlitēs	lapis	lapidēs	frāter	frātrēs
mīlitis	mīlitum	lapidis	lapidum	frātris	frātrum
mīlitī	mīlitibus	lapidī	lapidibus	frātrī	frātribus
mīlitem	mīlitēs	lapidem	lapidēs	frātrem	frātrēs
mīles	mīlitēs	lapis	lapidēs	frāter	frātrēs
mīlite	mīlitibus	lapide	lapidibus	frātre	frātribus

Hostis, *enemy.*

SINGULAR.	PLURAL.
hostis	hostēs
hostis	hostium
hostī	hostibus
hostem	hostēs, -īs
hostis	hostēs
hoste	hostibus

Pēs, *foot.*

SINGULAR.	PLURAL.
pēs	pedēs
pedis	pedum
pedī	pedibus
pedem	pedēs
pēs	pedēs
pede	pedibus

For the mode of distinguishing *vowel stems,* which are parisyllabic, from *consonant stems,* which are imparisyllabic, see (**131**).

GROUP II.

Feminines are: (1) nouns in **ās,** gen. **ātis: facultās, facultātis;**—(2) nouns in **iō** (*abstract and collective*): **legiō, legiōnis;**—(3) **ūs,** gen. **ūtis** or **ūdis: virtūs, virtūtis;**—(4) **dō** and **gō,** gen. **inis: multitūdō, multitūdinis;**—(5) some *monosyllables:* **pāx, lēx;**—(6) nouns in **ēs, ys, is,** and **s** (preceded by a *consonant*).

Facultās, *opportunity.*

SINGULAR.	PLURAL.
facultās	facultātēs
facultātis	facultātum
facultātī	facultātibus
facultātem	facultātēs
facultās	facultātēs
facultāte	facultātibus

Legiō, *legion.*

SINGULAR.	PLURAL.
legiō	legiōnēs
legiōnis	legiōnum
legiōnī	legiōnibus
legiōnem	legiōnēs
legiō	legiōnēs
legiōne	legiōnibus

Virtūs, *courage.*

SINGULAR.	PLURAL.
virtūs	virtūtēs
virtūtis	virtūtum
virtūtī	virtūtibus
virtūtem	virtūtēs
virtūs	virtūtēs
virtūte	virtūtibus

Lēx, *law.*

SINGULAR.	PLURAL.
lēx	lēgēs
lēgis	lēgum
lēgī	lēgibus
lēgem	lēgēs
lēx	lēgēs
lēge	lēgibus

Multitūdō, *multitude*.

SINGULAR.	PLURAL.
multitūdō	multitūdinēs
multitūdinis	multitūdinum
multitūdinī	multitūdinibus
multitūdinem	multitūdinēs
multitūdō	multitūdinēs
multitūdine	multitūdinibus

GROUP III.

Neuters are: (1) nouns in us, gen. eris or oris: latus, lateris; corpus, corporis;—(2) men, gen. minis: flūmen, flūminis;—(3) nouns in e, al, ar, ur.

Latus, *side*. Corpus, *body*.

SINGULAR.	PLURAL.	SINGULAR.	PLURAL.
latus	latera	corpus	corpora
lateris	laterum	corporis	corporum
laterī	lateribus	corporī	corporibus
latus	latera	corpus	corpora
latus	latera	corpus	corpora
latere	lateribus	corpore	corporibus

Flūmen, *river*. Insīgne, *badge*.

SINGULAR.	PLURAL.	SINGULAR.	PLURAL.
flūmen	flūmina	insīgne	insīgnia
flūminis	flūminum	insīgnis	insīgnium
flūminī	flūminibus	insīgnī	insīgnibus
flūmen	flūmina	insīgne	insīgnia
flūmen	flūmina	insīgne	insīgnia
flūmine	flūminibus	insīgnī	insīgnibus

459. Irregular nouns of the third declension.

Mīlia, *thousands*. Vīs, *force, vigor*. Iter, *march, journey*.

SINGULAR.	PLURAL.	SINGULAR.	PLURAL.	SINGULAR.	PLURAL.
mīlle	mīlia	vīs	vīrēs	iter	itinera
indeclinable	mīlium	vīs	vīrium	itineris	itinerum
adjective	mīlibus	—	vīribus	itinerī	itineribus
	mīlia	vim	vīrēs	iter	itinera
	mīlia	—	vīrēs	iter	itinera
	mīlibus	vī	vīribus	itinere	itineribus

460. Genitive plural in *um* and *ium*, third declension.
Vowel stems in i have ium.

Monosyllabic mute stems with the characteristic preceded by a *consonant* have ium: mōns, montium, urbs, urbium.

Monosyllabic mute stems with characteristics preceded by a *long vowel* have either um or ium: dōs, dōtis (*dowry*), dōtium ; lēx, lēgis, lēgum.

Monosyllabic mute stems with the characteristic preceded by a *short vowel* have um: dux, ducis, ducum.

Polysyllabic stems in āt have both um and ium: cīvitās, cīvitātis, cīvitātum or cīvitātium. *Polysyllabic stems* in nt and rt often have ium : cohors, cohortis, cohortium.

461. Fourth declension.—Nouns in us are *masculine*, a few *feminine* ; those in ū, *neuter*. The stem ends in u.

Manus, *hand, band.*

SINGULAR.	PLURAL.
manus	manūs
manūs	manuum
manuī (ū)	manibus
manum	manūs
manus	manūs
manū	manibus

Cornū, *horn, wing.*

SINGULAR.	PLURAL.
cornū	cornua
cornūs	cornuum
cornū	cornibus
cornū	cornua
cornū	cornua
cornū	cornibus

462. Fifth declension.—Nouns are *feminine*, except diēs. *day*, which is masculine or feminine in the singular and masculine in the plural. The stem ends in ē.

Diēs, *day.*

SINGULAR.	PLURAL.
diēs	diēs
diēī	diērum
diēī	diēbus
diem	diēs
diēs	diēs
diē	diēbus

Rēs, *thing.*

SINGULAR.	PLURAL.
rēs	rēs
reī	rērum
reī	rēbus
rem	rēs
rēs	rēs
rē	rēbus

PRONOUNS.

463 Personal pronoun, first person.

Ego, *I.*
SINGULAR.
Nom. ego
Gen. meī
Dat. mihi
Acc. mē
Abl. mē

Nōs, *we.*
PLURAL.
nōs
{ nostrum
{ nostrī
nōbīs
nōs
nōbīs

464. Demonstrative pronouns.

Is, ea, id, *he, this, that,* etc.; sometimes used as the personal pronoun, third person.

	SINGULAR.			PLURAL.		
Nom.	is,	ea,	id	eī (iī),	eae,	ea
Gen.	ēius			eōrum,	eārum,	eōrum
Dat.	eī			eīs (iīs)		
Acc.	eum,	eam,	id	eōs,	eās,	ea
Abl.	eō,	eā,	eō	eīs (iīs)		

Hīc, *this* (near the speaker).

	SINGULAR.			PLURAL.		
Nom.	hīc,	haec,	hōc	hī,	hae,	haec
Gen.	hūius			hōrum,	hārum,	hōrum
Dat.	huic			hīs		
Acc.	hunc,	hanc,	hōc	hōs,	hās,	haec
Abl.	hōc,	hāc,	hōc	hīs		

Ille, *that* (remote from the speaker).

	SINGULAR.			PLURAL.		
Nom.	ille,	illa,	illud	illī,	illae,	illa
Gen.	illīus			illōrum,	illārum,	illōrum
Dat.	illī			illīs		
Acc.	illum,	illam,	illud	illōs,	illās,	illa
Abl.	illō,	illā,	illō	illīs		

Īdem, *the same.*

SINGULAR.

Nom.	īdem,	eadem,	idem
Gen.	ēiusdem		
Dat.	eīdem		
Acc.	eundem,	eandem,	idem
Abl.	eōdem,	eādem,	eōdem

PLURAL.

Nom.	eīdem (iīdem),	eaedem,	eadem
Gen.	eōrundem,	eārundem,	eōrundem
Dat.	eīsdem (iīsdem)		
Acc.	eōsdem,	eāsdem,	eadem
Abl.	eīsdem (iīsdem)		

Ipse, *he, self* (with intensive force).

	SINGULAR.			PLURAL.		
Nom.	ipse,	ipsa,	ipsum	ipsī,	ipsae,	ipsa
Gen.	ipsīus			ipsōrum,	ipsārum,	ipsōrum
Dat.	ipsī			ipsīs		
Acc.	ipsum,	ipsam,	ipsum	ipsōs,	ipsās,	ipsa
Abl.	ipsō,	ipsā,	ipsō	ipsīs		

465. Relative, Interrogative, and Indefinite pronouns.

Relative **quī, quae, quod,** *who, which, that.*

	SINGULAR.			PLURAL.		
Nom.	quī,	quae,	quod	quī,	quae,	quae
Gen.	cūius			quōrum,	quārum,	quōrum
Dat.	cui			quibus		
Acc.	quem,	quam,	quod	quōs,	quās,	quae
Abl.	quō,	quā,	quō	quibus		

Interrogative and Indefinite **quis (quī),** *who?—any one.*

SINGULAR.

Nom.	quis (quī),	quae,	quid (quod)
Gen.	cūius		
Dat.	cui		
Acc.	quem,	quam,	quid (quod)
Abl.	quō,	quā,	quō

The plural is the same as that of the *relative.*

466. Adjectives.—First and second declensions.

Altus, *high, tall.*

SINGULAR.			PLURAL.		
altus,	-a,	-um	altī,	-ae,	-a
altī,	-ae,	-ī	altōrum,	-ārum,	-ōrum
altō,	-ae,	-ō	altīs,	-īs,	-īs
altum,	-am,	-um	altōs,	-ās,	-a
alte,	-a,	-um	altī,	-ae,	-a
altō,	-ā,	-ō	altīs,	-īs,	-īs

Crēber, *frequent.*

SINGULAR.			PLURAL.		
crēber,	-bra,	-brum	crēbrī,	-brae,	-bra
crēbrī,	-brae,	-brī	crēbrōrum,	-brārum,	-brōrum
crēbrō,	-brae,	-brō	crēbrīs,	-īs,	-īs
crēbrum,	-bram,	-brum	crēbrōs,	-ās,	-a
crēber,	-bra,	-brum	crēbrī,	-ae,	-a
crēbrō,	-brā,	-brō	crēbrīs,	-īs,	-īs

467. Adjectives continued.—Third declension.

Duplex, *double*—adjective of *one ending.*

SINGULAR.	PLURAL.
duplex, duplex, duplex	duplicēs, duplicēs, duplicia
duplicis	duplicium
duplicī	duplicibus
duplicem, -cem, duplex	duplicēs (-īs), -cēs (-īs), -cia
duplex	duplicēs, duplicēs, duplicia
duplicī	duplicibus

Fortis, *brave*—adjective of *two endings.*

SINGULAR.			PLURAL.		
fortis,	-tis,	-te	fortēs,	fortēs,	fortia
fortis			fortium		
fortī			fortibus		
fortem,	-tem,	-te	fortēs (-īs),	fortēs (-īs),	fortia
fortis,	-tis,	-te	fortēs,	fortēs,	fortia
fortī			fortibus		

Equester, *of cavalry*—adjective of *three endings.*

SINGULAR.			PLURAL.		
equester,	-tris,	-tre	equestrēs,	-trēs,	-tria
equestris			equestrium		
equestrī			equestribus		
equestrem,	-trem,	-tre	equestrēs (-īs),	-trēs (-īs),	-tria
equester,	-tris,	-tre	equestrēs,	-trēs,	-tria
equestrī			equestribus		

Pūgnāns (present participle), declined like an *adjective* of the *third declension*, with *one ending* in the nominative singular.

SINGULAR.			PLURAL.		
pūgnāns,	pūgnāns,	pūgnāns	pūgnantēs,	-tēs,	-tia
pūgnantis			pūgnantium		
pūgnantī			pūgnantibus		
pūgnantem,	-tem,	pūgnāns	pūgnantēs (-īs),	-tēs (-īs),	-tia
pūgnāns			pūgnantēs,	-tēs,	-tia
pūgnante (-ī)			pūgnantibus		

Altior, *taller*—comparative of altus.

SINGULAR.			PLURAL.
altior,	-ior,	-ius	altiōrēs, -ōrēs, -ōra
altiōris			altiōrum
altiōrī			altiōribus
altiōrem,	-ōrem,	altius	altiōrēs, -ōrēs, -ōra
altior,	-ior	-ius	altiōrēs, -ōrēs, -ōra
altiōre (-ī)			altiōribus

Adjectives of the third declension, parisyllabic and imparisyllabic, such as **duplex, fortis, equester,** etc., have ī in the *ablative singular*, **ia** in the *nominative plural neuter*, and īs or ēs in the *accusative plural masculine* and *feminine*.

Note carefully the corresponding endings of these cases in the present participle (**pūgnāns**), and the comparative of the adjective (**altior**).

468. Numeral adjectives.

Ūnus,[1] *one.* Duo, *two.* Trēs, *three.*

Nom.	ūnus, -a, -um	duo,	duae,	duo	trēs, trēs, tria
Gen.	ūnīus	duōrum,	-ārum,	-ōrum	trium
Dat.	ūnī	duōbus,	-ābus,	-ōbus	tribus
Acc.	ūnum, -am, -um	duōs (duo), -ās,		-o	trēs, trēs, tria
Abl.	ūnō, -ā, -ō	duōbus,	-ābus,	-ōbus	tribus

The numeral adjectives 4–100 are indeclinable; hundreds are declined like the *plural* of **altus**.

COMPARISON OF ADJECTIVES.

469. Regular adjectives.

POSITIVE.	COMPARATIVE.		SUPERLATIVE.	
altus, *tall*	altior,	-ior, -ius	altissimus,	-a, -um
certus, *certain*	certior,	-ior, -ius	certissimus,	-a, -um
dēnsus, *dense*	dēnsior,	-ior, -ius	dēnsissimus,	-a, -um
inīquus, *unfair*	inīquior,	-ior, -ius	inīquissimus,	-a, -um
parātus, *ready*	parātior,	-ior, -ius	parātissimus,	-a, -um
tardus, *slow*	tardior,	-ior, -ius	tardissimus,	-a, -um
tūtus, *safe*	tūtior,	-ior, -ius	tūtissimus,	-a, -um
fortis, *brave*	fortior,	-ior, -ius	fortissimus,	-a, -um
gravis, *severe*	gravior,	-ior, -ius	gravissimus,	-a, -um
potēns, *powerful*	potentior,	-ior, -ius	potentissimus,	-a, -um
amāns, *loving*	amantior,	-ior, -ius	amantissimus,	-a, -um

470. Adjectives ending in *er.* — These add rimus, -a, -um to the *nominative singular masculine* of the positive.

POSITIVE.	COMPARATIVE.		SUPERLATIVE.	
ācer, *sharp*	ācrior,	-ior, -ius	ācerrimus,	-a, -um
asper, *rough*	asperior,	-ior, -ius	asperrimus,	-a, -um
celer, *swift*	celerior,	-ior, -ius	celerrimus,	-a, -um
miser, *wretched*	miserior,	-ior, -ius	miserrimus,	-a, -um
pulcher, *beautiful*	pulchrior,	-ior, -ius	pulcherrimus,	-a, -um

---

[1] The voc. sing. mas. ūne is found but rarely.

471. Adjectives ending in *ilis*.—*Six* adjectives in ilis add the superlative ending limus to the *stem*, stripped of its final vowel, viz.: facilis, *easy;* difficilis, *difficult;* similis, *like;* dissimilis, *unlike;* gracilis, *slender;* humilis, *low.*

POSITIVE.	COMPARATIVE.		SUPERLATIVE.	
facilis	facilior,	-ior, -ius	facillimus,	-a, -um
difficilis	difficilior,	-ior, -ius	difficillimus,	-a, -um
similis	similior,	-ior, -ius	simillimus,	-a, -um
dissimilis	dissimilior,	-ior, -ius	dissimillimus,	-a, -um
gracilis	gracilior,	-ior, -ius	gracillimus,	-a, -um
humilis	humilior,	-ior, -ius	humillimus,	-a, -um

472. Irregular adjectives.

POSITIVE.	COMPARATIVE.		SUPERLATIVE.	
bonus, *good*	melior,	-ior, -ius	optimus,	-a, -um
malus, *bad*	pēior,	-ior, -ius	pessimus,	-a, -um
magnus, *great*	māior,	-ior, -ius	maximus,	-a, -um
multus, *much*	no mas. or *fem.*,	plūs	plūrimus,	-a, -um
parvus, *small*	minor,	-or, -us	minimus,	-a, -um
inferus, *lower*	inferior,	-ior, -ius	infimus or īmus	
superus, *upper*	superior,	-ior, -ius	suprēmus or summus	
novus, *new*	no comparative		novissimus, -a, -um	

Most adjectives ending in **us** preceded by a vowel, except those ending in **quus**, have no terminational comparison, and are compared by prefixing **magis**, *more*, and **māximē**, *most;* as,

POSITIVE.	COMPARATIVE.	SUPERLATIVE.
idōneus, *suitable*	magis idōneus	māximē idōneus

Adjectives ending in **quus** are regular; as,

| antīquus, *ancient* | antīquior | antīquissimus |

See also **inīquus, (469).**

478. COMPARISON OF ADVERBS.

POSITIVE.	COMPARATIVE.	SUPERLATIVE.
ācriter, *fiercely*	ācrius	ācerrimē
audācter, *boldly*	audācius	audācissimē
celeriter, *quickly*	celerius	celerrimē
dīligenter, *promptly*	dīligentius	dīligentissimē
diū, *a long time*	diūtius	diūtissimē
facile, *easily*	facilius	facillimē
fortiter, *bravely*	fortius	fortissimē
longē, *far*	longius	longissimē
māgnum, *greatly*	magis	māximē
multum, *much*	plūs	plūrimum
parvum, *a little, slightly*	minus	minimē
prope, *nearly*	propius	proximē

1. The accusatives of adjectives and pronouns are sometimes used as adverbs; as, **multum, multa,** *much;* **facile,** *easily;* **aliās,** *otherwise.*

2. Some adverbs were originally ablatives; as, **vērō,** *in truth, but, however;* **forte,** *by chance;* **iūre,** *rightly.*

3. Most adverbs are derived from adjectives, upon which they depend for comparison. Adjectives of the first and second declensions form the adverbs in **ē, ō, um**; as, **longus, longē; multus, multō,** and **multum.** Adjectives of the third declension form the adverbs in **ter**; as, **audāx, audāc-ter; fortis, forti-ter; dīligens, dīligen-ter.**

4. Some adverbs are formed by the union of prepositions with case forms; as, **inter-eā,** *meanwhile;* **post-eā,** *afterwards;* **paulis-per,** *for a little while.*

5. The comparative of the adverb is the accusative singular neuter of the comparative of the adjective; the superlative of the adverb is formed by changing the ending **us** of the superlative of the adjective to **ē**.

THE LATIN VERB.
FIRST CONJUGATION.

474. Active voice.—Amō, amāre, amāvī, amātum, *to love.*

Present indicative.
I love, do love, am loving.
amō
amās
amat
amāmus
amātis
amant

Imperfect indicative.
I was loving, loved.
amābam
amābās
amābat
amābāmus
amābātis
amābant

Future indicative.
I shall love.
amābō
amābis
amābit
amābimus
amābitis
amābunt

Perfect indicative.
I have loved, loved, did love.
amāvī
amāvistī
amāvit
amāvimus
amāvistis
amāvērunt (-ēre)

Pluperfect indicative.
I had loved.
amāveram
amāverās
amāverat
amāverāmus
amāverātis
amāverant

Future-perfect indicative.
I shall have loved.
amāverō
amāveris
amāverit
amāverimus
amāveritis
amāverint

Present subjunctive.
I may love.
amem
amēs
amet
amēmus
amētis
ament

Imperfect subjunctive.
I might love.
amārem
amārēs
amāret
amārēmus
amārētis
amārent

Perfect subjunctive.
I may have loved.
  amāverim
  amāveris
  amāverit
  amāverimus
  amāveritis
  amāverint

Pluperfect subjunctive.
I might have loved.
  amāvissem
  amāvissēs
  amāvisset
  amāvissēmus
  amāvissētis
  amāvissent

Imperative.

amā, *love (thou)*   amāte, *love (ye)*
amātō, *thou shalt love*   amātōte, *ye shall love*
amātō, *he shall love*   amantō, *they shall love*

Participle.

Present. amāns, *loving*
Future. amātūrus, -a, -um, *being about to love*

Infinitive.

Present. amāre, *to love*
Perfect. amāvisse, *to have loved*
Future. amātūrum, -am, -um esse, *to be about to love*

Gerund.

Gen. amandī, *of loving*
Dat. amandō, *to or for loving*
Acc. ad amandum, *for loving*
Abl. amandō, *by loving*

Supine.

amātum, *to love*   amātū, *to love*

475. Passive voice.—Amor, amārī, amātus sum.

Present indicative.
I am (being) loved.
  amor
  amāris (-re)
  amātur
  amāmur
  amāminī
  amantur

Imperfect indicative.
I was (being) loved.
  amābar
  amābāris (-re)
  amābātur
  amābāmur
  amābāminī
  amābantur

Future indicative.
I shall be loved.
amābor
amāberis (-re)
amābitur
amābimur
amābiminī
amābuntur

Present subjunctive.
I may be loved.
amer
amēris (-re)
amētur
amēmur
amēminī
amentur

Perfect indicative.
I have been loved, was loved.
amātus, -a, -um sum
                es
                est
amātī, -ae, -a sumus
               estis
               sunt

Imperfect subjunctive.
I might be loved.
amārer
amārēris (-re)
amārētur
amārēmur
amārēminī
amārentur

Pluperfect indicative.
I had been loved.
amātus, -a, -um eram
               erās
               erat
amātī, -ae, -a erāmus
             erātis
             erant

Perfect subjunctive.
I may have been loved.
amātus, -a, -um sim
               sīs
               sit
amātī, -ae, -a sīmus
            sītis
            sint

Future-perfect indicative.
I shall have been loved.
amātus, -a, -um erō
               eris
               erit
amātī, -ae, -a erimus
            eritis
            erunt

Pluperfect subjunctive.
I might have been loved.
amātus, -a, -um essem
               essēs
               esset
amātī, -ae, -a essēmus
            essētis
            essent

Imperative.

amāre, *be thou loved* amāminī, *be ye loved*
amātor, *thou shalt be loved*
amātor, *he shall be loved* amantor, *they shall be loved*

Present Infinitive.

amārī, *to be loved*

Perfect Infinitive.

amātum, -am, -um esse, *to have been loved*

Future Infinitive.

amātum īrī *to be about to be loved*

Perfect Participle.

amātus, -a, -um, *having been loved*

Gerundive.

amandus, -a, -um, *worthy to be loved*

SECOND CONJUGATION.

476. Active voice.—Moneō, monēre, monuī, monitum, *to advise.*

Present Indicative.	Imperfect Indicative.
I advise, do advise, am advising.	*I was advising, advised.*
moneō	monēbam
monēs	monēbās
monet	monēbat
monēmus	monēbāmus
monētis	monēbātis
monent	monēbant

Future indicative.
I shall advise.
monēbō
monēbis
monēbit
monēbimus
monēbitis
monēbunt

Perfect indicative.
I have advised, advised, did advise.
monuī
monuistī
monuit
monuimus
monuistis
monuērunt (-ēre)

Pluperfect indicative.
I had advised.
monueram
monuerās
monuerat
monnerāmus
monuerātis
monuerant

Future-perfect indicative.
I shall have advised.
monuerō
monueris
monuerit
monnerimus
monueritis
monuerint

Present subjunctive.
I may advise.
moneam
moneās
moneat
moneāmus
moneātis
moneant

Imperfect subjunctive.
I might advise.
monērem
monērēs
monēret
monērēmus
monērētis
monērent

Perfect subjunctive.
I may have advised.
monuerim
monueris
monuerit
monuerimus
monneritis
monuerint

Pluperfect subjunctive.
I might have advised.
monuissem
monuissēs
monuisset
monuissēmus
monuissētis
monuissent

Imperative.

monē, *advise (thou)*
monētō, *thou shalt advise*
monētō, *he shall advise*

monēte, *advise (ye)*
monētōte, *ye shall advise*
monentō, *they shall advise*

Participle.

Present. monēns, *advising*
Future. monitūrus, -a, -um, *being about to advise*

Infinitive.

Present. monēre, *to advise*
Perfect. monuisse, *to have advised*
Future. monitūrum, -am, -um esse, *to be about to advise*

Gerund.

monendī, *of advising*
monendō, *to or for advising*
ad monendum, *for advising*
monendō, *by advising*

Supine.

monitum, *to advise*   monitū, *to advise*

477. Passive voice.—Moneor, monērī, monitus sum.

Present Indicative.	Imperfect Indicative.
I am (being) advised.	*I was (being) advised.*
moneor	monēbar
monēris (-re)	monēbāris (-re)
monētur	monēbātur
monēmur	monēbāmur
monēminī	monēbāminī
monentur	monēbantur

Future indicative.
I shall be advised.
monēbor
monēberis (-re)
monēbitur
monēbimur
monēbiminī
monēbuntur

Perfect indicative.
I have been advised, was advised.
monitus, -a, -um sum
     es
     est
monitī, -ae, -a sumus
     estis
     sunt

Pluperfect indicative.
I had been advised.
monitus, -a, -um eram
     erās
     erat
monitī, -ae, -a erāmus
     erātis
     erant

Future-perfect indicative.
I shall have been advised.
monitus, -a, -um erō
     eris
     erit
monitī, -ae, -a erimus
     eritis
     erunt

Present subjunctive.
I may be advised.
monear
moneāris (-re)
moneātur
moneāmur
moneāminī
moneantur

Imperfect subjunctive.
I might be advised.
monērer
monērēris (-re)
monērētur
monērēmur
monērēminī
monērentur

Perfect subjunctive.
I may have been advised.
monitus, -a, -um sim
     sīs
     sit
monitī, -ae, -a sīmus
     sītis
     sint

Pluperfect subjunctive.
I might have been advised.
monitus, -a, -um essem
     essēs
     esset
monitī, -ae, -a essēmus
     essētis
     essent

THE LATIN VERB.

Imperative.

monēre, *be thou advised* monēminī, *be ye advised*
monētor, *thou shalt be advised*
monētor, *he shall be advised* monentor, *they shall be advised*

Present infinitive.

monērī, *to be advised*

Perfect infinitive.

monitum, -am, -um esse, *to have been advised*

Future infinitive.

monitum īrī, *to be about to be advised*

Perfect participle.

monitus, -a, -um, *having been advised*

Gerundive.

monendus, -a, -um, *worthy to be advised*

THIRD CONJUGATION.

478. **Active voice.**—Pōnō, pōnere, posuī, positum, *to place.*

Present indicative.	Imperfect indicative.
I place, do place, am placing.	*I was placing, placed.*
pōnō	pōnēbam
pōnis	pōnēbās
pōnit	pōnēbat
pōnimus	pōnēbāmus
pōnitis	pōnēbātis
pōnunt	pōnēbant

Future indicative.
I shall place.

pŏnam
pŏnēs
pŏnet
pŏnēmus
pŏnētis
pŏnent

Present subjunctive.
I may place.

pŏnam
pŏnās
pŏnat
pŏnāmus
pŏnātis
pŏnant

Perfect indicative.
I have placed, placed, did place.

posuī
posuistī
posuit
posuimus
posuistis
posuērunt (-ēre)

Imperfect subjunctive.
I might place.

pŏnerem
pŏnerēs
pŏneret
pŏnerēmus
pŏnerētis
pŏnerent

Pluperfect indicative.
I had placed.

posueram
posuerās
posuerat
posuerāmus
posuerātis
posuerant

Perfect subjunctive.
I may have placed.

posuerim
posueris
posuerit
posuerimus
posueritis
posuerint

Future-perfect indicative.
I shall have placed.

posuerō
posueris
posuerit
posuerimus
posueritis
posuerint

Pluperfect subjunctive.
I might have placed.

posuissem
posuissēs
posuisset
posuissēmus
posuissētis
posuissent

Imperative.

pōne, *place (thou)* pōnite, *place (ye)*
pōnitō, *thou shalt place* pōnitōte, *ye shall place*
pōnitō, *he shall place* pōnuntō, *they shall place*

Participle.

Present. pōnēns, *placing*
Future. positūrus, -a, -um, *being about to place*

Infinitive.

Present. pōnere, *to place*
Perfect. posuisse, *to have placed*
Future. positūrum, -am, -um esse, *to be about to place*

Gerund.

pōnendī, *of placing*
pōnendō, *to* or *for placing*
ad pōnendum, *for placing*
pōnendō, *by placing*

Supine.

positum, *to place* positū, *to place*

479. Passive voice.—Pōnor, pōnī, positus sum.

Present Indicative. **Imperfect Indicative.**

I am (being) placed. *I was (being) placed.*

pōnor pōnēbar
pōneris (-re) pōnēbāris (-re)
pōnitur pōnēbātur
pōnimur pōnēbāmur
pōniminī pōnēbāminī
pōnuntur pōnēbantur

Future indicative.
I shall be placed.
pōnar
pōnēris (-re)
pōnētur
pōnēmur
pōnēminī
pōnentur

Perfect indicative.
I have been placed, was placed.
positus, -a, -um sum
              es
              est
positī, -ae, -a sumus
              estis
              sunt

Pluperfect indicative.
I had been placed.
positus, -a, -um eram
              erās
              erat
positī, -ae, -a erāmus
              erātis
              erant

Future-perfect indicative.
I shall have been placed.
positus, -a, -um erō
              eris
              erit
positī, -ae, -a erimus
              eritis
              erunt

Present subjunctive.
I may be placed.
pōnar
pōnāris (-re)
pōnātur
pōnāmur
pōnāminī
pōnantur

Imperfect subjunctive.
I might be placed.
pōnerer
pōnerēris (-re)
pōnerētur
pōnerēmur
pōnerēminī
pōnerentur

Perfect subjunctive.
I may have been placed.
positus, -a, -um sim
              sīs
              sit
positī, -ae, -a sīmus
              sītis
              sint

Pluperfect subjunctive.
I might have been placed.
positus, -a, -um essem
              essēs
              esset
positī, -ae, -a essēmus
              essētis
              essent

Imperative.

pōnere, *be thou placed* pōniminī, *be ye placed*
pōnitor, *thou shalt be placed*
pōnitor, *he shall be placed* pōnuntor, *they shall be placed*

Infinitive.

Present. pōnī, *to be placed*
Perfect. positum, -am, -um esse, *to have been placed*
Future. positum īrī, *to be about to be placed*

Perfect participle.

positus, -a, -um, *having been placed*

Gerundive.

pōnendus, -a, -um, *worthy to be placed*

THIRD CONJUGATION. THE 'IŌ' VERB.

480. Active voice.—Capiō, capere, cēpī, captum, *to take.*

Present indicative.

I take, do take, am taking.

capiō
capis
capit
capimus
capitis
capiunt

Imperfect indicative.

I was taking, took.

capiēbam
capiēbās
[etc., regular]

Future indicative.

I shall take.

capiam
capiēs
[etc., regular]

Perfect indicative.

I have taken, did take, took.

cēpī
cēpistī
[etc., regular]

Pluperfect indicative.

I had taken.

cēperam
cēperās
[etc., regular]

Future-perfect indicative.
I shall have taken.
cēperō
cēperis
[etc., regular]

Present subjunctive.
I may take.
capiam
capiās
[etc., regular]

Imperfect subjunctive.
I might take.
caperem
caperēs
[etc., regular]

Perfect subjunctive.
I may have taken.
cēperim
cēperis
[etc., regular]

Pluperfect subjunctive.
I might have taken.
cēpissem
cēpissēs
[etc., regular]

Imperative.
cape, *take (thou)*
capitō, *thou shalt take*
capitō, *he shall take*
capite, *take (ye)*
capitōte, *ye shall take*
capiuntō, *they shall take*

Participle.
Present. capiēns, *taking*
Future. captūrus, -a, -um, *being about to take*

Infinitive.
Present. capere, *to take*
Perfect. cēpisse, *to have taken*
Future. captūrum, -am, -um esse, *to be about to take*

Gerund.
capiendī, *of taking*
capiendō, *to* or *for taking*
ad capiendum, *for taking*
capiendō, *by taking*

Supine.
captum, *to take*   captū, *to take*

481. Passive voice.—Capior, capī, captus sum.

Present indicative.
I am (being) taken.
capior
caperis (-re)
capitur
capimur
capiminī
capiuntur

Imperfect indicative.
I was (being) taken.
capiēbar
capiēbāris (-re)
[etc., regular]

Future indicative.
I shall be taken.
capiar
capiēris (-re)
[etc., regular]

Perfect indicative.
I have been taken, was taken.
captus, -a, -um sum
"   "   "   es
[etc., regular]

Pluperfect indicative.
I had been taken.
captus, -a, -um eram
"   "   "   erās
[etc., regular]

Future-perfect indicative.
I shall have been taken.
captus, -a, -um erō
"   "   "   eris
[etc., regular]

Present subjunctive.
I may be taken.
capiar
capiāris (-re)
[etc., regular]

Imperfect subjunctive.
I might be taken.
caperer
capererīs (-re)
[etc., regular]

Perfect subjunctive.
I may have been taken.
captus, -a, -um sim
"   "   "   sīs
[etc., regular]

Pluperfect subjunctive.
I might have been taken.
captus, -a, -um essem
"   "   "   essēs
[etc., regular]

Imperative.
capere, *be thou taken*
capitor, *thou shalt be taken*
capitor, *he shall be taken*
capiminī, *be ye taken*
capiuntor, *they shall be taken*

Infinitive.

Present. **capī,** *to be taken*
Perfect. **captum, -am, -um esse,** *to have been taken*
Future. **captum īrī,** *to be about to be taken*

Perfect participle.

captus, -a, -um, *having been taken*

Gerundive.

capiendus, -a, -um, *worthy to be taken*

FOURTH CONJUGATION.

482. Active voice.—**Mūniō, mūnīre, mūnīvī, mūnītum,** *to fortify.*

Present indicative.

I fortify, do fortify, am fortifying.

mūniō
mūnīs
mūnit
mūnīmus
mūnītis
mūniunt

Future indicative.

I shall fortify.

mūniam
mūniēs
mūniet
mūniēmus
mūniētis
mūnient

Imperfect indicative.

I was fortifying, fortified.

mūniēbam
mūniēbās
mūniēbat
mūniēbāmus
mūniēbātis
mūniēbant

Perfect indicative.

I have fortified, did fortify, fortified.

mūnīvī
mūnīvistī
mūnīvit
mūnīvimus
mūnīvistis
mūnīvērunt (-ēre)

THE LATIN VERB.

Pluperfect indicative.
I had fortified.
mūnīveram
mūnīverās
mūnīverat
mūnīverāmus
mūnīverātis
mūnīverant

Imperfect subjunctive.
I might fortify.
mūnīrem
mūnīrēs
mūnīret
mūnīrēmus
mūnīrētis
mūnīrent

Future-perfect indicative.
I shall have fortified.
mūnīverō
mūnīveris
mūnīverit
mūnīverimus
mūnīveritis
mūnīverint

Perfect subjunctive.
I may have fortified.
mūnīverim
mūnīveris
mūnīverit
mūnīverimus
mūnīveritis
mūnīverint

Present subjunctive.
I may fortify.
mūniam
mūniās
mūniat
mūniāmus
mūniātis
mūniant

Pluperfect subjunctive.
I might have fortified.
mūnīvissem
mūnīvissēs
mūnīvisset
mūnīvissēmus
mūnīvissētis
mūnīvissent

Imperative.

mūnī, *fortify (thou)*
mūnītō, *thou shalt fortify*
mūnītō, *he shall fortify*

mūnīte, *fortify (ye)*
mūnītōte, *ye shall fortify*
mūniuntō, *they shall fortify*

Participle.

Present. mūniēns, *fortifying*
Future. mūnītūrus, -a, -um, *being about to fortify*

Infinitive.

Present. mūnīre, *to fortify*
Perfect. mūnīvisse, *to have fortified*
Future. mūnītūrum, -am, -um esse, *to be about to fortify*

Gerund.

mūniendī, *of fortifying*
mūniendō, *to* or *for fortifying*
ad mūniendum, *for fortifying*
mūniendō, *by fortifying*

Supine.

mūnītum, *to fortify*   mūnītū, *to fortify*

483. Passive voice.—Mūnior, mūnīrī, mūnītus sum.

Present indicative.
I am (being) fortified.

mūnior
mūnīris (-re)
mūnītur
mūnīmur
mūnīminī
mūniuntur

Future indicative.
I shall be fortified.

mūniar
mūniēris (-re)
mūniētur
mūniēmur
mūniēminī
mūnientur

Imperfect indicative.
I was (being) fortified.

mūniēbar
mūniēbāris (-re)
mūniēbātur
mūniēbāmur
mūniēbāminī
mūniēbantur

Perfect indicative.
I have been, was fortified.

mūnītus, -a, -um sum
    es
    est
mūnītī, -ae, -a sumus
    estis
    sunt

THE LATIN VERB.

Pluperfect indicative.
I had been fortified.

mūnītus, -a, -um eram
               erās
               erat
mūnītī, -ae, -a erāmus
               erātis
               erant

Imperfect subjunctive.
I might be fortified.

mūnīrer
mūnīrēris (-re)
mūnīrētur
mūnīrēmur
mūnīrēminī
mūnīrentur

Future-perfect indicative.
I shall have been fortified.

mūnītus, -a, -um erō
               eris
               erit
mūnītī, -ae, -a erimus
               eritis
               erunt

Perfect subjunctive.
I may have been fortified.

mūnītus, -a, -um sim
               sīs
               sit
mūnītī, -ae, -a sīmus
               sītis
               sint

Present subjunctive.
I may be fortified.

mūniar
mūniāris (-re)
mūniātur
mūniāmur
mūniāminī
mūniantur

Pluperfect subjunctive.
I might have been fortified.

mūnītus -a, -um essem
               essēs
               esset
mūnītī, -ae, -a essēmus
               essētis
               essent

Imperative.

mūnīre, *be thou fortified*
mūnītor, *thou shalt be fortified*
mūnītor, *he shall be fortified*
mūnīminī, *be ye fortified*
mūniuntor, *they shall be fortified*

Infinitive.

Present. mūnīrī, *to be fortified*
Perfect. mūnītum, -am, -um esse, *to have been fortified*
Future. mūnītum īrī, *to be about to be fortified*

Perfect participle.

mūnītus, -a, -um, *having been fortified*

Gerundive.

mūniendus, -a, -um, *worthy to be fortified*

IRREGULAR VERBS.

484. Sum, esse, fuī, *to be.*

Present indicative.
I am.
sum
es
est
sumus
estis
sunt

Perfect indicative.
I have been, was.
fuī
fuistī
fuit
fuimus
fuistis
fuērunt (-ēre)

Imperfect indicative.
I was
eram
erās
erat
erāmus
erātis
erant

Pluperfect indicative.
I had been.
fueram
fuerās
fuerat
fuerāmus
fuerātis
fuerant

Future indicative.
I shall be.
erō
eris
erit
erimus
eritis
erunt

Future-perfect indicative.
I shall have been.
fuerō
fueris
fuerit
fuerimus
fueritis
fuerint

Present subjunctive.
I may be.
sim
sīs
sit
sīmus
sītis
sint

Imperfect subjunctive.
I might be.
essem
essēs
esset
essēmus
essētis
essent

Perfect subjunctive.
I may have been.
fuerim
fueris
fuerit
fuerimus
fueritis
fuerint

Pluperfect subjunctive.
I might have been.
fuissem
fuissēs
fuisset
fuissēmus
fuissētis
fuissent

Imperative.
es, *be thou*
estō, *thou shalt be*
estō, *he shall be*

este, *be ye*
estōte, *ye shall be*
suntō, *they shall be*

Participle.
Future. futūrus, -a, -um, *being about to be*

Infinitive.
Present. esse, *to be*
Perfect. fuisse, *to have been*
Future. futūrum, -am, -um esse, *to be about to be*

485. Possum, posse, potuī, *to be able.*

Present indicative.
I am able.

possum   possumus
potes   potestis
potest   possunt

Imperfect indicative.	**Present subjunctive.**
I was able.	*I may be able.*
poteram	possim
poterās	possīs
[etc., regular]	possit
	possīmus
Future indicative.	possītis
I shall be able.	possint
poterō	
poteris	**Imperfect subjunctive.**
[etc., regular]	*I might be able.*
	possem
Perfect indicative.	possēs
I have been, was able.	posset
potuī	possēmus
potuistī	possētis
[etc., regular]	possent
Pluperfect indicative.	**Perfect subjunctive.**
I had been able.	*I may have been able.*
potueram	potuerim
potuerās	potueris
[etc., regular]	[etc., regular]
Future-perfect indicative.	**Pluperfect subjunctive.**
I shall have been able.	*I might have been able.*
potuerō	potuissem
potueris	potuissēs
[etc., regular]	[etc., regular]

Infinitive.

Present. posse, *to be able*
Perfect. potuisse, *to have been able*

486. Eō, īre, īvī, itum, *to go.*

Present indicative.	Pluperfect indicative.
I go, am going, do go.	*I had gone.*
eō	īveram
īs	īverās
it	īverat
īmus	īverāmus
ītis	īverātis
eunt	īverant

Imperfect indicative.	Future-perfect indicative.
I was going, went.	*I shall have gone.*
ībam	īverō
ībās	īveris
ībat	īverit
ībāmus	īverimus
ībātis	īveritis
ībant	īverint

Future indicative.	Present subjunctive.
I shall go.	*I may go.*
ībō	eam
ībis	eās
ībit	eat
ībimus	eāmus
ībitis	eātis
ībunt	eant

Perfect indicative.	Imperfect subjunctive.
I have gone, went.	*I might go.*
īvī	īrem
īvistī	īrēs
īvit	īret
īvimus	īrēmus
īvistis	īrētis
īvērunt (-ēre)	īrent

Perfect subjunctive.
I may have gone.
īverim
īveris
īverit
īverimus
īveritis
īverint

Pluperfect subjunctive.
I might have gone.
īvissem
īvissēs
īvisset
īvissēmus
īvissētis
īvissent

Imperative.
ī, *go* (*thou*)
ītō, *thou shalt go*
ītō, *he shall go*

īte, *go* (*ye*)
ītōte, *ye shall go*
euntō, *they shall go*

Participle.
Present. iēns (gen. euntis), *going*
Future. itūrus, -a, -um, *being about to go*

Infinitive.
Present. īre, *to go*
Perfect. īvisse, *to have gone*
Future. itūrum, -am, -um esse, *to be about to go*

Gerund.
eundī, *of going*
eundō, *to or for going*
ad eundum, *for going*
eundō, *by going*

Supine.
itum, *to go*   itū, *to go*

487. Volō, velle, voluī, *to wish.*

Present indicative.
I wish, am wishing, do wish.
volō
vīs
vult
volumus
vultis
volunt

Imperfect indicative.
I was wishing, wished.
volēbam
volēbās
volēbat
volēbāmus
volēbātis
volēbant

Future indicative.	Present subjunctive.
I shall wish.	*I may wish.*
volam	velim
volēs	velīs
volet	velit
volēmus	velīmus
volētis	velītis
volent	velint

Perfect indicative.	Imperfect subjunctive.
I have wished, wished.	*I might wish.*
voluī	vellem
voluistī	vellēs
voluit	vellet
voluimus	vellēmus
voluistis	vellētis
voluērunt (-ēre)	vellent

Pluperfect indicative.	Perfect subjunctive.
I had wished.	*I may have wished.*
volueram	voluerim
voluerās	volueris
voluerat	voluerit
voluerāmus	voluerimus
voluerātis	volueritis
voluerant	voluerint

Future-perfect indicative.	Pluperfect subjunctive.
I shall have wished.	*I might have wished.*
voluerō	voluissem
volueris	voluissēs
voluerit	voluisset
voluerimus	voluissēmus
volueritis	voluissētis
voluerint	voluissent

Present participle.

volēns, *wishing*

Infinitive.

Present. **velle,** *to wish*
Perfect. **voluisse,** *to have wished*

488. Nōlō, nōlle, nōluī, *to be unwilling.*

Present indicative.
I am unwilling.
nōlō
nōn vīs
nōn vult
nōlumus
nōn vultis
nōlunt

Imperfect indicative.
I was unwilling.
nōlēbam
nōlēbās
[etc., regular]

Future indicative.
I shall be unwilling.
nōlam
nōlēs
[etc., regular]

Perfect indicative.
I have been, was, unwilling.
nōluī
nōluistī
[etc., regular]

Pluperfect indicative.
I had been unwilling.
nōlueram
nōluerās
[etc., regular]

Future-perfect indicative.
I shall have been unwilling.
nōluerō
nōlueris
[etc., regular]

Present subjunctive.
I may be unwilling.
nōlim
nōlīs
nōlit
nōlīmus
nōlītis
nōlint

Imperfect subjunctive.
I might be unwilling.
nōllem
nōllēs
[etc., regular]

Perfect subjunctive.
I may have been unwilling.
nōluerim
nōlueris
[etc., regular]

Pluperfect subjunctive.
I might have been unwilling.
nōluissem
nōluissēs
[etc., regular]

Imperative.

nōlī, *be (thou) unwilling* nōlīte, *be (ye) unwilling*
nōlītō, *thou shalt be unwilling* nōlītōte, *ye shall be unwilling*
nōlītō, *he shall be unwilling* nōluntō, *they shall be unwilling*

Present participle.
nōlēns, *being unwilling*

Infinitive.
Present. nōlle, *to be unwilling*
Perfect. nōluisse, *to have been unwilling*

489. Mālō, mālle, māluī, *to prefer.*

Present indicative.
I prefer, am preferring, do prefer.
mālō
māvīs
māvult
mālumus
māvultis
mālunt

Imperfect indicative.
I was preferring, preferred.
mālēbam
mālēbās
[etc., regular]

Future indicative.
I shall prefer.
mālam
mālēs
[etc., regular]

Perfect indicative.
I have preferred, preferred.
māluī
māluistī
[etc., regular]

Pluperfect indicative.
I had preferred.
mālueram
māluerās
[etc., regular]

Future-perfect indicative.
I shall have preferred.
māluerō
mālueris
[etc., regular]

Present subjunctive.
I may prefer.
mālim
mālīs
mālit
mālīmus
mālītis
mālint

Imperfect subjunctive.
I might prefer.
māllem
māllēs
māllet
māllēmus
māllētis
māllent

Perfect subjunctive.
I may have preferred.
  māluerim
  mālueris
  [etc., regular]

Pluperfect subjunctive.
I might have preferred.
  māluissem
  māluissēs
  [etc., regular]

Infinitive.

Present. mālle, *to prefer*
Perfect. māluisse, *to have preferred*

490. Active voice.—Ferō, ferre, tulī, lātum, *to bear.*

Present indicative.
I bear, am bearing, do bear.
  ferō
  fers
  fert
  ferimus
  fertis
  ferunt

Imperfect indicative.
I was bearing, bore.
  ferēbam
  ferēbās
  [etc., regular]

Future indicative.
I shall bear.
  feram
  ferēs
  [etc., regular]

Perfect indicative.
I have borne, bore.
  tulī
  tulistī
  [etc., regular]

Pluperfect indicative.
I had borne.
  tuleram
  tulerās
  [etc., regular]

Future-perfect indicative.
I shall have borne.
  tulerō
  tuleris
  [etc., regular]

Present subjunctive.
I may bear.
  feram
  ferās
  [etc., regular]

Imperfect subjunctive.
I might bear.
  ferrem
  ferrēs
  [etc., regular]

Perfect subjunctive.
I may have borne.
tulerim
tuleris
[etc., regular]

Pluperfect subjunctive.
I might have borne.
tulissem
tulissēs
[etc., regular]

Imperative.

fer, *bear (thou)*
fertō, *thou shalt bear*
fertō, *he shall bear*

ferte, *bear (ye)*
fertōte, *ye shall bear*
feruntō, *they shall bear*

Participle.

Present. **ferēns,** *bearing*
Future. **lātūrus, -a, -um,** *being about to bear*

Infinitive.

Present. **ferre,** *to bear*
Perfect. **tulisse,** *to have borne*
Future. **lātūrum, -am, -um esse,** *to be about to bear*

Gerund.

ferendī, *of bearing,* etc.

Supine.

lātum, *to bear*   **lātū,** *to bear*

491. Passive voice.—Feror, ferrī, lātus sum.

Present indicative.
I am (being) borne.
feror
ferris (-re)
fertur
ferimur
feriminī
feruntur

Imperfect indicative.
I was (being) borne.
ferēbar
ferēbāris (-re)
[etc., regular]

Future indicative.
I shall be borne.
ferar
ferēris (-re)
[etc., regular]

Perfect indicative.
I have been, was, borne.
lātus, -a, -um sum
es
[etc.]

Pluperfect indicative.
I had been borne.
lātus, -a, -um eram
  erās
  [etc.]

Future perfect indicative.
I shall have been borne.
lātus, -a, -um erō
  eris
  [etc.]

Present subjunctive.
I may be borne.
ferar
ferāris (-re)
[etc., regular]

Imperfect subjunctive.
I might be borne.
ferrer
ferrēris (-re)
[etc., regular]

Perfect subjunctive.
I may have been borne.
lātus, -a, -um sim
  sīs
  [etc.]

Pluperfect subjunctive.
I might have been borne.
lātus, -a, -um essem
  essēs
  [etc.]

Imperative.

ferre, *be thou borne*
fertor, *thou shalt be borne*
fertor, *he shall be borne*

feriminī, *be ye borne*

feruntor, *they shall be borne*

Infinitive.

Present. ferrī, *to be borne*
Perfect. lātum, -am, -um esse, *to have been borne*
Future. lātum īrī, *to be about to be borne*

Perfect participle.

lātus, -a, -um, *having been borne*

Gerundive.

ferendus, -a, -um, *worthy to be borne*

492. Active voice.—Faciō, facere, fēcī, factum, *to make.*

Present indicative.

I make, am making, do make.

faciō
facis
facit
facimus
facitis
faciunt

Imperfect indicative.

I was making, made.

faciēbam
faciēbās
[etc., regular]

Future indicative.

I shall make.

faciam
faciēs
[etc., regular]

Perfect indicative.

I have made, made.

fēcī
fēcistī
[etc., regular]

Pluperfect indicative.

I had made.

fēceram
fēcerās
[etc., regular]

Future-perfect indicative.

I shall have made.

fēcerō
fēceris
[etc., regular]

Present subjunctive.

I may make.

faciam
faciās
[etc., regular]

Imperfect subjunctive.

I might make.

facerem
facerēs
[etc., regular]

Perfect subjunctive.

I may have made.

fēcerim
fēceris
[etc., regular]

Pluperfect subjunctive.

I might have made.

fēcissem
fecissēs
[etc., regular]

Imperative.

fac, *make (thou)*
facitō, *thou shalt make*
facitō, *he shall make*

facite, *make (ye)*
facitōte, *ye shall make*
faciuntō, *they shall make*

Participle.

Present. faciēns, *making*
Future. factūrus, -a, -um, *being about to make*

Infinitive.

Present. facere, *to make*
Perfect. fēcisse, *to have made*
Future. factūrum, -am, -um esse, *to be about to make*

Gerund.

faciendī, *of making,* etc.

Supine.

factum, *to make*   factū, *to make*

493. Passive voice.—Fīō, fierī, factus sum.

Present indicative.
I am (being) made, become.
fīō
fīs
fit
fīmus
fītis
fīunt

Imperfect indicative.
I was (being) made, became.
fīēbam
fīēbās [etc.]

Future indicative.
I shall be made, shall become.
fīam
fīēs [etc.]

Perfect indicative.
I have been, was, made.
factus, -a, -um sum
    es [etc.]

Pluperfect indicative.
I had been made.
factus, -a, -um eram
    erās [etc.]

Future-perfect indicative.
I shall have been made.
factus, -a, -um erō
    eris [etc.]

Present subjunctive.
I may be made, may become
fīam
fīās
fīat
fīāmus
fīātis
fīant

Imperfect subjunctive.
I might be made, might become.
fierem
fierēs [etc.]

Perfect subjunctive.　　　Pluperfect subjunctive.
I may have been made.　　*I might have been made.*
factus, -a, -um sim　　　factus, -a, -um essem
　　　sīs [etc.]　　　　　　　　essēs [etc.]

Imperative.
fī, *be thou made*　　　　fīte, *be ye made*

Infinitive.
Present. fierī, *to be made, to become*
Perfect. factum, -am, -um esse, *to have been made*
Future. factum īrī, *to be about to be made*

Perfect participle.
factus, -a, -um, *having been made*

Gerundive.
faciendus, -a, -um, *worthy to be made*

DEPONENT VERBS.

494. First conjugation.—Populor, populāri, populātus sum, *to plunder.*

Present indicative.　　　**Future-perfect indicative.**
I plunder, am plundering, etc.　　*I shall have plundered.*
　populor　　　　　　　　　populātus erō [etc.]
　populāris (-re)　　　　**Present subjunctive.**
　populātur [etc.]　　　　*I may plunder.*
Imperfect indicative.　　　populer
I was plundering.　　　　populēris (-re)
　populābar [etc.]　　　　populētur [etc.]
Future indicative.　　　**Imperfect subjunctive.**
I shall plunder.　　　　*I might plunder.*
　populābor [etc.]　　　　populārer [etc.]
Perfect indicative.　　　**Perfect subjunctive.**
I have plundered.　　　　*I may have plundered.*
　populātus sum [etc.]　　populātus sim [etc.]
Pluperfect indicative.　　**Pluperfect subjunctive.**
I had plundered.　　　　*I might have plundered.*
　populātus eram [etc.]　　populātus essem [etc.]

Imperative.

populāre, *plunder (thou)*   **populāminī,** *plunder ye*
populātor, *thou shalt plunder*
populātor, *he shall plunder*   **populantor,** *they shall plunder*

Infinitive.

Present. **populārī,** *to plunder*
Perfect. **populātum, -am, -um esse,** *to have plundered*

Perfect participle.

populātus, -a, -um, *having plundered*

Gerundive.

populandus, -a, -um, *worthy to be plundered*

Active forms.

Present participle. **populāns,** *plundering*
Future participle. **populātūrus, -a, -um,** *being about to plunder*
First supine. **populātum,** *to plunder*
Second supine. **populātū,** *to plunder*   [*plunder*
Future infinitive. **populātūrum, -am, -um esse,** *to be about to*
Gerund. **populandī,** *of plundering* [etc.]

495. Second conjugation.—Vereor, verērī, veritus sum, *to fear.*

Present indicative.	Perfect indicative.
I fear, am fearing, etc.	*I have feared.*
vereor	**veritus sum** [etc.]
verēris (-re)	
verētur [etc.]	**Pluperfect indicative.**
Imperfect indicative.	*I had feared.*
I was fearing.	**veritus eram** [etc.]
verēbar [etc.]	**Future-perfect indicative.**
Future indicative.	*I shall have feared.*
I shall fear.	**veritus erō** [etc.]
verēbor [etc.]	

Present subjunctive.
I may fear.
verear
vereāris (-re)
vereātur [etc.]

Imperfect subjunctive.
I might fear.
verērer [etc.]

Perfect subjunctive.
I may have feared.
veritus sim [etc.]

Pluperfect subjunctive.
I might have feared.
veritus essem [etc.]

Imperative.
verēre, *fear (thou)*   verēminī, *fear (ye)*
verētor, *thou shalt fear*
verētor, *he shall fear*   verentor, *they shall fear*

Infinitive.
Present. verērī, *to fear*
Perfect. veritum, -am, -um esse, *to have feared*

Perfect participle.
veritus, -a, -um, *having feared*

Gerundive.
verendus, -a, -um, *worthy to be feared*

Active forms.
Present participle. verēns, *fearing*
Future participle. veritūrus, -a, -um, *being about to fear*
First supine. veritum, *to fear*
Second supine. veritū, *to fear*
Future infinitive. veritūrum, -am, -um esse, *to be about to fear*
Gerund. verendī, *of fearing*, etc.

496. Third conjugation.—Ūtor, ūtī, ūsus sum, *to use.*

Present indicative.
I use, am using, etc.
ūtor
ūteris (-re)
ūtitur
ūtimur
ūtiminī
ūtuntur

Imperfect indicative.
I was using.
ūtēbar [etc.]

Future indicative.
I shall use.
ūtar
ūtēris (-re)
ūtētur [etc.]

Perfect indicative.
I have used.
ūsus sum [etc.]

Pluperfect indicative.
I had used.
ūsus eram [etc.]

Future-perfect indicative.
I shall have used.
ūsus erō [etc.]

Present subjunctive.
I may use.
ūtar
ūtāris (-re)
ūtātur [etc.]

Imperfect subjunctive.
I might use.
ūterer [etc.]

Perfect subjunctive.
I may have used.
ūsus sim [etc.]

Pluperfect subjunctive.
I might have used.
ūsus essem [etc.]

Imperative.

ūtere, (*use thou*)　　　ūtiminī, *use (ye)*
ūtitor, *thou shalt use*
ūtitor, *he shall use*　　ūtuntor, *they shall use*

Infinitive.

Present. ūtī, *to use*
Perfect. ūsum, -am, -um esse, *to have used*

Perfect participle.

ūsus, -a, -um, *having used*

Gerundive.

ūtendus, -a, -um, *worthy to be used*

Active forms.

Present participle. ūtēns, *using*
Future participle. ūsūrus, -a, -um, *being about to use*
First supine. ūsum, *to use*
Second supine. ūsū, *to use*
Future infinitive. ūsūrum, -am, -um esse, *to be about to use*
Gerund. ūtendī, *of using*, etc.

497. Fourth conjugation.—Potior, potīri, potītus sum, *to capture.*

Present indicative.
I capture, am capturing, etc.
potior
potīris (-re)
potītur
potīmur
potīminī
potiuntur

Imperfect indicative.
I was capturing.
potiēbar [etc.]

Future indicative.
I shall capture.
potiar
potiēris (-re)
potiētur [etc.]

Perfect indicative.
I have captured.
potītus sum [etc.]

Pluperfect indicative.
I had captured.
potītus eram [etc.]

Future-perfect indicative.
I shall have captured.
potītus erō [etc.]

Present subjunctive.
I may capture.
potiar
potiāris (-re)
potiātur [etc.]

Imperfect subjunctive.
I might capture.
potīrer [etc.]

Perfect subjunctive.
I may have captured.
potītus sim [etc.]

Pluperfect subjunctive.
I might have captured.
potītus essem [etc.]

Imperative.

potīre, *capture (thou)*
potītor, *thou shalt capture*
potītor, *he shall capture*

potīminī, *capture (ye)*

potiuntor, *they shall capture*

Infinitive.

Present. potīrī, *to capture*
Perfect. potītum, -am, -um esse, *to have captured*

Perfect participle.

potītus, -a, -um, *having captured*

Gerundive.

potiendus, -a, -um, *worthy to be captured*

Active forms.

Present participle. potiēns, *capturing*
Future participle. potītūrus, -a, -um, *being about to capture*
First supine. potītum, *to capture*
Second supine. potītū, *to capture*
Future infinitive. potītūrum, -am, -um esse, *to be about to capture*
Gerund. potiendī, *of capturing,* etc.

PERIPHRASTIC CONJUGATION.

The *active voice* of the 'Periphrastic' is formed by annexing forms of **sum** to the *future active participle;* the *passive,* by annexing these forms to the *gerundive.*

498. Active voice.—Amātūrus sum, *I am about to love.*

Present indicative.
I am about to love.
amātūrus, -a, -um sum
     es
     est
amātūrī, -ae, -a sumus
     estis
     sunt

Imperfect indicative.
I was about to love.
amātūrus, -a, -um eram
     erās [etc.]

Future indicative.
I shall be about to love.
amātūrus, -a, -um erō
     eris [etc.]

Perfect indicative.
I have been, was, about to love.
amātūrus, -a, -um fuī
     fuistī [etc.]

Pluperfect indicative.
I had been about to love.
amātūrus, -a, -um fueram
     fuerās [etc.]

Future-perfect indicative.
I shall have been about to love.
amātūrus, -a, -um fuerō
     fueris [etc.]

Present subjunctive.
I may be about to love.
amātūrus, -a, -um sim
     sīs [etc.]

Imperfect subjunctive.
I might be about to love.
amātūrus, -a, -um essem
     essēs [etc.]

THE LATIN VERB.

Perfect subjunctive.
I may have been about to love.
amātūrus, -a, -um fuerim fueris [etc.]

Pluperfect subjunctive.
I might have been about to love.
amātūrus, -a, -um fuissem fuissēs [etc.]

Infinitive.

Present. amātūrum, -am, -um esse, *to be about to love*
Perfect. amātūrum, -am, -um fuisse, *to have been about to love*

499. Passive voice.—Amandus sum, *I deserve to be loved.*

Present indicative.
I am to be, ought to be, loved.
amandus, -a, -um sum
es
est
amandī, -ae, -a sumus
estis
sunt

Imperfect indicative.
I was to be, deserved to be, loved.
amandus, -a, -um eram

Future indicative.
I shall deserve to be, ought to be, loved.
amandus, -a, -um erō

Perfect indicative.
I was worthy to be, have deserved to be, loved.
amandus, -a, -um fuī

Pluperfect indicative.
I had deserved to be loved.
amandus, -a, -um fueram

Future-perfect indicative.
I shall have deserved to be loved.
amandus, -a, -um fuerō

Present subjunctive.
I may be worthy to be loved.
amandus, -a, -um sim

Imperfect subjunctive.
I might be worthy to be loved.
amandus, -a, -um essem

Perfect subjunctive.
I may have deserved to be loved.
amandus, -a -um fuerim

Pluperfect subjunctive.
I might have deserved to be loved.
amandus, -a, -um fuissem

Infinitive.

Present. amandum, -am, -um esse, *to deserve to be loved*
Perfect. amandum, -am, -um fuisse, *to have deserved to be loved*

QUANTITY RULES OF LATIN VOWELS AND SYLLABLES.

500. General rules of quantity.—1. A vowel before another vowel or h is *short:* except in the fifth declension, where ē follows a vowel, as diēī; ī in the genitive singular īus, see (286); ī in some forms of fīō, see (493).

2. Diphthongs and vowels formed by contraction are *long:* as ae in fossae, and ō in the penult of cōgō (= con + agō).

3. A syllable ending in a *short* vowel before a mute followed by l or r is *common*, i.e., long or short; as, pătris.

4. A vowel is *always long* before ns, nf, gn, and often long before scō, scor in inceptive verbs; as, regēns, īnferō, rēgnum, profīcīscor.

5. Compounds retain their *long* vowels; as, dē-dūcō.

6. Vowels are *long* in the nominative singular ending of nouns and adjectives which *increase long* in the genitive: vōx, vōcis; ferāx, ferācis.

7. A syllable is long by *nature* when it contains a long vowel or diphthong; long by *position* when it precedes two or more consonants or a double consonant.

501. Quantity of final syllables ending in a vowel.—In words of *more than one* syllable, final a, e, y are *short*, final i, o, u are *long*.

1. Final a is *short*, as vălla: except ablative of first declension, as tubā; imperative of first conjugation, as portā; most uninflected words, as posteā, intrā, but not so ita.

2. Final e is *short*, as mīlite: except ablative of fifth declension, as spē; imperative of second conjugation, as

QUANTITY RULES.

dēlē; most adverbs derived from adjectives of second declension, as māximē.

3. Final i is *long*, as flūminī: except nisi, cui; final i is common in mihĭ, tibĭ, sibĭ, ibĭ, ubĭ.

4. Final o is *long*, as pōnō: except homo, ego, modo, octo, duo.

5. Final u is always *long*, as adventū.

502. Quantity of final syllables ending in a consonant.—

1. All final syllables ending in a *single* consonant *other than s* are *short*, as amātur, reget.

2. Of final syllables in s, as, es, os are *long*, is, us, ys are *short*.

3. Final as is *long*, as tubās, audiās.

4. Final es is *long*, as amēs, diēs: except nominative and vocative singular, third declension, where the genitive ending is -etis, -idis, -itis, as obses, miles; es (from sum) and compounds of sum, as potes.

5. Final os is *long*, as virōs.

6. Final is is *short*, as militis, amātis: except dative and ablative plural, as puerīs, altīs; accusative plural, third declension, as finīs (= finēs); second person singular, present indicative active, fourth conjugation, as audīs; vīs (noun and verb from volō), fīs, sīs, velīs, nōlīs, mālīs, possīs, and īs (from eō).

7. Final us is *short*, as mūrus, amātus: except genitive singular, and nominative and accusative plural, fourth declension, as exercitūs; nominative third declension, when long u occurs in the genitive, as virtūs, virtūtis.

503. Quantity of monosyllables.—1. All monosyllables that end in a *vowel* are *long*, as ā, sī, dē, sē, etc.: except the enclitic que.

2. Declined or conjugated monosyllables that end in a *consonant* follow the rules given.

3. Monosyllabic nouns and adjectives have a *long* vowel in the nominative when they end in a *consonant*, as mōs, sōl, pēs, pār: but not so vir.

4. Monosyllabic *particles* that end in a consonant are *short*, as cis, in, nec, per, etc.: except nōn, quīn, and adverbs in c, as sīc.

504. Quantity of verb stems and endings.—1. A vowel is always *short* before final m, r, and t.

2. A vowel is always *short* before another vowel (except in certain forms of fīō), nd, and nt.

3. Final a, i, o, and u are *long;* final e is *short*, except in the imperative active, second person singular, in the second conjugation; as, monē.

4. Before final s, a and e are *long;* i and u are *short*, except that in the present indicative active, second person singular, in the fourth conjugation, i is long; as, audīs: see also (502), 6.

LATIN-ENGLISH VOCABULARY.

ā, ab, prep. + *abl.*, *from, by;* chapt. 7 (last sentence), *away.*

abdō, abdere, abdidī, abditum, *hide.*

absum, abesse, āfuī, *be distant.*

ac (before consonants only), conj., *and;* chapt. 19 (first sentence), *than.*

accēdō, -cēdere, -cessī, -cessum, *go towards, approach;* chapt. 13 (with ad + acc.); chapt. 7, *be inspired in* (with dat.).

accidō, -cidere, -cidī, (no supine), *happen.*

accipiō, -cipere, -cēpī, -ceptum, *receive, accept;* chapt. 33, *suffer.*

acclīvis, -is, -e, adj. (of two terminations), *sloping upward.*

acclīvitās, -tātis, fem., *slope (upward).*

accommodō, -āre, -āvī, -ātum, *adjust, fit, put on.*

acervus, -ī, mas., *a pile, a heap.*

aciēs, -ēī, fem., *line of battle, an army.*

ācriter, adv., *sharply, desperately.*

ad, prep. + *acc., to, towards, near;* ad + gerundive, *for;* chapt. 1, ad eōs, *against them;* chapt. 31, *according to.*

adaequō, -āre, -āvī, -ātum, *make equal to, equal.*

addūcō, see dūcō, *lead to, bring, lead* (with ad + acc.).

adeō, -īre, -īvī -iī, -itum, *go to;* chapt. 7, *reach.*

adiciō, -icere, -iēcī, -iectum, *throw to, hurl.*

aditus, -ūs, mas., *access, approach, admittance.*

adiuvō, -iuvāre, -iūvī, -iūtum, *aid, help.*

administrō, -āre, -āvī, -ātum. *execute, attend to.*

adorior, -orīrī, -ortus sum, depon., *rise up against, attack.*

Aduatucī, -ōrum, mas., a Belgic tribe living on the west bank of the Meuse.

adventus, -ūs, mas., *approach, arrival.*

adversus, -a, -um, adj., *opposite;* literally, *turned to* or *towards.*

aedificium, -ī, neut., *a building.*

aedificō, -āre, -āvī, -ātum, *build.*

Aeduī, -ōrum, mas., a Gallic tribe living between the upper waters of the Saone and Loire.

Aeduus, -a, -um, adj., *Aeduan.*

aegrē, adv., *with difficulty, barely.*

aequāliter, adv., *uniformly, evenly.*

aestās, -tātis, fem., *summer.*

aestuārium, -ī, neut., *a sea-marsh;*

literally, *relating to the tide* or *sea.*
aetās, -tātis, fem., *age, old age.*
afferō, -ferre, attulī, allātum, *bring to, carry to.*
affīnitās, -tātis, fem., *relationship (by marriage).*
ager, agrī, mas., *a field, land* (which is cultivated).
agger, aggeris, mas., *a mound, materials for a mound* (chapt. 20).
aggredior, -gredī, -gressus sum, depon., *approach, attack.*
agmen, -minis, neut., *the line of march (the marching column).*
agō, agere, ēgī, āctum, *drive;* chapt. 12, 30, *bring up;* 20, *do;* 21, *carry.*
aliās . . . aliās, adv., *at one time . . . at another.*
aliēnus, -a, -um, adj., *another's, of others.*
aliter, adv., *otherwise.*
alius, alia, aliud, adj., *other, another, different;* alius aliam in partem, *one in one direction, another in another.*
alter, -era, -erum, adj., *the other* (of two); *other, another.*
altitūdō, -dinis, fem., *height.*
altus, -a, -um, adj., *high,tall,deep.*
Ambiānī, -ōrum, mas., a Belgic tribe, from whose name is derived the modern *Amiens.*
amīcitia, -ae, fem., *friendship.*
amīcus, -ī, mas., *a friend.*
amīcus, -a, -um, adj., *friendly.*
āmittō, see mittō, *lose, let go* (away).

amplificō, -āre, -āvī, -ātum, *increase.*
amplius, neut. compar., used adverbially or as noun, *more.*
Andēs, -ium, mas., a Gallic tribe north of the Loire.
Andocumborius, -ī, mas., a chief man among the Remi.
angustus, -a, -um, adj., *narrow, difficult;* chapt. 25, in angustō, *at a crisis.*
animus, -ī, mas., *mind, courage, feelings;* chapt. 1, *character.*
annus, -ī, mas., *a year.*
ante, adv., *formerly;* prep.+acc., *before* (of place and time).
antīquitus, adv., *in olden times.*
apertus, -a, -um, adj., *open;* chapt. 23, *exposed, unprotected.*
appellō, -āre, -āvī, -ātum, *call* (name); chapt. 25, *address.*
appropinquō, -āre, -āvī, -ātum, *to draw near, approach.*
apud, prep. + *acc., near, among.*
arbitror, -trārī, -trātus sum, depon., *think, suppose.*
arbor, arboris, fem., *a tree.*
arcessō, -cessere, -cessīvī, -cessītum, *summon, invite.*
arduus, -a, -um, adj., *high, difficult* (of ascent), *steep.*
ariēs,-ietis, mas., *a battering ram.*
arma, -ōrum, neut., *arms, weapons.*
armātūra, -ae, fem., *equipment.*
armō, -āre, -āvī, -ātum, *arm, equip.*
ascendō, -cendere, -cendī, -cēnsum, *climb, ascend.*
ascēnsus, -ūs, mas., *an ascent;*

chapt. 33, *the way up, means of ascent.*
at, conj., *but.*
atque, conj., *and also, and;* chapt. 6, *as.*
Atrebātēs, -um, mas, a tribe in Northeastern Gaul.
attingō, -tingere, attigī, attāctum, *touch upon, reach, border upon.*
auctōritās, -tātis, fem., *influence, power, authority* (not military or political).
audācter, adv., *boldly.*
audeō, audēre, ausus sum, semidepon., *dare, venture.*
audiō, -īre, -īvī, -ītum, *listen to;* chapt. 12, *hear;* 31, *hear of* or *about.*
Aulercī, -ōrum, mas., a people of Central Gaul, consisting of several tribes.
Auruncolēius, -ī, mas., a lieutenant of Caesar.
aut, conj., *or;* aut ... aut, *either ... or.*
autem, conj., *but, moreover.*
auxilia, -ōrum, neut., *auxiliaries* (as opposed to the regular heavy-armed Roman infantry).
auxilium, -ī, neut., *help, aid, assistance.*
āvertō, -vertere, -vertī, -versum, *turn away from.*
Axona, -ae, fem., a river of Northern Gaul (now called Aisne) flowing into the Isara.

Baculus, -ī, mas., a centurion in Caesar's army.

Baleāris, -is, -e, adj., *Balearic;* the Balearic islands, famous for their slingers, lie in the Mediterranean off the coast of Spain.
barbarus, -a, -um, adj., *barbarian;* plur., *the barbarians* (used of the Gauls).
Belgae, -ārum, mas., *the Belgians,* a warlike people in the northern part of Gaul.
Bellovacī, -ōrum, mas., a powerful Belgic tribe, between the Seine and the Oise.
bellum, -ī, neut., *war.*
Bibrax, -actis, fem., a town of the Remi.
Boduōgnātus, -ī, mas., a leader of the Nervii.
Bratuspantium, -ī, neut., a town of the Bellovaci.
brevitās, -tātis, fem., *shortness;* with temporis, *want of time.*
Britannia, -ae, fem., *Britain.*

cadāver, -eris, neut., *a dead body.*
cadō, cadere, cecidī, cāsum, *fall, be killed.*
Caeroesī, -ōrum, mas., a tribe in Northern Gaul.
Caesar, -aris, mas., *Caesar,* Caius Julius Caesar, conqueror of Gaul.
calamitās, -tātis, fem., *calamity, disaster.*
Caletī, -ōrum, mas., a tribe in Normandy, on the Seine.
cālō, -ōnis, mas., *a camp-servant, groom.*

captīvus, -a, um, adj., *taken captive;* mas. as noun, *captive, prisoner.*
caput, capitis, neut., *the head;* less exactly, *person.*
Carnutēs, -um, mas., a tribe in Central Gaul.
castellum, -ī, neut., *a redoubt, stronghold.*
castra, -ōrum, neut., *a camp.*
cāsus, -ūs, mas., *event;* chapt. 21, *chance;* 31, *misfortune.*
causa, -ae, fem., *a cause, a reason;* causā, *for the sake of,* used like a prep., following the genitive.
cēdō, cēdere, cessī, cessum, *retreat, give way.*
celeritās, -tātis, fem., *swiftness, quickness.*
celeriter, adv., *quickly, speedily.*
cēlō, -āre, -āvī, ātum, *conceal, hide.*
centum, indeclin. num. adj., *a hundred.*
centuriō, -ōnis, mas., *a centurion;* a subordinate officer commanding a century (a hundred men).
certus, -a, -um, adj., *certain;* certiōrem (-ēs) facere, *inform* (with acc. + infin.).
(cēterus), -a, -um, adj., *the rest of;* usually plur. as noun, *the rest.*
Cimbrī, -ōrum, mas., a German tribe in Jutland, defeated by Marius B.C. 101.
circiter, adv., *about, not far from.*

circuitus, -ūs, mas., *a circuit, a circumference.*
circum, prep. + acc., *around, about.*
circumdō, see dō, *put around;* less exactly, *surround.*
circumiciō, -icere, -iēcī, -iectum, *place around, throw around.*
circummūniō, see mūniō, *fortify around, fortify.*
circumveniō, see veniō, *surround, outflank.*
cis, prep. + acc., *on this side of.*
citerior, -ior, -ius, adj. (comparative — two terminations), *hither, nearer.*
citrā, prep. + acc., *on this side of.*
cīvitās, -tātis, fem., *a state.*
clāmor, -ōris, mas., *a shout.*
claudō, claudere, clausī, clausum, *close, bring up.*
clēmentia, -ae, fem., *kindness, clemency.*
coacervō, -āre, -āvī, -ātum, *pile up.*
coepī, coepisse, coeptus sum, *began.*
cōgnōscō, -nōscere, -nōvī, -nitum, *find out, ascertain.*
cōgō, cōgere, coēgī, coāctum, *collect, assemble, force.*
cohors, -hortis, fem., *a cohort* (the tenth part of a legion).
cohortātiō, -ōnis, fem., *an encouraging, encouragement.*
cohortor, -tārī, -tātus sum, depon., *encourage, urge.*
collis, -is, mas., *a hill.*
comes, comitis, mas., *a comrade.*

commeātus, -ūs, mas., *supplies, provisions.*
commemorō, -āre, -āvī, -ātum, *remind one of, state, relate.*
committō, see mittō, *join ;* with proelium, *begin the battle.*
commodē, adv., *easily, readily.*
commoveō, see moveō, *alarm, disturb.*
commūnis, -is, -e, adj. (of two terminations), *common, general.*
commūtātiō, -ōnis, fem., *a change.*
comparō, -āre, -āvī, -ātum, *prepare, get ready.*
compellō, -pellere, -pulī, -pulsum, *drive together, drive.*
compleō, -ēre, -ēvī, -ētum, *fill.*
complūrēs, -rēs, -ria (-ra), adj. (of two terminations), *very many, a great many.*
concīdō, -cīdere, -cīdī, -cīsum, *cut to pieces.*
concilium, -ī, neut., *a council* (of war), *an assembly.*
concurrō, -currere, -currī (-cucurrī), -cursum, *run together, rush up.*
condiciō, -ōnis, fem., *terms, condition.*
Condrūsī, -ōrum, mas., a Belgic tribe on the Meuse.
condūcō, see dūcō, *bring together, hire.*
cōnferō, -ferre, -tulī, collātum, *bring together, collect;* sē cōnferre, *betake one's self.*
cōnfertus, -a, -um, adj., *crowded, dense.*
cōnficiō, -ficere, -fēcī, -fectum, *accomplish;* chapt. 4, *raise;* 23, 25, 27, *exhaust.*
cōnfīdō, -fīdere, -fīsus sum, semi-depon., *believe in, trust.*
cōnfīrmō, -āre, -āvī, -ātum, *establish ;* chapt. 15, *assure ;* 19, *encourage.*
cōnflīgō, -flīgere, -flīxī, -flīctum, *fight, contend.*
congredior, -gredī, -gressus sum, depon., *engage* (in battle), *fight*
cōniciō, -icere, -iēcī, -iectum, *throw together;* chapt. 6, 27, *hurl;* 23, *drive;* 16, 28, *place.*
coniungō, -iungere, -iūnxī, -iūnctum, *join, unite.*
coniūrō, -iūrāre, -iūrāvī, -iūrātum, *conspire, swear together.*
conlocō, -āre, -āvī, -ātum, *place, station* (of troops).
cōnor, -nārī, -nātus sum, depon., *attempt, undertake, try.*
cōnsanguineus, -a, -um, adj., *akin* (by blood); plur. as noun, *kinsmen.*
cōnscrībō, see scrībō, *enroll, enlist.*
cōnsēnsus, -ūs, mas., *consent, agreement.*
cōnsentiō, -sentīre, -sēnsī, -sēnsum, *agree, combine, conspire.*
cōnsequor, see sequor, depon., *follow, secure, obtain.*
cōnsorvō, -āre, -āvī, -ātum, *spare, save.*
cōnsīdō, -sīdere, -sēdī, -sessum, *settle, encamp.*
cōnsilium, -ī, neut., *wise counsel, a plan;* chapt. 17, *a suggestion.*

cōnsimilis, -is, -e, adj. (of two terminations), *very like, quite similar.*

cōnsistō, -sistere, -stitī, -stitum, *halt, make a stand;* chapt. 33, *depend upon.*

cōnspectus, -ūs, mas., *sight, view.*

cōnspiciō, -spicere, -spēxī, -spectum, *see, behold.*

cōnspicor, -cārī, -cātus sum, depon., *see, observe.*

cōnstanter, adv., *uniformly, steadily.*

cōnstituō, -tuere, -tuī, -tūtum, *decide;* chapt. 12, 30, *set up;* 8, 19, *arrange, station.*

cōnsuēscō, -suēscere, -suēvī, -suētum, *become accustomed;* in the perf. tenses, *be accustomed.*

cōnsuētūdō, -dinis, fem., *custom, habit.*

contemptus, -ūs, mas., *contempt, scorn.*

contendō, -tendere, -tendī, -tentum, *struggle, fight, hasten.*

contineō, -tinēre, -tinuī, -tentum, *hold in, keep* (within bounds), *keep.*

contrā, adv. and prep. + acc., *against, in opposition.*

contrārius, -a, -um, adj., *opposite.*

contumēlia, -ae, fem., *an insult, an outrage.*

conveniō, see **veniō**, *meet, assemble;* chapt. 19, *be agreed upon.*

convertō, -vertere, -vertī, -versum, *turn;* signa convertere, *face about.*

convocō, -āre, -āvī, -ātum, *summon, call together.*

cōpia, -ae, fem., *an abundance, plenty;* (plur.) *forces.*

cornū, -ūs, neut., *a horn, a wing* (of an army).

corpus, -oris, neut., *the body;* chapt. 10, 27, *a* (dead) *body.*

cortex, -ticis, mas. and fem., *bark.*

cotīdiē, adv., *daily, every day.*

Cotta, -ae, mas., a lieutenant of Caesar.

Crassus, -ī, mas., a son of the Triumvir and a lieutenant in Caesar's army.

crēber, -bra, -brum, adj., *frequent, numerous, thick.*

crēdō, crēdere, crēdidī, crēditum, *believe, trust.*

Crēs, Crētis, mas., *a Cretan* (an inhabitant of Crete).

cruciātus, -ūs, mas., *torture, suffering.*

cum, prep. + abl., *with;* conj., *when, while, after, since;* chapt. 29, second sentence, *although;* cum prīmum, *as soon as.*

cūnctus, -a, -um, adj., *all, all together.*

cupiō, cupere, -pīvī, -pītum, *desire eagerly, be eager.*

Curiosolitēs, -um, mas., a people of the West of Gaul.

cursus, -ūs, mas., *a running, speed.*

custōdia, -ae, fem., *protection, guard* (the state of being guarded).

dē, prep. + abl., *from, with respect to;* chapt. 7, *about, for;* 32, *from.*
dēbeō, -bēre, -buī, -bitum, *owe, ought, must.*
decem, indecl. num. adj., *ten.*
dēcernō, -cernere, -crēvī, -crētum, *decree, decide.*
dēcertō, -āre, -āvī, -ātum, *contend, fight.*
decimus, -a, -um, num. adj., *tenth.*
dēclīvis, -is, -e, adj. (of two terminations), *sloping down.*
decumānus, -a, -um, adj., *decuman* (*belonging to the tenth*): porta decumāna, *the rear gate of the camp, near which the tenth legion was posted.*
dēcurrō, -currere, -currī (-cucurrī), -cursum, *run down.*
dēditīcius, -a, -um, adj., *surrendered;* chapt. 17, as noun, *prisoners;* 32, *subjects.*
dēditiō, -ōnis, fem., *surrender.*
dēdō, dēdere, dēdidī, dēditum, *surrender.*
dēdūcō, see dūcō, *lead down or away;* chapt. 10, 31, *bring;* 33, *take away;* 35, *place.*
dēfendō, -fendere, -fendī, -fēnsum, *defend, protect.*
dēfēnsiō, -ōnis, fem., *a defence, a protection.*
dēfēnsor, -ōris, mas., *a defender.*
dēferō, see ferō, *carry down, report;* chapt. 4, *confer, bestow.*
dēficiō, -ficere, -fēcī, -fectum, *fail, fall away;* chapt. 14, *revolt.*

dēiciō, -icere, -iēcī, -iectum, *throw down.*
dēiectus, -ūs, mas., *a slope, a declivity.*
deinde, adv., *then, next.*
dēleō, -lēre, -lēvī, -lētum, *destroy.*
dēligo, -ligere, -lēgī, -lēctum, *choose, select.*
dēmōnstrō, -āre, -āvī, -ātum, *explain, show, state.*
dēnique, adv., *at last, finally;* chapt. 33, *at any rate.*
dēnsus, -a, -um, adj., *dense, thick.*
dēpōnō, see pōnō, *lay down* (*aside*).
dēpopulor, -lārī, -lātus sum, depon., *lay waste.*
dēprecor, -cārī, -cātus sum, depon., *avert by prayer, beseech, beg.*
dēserō, -serere, -seruī, -sertum, *desert, abandon, give up.*
dēsistō, -sistere, -stitī, -stitum, *stop, desist from, cease.*
dēspectus, -ūs, mas., *a view* (from above), *a prospect.*
dēspērō, -āre, -āvī, -ātum, *give up hope;* chapt. 24, *despair of.*
dēspoliō, -āre, -āvī, -ātum, *despoil, strip, deprive.*
dēsum, -esse, -fuī, *be lacking, be wanting.*
dēterreō, -terrēre, -terruī, -territum, *frighten off, prevent.*
dētrahō, -trahere, -trāxī, -trāctum, *take, snatch* (away).
dētrūdō, -trūdere, -trūsī, -trūsum, *remove, slip off.*

dēveniō, see veniō, *come away, come* (from one place to another).
dexter, -tra, -trum, adj., *right.*
diciō, -ōnis, fem., *control, sway.*
dīco, dīcere, dīxī, dictum, *say, mention, speak.*
diēs, -ēī, mas. and fem., *a day.*
difficilis, -is, -e, adj. (of two terminations), *difficult.*
difficultās, -tātis, fem., *difficulty.*
dīligenter, adv., *carefully, with care.*
dīmētior, -mētīrī, -mēnsus sum, depon., *measure, measure off.*
dīmicō, -āre, -āvī, -ātum, *fight, contend* (to a finish).
dīmittō, see mittō, *let go away, send out, dismiss.*
dīripiō, -ripere, -ripuī, -reptum, *plunder, pillage.*
discēdō, -cēdere, -cessī, -cessum, *depart.*
discessus, -ūs, mas., *a departure.*
dissipō, -āre, -āvī, -ātum, *scatter, disperse.*
distineō, -tinēre, -tinuī, -tentum, *keep apart, separate, divide.*
diū, adv., *for a long time;* diūtius, *longer.*
dīversus, -a, -um, adj., *diverse;* chapt. 22, *separated;* 23, *different;* 24, *routed.*
dīvīnus, -a, -um, adj., *divine.*
Dīvitiācus, -ī, mas., a leader of the Aedui, brother of Dumnorix.
dō, dare, dedī, datum, *give;* obsidēs inter sē dare, *exchange hostages.*
doceō, -cēre, -cuī, doctum, *teach;* chapt. 5, *explain;* 20, *direct.*
domesticus, -a, -um, adj., (*of the house*), *domestic, native.*
domicilium, -ī, neut., *an abode, a dwelling-place.*
dominor, -nārī, -nātus sum, depon., *rule.*
domus, -ūs, (-ī), fem., *a home, a house;* locative domī, *at home.*
dubitō, -āre, -āvī, -ātum, *have doubt;* with the infin., *hesitate;* with the subjunc., *doubt.*
ducentī, -ae, -a, num. adj., *two hundred.*
dūcō, dūcere, dūxī, ductum, *lead, conduct.*
dum, conj., *while.*
duo, -duae, -duo, num. adj., *two.*
duodecimus, -a, -um, num. adj., *twelfth.*
duodēvigintī, indecl. num. adj., *eighteen.*
duplex, gen. duplicis, adj. of one termination, *double, twofold.*
dux, ducis, mas., *a leader, a guide, a commander.*

ē, ex, prep. + abl., *from, out of;* chapt. 6, second sent., *after.*
Eburōnēs, -um, mas., a Belgic tribe situated between the Meuse and the Rhine.
ēditus, -a, -um, adj., *raised, elevated.*
ēdūcō, see dūcō, *lead out, lead forth.*
efficiō, -ficere, -fēcī, -fectum, *accomplish, bring* (*it*) *about.*

ēgredior, -gredī, -gressus sum, depon., *go forth, march out.*

ēgregiē, adv., *remarkably, excellently.*

ēligō, -ligere, -lēgī, -lēctum, *select, choose.*

ēmittō, see mittō, *let go, hurl.*

emō, emere, ēmī, ēmptum, *buy.*

ēnāscor, -nāscī, -nātus sum, depon., *grow out, sprout forth.*

enim, conj., *for.*

eō, adv., *thither, there.*

eō, īre, īvī (iī), itum, *go.*

eques, equitis, mas., *a horseman*, plur., *cavalry* (consisting of *Roman* troops).

equester, -tris, -tre, gen., equestris, adj. (of three terminations), *of cavalry, cavalry.*

equitātus -ūs, mas., *cavalry.*

ergō, adv., *therefore, then.*

ēruptiō, -ōnis, fem., *a sally, a sortie.*

Esuviī, -ōrum, mas., a Gallic tribe in Normandy.

et, conj., *and;* et ... et, *both ... and.*

etiam, conj., *also, even.*

ēventus, -ūs, mas., *result, issue.*

ex, see ē.

exagitō, -āre, -āvī, -ātum, *harass, persecute.*

exanimō, -āre, -āvī, -ātum, *make breathless, exhaust.*

exaudiō, see audiō, *hear distinctly.*

excēdō, -cēdere, -cessī, -cessum, *withdraw, retire.*

excursiō, -ōnis, fem., *a sally.*

excūsō, -āre, -āvī, -ātum, *excuse.*

exeō, -īre, -īvī -iī, -itum, *go out, go forth.*

exercitō, -āre, -āvī, -ātum, *train, drill.*

exercitus, -ūs, mas., *an army.*

exiguitās, -tātis, fem., *scantiness;* with temporis, *want of time.*

eximius, -a, -um, adj., *excellent, remarkable.*

existimō, -āre, -āvī, -ātum, *think, suppose, believe.*

expedītus, -a, -um, adj., *unincumbered, light-armed.*

expellō, -pellere, -pulī, -pulsum, *drive out.*

experior, -perīrī, -pertus sum, depon., *try, risk.*

explōrātor, -tōris, mas., *a scout.*

explōrō, -āre, -āvī, -ātum, *search, find out.*

expūgnō, see pūgnō, *storm.*

exspectō, -āre, -āvī, -ātum, *await, wait to see* (sī, *whether*, etc.).

exstruō,-struere,-strūxī,-strūctum, *pile up, build up.*

extrēmus, -a, -um, adj., *farthest.*

facile, adv., *easily.*

facilis, -is, -e, adj. (of two terminations), *easy.*

faciō, facere, fēcī, factum, *make, do.*

facultās, -tātis, fem., *opportunity;* chapt. 1, *means.*

fallō, fallere, fefellī, falsum, *fail, deceive, disappoint.*

fastīgātus, -a, -um, adj., *sloping, inclined.*

ferāx, gen., **ferācis**, adj. (of one termination), *fertile*.
ferē, adv., *nearly, almost*.
ferō, ferre, tulī, lātum, *carry, bear, endure*.
fertilitās, -tātis, fem., *fertility, productiveness*.
ferus, -a, -um, adj., *wild, fierce*.
fidēs, -eī, fem., *faith, confidence, protection*.
fīlius, -ī, mas., *a son*.
fīnis, -is, mas., *an end;* (plur.) *boundaries, territory*.
fīnitimus, -a, -um, adj., *neighbouring;* mas. plur. as noun, *neighbours*.
fīō, fierī, factus sum, *be made, happen, become*.
flūmen, -minis, neut., *a river*.
fors, fortis, fem., *chance, fate*.
forte, old abl. as adv., *by chance*.
fortis, -is, -e, adj. (of two terminations), *brave, courageous*.
fortiter, adv., *bravely*.
fortūna, -ae, fem., *fortune, fate*.
fossa, -ae, fem., *a ditch, a trench*.
frāter, frātris, mas., *a brother*.
fremitus, -ūs, mas., *a noise, an uproar*.
frōns, frontis, fem., *brow, front;* **ā fronte**, *in front*.
frūmentarius, -a, -um, adj., *of grain;* **rēs frūmentāria**, fem., *supply*.
frūmentum, -ī, neut., *corn, grain*.
fuga, -ae, fem., *flight*.
fugiō, fugere, fūgī, fugitum, *flee, fly, escape*.
fugō, -āre, -āvī, -ātum, *rout, put to flight*.

fūmus, -ī, mas., *smoke*.
funditor, -tōris, mas., *a slinger*.
furor, -ōris, mas., *madness, frenzy*.

Galba, -ae, mas., *a legatus of Caesar;* chapt. 4, 13, King of the Suessiones.
galea, -ae, fem., *a helmet* (of leather, worn by cavalry).
Gallia, -ae, fem., *Gaul* (country occupying all Northern Italy).
Gallus, -a, -um, adj., *of Gaul;* as noun, *a Gaul, the Gauls*.
gēns, gentis, fem., *a tribe, a class*.
Germānus, -a, -um, adj., *German;* plur. as noun, *the Germans*.
gerō, gerere, gessī, gestum, *carry on, wage* (war).
gladius, -ī, mas, *a sword*.
grātia, -ae, fem., *favor, influence, popularity*.
gravis, -is, -e, adj. (of two terminations), *heavy, severe, serious*.

habeō, -ēre, -buī, -bitum, *have, hold, possess*.
hībernācula, -ōrum, neut., *winter-quarters*.
hībernus, -a, -um, adj., *of winter;* neut. plur. (with **castra**), *winter-quarters*.
hīc, haec, hōc, demons. pron., *this, he*, etc.
hiemō, -āre, -āvī, -ātum, *winter, pass the winter*.
homō, hominis, mas., *a man*.
honor, -ōris, mas., *honor, respect*.

hostis, -is, mas., *an enemy* (of the state), *the enemy*.

iaceō, iacēre, iacuī, iacitum, *lie, lie dead;* chapt. 27, iacentibus, (pres. participle), *the slain*.

iaciō, iacere, iēcī, iactum, *hurl;* chapt. 12, *throw up*.

iam, adv., *now, already*.

ibi, adv., *there*.

Iccius, -I, mas., a nobleman of the Remi.

idem, eadem, idem, demons. pron., *the same*.

identidem, adv., *again and again*.

idōneus, -a, -um, adj., *suitable, fit*.

ignis, -is, mas., *fire;* chapt. 7, *camp-fire;* 33, *signal-fire*.

ille, illa, illud, demons. pron., *he, that*.

Illyricum, -I, neut., *Illyria* (country east of the Adriatic, belonging to Caesar's province).

impedīmentum, -I, neut., *a hindrance;* plur., *baggage, baggage-train, pack-animals*.

impediō, -īre, -īvī, -ītum, *entangle, hinder*.

impellō, -pellere, -pulī, -pulsum, *drive on, incite, influence*.

imperātor, -tōris, mas., *a commander* (in chief), *a general*.

imperātum, -I, neut., *a command, an order*.

imperium, -I, neut., *command, control, power*.

imperō, -āre, -āvī, -ātum, *command, require, direct*.

impetrō, -āre, -āvī, -ātum, *obtain* (a request), *obtain* (anything by a request).

impetus, -ūs, mas., *an attack, a charge;* chapt. 6, *fury*.

imprōvīsus, -a, -um, adj., *unforeseen;* dē imprōvīsō, *unexpectedly*.

in, prep. + acc and abl.; with acc., *into, against, upon* (with verbs of motion); with abl., *in, on, among;* chapt. 32, *in the case of*.

incendō, -cendere, -cendī, -cēnsum, *burn, set fire to*.

incidō, -cidere, -cidī, -cāsum, *fall in with, befall, happen*.

incīdō, -cīdere, -cīdī, -cīsum, *notch, cut into*.

incipiō, -cipere, -cēpī, -ceptum, *begin*.

incitō, -āre, -āvī, -ātum, *urge on;* incitātō cursū, *at full speed*.

incolō, -colere, -coluī, (no supine), *inhabit, live*.

incrēdibilis, -is, -e, adj. (of two terminations), *incredible, marvellous*.

increpitō, -āre, -āvī, -ātum, *taunt, upbraid*.

incūsō, -āre, -āvī, -ātum, *blame, chide*.

inde, adv., *thence, after that, then*.

indignitās, -tātis, fem., *disgrace, outrage*.

indīligenter, adv., *carelessly, negligently*.

indūcō, see dūcō, *draw on, cover*.

induō, -duere, -duī, -dūtum, *put on*.

ineō, -ire, -ivi (-iī), -itum, *enter upon, undertake, begin.*
inermis, -is, -e, adj. (of two terminations), *unarmed.*
inferior, -ior, -ius, adj. (comparative—two terminations), *lower;* chapt. 8, *inferior.*
inferō, -ferre, -tulī, illātum, *bring in;* chapt. 14, *bring upon;* 15, *import;* 25, (signa) inferre, *carry forward;* 25, (spē) illātā, *inspire in;* 29, *wage;* 32, *inflict.*
infimus, -a, -um, adj., *lowest;* chapt. 18, *at the bottom.*
inflectō, -flectere, -flēxī, -flexum, *bend down.*
ingredior, -gredī, -gressus sum, depon., *enter, march in.*
inimicus, -a, -um, adj., *unfriendly;* as noun, *an enemy* (personal).
iniquitās, -tātis, fem., *unevenness, inequality.*
iniquus, -a, -um, adj., *unfavourable, unfair.*
initium, -ī, neut., *a beginning.*
iniūria, -ae, fem., *injustice, wrong.*
innītor, -nitī, -nisus (-nixus) sum, depon., *lean upon.*
insequor, see sequor, depon., *pursue, follow up.*
insidiae, -ārum, fem., *an ambush, a trap.*
insigne, -is, neut., *a badge, a decoration.*
insistō, -sistere, -stitī, (no supine), *stand upon.*
instar, neut. indeclin. (*an image*);

like, in the manner of (with gen.).
instō, -stāre, -stitī, -stātum, *press forward, press on.*
instruō, -struere, -strūxī, -strūctum, *draw up* (of troops); chapt. 30, *build.*
intellegō, -legere, -lēxī, -lēctum, *know, learn.*
inter, prep. + acc., *between, among.*
intercēdō, -cēdere, -cessī, -cessum, *go between, move between.*
intercipiō, -cipere, -cēpī, -ceptum, *intercept* (obstruct in motion).
interclūdō, -clūdere, -clūsī, -clūsum, *cut off, shut off.*
intereā, adv., *meanwhile, in the mean time.*
interficiō, -ficere, -fēcī, -fectum, *kill, put to death.*
intericiō, -icere, -iēcī, -iectum, *throw in* (between); chapt. 17, *place among;* 22, *intervene.*
interim, adv., *meanwhile.*
interior, -ior, -ius, adj. (comparative—two terminations), *interior, inner.*
intermittō, see mittō, *cease, discontinue.*
interneciō, -ōnis, fem., *extermination, annihilation.*
interscindō, -scindere, -scidī, -scissum, *cut down, demolish.*
intersum, see sum, *be between;* impers., *it concerns* (with gen.).
intervāllum, -ī, neut., *distance* (between two things).

intexō, -texere, -texuī, -textum, weave together.
intrā, prep. + acc., within.
intrō, -āre, -āvī, -ātum, enter, penetrate.
intrōdūcō, see dūcō, lead in, bring in.
intrōmittō, see mittō, let go in, send in.
intrōrsus, adv., within, inside.
inūsitātus, -a, -um, adj., unusual, unwonted.
inūtilis, -is, -e, adj. (of two terminations), useless; chapt. 16, incapable.
inveniō, see veniō, come upon, find, learn.
inveterāscō, -rāscere, -rāvī, (no supine), grow old in, gain a firm footing.
invideō, see videō, envy (with dat.), be jealous of.
ipse, -a, -um, intensive pron., he, self.
irrīdeō, -rīdēre, -rīsī, -rīsum, laugh at, taunt.
is, ea, id, demons. or personal pron., he, that.
ita, adv., thus, so; chapt. 1, ita utī, as, just as.
Ītalia, -ae, fem., Italy.
itaque, adv., therefore.
item, adv., likewise.
iter, itineris, neut., a road, a march; iter facere, to march.
iubeō, iubēre, iussī, iussum, order, bid, command.
iūdicō, -āre, -āvī, -ātum, judge, think, decide.

iugum, -ī, neut., a yoke; a ridge (of a row or chain of hills).
iūs, iūris, neut., right, justice, law.
iūstitia, -ae, fem., justice, fair dealing.
iuvō, iuvāre, iūvī, iūtum, aid, help, assist.
iūxtā, adv., near by, next.

L, initial letter of Lūcius.
Labiēnus, -ī, mas., a legatus of Caesar in Gaul.
lapis, lapidis, mas., a stone.
lassitūdō, -dinis, fem., fatigue.
lateō, -tēre, -tuī, (no supine), lie concealed, be concealed.
lātitūdō, -dinis, fem., width, breadth.
lātus, -a, -um, adj., broad, wide.
latus, -eris, neut., the side; ab latere, on the flank.
laxō, -āre, -āvī, -ātum, open out, widen, extend.
lēgātiō, -ōnis, fem., an embassy, a legation.
lēgātus, -ī, mas., an ambassador, an envoy, a lieutenant.
legiō, -ōnis, fem., a legion.
legiōnārius, -a, -um, adj., legionary, of a legion.
lēniter, adv., gently.
levis, -is, -e, adj. (of two terminations), light.
levitās, -tātis, fem., lightness, fickleness, inconstancy.
lēx, lēgis, fem., a law, a statute.
līberāliter, adv., kindly, generously.
līberī, -ōrum, mas., children (of free parents).

littera, -ae, fem., *a letter* (of the alphabet); plur., *letters, letter* (an epistle).
locus, -I, mas., *a place;* neut. plur., loca, -ōrum; chapt. 26, *condition.*
longē, adv., *far, at a distance.*
longus, -a, -um, adj., *long.*
loquor, loquī, locūtus sum, depon., *speak, talk.*
Lūcius, -I, mas., a Roman praenomen (the first name).
lūx, lūcis, fem., *light;* prīmā lūce, *at early dawn, at daybreak.*
lūxuria, -ae, fem., *luxury.*

māchinātiō, -ōnis, fem., *a machine, an engine, a contrivance.*
magis, adv., *more, rather;* magis ... quam, *rather ... than.*
magistrātus, -ūs, mas., *a magistracy, a magistrate.*
māgnitūdō, -dinis, fem., *greatness, size.*
māgnopere, adv., *very much, very earnestly;* māgnō opere (see opus).
māgnus, -a, -um, adj., *great, large.*
māior, māior, māius, adj., *greater;* māiōrēs (nātū), *elders.*
maleficium, -I, neut., *harm, mischief.*
mālō, mālle, māluī, (no supine), *prefer, wish rather.*
mandō, -āre, -āvī, -ātum, *direct, instruct;* chapt. 24, *consign.*
manipulus, -I, mas., *a company* (a third of a cohort), *a maniple.*

mānsuētūdō, -dinis, fem., *kindness, gentleness.*
manus, -ūs, fem., *the hand; a band, a company.*
maritimus, -a, -um, adj., *maritime, of the sea.*
mātūrō, -āre, -āvī, -ātum, *hasten, make haste.*
māximē, adv., *especially, very.*
medius, -a, -um, adj., *middle of.*
memoria, -ae, fem., *memory, recollection.*
Menapii, -ōrum, mas., a Gallic tribe between the Meuse and the Scheldt.
mercātor, -tōris, mas., *a trader* (who carries his own goods abroad).
meritum, -I, neut., *merit, desert.*
mīles, -itis, mas., *a soldier.*
mīlitāris, -is, -e, adj. (of two terminations), *of the soldiers, military;* see rēs.
mīlle, indecl. num. adj., *a thousand;* plur. as noun, mīlia, mīlium.
minimē, adv., *least, very little.*
minus, neuter acc. of the comparative minor, used as an adv., *less;* chapt. 9, *not.*
miser, -era, -erum, adj., *wretched, miserable.*
misericordia, -ae, fem., *pity, clemency, compassion.*
mittō, mittere, mīsī, missum, *send, despatch.*
mōbilitās, -tātis, fem., *inconstancy, mobility.*
modo, adv., *merely, only;* nōn modo, *not only.*

modus, -ī, mas., *manner;* ad hunc modum, *after this fashion.*
moenia, -ium, neut., *fortifications, walls* (of a city).
molestē adv., *heavily;* molestē ferre, *be vexed* or *annoyed.*
moneō, monēre, monuī, monitum, *direct, advise, warn.*
mōns, montis, mas., *a mountain.*
mora, -ae, fem., *delay.*
Morinī, -ōrum, mas., a Belgic tribe on the seacoast opposite Kent.
moror, -rārī, -rātus sum, depon., *delay, linger, stay.*
mōs, mōris, mas., *custom;* plur., *habits, character.*
moveō, movēre, mōvī, mōtum, *move;* castra movēre, *break camp.*
mulier, -eris, fem., *a woman.*
multitūdō, -dinis, fem., *a multitude, a great number.*
multus, -a, -um, adj., *much, many.*
mūnīmentum, -ī, neut., *a defence, a fortification.*
mūniō, -īre, -īvī, -ītum, *fortify;* with castra, *make.*
mūnītiō, -ōnis, fem., *a fortification, works.*
mūrus, -ī, mas., *a wall* (a city wall).

nam, conj., *for.*
nāscor, nāscī, nātus sum, depon., *be born, spring up.*
nātiō, -ōnis, fem., *a nation, a tribe.*

nātūra, -ae, fem., *nature, character.*
nātus, -ūs, mas., *birth;* māiōrēs (nātū), *elders, old men.*
nāvō, -āre, -āvī, -ātum, *do with zeal;* operam nāvāre, *do one's best.*
nē, conj., *that ... not;* with verbs of fearing, *that, lest;* with the imperative, *not* (negative adv.).
necessārius, -a, -um, adj., *necessary, urgent.*
necessitās, -tātis, fem., *necessity;* chapt. 11, *compulsion;* 22, *urgency.*
negōtium, -ī, neut., *business;* chapt. 17, *trouble;* negōtium dare, *employ.*
nēmō, nēminis, mas. and fem., *no one.*
neque (nec), adv., *and not;* neque ... neque, *neither ... nor.*
nēquīquam, adv., *in vain.*
Nervius, -a, -um, adj., *Nervian;* plur., *the Nerviī,* a powerful tribe of Belgic Gaul.
neuter, -tra, -trum, gen. neutrīus, adj., *neither;* plur. mas., as a noun, *neither party.*
nēve (neu), conj., *and ... not* (continuing a *negative*); chapt. 21, *and that ... not.*
nihil, indecl. neut., *nothing;* acc. as adv., *not at all.*
nisi, conj., *unless, if not, except.*
nōbilitās, -tātis, fem., *nobility;* concretely, *the nobles.*
noctū, abl. used adverbially, *by night.*

nōlō, nōlle, nōluī, (no supine), *be unwilling, not wish.*
nōmen, -minis, neut., *a name.*
nōminātim, adv., *by name (individually).*
nōminō, -āre, -āvī, -ātum, *name, mention, call by name.*
nōn, adv., *not;* **nōn modo,** *not only.*
nōndum, adv., *not yet.*
nōnnūllus, -a, -um, adj., *some;* plur., as a noun, *some persons.*
nōnus, -a, -um, num. adj., *ninth.*
nōs, pers. pron. of the first pers. (plur. of **ego**), *we.*
noster, -tra, -trum, poss. adj. pron., *our;* plur., **nostrī,** *our men* (as a noun).
novem, indecl. num. adj., *nine.*
Noviodūnum, -ī, neut., a town of the Suessiones on the Aisne.
novus, -a, -um, adj., *new;* chapt. 31, *strange, novel.*
novissimus, -a, -um (superl. of **novus**), *the last, latest;* with **agmen,** *the rear;* plur. mas. as a noun, **novissimī,** *men or soldiers in the rear.*
nox, noctis, fem., *night.*
nūdō, -āre, -āvī, -ātum, *strip, lay bare;* chapt. 23, *expose, leave unguarded.*
nūllus, -a, -um, gen. **nūllīus,** adj., *not any, no;* as a noun, *no one.*
numerus, -ī, mas., *a number.*
Numida, -ae, mas., *a Numidian* (employed in the Roman army as cavalry).
nunc, adv., *now.*

nūntiō, -āre, -āvī, -ātum, *announce, report, send news.*
nūntius, -ī, mas., *message, messenger, news.*
ob, prep. + acc., *on account of.*
obdūcō, see **dūcō,** *lead against;* with **fossam,** *dig, construct.*
obitus, -ūs, mas., *a going to* (death), *destruction, death.*
obses, -idis, mas. and fem., *hostage* (one under guard).
obtineō, -tinēre, -tinuī, -tentum, *hold, occupy, possess.*
obveniō, see **veniō** (with dat.), *encounter, fall in with, meet.*
occāsus, -ūs, mas., *a falling, a setting* (of the sun).
occīdō, -cīdere, -cīdī, -cīsum, *slay, kill.*
occultus, -a, -um, adj., *concealed;* in **occultō,** *in secret.*
occupō, -āre, -āvī, -ātum, *seize, occupy* (in a military sense); chapt. 19, *be engaged.*
occurrō, -currere, -currī, -cursum (with dat.), *meet, come upon, fall in with.*
Ōceanus, -ī, mas., *the ocean.*
octāvus, -a, -um, num. adj., *eighth.*
octō, indecl. num. adj., *eight.*
offerō, offerre, obtulī, oblātum, *bring before, offer, carry, bring.*
omittō, see **mittō,** *let go by, neglect* (with **cōnsilium**).
omnis, -is, -e, adj. (of two terminations), *all, the whole of.*
onus, -eris, neut., *a burden, a load.*

LATIN-ENGLISH VOCABULARY. 331

opera, -ae, fem., *pains, service;*
operam nāvāre, *do one's best.*
opīniō, -ōnis, fem., *notion;*
chapt. 3, *expectation;* 8, 24,
reputation; 85, *impression.*
oportet, oportēre, oportuit,
impers., *it behooves, it ought.*
oppidānus, -a, -um, adj., *of the
town;* plur. mas. as a noun, *the
townsmen.*
oppidum, -I, neut., *a town*
(usually fortified).
opportūnus, -a, -um, adj., *convenient, opportune, suitable*
oppūgnātiō, -ōnis, fem., *a siege,
an attack* (in a formal manner
against a fortified place).
oppūgnō, -āre, -āvī, -ātum, *attack* (a defended position).
(ops), opis, fem., *help;* chapt.
14, *resources;* 31, *aid.*
optimus, -a, -um, adj. (superl. of
bonus), *best.*
opus, -eris, neut., *work;* māgnō
opere (māgnopere), *very much;*
quantō opere (quantopere),
how greatly.
opus, indecl. neut., *need;* opus
est, *there is need.*
ōrātiō, -ōnis, fem., *a speech, a
talk, an address.*
ōrdō, dinis, mas., *a row, an order,
a company, a rank* (of soldiers).
orior, orīrī, ortus sum, depon.,
arise; chapt. 4, *be descended
from.*
Osismī, -ōrum, mas., a Gallic
tribe in Brittany.

P., initial letter of Pūblius.

pābulum, -I, neut., *fodder* (for
animals).
pācō, -āre, -āvī, -ātum, *subdue,
pacify.*
Paemānī, -ōrum, mas., a tribe of
the Belgians.
paene, adv., *almost, nearly.*
palūs, -ūdis, fem., *a swamp, a
marsh.*
pandō, pandere, pandī, passum,
spread out; perf. particip.,
passus, *outstretched* (as an
adj.).
pār, paris, adj. (of one termination), *equal.*
parātus, -a, -um, adj., *prepared,
ready.*
pars, partis, fem., *part, side;*
less exactly, *direction.*
partim, acc. as adv., *partly, in
part.*
parvulus, -a, -um, adj., *slight,
small, unimportant.*
passus, -a, -um, see pandō.
passus, -ūs, mas., *a pace* (five
Roman feet); mīlia passuum,
a mile.
patefaciō, see faciō, *open, lay
open.*
pateō, -tēre, -tuī, (no supine),
extend, be open, spread.
pater, patris, mas., *a father;*
plur., *ancestors.*
patior, patī, passus sum, depon.,
endure, permit; chapt. 15,
allow; 31, *suffer.*
patrius, -a, -um, adj., *ancestral,
of one's fathers.*
paucus, -a, -um, adj. (mostly in
the plur.), *few; a few.*

paulātim, adv., *gradually, little by little.*
paulisper, adv., *a short while.*
paulō, abl. as adv., (by) *a little, just a little.*
paululum, adv., *slightly, a very little.*
paulum, adv., *a little, somewhat.*
pāx, pācis, fem., *peace.*
pedes, -itis, mas., *a footman;* plur. collectively, *the infantry.*
pedester, -tris, -tre, adj. (of three terminations), *of infantry, infantry.*
Pedius, -I, mas., a nephew and legatus of Caesar.
pellis, -is, fem., *a skin, a hide* (of an animal).
pellō, pellere, pepulī, pulsum, *drive, defeat, rout.*
per, prep. + acc., *through, by means of;* chapt. 10, *over.*
perferō, see ferō, *carry through;* chapt. 14, *endure;* 35, *spread among.*
periclitor, -tārī, -tātus sum, depon., *test, try, make a trial.*
periculum, -I, neut., *a trial, an attempt;* hence, *danger, peril.*
permittō, see mittō, *give up (over), entrust.*
permoveō, see moveō, *alarm, (move thoroughly).*
perspiciō, -spicere, -spēxī, -spectum, *see through, learn, find, see.*
persuādeō, -suādēre, -suāsī, -suāsum, *persuade* (with dat.), *induce.*

perterreō, -terrēre, -terruī, -territum, *terrify, frighten greatly.*
pertineō, -tinēre, -tinuī, (no supine), *extend, reach* (out), *tend.*
perturbō, -āre, -āvī, -ātum, *throw into disorder, alarm.*
perveniō, see veniō, *reach, arrive at.*
pēs, pedis, mas., *a foot.*
petō, petere, petīvī or petiī, petītum, *seek, ask for, beg.*
pīlum, -I, neut., *a javelin.*
plānitiēs, -ēī, fem., *a plain.*
plērumque, acc. sing. neut. as adv., *generally, usually.*
plērusque, -aque, -umque, adj. (only in the plur.), *most of, very many.*
plūrimus, -a, -um, adj. (superl. of multus), *most;* acc. sing. neut. as adv. (plūrimum), *most, very much;* plūrimum valēre, *have very great influence;* plūrimum posse, *be very powerful.*
polliceor, -licērī, -licitus sum, depon., *promise, offer.*
pondus, -eris, neut., *weight.*
pōnō, pōnere, posuī, positum, *place, put, pitch.*
pōns, pontis, mas., *a bridge.*
populor, -lārī, -lātus sum, depon., *lay waste, plunder.*
populus, -I, mas., *a people.*
porrēctus, -a, -um, adj., *stretched forth, extensive, long.*
porta, -ae, fem., *a gate.*
portō, -āre, -āvī, -ātum, *carry, bring.*

poscō, poscere, poposcī, (no supine), *demand, claim.*
possideō, -sidēre, -sēdī, -sessum, *possess, occupy* (in a military sense).
possum, posse, potuī, *can, be able;* plūrimum posse, *be very powerful.*
post, prep. + *acc., after, behind.*
posteā, adv., *afterwards.*
postquam, adverbial conj., *after, after that, when.*
postrēmō, adv., *finally, lastly, at last.*
postrīdiē, adv., *the next day.*
postrīdiē, adv., *the next day;* postrīdiē ēius diēī, adv. phrase, *the next day after that.*
postulō, -āre, -āvī, -ātum, *demand, claim, ask.*
potēns, potentis, adj. (of one termination). *powerful, mighty.*
potestās, -tātis, fem., *power, control;* chapt. 6, *ability.*
potior, potīrī, potītus sum, depon., *capture* (with *abl.*), *get control of.*
potius, adv., *rather;* potius . . . quam, *rather . . . than.*
prae, prep. + *abl., in comparison with.*
praeacūtus, -a, -um, adj., *sharpened* (to a point), *pointed.*
praebeō, -bēre, -buī, -bitum, *furnish, offer.*
praeceps, -cipitis, adj. (of one termination), *headlong, in haste.*
praedor, -dārī, -dātus sum, depon., *plunder, raid, take booty.*

praefectus, -ī, mas., *a general, an officer, a commander.*
praeferō, see ferō, *place before;* with sē, *outdo* (*show one's self better than*).
praeficiō, -ficere, -fēcī, -fectum, *place in command of.*
praemittō, see mittō, *send forward, send ahead.*
praescrībō, see scrībō, *give directions, order, direct.*
praesertim, adv., *especially.*
praesidium, -ī, neut., *defence, guard, protection.*
praestō, -stāre, -stitī, -stitum, *stand before;* chapt. 15, *excel;* 27, *display;* 31, impers., *it is better.*
praesum, see sum, *be in command of* (with the *dat.*).
praetereā, adv., *besides, furthermore.*
premō, premere, pressī, pressum, *press hard, attack fiercely.*
prīmipīlus, -ī, mas., *the chief* or *first centurion.*
prīmō, adv., *at first.*
prīmum, adv., *first, in the first place;* cum prīmum, *as soon as.*
prīmus, -a, -um, adj., *first;* plur. mas., prīmī, *the foremost men, the chief* or *leading men.*
princeps, -ipis, mas. (adj. of one termination used as a noun), *chief man, chief, leader.*
prior, -ior, -ius, adj. (comparative—two terminations), *former;* plur. mas. as a noun, priōrēs, *men* (*soldiers*) *in front.*

prīstĭnus, -a, -um, adj, *former, old, old time.*

priusquam, conj., adv., *before;* prius and quam are often separated by intervening words.

prō, prep. + abl., *in front of;* chapt. 14, *in behalf of;* 25, *in proportion to;* 31, *according to.*

prōcēdō, -cēdere, -cessī, -cessum, *go forward, advance, proceed.*

procul, adv., *afar off, at a distance.*

prōcumbō, -cumbere, -cubuī, -cubitum, *lean forward, fall, sink down* (to the ground).

proelior, -ārī, -ātus sum, depon., *fight* (in war).

proelium, -ī, neut., *a battle, contest, engagement.*

profectĭō, -ōnis, fem., *a departure, a setting out.*

proficīscor, proficīscī, profectus sum, depon., *set out, go.*

prōflīgō, -āre, -āvī, -ātum, *rout, put to flight, defeat.*

profugĭō, see fugĭō, *flee, escape.*

prōgnātus, -a, -um, adj., *descended from, sprung from.*

prōgredior, -gredī, -gressus sum, depon., *advance, march forward, go forward.*

prohibeō, -hibēre, -hibuī, -hibitum, *prevent, cut off, keep from.*

prōicĭō, -icere, -iēcī, -iectum, *throw away, abandon, give up.*

prōmoveō, see moveō, *move forward, push forward.*

prope, adv., *almost, nearly.*

properō, -āre, -āvī, -ātum, *hasten.*

propinquitās, -tātis, fem., *nearness, relation* (by blood), *kinship.*

propinquus, -a, -um, adj., *near, close, related* (by blood).

prōpōnō, see pōnō, *place before;* chapt. 2, *display, raise.*

propter, prep. + acc., *on account of.*

proptereā, adv., *on this account;* with quod, *because.*

prōpugnō, see pugnō, *fight* (rush out fighting), *fight in defence.*

prōsequor, see sequor, *pursue;* chapt. 5, *address.*

prōspectus, -ūs, mas., *view, outlook.*

prōtinus, adv., *immediately, instantly.*

prōturbō, -āre, -āvī, -ātum, *rout, drive off* (in confusion).

prōvideō, see videō, *foresee, provide, arrange beforehand.*

prōvincia, -ae, fem., *a province* (governed by a Roman magistrate).

prōvolō, -āre, -āvī, -ātum, *fly* (rush) *forth, hurry forward.*

proximē, adv., *recently, last, lately.*

proximus, -a, -um, adj., *next, nearest (last).*

prūdentia, -ae, fem., *discretion, wisdom, foresight.*

pūblicus, -a, -um, adj., *public;* rēs pūblica, fem., *the state.*

Pūblius, -ī, mas., *a Roman praenomen* (the first name).

puer, puerī, mas., *boy;* plur., *children.*

pūgna, -ae, fem., *a fight, a battle.*
pūgnō, -āre, -āvī, -ātum, *fight, engage, contend.*

Q, initial letter of Quīntus.
quā, adv., *where* (chapt. 33).
qua, indefinite pron., see quis.
quadringentī, -ae, -a, num. adj., *four hundred.*
quaerō, quaerere, quaesīvī, quaesītum, *ask, inquire.*
quam, adv., *than, as* (after comparatives and comparative expressions); chapt. 32, 2d sent, and chapt. 33, indef. pron., *any.*
quamvīs, indef. pron. from quīvīs, quaevīs, etc. (which see); chapt. 31, *any you please.*
quantopere, adv., *how greatly, how very much;* see opus.
quantus, -a, -um, adj., *how great?, how much (many)?*
quartus, -a, -um, num. adj., *fourth.*
quattuor, indecl. num. adj., *four.*
que, enclitic conj., *and* (always appended to the word or to some part of the phrase or sentence which it connects).
quī, quae, quod, rel. pron., *who, which, what, that.*
quīdam, quaedam, quoddam, indef. pron., *a certain, certain.*
quidem, adv., *indeed, certainly;* nē . . . quidem, *not . . . even* (emphasizing the word placed between them).
quīn, conj., *but that, that, from* (after negative verbs of *preventing, hindering, doubting,* etc.).

quīnam, quaenam, quodnam, interrog. pron., *who?, what?*
quīndecim, indecl. num. adj., *fifteen.*
quīngentī, -ae, -a, num. adj., *five hundred.*
quīnquāgintā, indecl. num. adj., *fifty.*
quīnque, indecl. num. adj., *five.*
Quīntus, -ī, mas., a Roman praenomen (the first name).
quis, quae, quid, interrog. pron., *who?, which?, what?* ; indef. pron., *any, any one, anything* (after sī, nisī, nē, num).
quisquam, (no fem.), quidquam (quicquam), indef. pron., *any one, anything* (in negative clauses).
quisque, quaeque, quidque, indef. pron., *each, each one.*
quisquis, quaequae, quicquid (quidquid), indef. pron., *whoever, whatever.*
quīvīs, quaevīs, quidvīs, indef. pron., *who you please, any one.*
quō, adv., *whither, where;* chapt. 25, = ut eō, *so that thereby,* (*so that by it*).
quod, conj., *because;* chapt. 17, *the fact that.*
quoque, conj., *also* (emphasizing the word which it follows).

rāmus, -ī, mas., *a branch, a bough.*
ratiō, -ōnis, fem., *a reckoning, a plan, a reason.*
recipiō, -cipere, -cēpī, -ceptum, *take back, receive;* sē recipere,

betake one's self; chapt. 12, sē
recipere, *recover.*
reddō, reddere, reddidī, redditum, *give back, render.*
redeō, -ire, -īvī (-iī), -itum, *go back, return;* less exactly, *decline* (slope).
redigō, -igere, -ēgī, -āctum, *reduce;* chapt. 27, *render.*
redintegrō, -āre, -āvī, -ātum, *renew, restore.*
Redonēs, -um, mas., a Gallic people in Brittany.
redūcō, see dūcō, *lead back, bring back.*
referō, -ferre, rettulī, relātum, *bring back, report, announce.*
refringō, -fringere, -frēgī, -frāctum, *break in, break open.*
regiō, -ōnis, fem., *a region, a district,* a part (of the country).
regō, regere, rēxī, rēctum, *to rule, have control of.*
rēgnum, -ī, neut., *kingdom, power;* plur., *sovereignty.*
rēicio, -icere, -iēcī, -iectum, *drive back, hurl back, drive off.*
relanguēscō, -languēscere, -languī, (no supine), *be weakened, languish away.*
relinquō, -linquere, -līquī, -lictum, *leave behind, leave.*
reliquus, -a, -um, adj., *remaining, the rest of;* as a noun (usually plur.), *the rest.*
Rēmī, -ōrum, a leading tribe of the Belgae.
remittō, see mittō, *send or hurl back;* chapt. 15, *relax, give up.*
Rēmus, -ī, mas., one of the Remi.

renūntiō, āre, -āvī, ātum, *bring back word, report, announce.*
repellō, -pellere, reppulī, repulsum, *drive back, repulse.*
repentīnus, -a, -um, adj., *sudden;* abl. repentīnō (as adv.), *suddenly.*
reperiō, -perīre, repperī or reperī, repertum, *find out, ascertain, find.*
rēs, reī, fem., *a thing, a fact;* rēs frūmentāria, *a grain supply;* rēs pūblica, *the state.*
resistō, sistere, stitī, (no supine), *resist* (with dat.), *withstand.*
respiciō, -spicere, -spēxī, -spectum, *look back, look behind* one.
respondeō, -spondēre, -spondī, -spōnsum, *answer, reply.*
retineō, -tinēre, -tinuī, -tentum, *hold back, restrain;* chapt. 21, with memoriam, *preserve.*
revertor, -vertī, -versus sum, depon., *go back, return;* active forms in the *perfect system,* revertī, reverteram, etc.
revocō, -āre, -āvī, -ātum, *call back, call away, recall.*
rēx, rēgis, mas., *a king.*
Rhēnus, -ī, mas., *the Rhine.*
rīpa, -ae, fem., *a bank, a river-bank.*
rogō, -āre, -āvī, -ātum, *ask, ask for.*
Rōmānus, -a, -um, adj., *Roman;* as a noun, *a Roman.*
rubus, -ī, mas., *a bramble-bush, a bramble.*
rūmor, -ōris, mas., *a report, a rumour.*
rūpēs, -is, fem., *a cliff, a rock.*

rūrsus, adv., *again, in turn, back again.*
rūs, rūris, neut., *country;* locative, rūri, *in the country.*

Sabīnus, -ī, mas., a lieutenant of Caesar.
Sabis, -is, mas., (now) *the Sambre,* a river in Gaul flowing into the Meuse.
saepēs, -is, fem., *a hedge.*
sagittārius, -ī, mas., *a bowman, an archer.*
salūs, -ūtis, fem., *safety, welfare.*
sarcina, -ae, fem., *a package, a pack;* plur., *baggage* (the load carried on the back of each soldier).
saxum, -ī, neut., *a rock.*
scientia, -ae, fem., *skill, knowledge.*
scrībō, scrībere, scrīpsī, scrīptum, *write;* chapt. 29, *give an account* (in writing).
scūtum, -ī, neut., *a shield* (of the Roman legion) made of wood, covered with leather, convex and oblong (2½ by 4 ft.).
sectiō, -ōnis, fem., *a cutting;* hence, from dividing in lots, *booty.*
secundum, prep. + acc., *along;* chapt. 18, *next to.*
secundus, -a, -um, num. adj., *second;* chapt. 9, *favourable.*
sed, conj., *but.*
senātor, -tōris, mas., (*an elder*), *a senator.*
senātus, -ūs, mas., *a senate*

(council of old men), especially the Roman senate.
Senonēs, -um, mas., a powerful Gallic tribe west of the Seine.
sententia, -ae, fem., *an opinion, a view.*
sentis, -is, mas., *a briar, a thornbush* (mostly plur.).
septimus, -a, -um, num. adj., *seventh.*
Sequanus, -a, -um, adj., *of the Sequani;* mas. plur., *the Sequani,* a Gallic tribe on the Rhone.
sequor, sequī, secūtus sum, depon., *follow;* chapt. 22, with ēventus, *ensue.*
servitūs, -tūtis, fem., *slavery, subjection.*
servō, -āre, -āvī, -ātum, *watch;* chapt. 33, with praesidia, *maintain.*
sēsē, see suī.
sex, indecl. num. adj., *six.*
sexāgintā, indecl. num. adj., *sixty.*
sexcentī, -ae, -a, num. adj., *six hundred.*
sī, conj., *if;* chapt. 9, *whether.*
sīc, adv., *so, thus, as follows.*
signifer, -ferī, mas., *a standard-bearer.*
significātiō, -ōnis, fem., *signal, warning.*
significō, -āre, -āvī, -ātum, *show, indicate, announce.*
signum, -ī, neut., *sign, standard;* signa convertere, *face about;* signa inferre, *advance (to the attack).*

silva, -ae, fem., *a forest, woods.*
silvester (-tris), -tris, -tre, adj. (of three terminations), *woody, wooded.*
simul, adv., *at the same time.*
sine, prep. + *abl., without.*
singulāris, -is, -e, adj. (of two terminations), *remarkable, unique.*
singulī, -ae, -a, adj., *single, several, each, one at a time.*
sinister, -tra, -trum, adj., *left.*
sōl, sōlis, mas., *the sun.*
sollicitō, -āre, -āvī, -ātum, *incite, stir up, instigate.*
sōlum, acc. neut. as adv., *only;* nōn sōlum . . . sed etiam, *not only . . . but also.*
sōlus, -a, -um, adj., gen. sōlīus, *only, alone.*
spatium, -ī, neut., *space, distance;* less exactly, *time.*
speciēs, -iēī, fem., *an appearance, a sight, a show.*
speculātor, -tōris, mas., *a spy, a scout.*
spēs, speī, fem., *hope, expectation.*
spīritus, -ūs, mas., *breath;* plur., *pride, arrogance.*
statim, adv., *at once, immediately.*
statiō, -ōnis, mas., *a post, a picket;* in statiōne, *on guard.*
statuō, -tuere, -tuī, -tūtum, *decide, determine.*
statūra, -ae, fem., *stature, height, size.*
strepitus, -ūs, mas., *noise, din.*
studeō, -dēre, -duī, (no supine), (with *dat.*), *desire;* chapt. 17, *pay attention to.*

studium, -ī, neut., *eagerness, desire, fondness* (for a thing).
sub, prep. + *abl.* and *acc., under;* chapt. 13, 38, *towards, near to.*
subeō, see eō, *undergo, approach, enter.*
subitō, adv., *suddenly, hastily.*
submittō, see mittō, *send up, send, despatch* (with dat.).
subruō, -ruere, -ruī, -rutum, *undermine, dig under.*
subsequor, see sequor, *follow up, pursue, follow on.*
subsidium, -ī, neut., *relief, assistance, help.*
succēdō, -cēdere, -cessī, -cessum, *come up, approach, draw near.*
successus, -ūs, mas., *a coming up, an advance, a close approach.*
Suessiōnēs, -um, mas., a tribe of the Belgae between the Marne and the Isère.
suī, sibi, sē (sēsē), reflex. pron., *himself, themselves,* etc.
sum, esse, fuī, *be, am.*
summa, -ae, fem., *the sum, the total;* chapt. 4, *control;* chapt. 23, with imperiī, *chief command.*
summus, -a, -um, adj., *highest, top of.*
sūmō, sūmere, sūmpsī, sūmptum, *take, assume, claim.*
superior, -ior, -ius, adj. (comparative — two terminations), *higher, former, preceding.*
superō, -āre, -āvī, -ātum, *overcome, defeat, conquer.*

LATIN-ENGLISH VOCABULARY. 339

supersedeō, -sedēre, -sēdī, -sessum, *refrain from.*
supersum, see sum, *survive, remain.*
supplex, -plicis, adj. (of one termination), *humble;* used as a noun, mas. and fem., *a suppliant.*
supplicātiō, -ōnis, fem., *a thanksgiving* (a supplication).
suprā, adv., *above, before.*
sustentō, -āre, -āvī, -ātum, *hold out.*
sustineō, -tinēre, -tinuī, -tentum, *withstand;* chapt. 6, with sēsē, *hold out;* chapt. 25, with sē, *stand up.*
suus, -a, -um, possess. adj. pron., *his* (*own*), *their* (*own*), (reflex.).

T., initial letter of Titus.
tam, adv., *so.*
tamen, adv., *however, nevertheless, still.*
tantulus, -a, -um, adj., *so small, so little.*
tantus, -a, -um, adj., *so great, so much.*
tardō, -āre, -āvī, -ātum, *check, retard.*
tardus, -a, -um, adj., *slow, sluggish;* chapt. 25, *exhausted.*
tegimentum, -ī, neut., *a covering, a cover.*
tēlum, -ī, neut., *a weapon, a missile, a javelin.*
tempus, -oris, neut., *time;* chapt. 22, *occasion;* ūnō tempore, *at one and the same time;* eōdem tempore, *at the same time.*

tendō, tendere, tetendī, tēnsum and tentum, *extend, stretch out.*
teneō, tenēre, tenuī, tentum, *hold, keep.*
tener, -era, -erum, adj., *tender, young, delicate.*
terror, -ōris, mas., *fright, terror, alarm.*
tertius, -a, -um, num. adj., *third.*
testūdō, -dinis, fem., *testudo (a covering of shields).*
Teutonī, -ōrum, (-ēs, -um), mas., a German people in Jutland, defeated by Marius in B.C. 102.
timeō, timēre, timuī, (no supine), *fear, be afraid.*
Titūrius, -ī, mas., *Quintus Titurius Sabinus;* see Sabinus.
Titus, -ī, mas., a Roman praenomen (the first name).
tormentum, -ī, neut., *an engine of war* (for throwing missiles).
totidem, indecl. adj., *just as many, as many.*
tōtus, -a, -um, gen. tōtīus, adj., *entire, the whole of.*
trabs, trabis, fem., *a timber, a beam;* (nom. sing. sometimes, trabēs).
trādō, trādere, trādidī, trāditum, *hand over, give up.*
trādūcō, see dūcō, *lead across, bring over.*
trāns, prep. with acc., *across, over, beyond.*
trānseō, see eō, *cross over, go across, cross.*
trānsgredior, -gredī, -gressus sum, depon., *go across, cross.*

trānsversus, -a, -um, adj., *across;* with fossa, *a cross-ditch.*
trēs, trēs, tria, gen. trium, num. adj., *three.*
Trēverī, -ōrum, mas., a powerful tribe of the Belgians on the Moselle.
tribūnus, -ī, mas., *a tribune;* with militum, *a military tribune.*
triduum, -ī, neut., *three days' time, three days.*
triplex, gen. triplicis, adj. (of one termination), *triple, threefold.*
tuba, -ae, fem., *a trumpet* (a straight instrument for infantry).
tum, adv., *then;* chapt. 4, cum ... tum, *both ... and.*
tumultus, -ūs, mas., *an uproar, confusion, a commotion.*
tumulus, -ī, mas., *a hill, a mound.*
Turonēs, -um (-ī, -ōrum), mas., a Gallic tribe on the Loire.
turpitūdō, -dinis, fem., *disgrace, baseness, dishonour.*
turris, -is, fem., *a tower.*
tūtus, -a, -um, adj., *safe, secure, protected.*

ubi, adv., *when, where.*
ūllus, -a, -um, gen. ūllīus, adj., *any one, any.*
ūnā, adv. (ūnā cum), *together with, along with* (them).
ūndecimus, -a, -um, num. adj., *eleventh.*
undique, adv., *from (on) all parts, on all sides.*

ūniversus, -a, -um, adj., *whole, all.*
ūnus, -a, -um, gen. ūnīus, num. adj., *one, only, alone.*
urgeō, urgēre, ursī, (no supine), *press hard.*
ūsus, -ūs, mas., *use, practice, advantage.*
ut (utī), conj., with indic. *as, when;* with subjunc., *so that, in order that.*
uterque, -traque, -trumque, gen. utrīusque, adj., *each of two, both.*
ūtor, ūtī, ūsus sum, depon., *use, employ, enjoy* (with abl.).

vacuus, -a, -um, adj., *empty, free;* chapt. 12, with ab + abl., *destitute of.*
vadum, -ī, neut., *a ford, shallows.*
valeō, valēre, valuī, valitum, *be strong;* plūrimum valēre, *have very great influence.*
vāllum, -ī, neut., *a rampart, a palisade.*
varius, -a, -um, adj., *diverse, different, various.*
vāstō, -āre, -āvī, -ātum, *lay waste, ravage.*
Veliocassēs, -ium, (-ī, -ōrum), mas., a Gallic tribe on the right bank of the Seine.
vēndō, vēndere, vēndidī, vēnditum, *sell.*
Venellī (Unellī), -ōrum, mas., a tribe along the west coast of Gaul.
Venetī, -ōrum, mas., a Gallic tribe on the west coast.

LATIN-ENGLISH VOCABULARY. 341

veniō, venīre, vēnī, ventum, come, approach, go.
verbum, -ī, neut., *a word, a discourse.*
vereor, verērī, veritus sum, depon., *fear, be afraid.*
vergō, vergere, (no perfect, no supine), *incline, slope, lie towards.*
vērō, adv., *in fact, in truth.*
versō, -āre, -āvī, -ātum, *turn, deal with;* frequently as a depon., *be (remain);* chapt. 24, *be engaged.*
vesper, -erī, mas., *the evening.*
vetō, vetāre, vetuī, vetitum, *forbid.*
vēxillum, -ī, neut., *a flag.*
vexō, -āre, -āvī, -ātum, *harass, annoy.*
victor, -tōris, mas., *a conqueror;* chapt. 24 (as adj.), *victorious.*
vīcus, -ī, mas., *a village.*
videō, vidēre, vīdī, vīsum, *see;* as depon. in the present system of the passive, *seem.*
vigilia, -ae, fem., *a watch* (one of the four divisions of the night).
vīmen, -minis, neut., *a pliant twig.*

vincō, vincere, vīcī, victum, *conquer, defeat.*
vīnea, -ae, fem., *vinea* (a movable shed covering a besieging party).
vīnum, -ī, neut., *wine.*
vir, virī, mas., *a man.*
Viromanduī, -ōrum, mas., a tribe of the Belgians north of the Oise.
virtūs, -tūtis, fem., *courage, valour* (manliness).
vīs, (vīs), (plur. vīrēs), *vigour, strength, force.*
vītō, -āre, -āvī, -ātum, *avoid, escape.*
vix, adv., *scarcely, with difficulty.*
volō, velle, voluī, (no supine), *wish, be willing.*
voluntās, -tātis, fem., *desire, will* (good will), *approval.*
vōx, vōcis, fem., *voice;* plur., *words, shouts*
vulgō, adv. (abl. of vulgus), *generally, everywhere.*
vulnerō, -āre, -āvī, -ātum, *wound, injure, hurt.*
vulnus, -eris, neut., *a wound.*

ENGLISH-LATIN VOCABULARY.

about, *circiter*, adv.; *dē*, prep. + *abl.*
about midnight, *dē mediā nocte.*
above, *suprā*, adv.
abundance, *cōpia*, *-ae*, fem.
access, *aditus*, *-ūs*, mas.
across, *trāns*, prep. + *acc.*
address, *prōsequor*, (3).
advance, *prōgredior*, (3).
after, *cum*, conj. + pluperf. subjunc.; *post*, prep. + *acc.*
afterwards, *posteā*, adv.
again, *rūrsus*, adv.
against, *contrā*, prep. + *acc.*
aid, *auxilium*, *-ī*, neut.; *iuvō*, *adiuvō*, (1).
alarm, *commoveō*, (2).
all, *omnis*, *-is*, *-e*, adj.
almost, *paene*, adv.
alone, *sōlus*, *-a*, *-um*, adj.
ambassador, *lēgātus*, *-ī*, mas.
ambush, *īnsidiae*, *-ārum*, fem.
among, *inter*, prep. + *acc.*
and, *et*, *que*, *ac*, *atque*, conj.
announce, *nūntiō*, *renūntiō*, (1).
another (other), *alter*, *-era*, *-erum*, adj.
any, *ūllus*, *-a*, *-um*, adj.
approach, *adventus*, *-ūs*, mas.
archer, *sagittārius*, *-ī*, mas.
arms, *arma*, *-ōrum*, neut.

army, *exercitus*, *-ūs*, mas.; *aciēs*, *aciēī*, fem.
arrival, *adventus*, *-ūs*, mas.
arrive, *perveniō*, (4).
arrogance, *spīritus*, *-ūs*, mas. (in the *plur.*).
as, *ut*, conj. + indic.
as soon as, *cum prīmum*, conj.
ask, *rogō*, (1); *quaerō*, (3).
ask for, *petō*, (3).
assemble, *conveniō*, (4); *cōgō*, (3).
attack, *impetus*, *-ūs*, mas.; *oppūgnō*, (1); *aggredior*, (3).
attempt, *cōnor*, (1).
at early dawn, *prīmā lūce.*
at first, *prīmō*, adv.
at one and the same time, *ūnō tempore.*
at once, *statim*, adv.
at the foot of the mountain, *sub monte.*
at the same time, *eōdem tempore.*
auxiliaries, *auxilia*, *-ōrum*, neut.
avoid, *vītō*, (1).
await, *exspectō*, (1).

badge, *īnsigne*, *-is*, neut.
baggage, *impedīmenta*, *-ōrum*, neut.
band, *manus*, *-ūs*, fem.
bank, *rīpa*, *-ae*, fem.

battle, *proelium*, -*i*, neut.
be, *sum;* be able, *possum*.
be in command of, *praesum* + *dat.*
be very powerful, *plūrimum posse; plūrimum valēre.*
be unwilling, *nōlō.*
bear, *ferō.*
beginning, *initium*, -*i*, neut.
begin battle, *proelium committere.*
behind, *post*, prep. + *acc.*
beloved, *amātus*, -*a*, -*um*, adj.
betake one's self, *sē recipere; sē conferre.*
between, *inter*, prep. + *acc.*
blame, *incūsō*, (1).
body, *corpus*, -*oris*, neut.
boldly, *audācter*, adv.
borders, *fīnis*, -*is*, mas. (in the plur.).
both . . . and, *et* . . . *et*, conj.
boundary, *fīnis*, -*is*, mas. (in the plur.).
bowman, *sagittārius*, -*i*, mas.
boy, *puer*, *puerī*, mas.
bravely, *fortiter*, adv.
break camp, *castra movēre.*
bridge, *pōns*, *pontis*, mas.
bring, *ferō.*
bring to, *addūcō*, (3).
bring up, *agō*, (3).
broad, *lātus*, -*a*, -*um*, adj.
brother, *frāter*, -*tris*, mas.
build, *aedificō*, (1).
building, *aedificium*, -*i*, neut.
burn, *incendō*, (3).
business, *negōtium*, -*i*, neut.; with *dare*, to employ.
but, *sed*, conj.

but also, *sed etiam*, conj.
by, *ā*, *ab*, prep. + *abl.* (with passive verb).
by night, *noctū* (as adv.).

calamity, *calamitās*, -*tātis*, fem.
call, *appellō*, (1).
camp, *castra*, -*ōrum*, neut.
captive, *captīvus*, -*i*, mas.
carry, *portō*, (1).
cavalry, *eques*, *equitis*, mas.; *equitātus*, -*ūs*, mas.
cause, *causa*, -*ae*, fem.
centurion, *centuriō*, -*ōnis*, mas.
certain, *certus*, -*a*, -*um*, adj.
chief, *princeps*, -*cipis*, mas.
children, *līberī*, -*ōrum*, mas.
choose, *dēligō*, (3).
cohort, *cohors*, -*hortis*, fem.
collect, *cōgō*, (3).
command, *imperium*, -*i*, neut.; *imperō*, (1).
commander, *imperātor*, -*tōris*, mas.
come, *veniō*, (4).
common, *commūnis*, -*is*, -*e*, adj.
conceal, *cēlō*, (1).
concerning, *dē*, prep. + *abl.*
confidence, *fidēs*, *fideī*, fem.
conquer, *pellō, vincō*, (3); *superō*, (1).
conspire, *coniūrō*, (1); *cōnsentiō*, (4).
contend, *dēcertō*, (1); *contendō*, (3).
convenient, *opportūnus*, -*a*, -*um*, adj.
corn, *frūmentum*, -*i*, neut.
council of war, *concilium*, -*i*, neut.

courage, *virtūs, -tūtis*, fem.
covering, *tegimentum, -i*, neut.
covering (of shields), *testūdō, -dinis*, fem.
cross, *trānseō*.
custom, *mōs, mōris*, mas.; *cōnsuētūdō, -dinis*, fem.
cut down, *interscindō*, (8).
cut off, *interclūdō*, (3); *prohibeō*, (2).

danger, *periculum, -i*, neut.
dare, *audeō*, (2).
dart, *tēlum, -i*, neut.
day, *diēs, diēi*, mas. and fem.
decide, *cōnstituō*, (8).
deep, *altus, -a, -um*, adj.
defeat, *pellō, vincō*, (8); *superō*, (1).
defence, *praesidium, -i*, neut.; *mūnimentum, -i*, neut.
defend, *dēfendō*, (3).
defender, *dēfēnsor, -sōris*, mas.
delay, *mora, -ae*, fem.; *moror*, (1).
demand, *poscō*, (8); *postulō*, (1).
depart, *ēgredior, proficīscor*, (8); *discēdō*, (3).
departure, *profectiō, -ōnis*, fem.
deprive, *dēspoliō*, (1).
descend (be descended) *orior*, (4).
desire, *studeō*, (2); *studium, -i*, neut. (fondness).
deter, *dēterreō*, (2).
different, *dīversus, -a, -um*, adj.
dig (extend), *obdūcō* (with *fossam*), (3).
direct, *mandō*, (1).
ditch, *fossa, -ae*, fem.
divide, *distineō*, (2).
do, *faciō*, (3).
draw near to, *appropinquō*, (1);

for construction with verb, see chapt. 10, next to last sent.; 19, second sent.; 31, first sent.
draw up, *īnstruō*, (8).
drive, *compellō*, (3).
drive back, *repellō*, (3).
drive out, *expellō*, (8).

each (of the two), *uterque*, adj.
easily, *facile*, adv.
easy, *facilis, -is, -e*, adj.
eight, *octō*, indecl. num. adj.
either . . . or, *aut . . . aut*, conj.
employ, *negōtium dare*.
empty, *vacuus, -a, -um*, adj.
encourage, *cohortor*, (1); with *ut* + subjunc.
end, *fīnis, -is*, mas.
ends of the ditches, *extrēmae fossae*.
enemy, *hostis, -is*, mas. (usually plur.).
engine of war, *tormentum, -i*, neut.
enroll, *cōnscrībō*, (3).
enter, *intrō*, (1).
enter upon, *ineō*.
entire, *tōtus, -a, -um*, adj.
entrust, *permittō*, (3).
envoy, *lēgātus, -i*, mas.
equal, *adaequō*, (1); for construction with verb, see chapt. 32, last sent.
erect, *cōnstituō*, (3).
especially, *maximē*, adv.
establish, *cōnfīrmō*, (1).
even, *etiam*, conj.
evening, *vesper, -eri*, mas.
exchange hostages, *obsidēs inter sē dare*.

ENGLISH-LATIN VOCABULARY. 345

execute, *administrō*, (1).
expect, *exspectō*, (1).

face about, *signa convertō*, (8).
fail, *fallō*, (8).
farthest, *extrēmus, -a, -um*, adj.
father, *pater, -tris*, mas.
fear, *vereor, timeō*, (2).
fertility, *fertilitās, -tātis*, fem.
few, *paucus, -a, -um*, adj.; *plur.* only.
fickleness, *levitās, -tātis*, fem.
field, *ager, agrī*, mas.
fierce, *ferus, -a, -um*, adj.
fight, *pūgna, -ae*, fem.; *pūgnō, dēcertō, dīmicō*, (1), *contendō, cōnflīgō*, (3).
fill, *compleō*, (2).
find, *reperiō, inveniō*, (4).
find out, *cōgnōscō*, (8); *explōrō*, (1).
fire, *īgnis, -is*, mas.
first, *prīmus, -a, -um*, adj.
five, *quīnque*, indecl. num. adj.
flee, *fugiō*, (3).
flight, *fuga, -ae*, fem.
fodder, *pābulum, -ī*, neut.
follow after, *subsequor*, (8).
foot, *pēs, pedis*, mas.
for, *nam*, conj.
for the sake of, *causā* (as a prep., following a *gen.*).
force (vigor), *vīs, vīs*, fem.; (plur. *vīrēs*).
forces, *cōpiae, -ārum*, fem.
ford, *vadum, -ī*, neut.
foremost (men), *prīmī, -ōrum*, (mas. plur. of *prīmus*).
forest, *silva, -ae*, fem.
former, *prīstinus, -a, -um*, adj.

fortification, *mūnītiō, -ōnis*, fem.
fortify, *mūniō*, (4).
free, *vacuus, -a, -um*, adj.
frequent, *crēber, -bra, -brum*, adj.
fresh, *integer, -gra, -grum*, adj.
friend, *amīcus, -ī*, mas.
friendly, *amīcus, -a, -um*, adj.
friendship, *amīcitia, -ae*, fem.
frighten, *perterreō*, (2).
from, *ā, ab*, prep. + abl.
from (on) all sides, *undique*, adv.

gate, *porta, -ae*, fem.
Gaul, (country), *Gallia, -ae*, fem.; (person), *Gallus, -ī*, mas.
general, *praefectus, -ī*, mas.
general (common), *commūnis, -is, -e*, adj.
give, *dō*, (1).
give hostages to one another, *obsidēs inter sē dare*.
give up, *permittō, trādō*, (3).
great, *māgnus, -a, -um*, adj.

halt, *cōnsistō*, (3).
hand over, *trādō*, (3).
hasten, *mātūrō*, (1); *contendō*, (3).
have, *habeō*, (2).
have very great power or influence, *plūrimum posse, plūrimum valēre*.
he, self, *ipse, -a, -um*, intensive pron.
he, she, it, *is, ea, id*, (used as pers. pron., third person).
hedge, *saepēs, -is*, fem.
height, *altitūdō, -dinis*, fem.
helmet, *galea, -ae*, fem.
help, *auxilium, -ī*, neut.; *iuvō*, (1).

hesitate, *dubitō*, (1).
high, *altus, -a, -um*, adj.
hill, *collis, -is*, mas.
hinder, *impediō*, (4).
hire, *condūcō*, (3).
his, *ēius* (not reflex.); *suus, -a, -um*(reflex.), possess. pronouns.
hither, *citerior, -ior, -ius*, adj.
hold, *obtineō*, (2).
hold out, *sustentō*, (1).
home, *domus, -ūs* (*-ī*), fem.
hope, *spēs, spei*, fem.
horse, *equus, -ī*, mas.
hostage, *obses, -idis*, mas.
how great, *quantus, -a, -um*, adj.
hurl, *cōniciō*, (3).

immediately, *prōtinus, statim*, adv.
in, on, upon, *in*, prep. + *abl.*
incite, *sollicitō*, (1).
infantry, *pedes, -itis*, mas. (usually *plur.*).
influence, *addūcō*, (3).
inform, *certiōrem (-ēs) facere.*
in front of, *prō*, prep. + *abl.*
inhabit, *incolō*, (3).
injury, *iniūria, -ae*, fem.
inquire, *quaerō*, (3).
instruct, *mandō*, (1).
into, *in*, prep. + *acc.*
investigate, *cōgnōscō*, (3).

javelin, *pilum, -ī*, neut.
join, *coniungō*, (3).
just as, as, *ita . . . ut.*

keep, *contineō*, (2).
keep apart, *distineō*, (2).
keep back, *retineō*, (2).
kill, *interficiō*, (3).

kindly, *liberāliter*, adv.
king, *rēx, rēgis*, mas.
kingdom, *rēgnum, -ī*, neut.; (plur. sovereignty).
kinsmen, *cōnsanguineī, -ōrum*, mas.

large, *māgnus, -a, -um*, adj.
last, lately, *proximē*, adv.
lay waste, *vāstō, populor*, (1).
lead, *dūcō*, (3).
lead across, *trādūcō*, (3).
leader, *dux, ducis*, mas.
lead out, *ēdūcō*, (3).
leave, *relinquō*, (3).
legion, *legiō, -ōnis*, fem.
left, *sinister, -tra, -trum*, adj.
less, *minus*, adv.
less easily, *minus facile, minus commodē*, adv.
letter, *littera, -ae*, fem.; (usually *plur.*).
lieutenant, *lēgātus, -ī*, mas.
light, *lūx, lūcis*, fem.
light-armed, *expedītus, -a, -um*, adj.
likewise, *item*, adv.
line of battle, (army), *aciēs, aciēī*, fem.
line of march, *agmen, -minis*, neut.
long, a long time, *diū*, adv.
longer, *diūtius*, adv.
love, *amō*, (1).

make, *faciō*, (3).
make (take) a stand, *cōnsistō*, (3).
make an attack upon, *facere impetum in* + *acc.*
make more certain (see '*inform*'), *certiōrem (-ēs) facere.*

ENGLISH-LATIN VOCABULARY. 347

man, *homō, hominis*, mas.; *vir, virī*, mas.
march, *iter, itineris*, neut.; *iter facere*.
marsh, *aestuārium, -ī*, neut.
meanwhile, *interim*, adv.
memory, *memoria, -ae*, fem.
(men) in the front, *priōrēs, -um*, mas. (compar. adj. as noun).
(men) in the rear, *novissimī, -ōrum*, mas. (superl. adj. as noun).
merchant, *mercātor, -tōris*, mas.
message, messenger, *nūntius, -ī*, mas.
middle of, *medius, -a, -um*, adj.
mind, *animus, -ī*, mas.
most of, *plērusque, -aque, -umque*, adj. (in the plur. only).
mountain, *mōns, montis*, mas.
move, *moveō*, (2).
movable shed, *vīnea, -ae*, fem.
multitude, *multitūdō, -dinis*, fem.
much, many, *multus, -a, -um*, adj.

name, *nōmen, -minis*, neut.
nature, *nātūra, -ae*, fem.
near by, *iūxtā*, adv.
nearness, *propinquitās, -tātis*, fem.
neighbouring, *fīnitimus, -a, -um*, adj.; in the mas. plur., noun, *neighbours*.
neither, *neuter, -tra, -trum*, adj.
neither . . . nor, *neque (nec)* . . . *neque (nec)*.
new, *novus, -a, -um*, adj.
next, *proximus, -a, -um*, adj.
night, *nox, noctis*, fem.
no, none, *nūllus, -a, -um*, adj.

not, *nōn*, adv.; *nē* (regular negative of the *imperative*).
not only, *nōn modo*.
not yet, *nōndum*.
number, *numerus, -ī*, mas.

obtain, *impetrō*, (1).
of cavalry, *equester, -tris, -tre*, adj. (of three terminations).
of corn, *frūmentārius, -a, -um*, adj.
officer, *magistrātus, -ūs*, mas.
on, *see* in, upon.
one (alone), *ūnus, -a, -um*, num. adj.
only, alone, *sōlus, -a, -um*, adj.; *ūnus, -a, -um*, adj.
on all sides, *undique*, adv.
on account of, *propter*, prep. + acc.
on the flank, *ab latere* (from *latus*, the noun).
on the left side, *ab sinistrā parte*.
on the right wing, *ā dextrō cornū*.
on the top of the hill, *in summō colle*.
on this side of, *cis*, prep. + acc.
opportunity, *facultās, -tātis*, fem.
opposite, *adversus, -a, -um*, adj.
order, *imperātum, -ī*, neut.; *imperō*, (1); *iubeō*, (2).
other (another), *alter, -era, -erum; alius, -a, -ud*, adj.
our, *noster, -tra, -trum*, adj.; mas. plur. as noun, our men.
out of, *ē, ex*, prep. + abl.
outstretched, *passus, -a, -um*, adj.
overcome, *superō*, (1).

pace, *passus, -ūs,* mas.
part, *pars, partis,* fem.
peace, *pāx, pācis,* fem.
people, *populus, -ī,* mas.
pitch (place), *pōnō,* (3).
place, *locus, -ī,* mas.; neut. plur., *loca;* conlocō, (1); *pōnō,* (3).
place in command of, *praeficiō,* (3), (with *dat.*).
plain, *plānitiēs, plānitiēī,* fem.
power, *imperium, rēgnum, -ī,* neut.; *potestās, -tātis,* fem.
powerful, *potēns,* gen. *potentis,* adj. (of one termination).
prepare, *parō,* (1); prepared, *parātus, -a, -um* (particip. as adj.)
prevent, *prohibeō, dēterreō,* (2); *impediō,* (4).
promise, *polliceor,* (2).
protection, *fidēs, fideī,* fem.
province, *prōvincia, -ae,* fem.
pursue, *prōsequor,* (3).
put on, *induō,* (3).

quickly, *celeriter,* adv.

rampart, *vāllum, -ī,* neut.
ready, *parātus, -a, -um,* adj.
rear, *novissimum agmen, novissimī agminis,* neut.
receive, *accipiō,* (3).
recently, *proximē,* adv.
redoubt, *castellum, -ī,* neut.
reduce, *redigō,* (3).
refrain from, *supersedeō,* (2).
region, *regiō, -ōnis,* fem.
relief, *subsidium, -ī,* neut.
remaining, *reliquus, -a, -um,* adj.
Remian (a), *Rēmus, -ī,* mas.; plur., the Remi.

renew, *redintegrō,* (1).
report, *rūmor, -ōris,* mas.; *nūntiō, renūntiō,* (1).
rest, the rest, *cēterus, -a, -um,* adj.; usually mas. plur. as a noun.
restrain, *retineō,* (2).
resist, *resistō,* (3), (with *dat.*).
return, *revertor,* (3).
revolution, *rēs nova, reī novae,* fem.
right, *dexter, -tra, -trum,* adj.
river, *flūmen, -minis,* neut.
Roman, *Rōmānus* (adj. or noun).
rout, *fugō, prōflīgō,* (1); *pellō,* (3).
rumor, *rūmor, -ōris,* mas.
run down, *decurrō,* (3).
rush forth, *prōvolō,* (1).

safety, *salūs, -ūtis,* fem.
sally, *excursiō, -ōnis,* fem.
say, *dīcō,* (3).
scout, *explōrātor, -tōris,* mas.
second, *secundus, -a, -um,* adj.
see, *videō,* (2).
seek, *petō,* (3).
seem, *videor,* (2).
seize, *occupō,* (1).
senate, *senātus, -ūs,* mas.
send, *mittō,* (3).
send forward, *praemittō,* (3).
separate, *distineō,* (2).
servant, *servus, -ī,* mas.
settle, *cōnsīdō,* (3).
set out, *proficīscor,* (3).
set up (arrange), *cōnstituō,* (3).
seventh, *septimus, -a, -um,* num. adj.
shield, *scūtum, -ī,* neut.
side, *latus, -eris,* neut.

ENGLISH-LATIN VOCABULARY. 349

sight, *cōnspectus, -ūs,* mas.
signal, *signum, -ī,* neut.
since, *cum* + subjunc.
shortness, *brevitās, exiguitās, -tātis,* fem.
slave, *servus, -ī,* mas.
slavery, *servitūs, -tūtis,* fem.
slay, *occīdō,* (3).
slight, *parvulus, -a, -um,* adj.
slinger, *funditor, -tōris,* mas.
so (thus), *tam, ita,* adv.
so great, *tantus, -a, -um,* adj.
some, *nōnnūllus, -a, -um,* adj.
so that, *ut* + subjunc.
so that . . . not, *nē* + subjunc.
sovereignty, *rēgnum, -ī,* neut., (in the plur.).
speech, *ōrātiō, -ōnis,* fem.
speed, *cursus, -ūs,* mas.
state, *cīvitās, -tātis,* fem.
stone, *lapis, -idis,* mas.
stop (cease), *dēsistō,* (3).
storm, *expūgnō,* (1).
strength, *vīs, (vīs),* fem.
strip, *nūdō,* (1).
strong (to be), *valeō,* (2); to have very great influence, *plūrimum valēre.*
subdue, *superō,* (1) ; *vincō, pellō,* (3).
subjection, *servitūs, -tūtis,* fem.
suddenly, *subitō,* adv.
suitable, *idōneus, -a, -um,* adj.
summer, *aestās, -tātis,* fem.
summon, *convocō,* (1).
supply (plenty), *cōpia, -ae* fem.; (in the plur.) forces.
supply of corn, *rēs frūmentāria, reī frūmentāriae,* fem.
supplies, *commeātus, -ūs,* mas.

surrender, *dēditiō, -ōnis,* fem.; *dēdō, trādō,* (3).
surround, *circumdō,* (1); *circumveniō,* (4).
swamp, *palūs, -ūdis,* fem.
sword, *gladius, -ī,* mas.

tall, *altus, -a, -um,* adj.
tenth, *decimus, -a, -um,* num. adj.
terms, *condiciō, -ōnis,* fem.
territory, *fīnis, -is,* mas. (in the plur.).
testudo, *testūdō, -dinis,* fem.
that, *is, ea, id,* demons. pron., or adj.
their, *eōrum,* (not reflex.), possess. pron.; *suus, -a, -um,* (reflex.), possess. pron.
there, *ibī,* adv.; *eō* (in sense of *thither*).
thing, *rēs, reī,* fem.
this, *hīc, haec, hōc,* demons. pron.
this side of, *cis,* prep. + acc.
thither, *eō,* adv.
(those) in the front, *priōrēs, -um,* mas. (compar. adj. as noun).
thousand, *mīlle;* declined only in plur., *mīlia, -ium,* neut.
three, *trēs, trēs, tria,* num. adj.
through, *per,* prep. + acc.
throw, *cōniciō,* (3).
time, *tempus, -oris,* neut.
to (towards), *ad,* prep. + acc.
tower, *turris, -is,* fem.
town, *oppidum, -ī,* neut.
townsmen, *oppidānī, -ōrum,* mas.
top of, *summus, -a, -um,* adj.
tribe, *gēns, gentis,* fem.
triple, *triplex,* gen. *triplicis,* adj. (of one termination).

trumpet, *tuba, -ae,* fem.
try, *cōnor,* (1); *experior,* (4).
two, *duo, duae, duo,* num. adj.

undermine, *subruō,* (3).
unexpectedly, *dē imprōvisō.*
unfavorable, *iniquus, -a, -um,*
 adj.
unfriendly, *inimīcus, -a, -um,*
 adj.
unite (conspire), *cōnsentiō,* (4).
unless, *nisi,* conj.
upon, *in + acc.,* with verbs of
 motion; *in + abl.,* with verbs
 of rest.
uproar, *tumultus, -ūs,* mas.
urge, *cohortor,* (1).
use, *ūsus, -ūs,* mas.; *ūtor,* (3).

very greatly, *māximē,* adv.
very like, *cōnsimilis, -is, -e,* adj.
 (of two terminations).
very many, *plūrimus, -a, -um,*
 adj. (in the plur.).
village, *vicus, -ī,* mas.
vinea, *vinea, -ae,* fem.

wait for, *exspectō,* (1).
wall, *mūrus, -ī,* mas.
war, *bellum, -ī,* neut.
watch, *vigilia, -ae,* fem.
weapon, *tēlum, -ī,* neut.
when, where, *ubi* (denoting *time*
 or *place*).
while, *cum +* imperf. subjunc.
who, *quī,* (rel. pron.); *quis,*
 (interrog. pron.).
width, *lātitūdō, -dinis,* fem.
wing, *cornū, -ūs,* neut.
winter, *hiemō,* (1).
winter-quarters, *hiberna, hibernā-
 cula, -ōrum,* neut.
wish, *volō, velle, voluī.*
with, *cum,* prep. *+ abl.; post-
 positive* with the *personal, relative* and *reflexive pronouns.*
within, *intrā,* prep. *+ acc.*
without, *sine,* prep. *+ abl.*
with respect to, *dē,* prep. *+ abl.*
withstand, *sustineō,* (2).
work, *opus, -eris,* neut.
wound, *vulnus, -eris,* neut.; *vulnerō,* (1).

INDEX.

References are to paragraphs.

Ā, ab: use of, 240
Ablative: separation, 221; quality, 376; time when or within which, 65; means or instrument, 43; attendance or accompaniment, 43; cause and manner, 210; place in which (place where), 47; place from which (whence), 386; place towards which (whither), 386; personal agent, 237; causā with the *gen.*, 7; quō with the comparative, 384; with opus and ūsus, 379; with depon. verbs, 353; with comparative adj., 369; abl. absolute, 287; abl. absol. analyzed, 288; abl. absol. written in four ways, 364; abl. absol. distinguished from the p. p. p. modifying subj. or obj., 323
Accusative: direct object, 16, *c*; extent in space, 342; duration of time, 342; adverbial acc., 374; end or limit of motion (place towards which), 386; subj. of infinitive, 301, 302
Ad: with verbs of motion, 59; with *gerundive* in affirm. purpose, 355

Adapted and Simplified Caesar: 408–447
Adjectives: agreement of, 4, 115; stem, how found, 188, 298; used as substantives, 258; in the predicate, 95, 97; governing the *dat.*, 126; with *gen.* in ius, *dat.* in ī, 286; of 1st and 2d declens. declined, 466; of 3d declens. declined, 467; numeral adjs. declined, 468; comparison of regular adjs., 298, 469; comparison of, ending in er, 308, 470; comparison of, ending in ilis, 314, 471, comparison of irregular, 472
Adverb: translated like adj., 216
Adverbial accusative: 374
Adverbial phrase: use of, 34
Adverbs compared: 473
Affirmative purpose: how expressed, 320; expressed in four ways, 355
Affirmative result: 321
Ager: declined, 454
Agmen: declined, 122
Altior: declined, 467
Altus: declined, 466
Amō: complete paradigms, 474, 475

Analysis of a complex sentence: 204
Apposition: 54

Capiō: complete paradigms, 480, 481
Cāsus: declined, 182
Causal clauses: 104, 276
Causal cum: 350, 359
Certior factus: 338
Certiōrem (-ēs) facere: 333
Cīvitās: declined, 122
Cohortor: use of, 347
Collis: declined, 180
Commands and exhortations: 389
Commands, etc., in O. O.: 390
Comparative adjective declined: 467
Comparison of adjectives: see 'Adjectives.'
Comparison of adverbs: 473
Complex sentence analyzed 204
Concessive cum. 350, 359
Conditions. more vivid future, 223, a, b; less vivid future, 335; conditions in O. O., 396
Conjugations:
  1st conjuga.: list of 92 verbs, 448; complete paradigms (amō), 474, 475; synopses, by stems (portō): (a) *active*—pres. syst., 75, perf. syst., 120, sup. syst. 133; (b) *passive* — pres. and perf. syst., 255
  2d conjuga.: list of 42 verbs, 449; complete paradigms (moneō), 476, 477; synopses, by stems (dēleō): (a) *active*—pres.

syst., 158, perf. syst., 163, sup. syst., 169; (b) *passive*—pres. and perf. syst., 270
  3d conjuga.: list of 157 verbs, 450; complete paradigms (pōnō), 478, 479; capiō (the 'iō' verb) complete, 480, 481; synopses, by stems (pōnō): (a) *active*—pres. syst., 192, perf. syst., 196, sup. syst., 197; (b) *passive*—pres. syst., 281, perf. syst., 284
  4th conjuga.: list of 19 verbs, 451; complete paradigms (mūniō), 482, 483; synopses, by stems (mūniō): (a) *active*—pres. syst., 225, perf. syst., 230, sup. syst., 231; (b) *passive*—pres. syst., 295, perf. syst., 296
Cornū: declined, 461
Corpus: declined, 458
Crēber: declined, 466
Cum clauses: historical **cum**, *when* (= *while* or *after*), 128, 203, 263, 359; temporal **cum**, *when*, 359; causal **cum**, *since*, 350, 359; concessive **cum**, *although*, 350, 359

Dative: indirect obj., 15; with adjs., 126; with **imperō** and **mandō**, 134, 145; with **negōtium dare**, 330; with compound verbs, 337; with special verbs, 348; with **persuādeō** (in the *active*), 345; with **persuādeō** (in the *passive*), 380; double dat. (purpose, end, service), 352; possession, 357; personal agent, 362

Declension of adjectives: 1st and 2d declensions, 466; 3d declension, including pres. particip. and comparative, 467; numerals, 468

Declension of nouns:
1st declension: stem, gender, paradigms, 453
2d declension: stem, gender, paradigms, 454
3d declension: stems, kinds of, 455; nom., how formed in *consonant* stems, 456, A, B, C; nom., how formed in *vowel* stems, 457; *nom. sing.* ending (all genders) of vowel stems in i, 457; *nom. plur.* (neut.) ending of vowel stems in i, 457; *gen. plur.* ending of vowel stems in i, 457; *acc. plur.* (mas. and fem.) endings in īs or ēs, 457 gen. plur. endings um and ium, all 3d-declension nouns, 460; general rules of gender, 458; paradigms: mīles, 112; cīvitās, agmen, lapis, mīles ferus, 122; pater, rūmor, latus, corpus, legiō, 124; collis, rēx, flūmen lātum, 130; multitūdō, vīs, iter, 138; frāter, hostis, pēs, facultās, virtūs, lēx, flūmen, īnsīgne, 458; mīlia (plur. of mīlle), 459. Third-declension paradigms (nouns) may be found in 112, 122, 124, 130, 138, 458, 459
4th declension: stem, gender, paradigms, 461
5th declension: stem, gender, paradigms, 462

Declension of pronouns: personal pron., 1st person, 463; demonst. and intensive, 464; rel., interrog., and indef., 465
Dēleō: for synopses by stems, both voices, see 'Conjugations,' 2d.
Demonstrative pronouns, 464
Deponent verbs
1st conjuga.: complete paradigms (populor), 494; for *active* forms and synopses, *by stems,* see 326, 327
2d conjuga.: complete paradigms (vereor), 495
3d conjuga.: complete paradigms (ūtor), 496
4th conjuga.: complete paradigms (potior), 497
Diēs: declined, 462
Direct discourse (Ōrātiō Rēcta), 301
Direct object: 15, 16, c
Direct question: 313
Duo: declined, 468
Duplex: declined, 467
Duration of time: 342

Ego: declined, 463
Eō: complete paradigms, 486
Equester: declined, 467
Extent in space: 342

Faciō: active paradigms, 492
Facultās: declined, 458
Fearing: verbs of, with ut or nē + subjunctive, 343
Ferō: complete paradigms, 490, 491
Fīō: passive of faciō; passive paradigms, 493

Flūmen: declined, 458
Flūmen lātum: declined, 130
Fortis: declined, 188
Fossa: declined, 1, 6
Frāter: declined, 458
Future participle, Future infinitive: how formed, 170; fut. infin. in O. O., 818, examples 3 and 4 with note; fut. infin. of depon. verb, 328

Galea: declined, 453
Gender: 1st declension, 453; 2d declension, 454; 3d declension, 458, I, II, III; 4th declension, 461; 5th declension, 462
Genitive: use of and meaning, 7; with the abl. causā, 7; partitive and exceptions, 378; ending in um and ium, 460
Gerund: defined and declined, 73
Gerundive construction: in agreement with noun, 253; with ad to represent affirmative purpose, 355
Gladius: declined, 454

Hic: declined, 464
Hinder: verbs of, with quīn or nē + subjunctive, 370
Historical cum: 128, 203, 263
Hortatory subjunctive: 395
Hostis: declined, 458
How to express 'ought' or 'must': pres. and past action, 385, 1, 2, 3
How words are combined: order and dependence, 92, 161, 176

Īdem: declined, 464
Ille: declined, 464

Imperō: with dat. and subjunctive clause, 145, 238
Impersonal verbs: 365
Impetum facere: with in + acc., 216
In: uses of, 35
Indefinite pronoun, quis: declined, 465
Indirect Discourse (Ōrātiō Obliqua): defined, 301; mood in, 392; pres. infin. (statement clauses), 302; perf. infin. (statement clauses), 305; fut. infin. (statement clauses), 318; subord. clauses in, 306, 397; substitute for fut. infin. in, 382; conditions in, 396; commands and exhortations in, 390; certiōrem (-ēs) facere, used as a verb of saying, 333; specimens of, 400–407
Indirect object: 15, 16, d
Indirect question: mood of, 313
Insigne: declined, 458
Integer: declined, 56
Intensive pronoun (ipse): declined, 464
Intermediate clauses: 276
Intermediate (subordinate) clauses in O. O.: 306
Interrogative pronoun (quis): declined, 465
Ipse: declined, 464
Irregular verbs: list of 26 verbs, 452
 eō, complete paradigms, 486
 faciō, " " 492
 ferō, " " 490, 491
 flō, " " 493
 mālō, " " 489

Irregular verbs:
nōlō, complete paradigms, 488
possum, " " 485
sum, " " 484
volō, " " 487
Is, ea, id: declined, 464
Iter: declined, 459
Iubeō: use of, 155
-ius: gen. ending of adjs., 286

Lapis: declined, 458
Latus: (noun) declined, 458
Legiō: declined, 458
Less vivid future condition: 335
Less vivid future condition in O.O.: 396, 2 and examples.
Lēx: declined, 458
-limus: adj. superl. ending, 471

Mālō: complete paradigms, 489
Mandō: with *dat.* and subjunctive clause, 145, 228
Manus: declined, 461
Mīles: declined, 458
Mīles ferus: declined, 122
Mīlia: declined, 459
Moneō: complete paradigms, 476, 477
Mood in O. O.: 392
More vivid future condition: 223, *a*, *b*
More vivid future condition in O. O.: 396, 1 and examples.
Motion, end or limit of: 386
Multitūdō: declined, 458
Mūniō: complete paradigms, 482, 483; for synopses, by stems, both voices, see 'Conjugations,' 4th.
'Must' or 'ought': how expressed, 385, 1, 2, 3

Nē: with subjunctive, neg. purpose, 211, 320; with subjunctive after imperō and mandō, 228; with imperative, neg. commands and exhortations, 389; nē + imperative (neg. commands, etc.) changed to O. O., 390; after verbs of fearing, 343; after verbs of hindering, etc., 370
Negative purpose: 211, 320
Negative result: 321
Negōtium dare: with *dat.* and subjunctive clause, 330
Nisi: in conditions, 223, 335
Nōlō: complete paradigms, 488

Object: direct, indirect, 15, 16
Oppidum: declined, 37
Opus and ūsus: with *abl.*, 379
Ōrātiō Oblīqua: see 'Indirect Discourse.'
Ōrātiō Rēcta: see 'Direct Discourse.'
Order of words: 16, 77, 92, 161, 176
'Ought' or 'must': how expressed, 385, 1, 2, 3,

Participles: pres. particip. declined, 467; substitutions for perf. act., 340, 372; formation of perf. pass., 257; use and agreem. of perf. pass., 316; perf. pass. in abl. absol., 287, 364; perf. pass., when mod. the subj. or obj., distinguished from abl. absol., 323; perf. pass. of depon., its use instead of perf. act., 340; perf. pass.

translated as finite or coordinate verb, 381; perf. pass. with habeō or teneō, 375
Partitive genitive: and exceptions, 378
Pater: declined, 124
Periphrastic conjugation: formation and meaning, 361; complete paradigms, 498, 499
Personal agent: with regular passive verb, 237; with gerundive (periphrast. pass.), 362
Personal pronoun (ego): declined, 463
Persuādeō: in the active, 345; passive, 380
Pēs: declined, 458
Place from—towards—which: 386
Place in which: 47
Pōnō: complete paradigms, 478, 479; for synopses, by stems, both voices, see 'Conjugations,' 3d
Populor: complete paradigms, 494
Possession: dat. of, 357
Possum: complete paradigms, 485
Postquam: in temporal clauses, 358
Potior: complete paradigms, 497
Predicate nominative: 95, 97
Pronouns: ego, 463; hīc, idem, ille, ipse, is, 464; quī, quis, 465; sē, 214
Puer: declined, 41
Pūgnāns: declined, 467
Purpose: relative clause of, 311; affirm. and neg. purpose, 320;
affirm. purpose expressed in four ways, 355

Quantity: general rules of, 500–504
Que: position, 215
Questions: direct, indirect, 313
Quī: declined, 465
Quis: declined, 465
Quod clauses: mood of; when *indic.*, 276; when *subjunc.*, 276, 306

Reflexive pronoun: *personal* suī, etc., declined, 214; *possessive* suus, etc., 189
Relative: quī, declined, 465; agreement of, with antecedent, 83; with castra, etc., 84, 85; agreement of, with pred. word, 373; rel. clause of purpose, 311; of cause or concession, 368; of result, 387; rel. as a connective at the beginning of a sent., 367
Review vocabularies: 78, 219, 332, 399
Rēs: declined, 462
Rēx: declined, 130
Rūmor: declined, 124

Scūtum: declined, 454
Sē: declined, 214
Sequence of tenses: rule of, 135; table of, 136; application of rule of, 137; use of, in O. O., 397
Servus: declined, 18, 25
Silva: declined, 453
Special verbs with dative: 348
Subordinate clauses: use and

dependence of, 110, 161, 166, 276; use of, in O. O., 306, 397

Substitution for future infinitive: in supineless and passive verbs, 382

Substitution for perfect active participle: by using depon. particip., abl. absol., or subord. clause, 340, 372

Suī: declined, 214

Sum: complete paradigms, 484; synopsis, pres. syst., 117; perf. syst., 127

Suus: use and meaning of, 189

Temporal clauses: postquam, ubi, etc. + indic., 358

Tōtus: declined, 286

Trēs: declined, 468

Ubi: use of, 203, 358

Ut: in purpose clauses, 53, 320, 355; with verbs of command, 145, 228; clauses of command in O. O., 389, 392, 2, a, b, c; in temporal clauses, verb indic., 358

Ūtor: complete paradigms, 496

Vir: declined, 454

Virtūs: declined, 458

Vīs: declined, 459

Volō: complete paradigms, 487

Vowel stems in i: (a) *nouns:* collis, declined, 130; hostis, declined, 458; gender, stem, and special endings of, 131, 457; (b) *adjectives:* fortis, declined, 467; stem and special endings of, 188

www.ingramcontent.com/pod-product-compliance
Lightning Source LLC
Chambersburg PA
CBHW032044220426

43664CB00008B/848